Europe in the Sixteenth Century

D1240169

Blackwell History of Europe

General Editor: John Stevenson

The series provides a new interpretive history of Europe from the Roman Empire to the end of the twentieth century. Written by acknowledged experts in their fields, and reflecting the range of recent scholarship, the books combine insights from social and cultural history with coverage of political, diplomatic and economic developments. Eastern Europe assumes its rightful place in the history of the continent, and the boundary of Europe is considered flexibly, including the Islamic, Slav and Orthodox perspectives wherever appropriate. Together, the volumes offer a lively and authoritative history of Europe for a new generation of teachers, students and general readers.

Published

Europe in the Sixteenth Century
Andrew Pettegree

Fractured Europe: 1600–1720
David J. Sturdy

In preparation

The Foundations of Europe
J. S. Richardson

Europe: 300–800
Peter Heather

Europe: 750–1000
John Contreni

Europe in Ferment: 950–1100
Jonathan Shepard

The Advance of Medieval Europe: 1099–1270
Jonathan Phillips

Europe: 1409–1523
Bruce Gordon

Europe from Absolutism to Revolution: 1715–1815
Michael Broers

Europe in the Age of Total War: 1900–1945
Conan Fischer

Europe: 1945–2000
Tom Buchanan

Europe in the Sixteenth Century

Andrew Pettegree

BLACKWELL
Publishers

First published 2002

2 4 6 8 10 9 7 5 3 1

Blackwell Publishers Ltd
108 Cowley Road
Oxford OX4 1JF
UK

Blackwell Publishers Inc.
350 Main Street
Malden, Massachusetts 02148
USA

British Library Cataloguing in Publication Data

A CIP catalogue record for this book is available from the British Library.

Library of Congress Cataloging-in-Publication Data

Pettegree, Andrew.
    Europe in the sixteenth century / Andrew Pettegree.
        p. cm. — (Blackwell history of Europe)
    Includes bibliographical references and index.
        ISBN 0–631–20701–5 (alk. paper) – ISBN 0–631–20704–X (pbk.: alk. paper)
        1. Europe–Politics and government–1492–1648.   2. Europe–Economic conditions–16th century.   3. Europe–Social conditions–16th century.   I. Title. II. Series.

    D228 .P42 2002
    940.2—dc21

                                                                                    2001001821

Picture Researcher Charlotte Morris

Typeset in 10.5/12.5pt Galliard
by Kolam Information Services Private Limited, Pondicherry, India.
Printed in Great Britain by TJ International Ltd, Padstow, Cornwall.

This book is printed on acid-free paper

Contents

Maps

Illustrations

Tables

Acknowledgements

I first became interested in the sixteenth century in the autumn of 1974, and it has been the centre of my studies and subsequent academic career pretty much from that day to this. So it is a pleasure to acknowledge with gratitude the support and stimulation provided by teachers, students, colleagues and friends during those times: at Oundle, Oxford, Hamburg, Cambridge, Emden, Leiden, in the United States and now at St Andrews. I am particularly grateful to the undergraduate Honours class at St Andrews that in the autumn of the year 2000 tested some of the text and provided valuable comments on structure and content. Christine Gascoigne and the staff of the St Andrews University Library Special Collections deserve special thanks for the outstanding service they provide to readers in the library, and particularly for help with the illustrations. My colleague Bruce Gordon was an influential voice and stimulating companion as the text took shape. Two academic colleagues, Scott Dixon and William Naphy, read the whole text in typescript, as did my former student Philip Conner. I thank them all for their many valuable comments and corrections. My family, Jane, Megan and Sophie have influenced my developing understanding of the past in many ways, and I thank Jane in particular for her help in the sections dealing with sixteenth century music and literature. Finally I want in this book to acknowledge a special debt to my first teacher, Alan Midgley, who was an inspiration and model as I first became a historian. I dedicate this book to him.

St Andrews
March 2001

1

Time and Space: Living in Sixteenth-century Europe

Landscape and People

For the inhabitants of sixteenth-century Europe life was dominated far more than it would be today by the physical landscape. In today's western society, landscape is to all intents and purposes an optional feature of existence: experienced most directly as a vacation diversion or digression from the everyday. In the sixteenth century, in contrast, the physical environment – urban or rural – was the overwhelming, determining fact of life, shaping lives as surely as any human capacities or limitations.

Experiencing the natural world as we do today, mostly voluntarily, we can delight in its grandeur – but it is a grandeur that we have rendered largely risk free. Only on very rare occasions can we experience the potency, the overwhelming force of nature. Our sixteenth-century forebears had a very different relationship with their environment, be it their physical location, the natural world or their own bodies. Civilization was prized precisely because it was so thin and brittle a veneer.

The physical landscape of Europe in the sixteenth century would have been, to our eye, imposing and dangerous: far more varied, full of stark contrasts, much less densely settled – above all, untamed. Far less of the surface area was urbanized; of the remainder, far less was intensely farmed. The population of Europe seems to have been 70 million in 1500; at this level it had barely recovered to the level it had attained some 200 years before, in 1300, before the ravages of the Black Death. By 1600, it had grown to around 89 million. But even at that level, there were six times fewer people in Europe than there would be in the year 2000. One has now to go to some of Europe's remotest regions – the Highlands of Scotland, for instance – to find overall population densities equivalent to those of the sixteenth century.[1]

Europe still possessed huge areas of natural wilderness: marshland and fen, undrained lakes, huge mountain ranges. A far higher proportion of the surface area was wooded, ranging from the huge impenetrable forests of southern Germany and eastern Europe, to the more domesticated, but still vastly impressive mature woodland of southern England. Roads were rudimentary or haphazard; rivers could be either vital arteries of communication, or impassable barriers. For many of Europe's peoples, the physical landscape created an immediate context for life that was in our terms quite narrowly defined. Many would live, work, marry and die within a few kilometres of where they were born. The difficulties of transporting goods long distances meant that most of the necessities of life were grown, farmed or manufactured within a very small radius.

In communities defined by their physical location, places could be quite close to each other and yet utterly remote. The southern French towns of Carcassonne and Mazamet, less than 50 km apart, are nevertheless separated by an imposing set of wooded mountains that would have inhibited any real contact. The port town of La Rochelle was connected to the outside world only by the sea, for impenetrable marshes separated it from its rural hinterland. Landscape created boundaries far more than did borders. The concept of a border between territories or kingdoms as a line rather than a zone only really began to take root in the eighteenth century, when advances in government and cartography made such a concept meaningful. In the sixteenth century, lives were bounded by natural features, and when none existed (or even, in the case of rivers, where they did), people moved between different jurisdictions with considerable freedom. Until the treaties of Madrid (1526) and Cambrai (1529) it was impossible to speak of a frontier between France and the Netherlands in any sense we would recognize. Fifty years later during the Wars of Religion citizens of both lands would continue to exploit the lack of controls or border markings to take themselves beyond the reach of trouble almost at will. In eastern and central Europe geographical borders between states were even more uncertain. Following the Ottoman conquest of much of Hungary in the 1520s and 1530s, boundaries between areas of Turkish and Habsburg overlordship remained cloudy for generations. This allowed many Hungarian lords to continue to exercise jurisdiction over parts of their lands now under nominal Turkish control. A sixteenth-century traveller would have measured progress far more in terms of places of refreshment (towns, inns or taverns) or economic barriers (tolls and ferries) than jurisdictional boundaries.

In a world defined, shaped and dominated by natural features, towns stood out. Sixteenth-century peoples were proud of their towns, as is demonstrated by the new (and very expensive) genre of topographical woodcuts, which represented Europe's great cities, majestic behind their great walls, a honeycomb of churches and imposing civic buildings. Here European peoples created intricate, densely populated societies of considerable sophistication and drive. All were by today's standards small. The city of London comprised a bare square mile, and its population of some 60,000 at the beginning of the sixteenth century was only then beginning to sprawl beyond the walls. The great imperial cities of Nuremberg and Strasbourg housed populations of 20,000 to 25,000 in an even smaller space. Many cities were only just beginning to outgrow the natural features, the island or hilltop, that had defined the ancient settlement, and the extramural suburbs were often little more than slum shanty towns, heartily disapproved of by the urban grandees, and easily sacrificed in time of war.

Between these towns and cities by 1500 there existed networks of communication and trade that were often intricate and sophisticated. Much of this trade was river borne, reflecting the poor quality and danger of sixteenth-century roads. But all travel was attended by a level of risk, uncertainty and physical danger that is hard to contemplate today. Travellers' tales were popular precisely because roads were such perilous and eventful places.

Nevertheless one should not believe that because of these impediments people in this period led bounded, limited lives. It is possible to reconstruct not untypical careers, where men and women lived their entire lives in the same settlement. Their range of acquaintance was defined by homestead, village, kin and civil authority: essentially a series of concentric circles with contact of diminishing frequency away from the central core. But even this limited worldview implies a degree of connectedness with the outside world. Even in an essentially static life, every community would receive visitors: travelling salesmen, migrant workers, roving players, quack doctors or teeth pullers, fairground performers. If they were less fortunate, they would experience the disruption caused by organized bands of troops or beggars. All, for good or ill, would bring their experience of the world beyond the village.

In truth, travel was a ubiquitous part of sixteenth-century life. Many people would themselves have experienced, or known someone who had made a long journey. Mediaeval Europe offered many opportunities for pilgrimage, and whole communities existed to service this religious *Wanderlust*. The Scottish burgh of St Andrews had grown up around this industry, its very remoteness (which incurred pious hardship for the dedicated pilgrim) here turned to advantage. Pilgrims who made the journey to see St Andrew's bones under the High Altar of the Cathedral – one of the largest ecclesiastical buildings in northern Europe – could buy a pleasing variety of souvenir trinkets from local tradesmen. In fifteenth-century Worms the first successful business enterprise of Johannes Gutenberg, later inventor of printing, was the mass production of pilgrims' mirrors.

In towns the effect of population movements was even more profound. Sixteenth-century towns experienced vast inward migration: often young men looking for work, sometimes whole families. Many incomers had their hopes of finding fortune in the city cruelly dashed, and ended up begging or on the poor rolls. The reorganization of poor relief, one of the principal bureaucratic achievements of the age, was partly stimulated by this vast flow of peoples towards the cities. But if migrants impinged on the consciousness of the city fathers

Figure 1 Pilgrim badge of St Andrew. Courtesy St Andrews Museum. Pilgrims collected such badges as tokens of their visits to Europe's many pilgrimage centres. Pilgrimage was big business; Johann Gutenberg made the fortune that first floated his experiments in printing from the manufacture of pilgrims' mirrors.

largely when they became a problem, they were also a necessity, because sixteenth-century towns could not sustain themselves by the natural cycle of birth and death. Sixteenth-century cities were great killing fields, particularly prone to epidemic disease and the illnesses caused by poor sanitation and dirty water. To the extent that the sixteenth century saw a growth of urbanization, it probably also saw a general reduction of life expectancy.

To this normal, traditional pattern of people movements the sixteenth century added another more turbulent: the phenomenon of religious exile. The religious convulsions of the period, and particularly the second half of the century, saw very considerable population shifts as people fled persecution, or made a pre-emptive bid for religious freedom. An estimated 50,000 people left the Netherlands in the wake of the collapse of the first brief experiment of religious coexistence in 1566–7, and France experienced a similar exodus after the St Bartholomew's Day massacre in 1572. Such mobility had a very profound economic impact, not least because these migrants included a disproportionately large number of skilled artisans and men with working capital, often travelling without or ahead of their families. Shrewd governments took positive steps to recruit such workers to revitalize flagging local economies. Overall, the impact on the European economy was overwhelmingly positive, spreading new technologies and deepening the web of connections between the central powerhouse economies such as the textile towns of Flanders and more peripheral places. But the immediate context was a great deal of individual hardship.

We can experience the harsh realities of divided families and loved ones left behind in a rare survival from the Royal Archives in Brussels. This dossier consists of some 79 letters written by men and women in the towns and villages around Saint-Omer to their friends and relations who had taken flight to England from religious persecution in the Low Countries. A sister writes to her brother that their mother desired urgently his return, 'because she has cried almost from the hour and day of your departure, praying God for your return'. The wife of Plennart Martin related that the younger of their two little girls asked constantly for their father: the older sister told her that Daddy could not come back because he had bad feet. One can almost hear the children's voices in this kindly, nonsensical explanation. The poignancy of these simple familial greetings is only increased by the fact that we know that the letters will never reach their destination. Intercepted by the Catholic authorities the whole consignment of letters was deposited in the Royal Archive, where it remains today.[2]

Time

What impresses about much of this confiscated correspondence is the speed with which it reached its destination. One letter in this bundle is a reply, dated 6 January, to a letter of 26 December – and remember that this particular correspondence relied wholly on an unofficial and largely underground postal network. The Dutch church in London logged in letters received on 12 January despatched from Antwerp on 9 January, an apparent speed of transmission that would do credit to a modern postal service.

Yet here we need to exercise a measure of caution, because dating sixteenth-century documents presents many pitfalls for the unwary. When a document is dated 9 January in the latter sixteenth century, this can be 'New' or 'Old' Style, a consequence of the long gestated calendar changes introduced during this era. Still more confusingly, much of Europe continued the practice of dating the New Year from Easter rather than 1 January; in which case a letter of 9 January 1561 would in fact emanate from 1562 according to our method of calculation. These are pitfalls for the unwary historian; but in fact sixteenth-century peoples themselves had great problems with time.

Let us begin with what was shared, and obvious. In the sixteenth century peoples' sense of time was dominated by the natural day, and by the rhythms of the agricultural year. This was an age when light, other than that provided by the sun, was vastly expensive, and carefully rationed. So too of course was fuel – within living space the need to maximize light had to be carefully balanced against the equally imperative need to keep out the cold. In consequence workmen, in town or country, worked long hours in summer, and a much shorter day in winter. Country life especially was dominated by the rhythms of the seasons: planting, tending, harvest and slaughtering. Just as had the church in the Middle Ages, so the new emerging apparatus of government and commerce in the sixteenth century silently acknowledged the power of nature's calendar by setting their dates, for taxation and interest, for instance, to the traditional year.

Nevertheless the sixteenth century was certainly characterized by a steadily more intricate sense of time. The governing of a large conglomeration of territories required the transmission of instructions over long distances. Complex legal issues might rest on when such instructions came into force. Printed versions of French royal proclamations carefully recorded the dates in the various stages of onward transmission: signed in the Royal Council on 30 March, registered in the Parlement of Paris on 3 April, proclaimed on the streets and in the marketplaces of Lyon on 30 April. In Spain's global empire the passage back and forth of advice and orders might well take months, a physical limitation which does much to explain both the problems experienced in the Netherlands, and the freewheeling spirit of the conquistadors.

In grappling with these problems the sixteenth century developed an ever more exact and exacting sense of time. The two centuries before this had seen the invention, perfection and gradual domestication of the mechanical clock. Although still a luxury item, by 1400 most large cities had invested in a prominent public timepiece, whose visible presence and chiming of the hours permitted a far more exact and objective measurement of the business day. Such clocks were commonplace by the beginning of the sixteenth century, and in the years that followed it was government initiative that lay behind the installation of such public clocks in the smaller towns and villages. The motivation was clearly spelt out in the Ecclesiastical Constitutions of Saxony: 'In villages without a clock, the pastor should admonish the church, and in particular the people who can afford it, to buy one, so that the church-offices can be carried out at the appropriate time in accord with the clock, and the people in other respects, too, should be guided by it in their housekeeping'.[3]

Clocks were seen as conducive to good order. A familiar if rather obscure saying of Holy Roman Emperor Charles V makes the point: 'Portae, pulsus, pueri: gates, bell strokes, children.' Solid walls, proper schools, and the orderly measurement of time were for the emperor the characteristics of a well-governed city. Conversely the removal or dismantling of a tower and bell as punishment for rebellion amounted to a loss of legal status and disenfranchisement. At the end of the century one of the most knotty problems encountered in communities divided between Protestants and Catholics was control of the bell tower. The commissioners of Henry IV of France despatched to enforce the Edict of Nantes after 1598 were often forced to resolve these complicated 'bell wars'.

It would be wrong to infer from this, however, that the pressure for more exact timekeeping came only from above. The generalization of printing technology also opened the way for mass-produced calendars, with their standardized renderings of months and astrological seasons, feast days, fairs and the phases of the moon. The enormous popularity of such calendars and almanacs reveal the increased importance attached to time and timekeeping through all social orders. The rapidly rising production of small personal timekeepers opens a further chapter in the history of time consciousness.

Nevertheless, the sixteenth century had a major problem with time. For while the Roman reordering of the calendar year had served Christendom well (the emperor Augustus had finally fixed the names of the months and their lengths) it was by the sixteenth century common knowledge that the calendar year had drifted away from the true seasons. The error – the difference of the true summer from the calendar date – was now of the very significant order of 11 days. But how should this drift be corrected? Various papal commissions grappled with the problem, before the matter was finally taken in hand by Gregory XIII in 1581. For decades theologians had wrestled with the technically difficult and theologically charged issue of determining the true astronomical year, and by now they had both their measurements and a solution. On 1 March 1582 Gregory signed the bull proclaiming the new Gregorian calendar: at midnight on 4 October the calendar year would leap forward to 15 October.

The effect was, to say the least, traumatic. Many felt that ten days had, quite literally been snatched away from them: in the German city of Frankfurt people rioted against the pope and mathematicians. And how was one to calculate interest in a month reduced to 21 days? Europe's Catholic countries by and large fell into line: Spain, Portugal and the Italian states on the specified day, France and Flanders at the end of the year. Bavaria and the Austrian lands converted in 1583, as did Würzberg, Münster and Mainz (though each dropped a different set of ten days). But for Protestant states the Gregorian calendar was just one further example of papal arrogance and power, and they emphatically rejected the reform (as did the Eastern Orthodox). For over a century Protestant and Catholic Europe would march to different time. This had some bizarre consequences. A traveller journeying from Catholic Regensburg to Protestant Nuremberg, a journey of 70 km, would set off on 1 January and arrive on 21 December the previous year. It says a great deal for the intensity of religious passions, that these absurdities were not resolved for the best part of 200 years. England was the last major Protestant state to adopt the Gregorian calendar, in 1752. The Eastern Orthodox churches remained utterly opposed to the 'new' calendar time until the twentieth century, and even now continue to celebrate Easter on a different day.

Opposition to calendar reform was not the limit of the Protestant assault on 'Catholic' time. Protestant reformers looked with considerable disfavour on a year measured through Catholic feast days. The traditional holidays associated with saints' days were an early victim of reforming fervour, but the name days of saints were still universally cited in calendars and almanacs. Only in Calvinist Geneva was the matter taken efficiently in hand, with the development of a new calendar that swept away the traditional name days, and substituted an eccentric miscellany of biblical and classical events, together with commemorations of heroes of the new movement. Thus January noted the Circumcision of Christ, Nebuchadnezzar's siege of Jerusalem (10th), and the conversion of St Paul; but also that on 24 January the emperor Caligula had been assassinated, and the Duke of Somerset executed in London in 1552. On 18 February the calendar called our attention to the fact that on this historically busy day the Romans celebrated the festival of fools, Noah sent out the dove that brought back the olive branch, and Martin Luther died in 1546.

Living and Dying

Even Geneva's most pious citizens would probably have taken no more than a casual interest in the making of this new model calendar. For most, life was full of far more pressing concerns. After all, a throbbing toothache was just as painful on the date of the execution of the Duke of Somerset as it would have been on the feast day of St Anthony. Illness, disease, incapacitating accidents, disability, keeping clothed and fed, all of these were infinitely more perilous that they are for many of us today. In this at least, rich and poor, townsmen and country folk, shared common concerns.

For the vast majority of Europe's population, diet was much less varied than it is today. Most of Europe's peoples subsisted on a limited diet of grains, milk products, and a little fish. Bread, usually made of cheap inferior grains, composed a large proportion of the countryman's diet. Even in the eighteenth century, up to 95 per cent of the diet of the rural poor in France was cereal in various forms. Within this general context there were clear regional variations. Germans, according to the chronicler Sebastian Franck, subsisted on black

bread made of rye, oatmeal porridge and boiled peas. Bretons preferred buckwheat porridge, the Burgundians ate bread made of rye and
oatmeal, supplemented by maize porridge. Only in times of dearth
would country folk resort to peas and beans, normally only fed to
animals. The ubiquity of bread in the diet of the poor, and the fact that
few would have an oven to bake at home, meant that bread was the
most heavily regulated of consumer products. The size, weight and
quality of a loaf were all closely regulated, and infractions of the
regulations severely punished. Only in the nineteenth century would
the potato begin to offer a cheap alternative source of basic nutrition.

If diet was unvaried, then in truth this was less of a concern than one
might imagine. Monotony at least implies regularity, which, given the
vagaries of weather, could hardly be guaranteed. Times of dearth were
terrifying, and, for many on the economic margins, potentially deadly.
A shortfall in the harvest of 20 per cent could raise prices by 80 per
cent. A 50 per cent shortfall would send prices leaping up to 450 per
cent above normal levels. These were deadly figures. No wonder town
governments in the sixteenth century gave considerable attention to
the establishment of municipal grain reserves, which could be used to
turn back the ire of the poor in times of extreme want. Even in normal
times lack of protein and vitamins led to near permanent undernour-
ishment among many rural populations. In the poorer parts of Europe
the poor assuaged the gnawing pangs of hunger with bread so adulter-
ated with field grasses that it may well have had halucinatory qualities;
if so, this 'bread of dreams' offered no more than a brief respite from
life's harsher realities.[4]

The rich, of course, fared better, none more so than the rural
aristocracy who could draw on their estates for varieties of game,
meat and quality grains (wheat), and, depending on location, the
manufacture of beer or wine. They also enjoyed the underappreciated
boon of abundant supplies of unadulterated water. Employment in the
households of the rich was in the sixteenth century as reliable a
passport to regular nourishment as had been life in a medieval monastic community, for conspicuous consumption left much surplus food
to be redistributed according to the careful hierarchies in which
sixteenth-century society so excelled. Surviving accounts of magnate
kitchens allow us to experience vicariously the best that sixteenth-
century eating had to offer. At the palaces of the family d'Albret in
the south of France the retinue of the kings of Navarre 'feasted from
platters heaped high with every imaginable wild beast of the field, bird
of the air, and on holy days, fish of the sea'.[5] At a normal winter meal,

family and guests would be served at least a dozen types of meat, game and fowl, along with elaborately prepared patés. Such a household could be a mainstay of the local economy, as merchants strove to outdo each other with ever more exotic delicacies. An extant purveyorship contract specifies 187 different kinds and cuts of meat, fish and fowl that merchants were prepared to bring to the d'Albret table. Nor need a fish day necessarily be a fast day: oysters, salmon and sole, even whale, decorated the table on Fridays. But sixteenth century food culture also had its hazards for those with money to spare. Because meat eating was the prerogative of the well-off, they tended to do too much of it, leading to health conditions associated with vitamin deficiency such as scurvy and ulcers. Massive consumption of wine brought retribution in the agonies of gout.

Figure 2 Doctor visiting the sick. Woodcut from *Das Buch zu distillieren*, Strasbourg, 1519. Courtesy St Andrews University Library. The doctor at the bedside was more an indicator of the patient's social status than holding out any hope of effective treatment.

Bringing food to the table, especially in the growing cities, increasingly distant from their centres of supply, was for sixteenth century peoples just one of the many hazards of life. Illness, disease, disfiguring accidents or conditions, these were all endemic and all had to be borne with far less hope of effective treatment than we have today. In an age before anaesthetics there were few conditions that justified the agony and risk of a surgical operation. While theoretical texts on the body and its humours multiplied, most people had too much sense to allow doctors to practise what they preached, at least on them. Most perilous of all was childbirth, both for infant and mother. Multiple, sequential pregnancies were the Russian roulette of the pre-modern age. Most parents experienced the agony of losing children in infancy. Here, the basic demographic facts make chilling reading. In sixteenth-century Castile in the rural areas around Valladolid, 40 to 50 per cent of all children died before their seventh year; in Palencia for the period 1576–1600 this figure rises to 68 per cent. A not untypical experience was that of the French family Capdebosc. The parents, Jean and Marguerite, who married in 1560, had ten children, five of whom died before they were ten. The surviving children in their turn raised a total of 23 children, 10 of whom survived childhood.[6] Thus of the 33 children of this prolific family, only six children lived to found a family of their own. The social consequences of these pitiless statistics were profound. Those determined that a family name should live on often took the precaution of giving the same Christian name to several children, to maximize the chance that it should survive for posterity. Fathers left with young children would usually swiftly remarry, often to a younger wife; their death in turn allowed the widow to continue a chain of serial relationships of partners of unequal age.

To these regular hazards, epidemic disease added a further, terrifying element of uncertainty. Sixteenth-century Europe made no progress whatsoever in grappling with the scourge of epidemics. Indeed the growth of cities, unaccompanied by any breakthrough in public sanitation or public hygiene, may indeed have intensified its impact. Many cities suffered incidence of epidemics at least every ten years. In the middle of the sixteenth century England was twice laid low by the sweating sickness, a mysterious if deadly affliction which modern medical science has struggled precisely to identify. Most terrifying of all was the Black Death, the bubonic plague, introduced to Europe in 1348, and a regular visitor thereafter. Epidemics could kill up to one third of a city's population in one year, a rate of mortality that left few households untouched. While its cause was still unknown, the plague sent terror through communities that recognized the tell-tale signs of a new outbreak. Panic led to the wildest accusations: some believed that plague was deliberately spread by malign individuals, and communities turned on these plague spreaders with a ferocity that in the next century would be reserved for witches. Even Calvin's Geneva was not spared this sort of irrationality. Three times in the sixteenth century Geneva initiated proceedings against unfortunate individuals who it was alleged had deliberately spread plague in the city. Evidence collected under torture revealed a bizarre conspiracy to spread the disease by smearing door lintels with grease concocted

Figure 3   The Apothecary's Shop, from *Das Buch zu distillieren*, Strasbourg, 1519. Courtesy St Andrews University Library.

by rendering fat from the foot of a corpse removed from the town gibbet. Incredible though this might seem to us, the magistrates were in deadly earnest. In the third episode, in 1570, 115 persons were prosecuted and 44 executed.[7]

With all of these contending perils, it is perhaps surprising that life expectancy was not lower than it was. In fact, if an infant survived his or her first year (admittedly a considerable qualification), average life expectancies were not lower than those of our great grandparents' generation. Only in the last century has modern medicine and nutrition significantly lengthened the average adult life span. But issues of life and death were still perceived very differently. Firstly, the arbitrary quality that attended issues of mortality gave a different quality to life. Death was literally all around: few lives would have been untouched by the sudden brutalities of its sheer unpredictability. Furthermore, although lives were often long, they were, in health terms, qualitatively different. Pain and disability were the common lot, often to be endured over a long span of years. Pain was an everyday part of life to an extent we can scarcely understand. This is a circumstance that historians take insufficiently into account when we pass judgement on the actions of sixteenth-century opinion formers. When the real extent of the health problems with which they laboured can be deduced (which is infrequently, given the nature of the surviving evidence), one begins to wonder why policy-making was not more arbitrary and wilful than it was. A modern analysis of the illnesses of the Genevan reformer John Calvin reveals a body so riddled with debilitating conditions that it is a wonder that he could drag himself to the pulpit. For the last ten years he suffered from kidney stones so agonizing that movement was a torment. The only proposed medical solution was that he should attempt to dislodge them by vigorous horse-riding. The emperor, Maximilian, seems to have enjoyed robust good health until his late thirties, when he contracted syphilis. In 1501 he fell off his horse, damaging a leg, which gave him pain for the rest of his life. His major problem seems to have been morbid depression. After 1514 he always travelled with his coffin, which, considering he lived a further five years constantly on the move, must have been a great trial to his servants.[8]

Such conditions, when they can be deduced, can be factored into our analysis; but inferior healthcare also had less tangible and culturally more subtle effects. In an age when spectacles were a rare luxury and an inexact palliative, inferior eyesight was by and large a condition that had simply to be endured. In societies like our own which assume clear (or as least reliably corrected) eyesight, the cultural effect of this is hard to imagine. But it is possible to postulate that the sixteenth century in fact had a quite different hierarchy of the senses: the dissemination of information and shaping experiences relied far less on what was visually perceived, than on hearing, touch and taste.

This insight can be applied to all of the senses to a greater or lesser degree. In the sixteenth century medical diagnosis relied to a large extent on taste and smell, although, it need hardly be added, with erratic results. This was also a much more tactile age. There were fewer people but they lived, paradoxically, in conditions of far greater intimacy. Dwelling places had far fewer rooms; the concept of privacy had little meaning for most people of that time. Even among the well-born, polite society revolved round a complex ritual of greetings and physical contact. But it is most of all our elevation of visual experience that separates us from the past. Ours is a highly visual age, particularly in the field of information technology. It was not only because literacy was a less universal skill that the same reliance could not be placed on visually perceived information: people simply did not see as well, if indeed they could see at all. A sense of this would encourage a reinterpretation of the impact of many communal activities, from processions and pageants to sermons and public executions. In the world of the arts and public display colour would have been more important, the precision of line less so. The salutary impact of a public burning may have had more to do with the awful sounds and smell than the visual tableau. Certainly, and more prosaically, a sense of this reordered hierarchy of sensory experience points up the continued importance of aural communication – song and speech – in a world that was experiencing the creeping importance of print.

This World and the Next

If in the light of this review of the basic circumstances of existence we are to try now to get inside the minds of our sixteenth-century forebears, where does this leave us? A basic and obvious observation is that the sheer unpredictability of existence – an untamed landscape, the constant danger of sudden calamity – left far more space than we leave today for the operation of supernatural powers. The sixteenth century world had far more space for God. They saw God at work in many aspects of their day-to-day existence, where we now offer an undeified, scientific explanation. They saw God in the weather. They prayed urgently for a merciful sun at time of harvest, and gave grateful thanks for full bellies in winter. Floods, tempests, thunder and lightning were all seen as direct evidence of God's anger, for what else could it be? The All Saints flood of 1570 in the Netherlands was inevitably interpreted by Catholic authors as God's judgement on the recent iconoclastic attack on the churches during the first phase of the Dutch Revolt; Protestant commentators, naturally, did not agree. However interpreted, tales of natural calamities became one of the most popular classes of sensation literature as cheap printed books began to be mass-produced in the second half of the century.

The calamity of illness and epidemic, whether it struck at members of the family or livestock, were all laid at the door of an all powerful deity. Incidences of the plague invariably brought forth from the pulpits of the afflicted community loud calls for repentance, for it seemed a matter of course that such a severe affliction could only be a sign of God's special disfavour. In Dutch the plague was known simply as *De Gave Gods*: God's gift. Those spared in such circumstances gave grateful thanks; as did those who experienced the everyday miracle of the successful delivery of a healthy child. When the distinguished Nuremberg jurist Christoph Scheurl was blessed with a first surviving child at the age of fifty-one his ecstatic journal entry was careful to give credit where credit was due: 'By the will of the Lord God, to whom alone praise and honour is due in all things, my dear wife Katharina gave birth to an early son on the Friday after Misericordia Domini, April 19, at three and a quarter hours sunrise, or 8.15 a.m. by the tower clock.'[9]

For a family on the edge of subsistence the loss of livestock could be an even greater calamity than the loss of children. The medieval Cornish hermit Saint Brannoc knew what he was about when he manifested his sanctity by resurrecting a cow. His cult was still enthusiastically celebrated in the English West Country in the sixteenth century. Just as did individuals, so too communities saw manifestations of the divine will in good times and bad. Seeking an explanation of a recent influx of poor people, which threatened the fragile social order in the city, the city secretary of Strasbourg in 1534, Lucas Hackfurt, saw the hand of God behind the recent rise in prices: 'What drives the poor here in such numbers? Answer: the great need and the dearness of all things. And where does this dearness come from? From God. Why did he send it to us? Because of our disbelief and sins, our ingratitude and selfishness, from which develops great cruelty and unbrotherly hardship for our neighbours.'[10]

The Genevan reformer John Calvin would later in the century begin one section of his great work the *Institutes of the Christian Religion* with the exhortation 'let God be God'. To most of Europe's citizens this would have seemed strangely superfluous. For to them, God was everywhere, even as they schemed and plotted to achieve their own very human ends.

The question that troubled theologians more was not the presence, or ubiquity of God, but to what sort of God, or gods, were the mass of the population offering their allegiance. If God was ceaselessly active in the world, then so too was the Devil and all his instruments: these too had to be fought, warded off or, on occasion, propitiated.

Belief in the Devil was not simply the preserve of the superstitious common folk. According to a recent and revolutionary study of the German reformer Martin Luther, his whole life can accurately be described – in his own perception – as a struggle against Satan and his cohorts.[11] Luther, through his dramatization of the Christian struggle for salvation, in fact intensified the medieval belief in the Devil and lent it additional urgency. His lead was followed by a whole generation of Lutheran ministers, who effectively filled the world with Satan's cohorts by diabolizing all vices. Printing presses in Germany were soon turning out dozens of treatises on the various devils and their specialities. One writer, the learned Professor Martin Borrhaus, even took a census of hell, counting exactly 2,665,886,746 devils in the infernal kingdom.[12]

Those rooted in a progress-orientated view of history should consider this evidence well. By the second half of the sixteenth century, with something like 250,000 of these devil books in circulation, this one genre had captured something like 10 per cent of the Protestant book market in the empire. And it is clear that this post-Reformation fixation did not originate with the people, but was developed by the educated, and spread by them to the populace. Far from being a product of popular superstition, this obsession with the Devil, like the concurrent witch-craze, was the outcome of a prolonged educational campaign by the political and intellectual elites.

In such a cosmic understanding, belief slid easily into superstition, and peoples across Europe used a variety of instruments in the endless struggle with the forces of the night. In times of sickness the local wise woman was far more accessible and affordable than any physician, and probably, with a rudimentary knowledge of herbs and homeopathic remedies, far more efficacious. But healing and magic were closely intertwined, and the search for remedies often involved a complex

jumbling of potions and incantations. Even within the bounds of the
official church, the frantic search for assurance, both in this world and
the next, led to excesses which many churchmen found troubling. In a
world where death was so close, invariably had been experienced
within the immediate family, and where bodily pains gave constant
intimations of mortality, the two worlds were simply far more connected. Sixteenth-century men and women did not feel disconnected
from dead kin; they thought about them frequently, and gave great
pains to preparing the way for when they eventually slipped across the
narrow gate between life and death.[13] All commodities have their
price, and anxiety commands a very high price indeed. The sixteenth
century inherited from the medieval world a complex and vibrant
economy of the afterlife. By the turn of the century church life had
accrued a dense and intricate structure of memorial masses, altars and
pious associations dedicated to smoothing the path to salvation of
those who had gone before.

2

Europe in 1500: Political Organization

To be a member of one of Europe's elites in the sixteenth century was to be shielded from some of life's most conspicuous brutalities. There was enough to eat (if not always a very balanced diet), fuel to keep one warm, opulent clothing. Your residences were likely to be made of superior building materials, and, if often bleak and draughty, usually among the first to be fitted with glass windows and other modern conveniences. Servants tended to bodily needs and helped banish boredom with entertainments; revenues from land and taxes could be used to purchase artefacts of great beauty and craftsmanship.

But did this make for happiness? In many cases, the absence of material want had to be balanced against other harsh realities. Consider the case of Louis d'Orléans, cousin and later successor to King Charles VIII of France. As a member of a collateral branch of the royal house Louis had learned the harsh realities of power politics early, when the then king, Louis XI, had promised him in marriage to his own daughter Jeanne, a deformed cripple known to be incapable of bearing children. The marriage, which had been concluded when the appalled youth was 11 years old, blighted Louis's life for 25 years; only his own rather improbable accession to the throne in 1498 allowed him to secure the papal annulment that rescued him from this loveless match.

So it was in many of the ruling houses of Europe. Children were promised in marriage almost before they left the cradle. A happy childhood, secure in their own home, was seldom their lot. Children were used as pawns in diplomacy, sometimes quite literally. When Francis I of France was released from captivity by Charles V following his incarceration after the Battle of Pavia (1525), he left as hostages from his compliance with the terms of the treaty two of his sons. The two boys were respectively seven and eight, and since Francis had on his return to France instantly reneged on the treaty they remained prisoners in Spain, initially in harsh conditions, for three years. Marriage diplomacy often dictated a partner of very unequal age, and often marriage to a cousin, uncle, or other close kin. When Philip II married for the fourth time, his new wife Anna of Austria was his cousin, but also his niece.

The consequence of all this intermarriage is not difficult to imagine; indeed, it stares out at you in the bland, stupid features of many a royal portrait. In the Habsburg family the problem was particularly acute. Charles V acceded to the throne of Spain through the incapacity of his mother, Juana the Mad. Driven over the brink by the death of her husband, she remained incarcerated and secluded almost throughout her son's reign. Philip II's son Don Carlos exhibited similar symptoms of a dangerous instability as he grew to manhood. His health and alienation from his father became a major problem of state before he died in mysterious circumstances in 1568. No wonder; the unfortunate Don Carlos had four generations of inbreeding behind him. Instead of 8 great-grandparents he had only 4; instead of the usual 16 great-great-grandparents, he had only 6.[1]

The purpose of all this feverish and often ill-starred marriage diplomacy was state-building. The sixteenth century inherited from the mediaeval world no concept of 'natural' borders. A state was defined by such territories as a ruling house could acquire, or rather, to which it could make good its claim, for a complex patchwork of competing historic claims was the inevitable backcloth to any new negotiation or conflict. Geographical distance from the heart of one's existing territory, or a lack of any common cultural identity, would not in any way discourage an eager claimant.

Thus the beginning of the sixteenth century saddled Europe with some unlikely combinations of territories; others, no less improbable, emerged during the course of the century. There was nothing inevitable or pre-ordained about the political map that emerged during the course of the century. Seen from the mediaeval perspective, the gradual consolidation of territories into the kingdom of France – which by the end of the sixteenth century had reached a state quite close to its modern borders – would have seemed wildly improbable. Only a century before, the kings of France had been driven back to a small appenage on the Loire, in danger of being permanently eclipsed by the challenge of Burgundy. Yet, Burgundy, like other dynastic combinations that threatened briefly to become permanent features of the political map had itself dwindled away, its sixteenth century fate to be absorbed into the huge conglomeration of Habsburg territories. When the kingdoms of Aragon and Castile were united in the persons of Ferdinand and Isabella, a permanent union was by no means certain; a few years later in another part of Europe another such association, the united kingdom of Scandinavia, was rent asunder. In the second half of the century a free rebel state emerged in the northern Netherlands but not in the Huguenot stronghold of southern France. The most tantalizing and potentially formidable new combination was a united kingdom of England and the Netherlands, a combination which would have come into being had Queen Mary and her husband Philip of Spain had a male heir. In the event the union proved barren, and England had to settle for a union with another sworn enemy – Scotland – a half-century later.

At the centre of all this chopping and changing was a social code that put family – dynasty – at the centre of social organization. Family provided the key to the most unlikely accumulation of territories, and land was the cornerstone of wealth and fortune. In this respect the attitudes of Europe's rulers only mirrored those of the noble caste from which they had emerged, and to which they remained closely tied by bonds of obligation and service. At the dawn of the sixteenth century a number of Europe's nobilities were characterized by great fluidity. In France several major appanages were in danger of extinction. In England the senior ranks of the nobility were severely depleted by the murderous feuds of the Wars of the Roses. But this did little to shake their domination of society. Noble magnates acknowledged their duty to the ruler, and in return they held unchallenged sway over their regions of influence. Their marriage strategies replicated in miniature those of their monarchs, using female kin to build family connections, and younger sons to annexe lucrative offices in the church. Below them gentry families sought eagerly to trade wealth for position and begin the steady climb up the social ladder and into the noble estate. In an age where the survival of healthy children was so uncertain, noble status was surprisingly permeable and new families could rise with astonishing speed. They did so in a context where aristocratic values were largely unquestioned.

During the course of the sixteenth century the feudal logic underpinning the privileges of nobility – a fighting caste that would bring their feudal subjects to serve their lord in arms – gradually dissolved, but the values of that earlier society proved remarkably enduring. Throughout the social hierarchy men continued to look to their social betters for example, for inspiration, for favour, justice and patronage – and particularly for the last of these, for the growth of government brought with it a multiplication of offices and the spoils that went with them. The enduring dominance of the cultural values established by the social supremacy of the nobility could manifest itself in quite surprising ways. The chivalric code of mediaeval society continued to inform the thinking of Europe's most calculating ruling heads. It may seem bizarre to us that the emperor Charles V should on several occasions have offered to resolve his quarrel with the king of France by single combat, but there is no reason to doubt his sincerity. In all their dealings Europe's rulers continued to play lip-service to the vision of Christendom united against the infidel. The obligation to mount a joint crusade when European conflict was resolved was routinely written into a treaty of alliance, or the peace that concluded a war between two Christian princes.

This was an age in which personality and character mattered: rulers had to look the part. Bad kings, those who failed to measure up, could be quite ruthlessly dealt with. The English, after all, had removed no fewer than four kings in the last 300 years, all of them with far stronger claims to the throne than the current incumbent, an obscure Welsh gentleman who had succeeded almost by default in having himself recognized as Henry VII. As in this case, an energetic assertion of right could often overwhelm a weak legal case. Dubious legality clouded the succession of Spain's two most charismatic rulers of the period, Isabella of Castile and the emperor Charles. Charles's proclamation of his right to the Spanish throne was technically a usurpation since his mother was still alive, if incapable; the rule of Isabella the Catholic was a flagrant denial of the superior right of her half-sister. In both cases it suited the natural leaders of these societies to ignore legal niceties for the greater benefit of stability. A strong ruler could make a difference; a weak one could bring great tribulation.

A survey of Europe's political geography at the beginning of the century reveals a curiously unfamiliar and shifting pattern. The powers that would come to dominate this century were often relatively new and uncertain features of the European political scene.

Spain and Portugal

Most eye-catching, because most brilliantly successful, was the personal alliance that had knit together the Spanish kingdoms of Aragon

Figure 4   Sixteenth-century Europe, from Sebastian Münster, *Cosmographia Universalis*. Courtesy St Andrews University Library. Note that the convention of showing north at the top had not yet become established by this period.

and Castile. The marriage of Ferdinand and Isabella had already by the turn of the new century been crowned by a military success that resounded through Christendom: the campaign against the Moors of Granada. This had culminated in 1492 with the subjugation of the Moorish kingdom, and the final recovery of the Iberian peninsula.

For much of the fifteenth century it would have appeared highly unlikely that the Spanish kingdoms would shortly rank among the leading powers of Europe. The reign of Henry IV of Castile (1454–74) had been characterized by a rampant aristocratic factionalism that had threatened the gravest consequences for the dynasty. Opponents of the influence of the king's principal minister, Beltrán de la Cueva, attempted to set aside the rights of the king's daughter and heir, Juana, in favour of her half-sister Isabella. They justified this coup, ratified at Toros de Guisando in 1468, by the sordid claim that Juana was not the king's rightful heir, but a bastard of the favourite. To strengthen her hand Isabella married Ferdinand of Aragon, the youthful monarch of an equally troubled kingdom, but a potent ally in the future struggle for the succession. Ferdinand's military prowess would indeed prove decisive. When Henry died Juana's cause was championed by Afonso of Portugal, but Ferdinand won the only battle of the war, and the succession was assured. Afonso, who had married the hapless Juana, now agreed to put away his wife and abandon her cause. It was a grubby enough beginning to a great age of Spanish kingship.

For all the queen's personal sense of obligation Castile did not take easily to Ferdinand. A joint monarchy was reluctantly conceded, but in all other respects the kingdoms would remain separate. Isabella's death in 1504 would temporarily destroy Ferdinand's position in the larger kingdom, until he returned, technically as regent, in 1506. But the Catholic monarchs forged an effective partnership in government. Resumption of land granted out to the nobility during the previous generation of faction fighting did something to set the royal finances on a firmer footing, and purposeful action was taken to bring under royal control the three military orders. These were the most tangible institutional reminder of the reconquest. Founded in the thirteenth century, the military orders had been rewarded for their efforts in the struggle against the Moors by vast grants of lands in the reconquered territories. While gratefully accepting their assistance in the Granada campaign, the king and queen also took action to rein in their independence. Through steady pressure they secured for Ferdinand appointment of the reversion of title of Grand Master of all three main orders: Calatrava (1485), Santiago (1492) and Alcántara (1494). In 1524 their lands were formally incorporated into the royal patrimony.

The Catholic monarchs also succeeded in forging a co-operative working relationship with the Castilian towns. The political power of the towns of Castile requires some explanation, for the Iberian peninsula, arid and sparsely populated, was not a natural centre of an independent urban culture. Spain's history and development were shaped by difficult and forbidding terrain. The great central plain of Castile is an arid elevated plateau divided by a central mountain range. Spain was condemned to be an agricultural society in land ill suited to agriculture: in northern Castile by far the most productive farming was provided by the huge migratory flocks of sheep tended for their wool. The Iberian peninsula is also relatively poorly endowed with rivers, and these of irregular depth: more often they served as a barrier than as an aid to communication. The harshness of the terrain seems to have encouraged the growth of the cities. Already by 1500 Spain had 20 cities with more than 10,000 inhabitants, including Toledo,

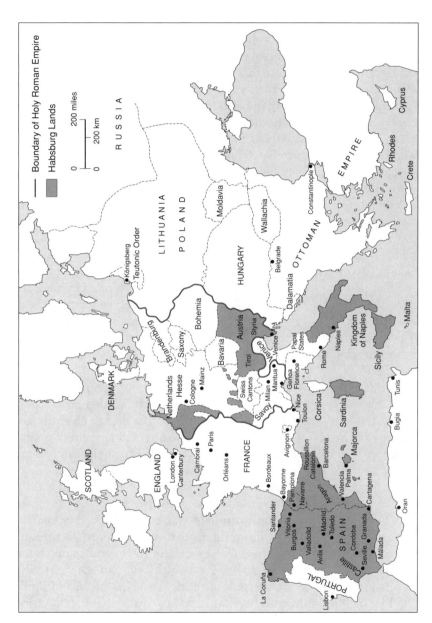

Map 1 Europe in 1500.

Valladolid and Salamanca. Out of a total population of some 6.8 million this represented a higher degree of urbanization than many parts of northern Europe.

For all that, the cities were scarcely the jealous guardians of urban values. In the later mediaeval period many nobles had gravitated to the cities, and they had effectively come to dominate the cities' political institutions. In the disturbances of the fifteenth century their interests had collided with those of the new feudal nobility gathered around the crown. Consequently the cities became the most enthusiastic supporters of Ferdinand and Isabella in their campaign to tame the grandees. The Catholic monarchs worked hard to extend this power base, expanding the noble caste by issuing new patents (*hidalguía*) normally for service in war. Meanwhile royal power in the towns was enhanced by the installation of royal judges (*corregidores*) to ensure their edicts were enforced. The representative assembly of the towns, the Cortes, met infrequently. After two meetings at the beginning of the reign there was an interval of 18 years until the towns met again. The intermittent nature of their meetings can be explained by the fact that the Catholic monarchs were not constrained by financial necessity: perhaps as much as four-fifths of their revenues came from the internal sales tax (the *alcabala*) which was theirs by custom. Through careful husbanding of this and other resources, the Catholic monarchs doubled the ordinary income of the crown between 1482 and 1504.

The fact that this was all accomplished without serious resistance probably owes a great deal to the quality of the leadership provided by the Catholic monarchs in the subjugation of Granada. This, the last crusade of the reconquest, required a sustained military effort unprecedented in Spanish history. From the siege of Alhama in 1482 to the fall of Granada ten years later Ferdinand and Isabella kept an army of some 50,000 virtually permanently in the field. The terrain was difficult and casualties high: the unification of the peninsula was hard won. But the consequent political dividend was considerable. Ferdinand's undeniable role in the campaign helped sustain his prestige through the difficult years following Isabella's death (1504) and the recognition that their daughter Juana was incapable of rule. In the short term Ferdinand was forced to concede authority to Juana's husband Philip the Fair of Burgundy, who had journeyed to Spain to assert his claim. But in 1506 Philip died, suddenly and unexpectedly, at the age of 28, and Ferdinand was restored, nominally as regent for the young son of Juana and Philip (the future Charles V), in effect as king.

In 1512 Ferdinand performed his last substantial service when, on the flimsiest pretext, he led Spanish forces into the independent Pyrenean kingdom of Navarre. Three years later the Cortes of Burgos formally admitted the conquered territories into the kingdom of Castile: the unification of the territories of Spain was complete. But the unification remained a purely personal one. No attempt was made to blend the separate administrative structures of the two kingdoms, nor would such an effort have been crowned with success, for the kingdom of Aragon defended its cherished liberties as doggedly as the Cortes of Castile. Aragon remained fundamentally Mediterranean in its orientation. Indeed, Ferdinand's successful conquest of Naples (1503) to join this southern state to his existing kingdom of Sicily made this eastern orientation more pronounced. The Spanish kingdoms inherited by Charles V in 1516 were thus as remarkable for their diversity as their coherence; diversity reflected in the variety of institutions, language, climate and culture, as well as geopolitical priorities. In this period 'Spain' was a term applied to all the peoples in the peninsula (including the Portuguese) and had no specific political meaning, any more than did 'Germany' or 'Italy'. For all that, the events on Europe's southern flank would have left no one in doubt that a formidable power had emerged: even before the consequences of the Habsburg succession combined to make this the basis of a potent European empire.

In all of these events Portugal – the other kingdom of the Iberian peninsula – was far from a mere passive spectator. Indeed, if it makes any sense to talk of the 'great powers' of the fifteenth century, then Portugal would have ranked among them, for Portugal was the first European nation to grow rich on the fruits of exploration. For all that, Portugal presents a paradox, since the confident expansion abroad took place against a backcloth of domestic turbulence and dynastic insecurity. The victory of the royal house of Avis at the end of the fourteenth century had brought Portugal little peace. The middle years of the fifteenth century were a time of almost constant tumult between the kin of King John and the bastard line. For 30 years during the reign of Afonso V the barons held sway; the persecuted king sought distraction in external affairs. The attempt to profit from the similar convulsions in Castile ended in ignominy, when Isabella asserted her claim through the alliance with Aragon. The humiliated Afonso was even forced to repudiate his wife, as we have seen. John II (1481–95) fared better only by a savage assault on the overmighty house of Bragança; his cousin and successor Manuel (1495–1521) finally achieved a tenuous security in successive marriages to the daughters of Ferdinand and Isabella, thus finally allying his house to that of Castile.

Portugal fared better abroad. In the first part of the fifteenth century Portuguese seafarers opened up Madeira and the Azores; Portuguese armies achieved notable successes against the Moors of Africa. Thus inspired, and assisted by the development of a new, hardier vessel, the caravel, the Portuguese pushed further down the coast of West Africa. The colonization of the Atlantic islands bore a rich dividend through the establishment of plantations of sugar, which now for the first time became a staple of the European diet. Late in the century the voyages of Vasco da Gama opened up the valuable spice trade to Portuguese exploitation.

The cumulative impact of these overseas voyages was to give the Portuguese crown an influence in European affairs that their fractious ruling classes scarcely deserved. Francis I of France would contemptuously refer to the king of Portugal as the 'roy epicier' (the spicer king), but spices were the key to wealth, and the Portuguese crown reaped the benefit. In the sixteenth century the kings of Spain would put aside the ancient antagonisms to seek in Portugal a succession of royal brides – and the dowries that came with them. These alliances finally settled the peace of the peninsula; though Portugal's rulers would not know that they would also hold the key to the later extinction of Portuguese independence.

France and Burgundy

To propose France as another of Europe's emergent powers in 1500 may seem extraordinary. This was, after all, one of the oldest established kingdoms of mediaeval Europe. But the intervening centuries had served France ill. Foreign invasion, military defeat and weak leadership had brought the kingdom to the brink of destruction. At the low point of French fortunes the area acknowledging the authority of the Valois king was reduced to a small enclave in the Loire valley.

By 1429 the tide had turned, and the expulsion of the English in 1453 completed the recovery of territory lost during the Hundred Years' War. Victory over Charles the Bold, Duke of Burgundy, in 1477 then secured the eastern flank. Ducal Burgundy was swiftly occupied, and though the heirs of Burgundy remained committed to its recovery, Burgundy would never again pass out of French hands.

With the final defeat of the Burgundian threat the focus of French ambition switched to Brittany on the north-western seaboard. The independence of Brittany was a long-running source of irritation. Although the dukes acknowledged a technical homage to the French king, and its nobles often sought service in France, it remained always a refuge for rebellious subjects. This was demonstrated in the reign of Charles VIII (1483–98) when his uncle Louis d'Orléans (the future Louis XII) took flight there after his frustrations at his exclusion from power boiled over into open defiance. This conflict provided the occasion for the final solution to the problem of Brittany. A French invasion brought Duke Francis to negotiations, and when he died Charles VIII claimed his daughter and heir, Anne, as his bride. On Charles's death in 1498 the new king moved swiftly to secure the royal widow, and on 8 January 1499 Anne of Brittany married her second king of France.[2] To achieve this goal Louis had first to dispose of his first wife, the saintly but ugly Jeanne of France. But Louis found a complaisant and worldly ally in the pope, Alexander VI, who provided the required dispensations. A grateful Louis made the pope's illegitimate son, Cesare Borgia, Duke of Valentinois.

The final assimilation of Brittany was a prize worth all of these sordid manoeuvres, but it did not complete the consolidation of French territory as we know it today. The northern and eastern frontiers remained wavering and uncertain, and many provinces and regions that acknowledged the authority of France were not yet in any meaningful sense integral parts of the kingdom. In the south, Dauphiné and Provence (annexed in 1481), east of the Rhône, were still not fully attached – the king was obeyed only as 'Dauphin' in the one and Count in the other. The great central fiefdom of the Bourbonnais was fully incorporated only after the treason and flight of the Duke of Bourbon in 1523.

Nor was the apparently inexorable progress towards an integral state irreversible. The marriage of Louis XII and Anne was blessed only by a daughter, Claude, who under Salic law could not succeed to the throne of France. In consequence for much of the king's reign the succession remained uncertain. The king's energetic marriage diplomacy necessarily concentrated on potential marriage partners for Claude, and in 1501 it was proposed to offer her to the young Charles of Ghent, newborn son of the emperor Maximilian. The dowry was to comprise Milan, Naples, Burgundy, Brittany and the county of Blois. This would have effected the dismemberment of France. When the treaty was renewed in 1504 further French territory was substituted for Naples. In the event wiser counsels prevailed, and in 1505 Claude of France was bestowed instead on Francis of Angoulême, the cousin who in 1515 would succeed as King Francis I.

The kingdom to which Francis succeeded was potentially one of the richest in Europe. In one single landmass it comprised a territory of 460,000 square kilometres (85 per cent of the present land mass of metropolitan France) and some 16 million people. Although France

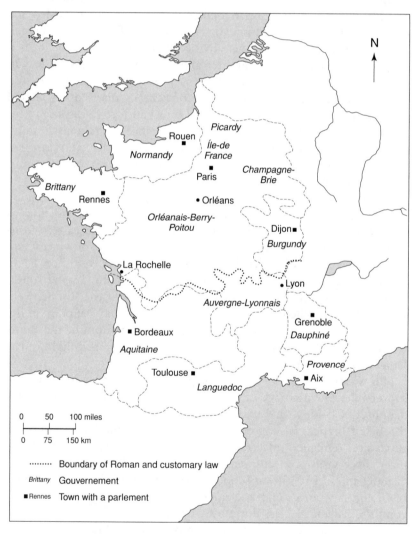

Map 2   Sixteenth-century France.

was for the most part an agricultural country, a considerable number of its inhabitants lived in cities. Fine provincial cities like Rouen, Orléans and Toulouse functioned as regional capitals in their own right, as did the rich entrepôt and banking centre of Lyon, with its close connections with the trading centres of Italy and Germany. These 4 cities each had between 40,000 and 70,000 inhabitants in the early sixteenth century, and there were another 20 or more with populations of between 10,000 and 30,000.

Another useful indicator of the vibrancy of provincial urban culture is the fact that by 1500 some 40 different French cities had a printing press. The capital, Paris, was one of the great cities of Europe, with a population of some 200,000, a rich intellectual life, and one of the most venerable and highly respected universities in Europe. Paris was the greatest of France's 15 universities, a high number that reflected the established influence of the church in French life. France had no fewer than 100 episcopal sees, and though some in the south were poor and impoverished, the best endowed bishops were venerable princes of the church.

Nevertheless, this was not a uniform state. France lacked a common language. The people of the north and south spoke quite separate dialects: the *langue d'oil* and the *langue d'oc*, and it was only gradually that the language of the north began to assert itself as what is now modern French. Brittany and the Basque country (Navarre) spoke different languages altogether. The piecemeal accumulation or reconquest of territories was also reflected in France's institutional development. While a large part of central and northern France was under the authority of the Parlement of Paris, the kingdom's highest law court, the recently acquired provinces generally had their own Parlement (there were six: at Toulouse, Grenoble, Bordeaux, Dijon, Rouen and Aix-en-Provence). These *pays d'état* also generally enjoyed a more favourable tax regime than the more integrated *pays d'élection*. Each province and even each locality had its own jealously guarded law code. Here, north and south marched to a different drum: the north generally followed customary law, whereas the south, a more Mediterranean culture in every respect, favoured Roman law. Whereas to outsiders France might have appeared a powerful and homogenous territory, the day-to-day reality was that in far-flung places the authority of the Crown was quite remote. It could not be otherwise when it took 10 to 14 days to travel between Paris and Marseilles. The south even had its own tradition of mediaeval heresy, with the mediaeval movement of the Cathars or Albigensians. This had been put down in a war of great brutality, but its spirit lived on in some mountainous regions, and even in the sixteenth century the Catholic Church struggled to exert its influence over a region of independent mind and spirit.

Such unity as there was was provided by the person of the king, rather than any particular institution. At the national level the only representative body was the Estates General, made up of elected representatives of three estates: the clergy, nobility and third estate (commons). But the Estates General met only at the pleasure of the king, and then only on extraordinary occasions. After a meeting in 1484 to settle the question of the regency during the minority of Charles VIII, they would not meet again until 1560. The king's income, though complex, was not dependent on consent. By 1500 the customary distinction between 'ordinary' revenue drawn from the king's lands and feudal dues, and 'extraordinary' levies, had largely disappeared. The extraordinary revenues comprised three main taxes: the *taille* (a property tax), the *gabelle* (on salt) and *aides* (duties on commodities). The *taille* was levied annually, in war and peace, at a level determined by the King's Council. The kings of France would have enjoyed an enviable financial position but for two constraints: their own habit of wanton war-making, and inefficiencies in the gathering of taxes that ensured that the tax take was always far below its nominal value. To achieve a steady flow of ready money the custom had developed of farming out taxes – in effect auctioning the right to collect on the king's behalf – and the tax farmer would always take a huge premium on what was in effect a short-term loan. The kings were able to raise their armies, but the financiers became some of the richest men in France.

The work of forging a coherent administration for these lands was painstakingly advanced by Louis XII. After his early career as a factious rebel, Louis's accession was not greeted with any particular expectation, but in fact he ruled with wisdom and discretion. Recognizing the need to reduce taxes from the high levels they had reached under Charles VIII, Louis kept a frugal court, to the disappointment of courtiers who spitefully dubbed him 'le roi roturier' (the commoner king). Louis was unrepentant. 'I much prefer', he was reported to have said, 'to make dandies laugh at my miserliness than to make the people weep at my open-handedness.' It was a lesson some of his sixteenth-century successors could have done well to learn. Louis also set in hand the codification and rationalization of customary law that would be carried steadily forward in the following century. All in all it was a self-confident and prosperous nation that Louis was able to pass to his successor on his death in 1515.

A hundred years before the lands of Burgundy had looked fair set to emerge as one of Europe's greatest powers. A series of ambitious and powerful dukes had built this cadet branch of the royal house of France into a formidable competitor. In the first half of the fifteenth century and in alliance with England during the Hundred Years' War it even seemed possible that the two together would preside over the dismemberment of the French kingdom. Even when English fortunes began to wane, Burgundy went from strength to strength. In 1473, when René II of Lorraine recognized Charles the Bold as his 'protector', it appeared that the juncture of the northern and southern Burgundian lands – Flanders and Burgundy proper – lay within reach. If this had been achieved, it would have created a rich and compact state straddling some of Europe's richest and most strategic territories.[3]

It was not to be. The defection of the Duke of Lorraine obliged Charles the Bold to attempt to subjugate the crucial central territories by force of arms; and it was here, at the Battle of Nancy in 1477 that the Burgundian vision was shattered. In the wake of Nancy ducal Burgundy was overrun, leaving the Free County (the Franche-Comté) as an isolated and apparently vulnerable remnant separated from the new heartland of Burgundian territories in Flanders and Holland. In fact, the mountainous and difficult terrain was an adequate defence, and the Franche-Comté would remain in Habsburg hands until 1679.

Nevertheless the defeat at Nancy left the Burgundian inheritance vulnerable and exposed, and there was little option for the grieving heiress, Mary, daughter of Charles the Bold, but to seek protection in a new dynastic combination. Within a few months Mary had married Maximilian of Habsburg, the future emperor, but for now eager to accept the new prize offered by such an advantageous marriage. For the Burgundian lands, though diminished, were still highly desirable, especially the lands in the Low Countries, the counties of Flanders, Brabant and Holland. This was not yet the 17 provinces of the sixteenth century, for only in the time of Charles V would the consolidation of these territories be completed, through conquest and negotiation, by the accession of Friesland (1524), Groningen (1536) and Gelderland (1543). But the fifteenth-century inheritance was certainly the most prosperous part of these sophisticated and cultured lands. Flanders and Brabant, especially, were a rich prize, among the most prosperous and most heavily urbanized territories in Europe. The basis of this wealth was the manufacture and finishing of cloth, for Flanders produced some of the finest cloth in Europe: this in turn fuelled the growth of the great cities of the Flanders plain, Bruges, Ghent and Brussels, and in Brabant, Antwerp and Louvain. These were sophisticated and cosmopolitan societies, closely connected by trade to the great cities of Italy, with which they also shared an advanced artistic tradition. This was a part of Europe unusually open to outside influences, as the early impact of Humanism would testify. But the tradition of urban independence was also reflected in a truculent, stubborn resistance to direction, and the loyalties of the estates were strained to breaking point by repeated financial exactions. Bruges and Ghent particularly embodied a tradition of urban protest that would flare fitfully in the sixteenth century.

Securing the obedience of these self-willed cities was a task that seemed at one point to be beyond Maximilian. Even before Mary's marriage the financial demands of her father had provoked rebellion, and Maximilian's arrival made him the new focus of these discontents. In 1482 Mary of Burgundy died in a hunting accident, leaving a young son, Philip. Maximilian's claim to the regency was contested by the Netherlandish estates. An opportunist attempt by the French to capitalize on his discomforture might have rebounded to his advantage, but both Bruges and Ghent continued to resist, at one point openly seeking a French alliance. Only in 1492, with the Peace of Kadzand, was the revolt finally ended. By this point Philip was fast reaching the age at which he could exercise his rule in person, and the issue of Maximilian's regency would be moot. Philip's marriage to Juana, daughter of Ferdinand of Aragon, completed a web of diplomatic alliance that seemed once and for all to secure the Netherlandish lands from the French threat.

One could well understand therefore the celebration that greeted the birth of a new Burgundian heir, Charles, in 1500. After perilous years the independent future of Netherlandish Burgundy seemed secure. No-one could have anticipated that this was the first link in a diplomatic chain that would ultimately see the Netherlands subsumed in a greater and increasingly Hispanic empire; and the beginning of an enduring relationship which would, in the case of Flanders and Brabant, continue through to the eighteenth century.

England and Scotland

England was at this time emerging from a period of turmoil that had brought its prestige very low. At the beginning of the sixteenth century the kingdom was enjoying a precarious peace after 30 years of murderous noble feuding known as the 'Wars of the Roses'. This was not a civil war in the modern sense, and fighting was far from continuous. But such fighting as there was proved surprisingly decisive, when one considers that from the time of Henry VI's mental breakdown in 1453 to Henry VII's defeat of a Yorkist challenge at the Battle of Stoke (1487) the crown of England changed hands six times. There were 14 pitched battles and a surprising number of casualties. In particular, the wars caused a veritable holocaust in the English nobility. In all 38 peers were killed in battle or executed by the victors. In a noble caste that was by European standards narrow, this was a very significant rate of attrition. The chaos in the upper nobility was compounded by the wholesale use during the wars of acts of attainder: a Parliamentary declaration of treason by which family goods and lands were forfeit to the crown. Acts of attainder were passed against some 397 individuals in this period – and although many were subsequently reversed, reversal was seldom complete. With necessary distribution of spoils to the victors, and frequent reversals of fortune, the wars left a morass of competing claims and expectations in this most sensitive area of noble culture.

So when in 1485 Henry Tudor, the relatively obscure descendent of the Lancastrian claim, managed to wrest the crown from Richard III, there was no reason to believe that this last, and in many respects, most unlikely twist, would prove decisive. The signs were not auspicious. The unlikely victory at Bosworth propelled to the throne a man of 28 who had spent his youth in Wales and the last 14 years as an exile in France and Brittany. Before his accession he may have visited England only once. His experience of government was non-existent; his connections with the English elites tenuous.

In fact, England had much to be grateful for in their new king. Thoughtful, calculating and cautious, Henry piloted the kingdom through a period of reconstruction and reconciliation with surprising assurance. To secure the loyalty of the remains of the English nobility he compelled many to enter into bonds and recognizances, specific financial obligations that would be called in only if they proved disloyal. Never before had such a fiscal dimension to the normal moral and social constraints of feudal obligation been so systematically employed: of 62 peerage families alive during the reign, some 46 were effectively at the king's mercy through this and other means. But in a period when the normal bonds of loyalty had been completely destroyed by 30 years of endemic rebellion, Henry's innovation was both justified and surprisingly effective.

Henry's natural caution also suited England well in its relations with other European powers, at a time when the kingdom was scarcely in a position to assert itself on the European stage. This required a certain intellectual adjustment. It was only a century before, after all, that England had possessed extensive possessions on continental Europe, and Henry could not entirely deny this heritage. The new king duly asserted his claim to France and in 1492 led an expedition across the Channel. But the resources for such foreign adventures were meagre, and Henry was happy to accept a diplomatic solution after only 33 days' campaigning. Henry's active diplomacy was well rewarded. His inclusion in the 1496 Holy League against France marked a recognition of his status as a European monarch of note, and in 1499 he secured the major prize of a notable Spanish bride (Catherine, daughter of Ferdinand of Aragon) for his son Arthur.

It is worth asking why the evident weakness of England during the period of dynastic chaos that preceded Henry VII was not more fully exploited by Europe's other powers. The probable answer is revealing for what it tells us of England's status among the European powers in this period. Put brutally, even at its most vulnerable during the Yorkist/Lancastrian conflicts there was little to encourage Europe's dynastic predators to exploit England's misfortune. It was not one of Europe's richest regions; its position on the Atlantic periphery placed it far from areas of strategic sensitivity. So although Europe's rulers were happy to meddle, this was more for the sake of mischief, and to establish one of the competing factions in a client relationship, than because any had serious designs on English territory. Louis XI of France had assisted the Earl of Warwick against Edward IV, and the Yorkist king subsequently took refuge in the Low Countries. Henry Tudor's successful invasion was made possible by 4,000 French troops. It was therefore inevitable that his defeated opponents would seek assistance at the Burgundian court, where Margaret of York, the dowager duchess (the widow of Charles the Bold), was an indefatigable promoter of the Yorkist cause. Yet the assurance with which Henry VII dealt with such intrigues (notably the attempt to set up the impostor Perkin Warbeck in 1497) demonstrated the futility of such attempts to destabilize the dynasty. In 1506 the Anglo-Burgundian *rapprochement* was sealed by the handing over to Henry of Edmund de la Pole, heir to the Yorkist claim, and a long-term exile in the Netherlands.

Most of all Henry revealed himself as a man with a natural gift for administration. He picked good men to serve him, but kept close watch on the details of royal financial administration; in consequence from the ruins of the dynastic wars he built a position of considerable stability. He was helped by a system of taxation that was by European standards relatively efficient: to the king's customary income from land could be added customs revenues, and more sporadic Parliamentary taxation. Although taxation issues inevitably caused debate and friction (and a measure of resistance), it is important to note that the fiscal base of royal finances was created without resort to either tax-farming or selling of offices: the two single greatest causes of the inefficiency of continental tax-gathering in this period.

England in the sixteenth century was an agrarian society, and a relatively prosperous one. The population in 1500 had recovered to around 2.5 million: still only half that of the high Middle Ages, before the Black Death had triggered a succession of crises of mortality. This was the beginning of a gentle recovery that would accelerate through the century. Local county societies were organized politically around the influence of the major regional magnates, and economically around a network of county towns, but these were on the whole small by continental standards. Only London attained the size and sophistication of the major European centres. Culturally, England was undoubtedly a backwater. It had only two universities, neither of them in the European front rank; the influence of Humanism arrived late. When Erasmus came to Cambridge in 1499 this was a great triumph for the small intellectual clique that had lured him across the Channel; but he made no secret of the fact that he felt he had arrived in frontier territory.

In contrast this was a state where the political organization of society was, despite the setbacks of the last half century, precociously advanced. By the sixteenth century the representative assembly, Parliament, was a fixed part of the political landscape. Its constituent parts were also fixed, and unvaried: the two chambers consisted of a House of Lords, to which were summoned secular peers and the leaders of the church, and a House of Commons, with representatives of county communities and boroughs. The monarch retained the whip hand: only he could determine when Parliament would be summoned and it was despatched at his pleasure. Sessions were short, and normally determined by the need to seek funds. Its function was taxation and legislation, rather than the making of policy. Henry VII would look to other bodies for counsel and advice – his Privy Council of intimates and, on occasion, a specially convened Grand Council of notables (such a Council was summoned five times during his reign). But the reliance on parliamentary taxation assured Parliament of a fixed place in the political framework; the events of the next reign, when Parliament found itself at the hub of the legislative change associated with the English Reformation, would further enhance its stature.

In marked contrast to its fractious southern neighbour, the dynastic history of Scotland presents a picture of relative tranquillity. Almost uniquely in the states of Europe, between 1371 and 1542 the crown of Scotland passed in an unbroken sequence from father to son in the same (in this case Stewart) dynasty: from James I (died 1437) to James V (1513–42). But the age of the five kings James was far more turbulent than a simple acknowledgement of this admittedly impressive dynastic achievement would suggest. For much of this time Scotland was forced to confront relentless assaults from the English neighbour, and the search for allies made Scotland an active partner in the diplomatic negotiations of the centuries. And, during this time, the English landed some telling blows, culminating in the three terrible Scottish defeats of Flodden (1513), Solway Moss (1542) and Pinkie (1547). The death of James IV at Flodden left the crown in the hands of an infant, his son James; when James V in turn died suddenly after Solway Moss the crown passed to another infant, the young Mary, Queen of Scots.

Under these pressures the survival of the dynasty depended to a large extent on the co-operation of the magnate class. More perhaps than any of Europe's ruling houses, the Stewart house of Scotland was obliged to rule in partnership with their leading subjects. The simple facts of geography and topography give a clear indication as to why this should have been so. The population of Scotland in 1500 was around 800,000, heavily concentrated in the Lowland zone of the present central belt between Edinburgh and Glasgow and the borderlands with England. This was fundamentally a rural society. Although the Scottish towns (burghs) had a well-established legal and political presence, only Edinburgh was of any real size by European standards, with a population of about 5,000 in 1500, growing to 15,000 by the end of the century. The other burghs were much smaller: Dundee and Aberdeen grew to 6,000 and 10,000 inhabitants by the end of the century, but all remained in the shadow of the capital. Edinburgh paid more taxation than the next three burghs (Dundee, Perth and Aberdeen) combined, and its proportion of the total customs revenue might amount to a half or more. Far more therefore than in richer or more populous lands, the social topography of Scotland was dominated by the buildings of the two great estates, the nobility and the church.

Their castles and cathedrals towered over other burgh housing and were the major human landmarks in the countryside. And in comparison with the other countries of Europe, the Scottish elite was both small, and compacted into a relatively small space. Most of the leading magnates would have their dwelling within a couple of days' hard riding of each other, and noble families were densely connected by marriage and kinship loyalties.

All of this made for a comparatively sophisticated political culture. Scottish lairds were more used than their European brethren to dealing directly with each other in person; they expected to see the king, and know him personally. Meetings of the Scottish Parliament would be intimate occasions, and they occurred often: the custom of annual meetings was only abandoned at the end of the fifteenth century. But this was not a closed society. The incessant pressure from the English encouraged the development of quite intricate connections with potential European allies or protectors: most famously France, but also the rulers of the Netherlands and Scandinavia. It was to the northern kingdoms that. Scotland was most closely linked by trade, and the marriage alliance between James III and Margaret, daughter of Christian I of Denmark and Norway (1468) was a recognition of this. As part of the dowry settlement Orkney and Shetland were pawned to the Scottish crown, thus finally passing out of Norwegian hands. The long alliance with France brought less obvious benefit. Scotland was obviously the junior partner, and merely one of France's multiple foreign policy concerns and opportunities. A connection that was crucial to Scottish security could be treated with unsentimental disdain at the French court. After Flodden Louis XII made preparations for either war or peace with England – if he opted for the latter, then the alliance that had led Scotland to disaster would have been abandoned without settlement or compensation.

In the event the most tangible benefit of the long continental alliance would be more cultural than territorial. Scottish magnates and their representatives spent long months at the continental courts, as supplicants or exiles, and brought back with them French tastes and styles. When Mary of Guise (widow of James V and regent of Scotland in the mid-sixteenth century) praised the palace of Linlithgow as the finest building she had seen outside the Château of the Loire, she may for the most part have been exercising her innate courtesy. But there are some fine Renaissance buildings in Scotland, not least the Castle/Palace of St Andrews, rebuilt in the modern style about this time. But in truth the connections with England were also close, and sometimes more

Figure 5 St Andrews Castle. Courtesy St Andrews University Library. Although now decayed, the front of this once impressive building shows the broad geographic spread of Renaissance architectural influence.

amicable than the simple narration of wars and battles would suggest. James III (1460–88) had consciously pursued a friendship with England, and though James IV (1488–1513) had reversed this policy, notably by ill-judged support for Perkin Warbeck, the English king Henry VII had refused to be provoked, and friendship was renewed with the marriage of James to Margaret Tudor. Thus the English amity was a strand of Scottish policy-making well established by the sixteenth century, offering a plausible alternative to the Auld Alliance even before the coming of the Reformation.

Northern Europe and the Empire

Still more remote on Europe's northern flank were the kingdoms of Scandinavia. These cold, harsh and desolate lands present a paradox. Sparsely populated and unsophisticated societies, they were nevertheless incredibly rich in natural resources: from the end of the sixteenth century onwards they would form an essential part in the network of European trade, with their apparently limitless abundance of iron ore, tar, pitch, hemp and timber. But in 1500 all this lay in the future: before the great age of European trade and naval conflict, when even Portugal and Spain still had enough timber to build their own ships, few bothered to acquaint themselves with the perilous northern voyages for the sake of herrings and whalebone.

From 1397 the northern kingdoms of Denmark, Norway, Sweden and Finland had been united under the crown of Denmark. Together the united kingdom covered an impressive proportion of Europe's surface area but numbered only a tiny proportion of its population. Only about 1.5 million people populated this huge area, much of it dense forest or frozen tundra. Centres of population were concentrated in Denmark, and on the southern coastal fringe of Norway and Sweden, where the sea and rivers offered at least some protection from the harshest aspects of the climate, and connections with the outside world.

All parts of this vast region had in 1397 been brought to acknowledge the authority of King Eric, after a long and brilliant campaign by his mother, the redoubtable Margaret. But this technical unity masked significant differences between the constituent kingdoms. In Denmark both landownership and society were dominated by the nobility. Denmark was of all the kingdoms closest in culture, social structure and political custom to Germany, to which it was closely linked by trade. In Sweden, in contrast, 50 per cent of the land remained in the hands of an independent peasantry, many of them still enthusiastically carving out new farms in the northern forests. Norway, meanwhile, had been so devastated by the Black Death that many farms remained desolate for generations. The depopulation permanently altered the balance in the union between Norway and Denmark.

The fifteenth century was an exceptionally turbulent time. The unification of the Scandinavian crowns having been completed, there was no intrinsic reason why the accumulation of territory should end there, and successive fifteenth-century kings pursued a variety of claims and aspirations within the Empire: for Schleswig, Holstein, and Pomerania. The high costs of this ambitious foreign policy put power in the hands of the magnates, and it was they who on the deposition of King Eric and the death of his usurper Christopher offered the crown to Christian of Oldenburg (1448). Thus the ruler of an obscure German dynasty founded a royal line that was to continue in Denmark for four centuries.

Figure 6 Scandinavia, from *Histoia Joannis Magni Gothi*, Rome, 1554. Courtesy St Andrews University Library.

Sweden remained restive, and never really fully accepted the Union. A succession of leading nobles, recognized as Guardian, continued the tradition of independence. In 1520 Christian II (1513–23) achieved a military victory over these forces which allowed him finally to be crowned King of Sweden in Stockholm. He attempted to secure his position by arresting those of his former opponents who had attended the festivities and condemning them to death: this famous and perfidious bloodbath claimed 82 high-born victims. Even after this, the cull of Sweden's elite was pursued with such energy that the final death toll approached 600. But one young noble, Gustavus Vasa, remained at large, and he succeeded in rallying the Swedish peasantry to his cause. In July 1523 an assembly of the realm elected him King. When the Danish nobility also tired of their erratic king, even his Imperial connections (his wife was sister of Charles V) could not save him: Christian II was overthrown and condemned to a discontented exile. The separation of Denmark and Sweden now became a permanent feature of the northern political landscape.

While Scandinavia defined Europe's northern reaches, the Holy Roman Empire sprawled over a vast area of the most populous parts of central Europe. At the beginning of the sixteenth century the Empire technically encompassed significant territories whose residual connection was tenuous in the extreme. The Netherlands, for instance, had been ruled as an independent state by the Burgundian counts, but were only legally removed from the Empire by their new Habsburg rulers in 1548. The Swiss Confederation made good its claim to independence on the field of battle: this achieved *de facto* recognition in 1499, but *de jure* only with the Peace of Westphalia in 1648. In the east Habsburg lands within the Empire blended seamlessly into territories outside its boundaries. Most curiously of all the whole of the north Italian plain was still technically part of the Empire. By the fifteenth century none of the Italian territories south of the Alps acknowledged the authority of the Emperor, with the exception of small enclaves such as the ecclesiastical territory of Trent; though that anomaly, as we shall see, actually allowed it to play a crucial role in the geopolitical affairs of the age.

The ambiguity that attached even to its boundaries reveals an essential part of the Empire's political nature: that by the late Middle Ages the Empire was a political entity in name alone. It is best described as a conglomeration of diverse and multitudinous territories that for the most part were independent and autonomous, but which recognized a loose allegiance to Imperial institutions and the personal authority of the Emperor. Although the part played by the Emperor in the political life of any individual territory was necessarily sporadic, he nevertheless was a presence, if only as a final point of appeal in disputes between territories, or as the figure most likely to rally forces against an external threat.

At the dawn of the sixteenth century there was at least the chance for the Empire to become rather more than the sum of its disparate parts. The gradual erosion of authority over the non-German lands on the periphery had the potential to accentuate the German character, and sense of common interest, of what remained. There is clear sign of growth of a German cultural identity in the second half of the fifteenth century, which sought, not altogether successfully, for some sort of concrete political manifestation. With the Imperial crown settled in the hands of an ambitious and dynamic ruling house, the Habsburgs, they could be expected to give energetic leadership, not least against the looming threat from Turkish encroachment towards the Empire's eastern border.

Nevertheless the institutional barriers to such a development were considerable, and ultimately decisive. Germany in 1500 had about 16 million inhabitants, but these were divided between several hundred political units of wildly variant sizes. Towards the top end were around 30 major secular states, some of which, in the north east and south of the Empire, had accumulated quite significant territories. First in terms of size and prestige were the four electoral states of Saxony, Bohemia, the Palatinate and Brandenburg, though the thrusting and ambitious state of Bavaria was also a force to be reckoned with. These princes were themselves strongly committed to advancing the cause of state-building, but within their own borders. Borders were in any case, still remarkably fluid; few states within the Empire had significant natural boundaries, and territories might be interwoven with a patchwork of smaller, independent jurisdictions: there were several hundred such in the Empire as a whole.

Most of all the leading princes aspired to bring under their control any cities within the borders of their territories that enjoyed an independent existence. Germany was one of the most heavily urbanized parts of Europe: there were some 4,000 towns in all, but these again varied greatly. At their apex were the 65 towns recognized as Imperial Free Cities (*Reichstädte*). They enjoyed functional independence, and were separately represented at the Imperial Diets. There were important concentrations of Imperial cities in the south of Germany, including some of the largest and most important cities, such as Nuremberg, Augsburg and Strasbourg, and a curtain of northern coastal ports, including Hamburg, Lübeck and Rostock. Some of the cities possessed a considerable territory in their hinterland outside the city walls but they exercised their influence through economic power, and especially in the wider European economy. The southern towns flourished through transcontinental trade, and through the associated business of banking and exchange. The northern cities had a rather separate economic orientation, as part of the Hanseatic League, an association that comprised cities in the Empire, but also the Netherlands and Scandinavia. Inevitably their wider political concerns were bound up with the politics of the Baltic and Scandinavia. The Imperial cities were the elite; the position of the remaining towns (*Landesstädte*) was much less certain and they remained vulnerable to the ambitions of their princely neighbours. A last and not to be underestimated group was made up by the ecclesiastical territories. There were some 90 in all, and again the largest were considerable bodies of territory, over which their bishop or archbishop exercised authority much as if he were a secular lord. Their rulers had similar political concerns and priorities to those of secular princes, to whom indeed they were often allied by ties of family.

In all the circumstances there is the question why anyone should have aspired to rule over such a loose and unwieldy association – never mind spend, as Charles V and Francis I of France both did in 1519, considerable sums to win the loyalty of the seven hereditary electors.[4] Part of the explanation lay in the historical prestige of the office: the Holy Roman Emperor was still recognized as the first prince of western Christendom, and received the diplomatic precedence appropriate to that rank. Also those who held the office still cherished the hope that in this age of state-building the Empire might still achieve a greater coherence and reality. This goal was most energetically pursued by Maximilian I (Emperor 1493–1519) though it remained a live aspiration for his grandson Charles V. The Habsburg Emperors also derived great authority from their own family lands: even without the Imperial dignity they would have been very considerable figures in central European politics.

The cause of Imperial unity was most energetically, if inconsistently, pursued by Maximilian. He followed into the Imperial office his father Frederick III and for the next 30 years was a major player in Europe's dynastic quarrels. Charming, stylish, devious, generous and impecunious, Maximilian was in many respects the archetype of the Renaissance prince. At various times in his eventful period as Emperor he would attempt both to exert his authority, and to be a major player in Europe's wider dynastic conflicts and alliances. In the event, almost inevitably, he fell between two stools: always distracted from his

German responsibilities by military adventures in Italy, always thwarted in attempts to assert his authority over the German princes and towns by his embarrassing need for their co-operation in funding his schemes. As a result the Imperial reform movement, which reached its zenith in the 1480s and 1490s, proceeded without substantial support from the Emperor, and followed paths that at times he strongly opposed. Maximilian supported Imperial reform largely as a means of guaranteeing him regular tax income, and bolstering his authority. The states obviously had other priorities, and it was these that lay behind the re-establishment of the *Reichskammergericht* (Imperial Chamber court) to deal with disputes within the Empire. This was part of a wider campaign to combat lawlessness within the politically fragmented lands of Germany: the Imperial Diet, which the reformers insisted should meet annually, also succeeded in making permanent a declaration of general peace within the Empire (*Reichslandfrieden*). But plans for a standing central Council (*Reichsregiment*) and Imperial standing army were effectively obstructed by Maximilian – like any other German prince when it came to it he was more comfortable building administrative institutions within his own lands, where they could not be used to challenge his authority. So compared to the state-building accomplished or initiated elsewhere in Europe during this period, the Imperial reform movement was destined for failure. The enduring legacy of Maximilian's time would be in the more traditional areas of princely pursuits; part cultural, through his patronage of Dürer and other notable contemporaries, and part in the web of marriage alliances that would shape Europe's dynastic future to a quite improbable extent.

The position of the Habsburg Emperors was complicated by a confusion of purpose even in their strategy for political reform within the Empire. While they seemed to aspire to a closer institutional unity for the whole German core of the Empire, they also had the opportunity to carve out for themselves a more closely knit princely state, based on the Habsburg lands of Austria and south Germany. This was the most tantalizing of the states that failed to be in sixteenth-century Europe, and it was ultimately thwarted by the collapse of co-operation between the Habsburgs and the towns, as their relationship came under strain in the era of the Reformation.[5]

For the towns, at the beginning of the century the power of the Emperor was less resented than perceived as a possible protection against the greedy designs of the territorial princes. When this relationship came under strain a possible alternative was to band together as a free association, either together, or in an expanded Swiss Confederation. For of course there was no particular logical limit to the Swiss Confederation, already a fairly motley collection of urban and rural cantons, spanning a wide range of physical environments and language groups.

The core of the Swiss Confederation had been created by the resistance of the inner mountain cantons to Austrian authority at the end of the thirteenth century. Over the next hundred years, other, more urban cantons (including Berne, Zurich, Lucerne and Zug), adhered to the original association. But independence was only assured by the smashing victory over Maximilian in 1499, when the famous Swiss peasant infantry (the *Landsknechte*) proved their worth. Thereafter the Swiss Confederation guaranteed internal peace by a carefully nurtured respect for diversity: a harmony only really threatened once, by the attempt to coerce the Catholic cantons into reform in the first generation of the Reformation. This Zurich imperialism (for so it appeared to the more sceptically minded) met its nemesis with Zwingli's death on the battlefield at Kappel in 1531. Thereafter the Swiss Confederation settled into the backcloth of European politics. For those who could pay regular wages Swiss mercenaries continued to be much sought after in the larger struggles of European states; the Swiss model of government found admirers but no imitators.

This rapid survey of Europe's nations and territories concludes without venturing further east than Vienna – eastern Europe is reserved to a later chapter – or into Italy. This may seem perverse in that at the dawn of the sixteenth century Italy remained the fulcrum of European politics, and a model and inspiration in many areas of European life. For these reasons Italy has been reserved for a separate chapter.

3

The Struggle for Italy

The Lure of Italy

At the dawn of the sixteenth century, Italy was arguably not only the heart of Europe, but its mind and soul as well. For this was a period in which Italy provided not only the normative culture, but admired models of government, advanced education method, and – in the person of the pope – the ultimate spiritual authority. If this last had been somewhat battered by the struggle over church authority in the late Middle Ages, the vision of a more distant classical past burned ever more brightly. For Rome was the undisputed centre of that classical world that was so eagerly reconstructed in the minds and work of Renaissance scholarship.

For Europe's leading citizens – its rulers, churchmen and aspiring scholars – Italy at the end of the fifteenth century exercised an extraordinary magnetic attraction. Merchants, students, pilgrims and artists from all over Europe all journeyed to Italy in the hope of profit, enlightenment, or spiritual fulfilment. Even in an age where journeying was costly and hazardous – and since visiting Italy meant crossing the Alps, in this case especially arduous – the imperative behind this speculative migration is not hard to discern. For at the end of the fifteenth century the cities and states of Italy could plausibly claim leadership in four crucial areas of European life: the economy, education, culture and religion.

Most of these aspects of Italian life were inevitably concentrated in the cities, and it was indeed the cities that overwhelmingly dominated contemporary perceptions of Italy, both in the minds of foreigners and Italians themselves. In the peninsula as a whole over 1.3 million people lived in cities of over 10,000 inhabitants. In a total population of around ten million this represented a level of urbanization matched only in the Low Countries. The density of urban settlement was reflected in the fact that a third of all Europe's large conurbations (44 of 154) were to be found in the peninsula, and these of course included some of the greatest of them all. A pilgrim or traveller following the itinerary of one of the newly popular genre of travel guides would be led through some of Europe's greatest places: Milan, the gateway to Italy, famed for its wealth and industry; Florence, Pisa, Bologna and Rome itself. To the south lay Naples, a city of some 120,000 inhabitants; to the east the great Mediterranean power of Venice.

These were societies in which life was lived on a sophisticated level. Italy provided Europe with the model of the independent city republic, communities that enjoyed a high level of public political involvement, and an advanced level of administrative and economic development. Despite a notable trend towards oligarchy in the course of the fifteenth century, Italian cities still preserved a high level of popular representation and considerable social mobility. The greater council in Venice in 1500 had around 2,000 members; in a total city population of 100,000 this represented an impressive level of participation for native-born male citizens. In Florence there were some 3,000 offices to be filled from a much smaller core of politically emancipated citizens. With highly developed political institutions went a precociously active bureaucracy and record keeping, and some sophisticated institutions of public finance. Although institutions like the Florentine *Monte dei Doti* (Dowry Fund) did not entirely replace short-term financial expedients in time of crisis, they did point to an important success in the extent to which the Italian city states had succeeded in domesticating public debt. This was an example that the new monarchies of western Europe would struggle to emulate in the next hundred years.

The wealth of the peninsula was built on trade. Much of this trade was internal to the peninsula, between and among the cities and towns of the northern plain. By the fifteenth century many of the leading merchant families had taken to establishing permanent outposts in other towns, a model for a development that spread to other parts of Europe where demand for Italian manufactures was intense. Italians were always prominent in the great international trade fairs of mediaeval Geneva and Lyon, and considerable colonies of Italians made these cities their permanent home. In northern Europe, London, Paris and Antwerp also played host to small but wealthy communities drawn from Italy's leading trading towns. Here and elsewhere it was Italy's dominant role in extra-European trade that consolidated the place of the great Italian trading families in the wider European economy. Much of the trade of the Levant – spices, fine fabrics, exotic comestibles – flowed through the peninsula, bringing wealth to places like Genoa, and making Venice a considerable imperial power. The phenomenal wealth generated by trade in precious merchandise allowed the Italians to develop quite naturally specialist skills associated with international trade and the money market: banking, exchange and financial services.

By the dawn of the sixteenth century the Italian pre-eminence in many areas of long-distance trade was no longer absolute. German and Netherlandish families were increasingly coming to the fore, and in Lyon native French merchants were beginning to take back influence from the immigrant families. But the influence of Italy was still profound, not least because in many parts of Europe the presence of a local Italian merchant community was the most immediate point of contact with the sophisticated social practice and culture of the peninsula. For many young members of German merchant families a period in Italy was an essential part of their apprenticeship. In this way too the influence of Italian business practice became generalized throughout Europe.

If trade brought many a hopeful youth south, still more travelled for intellectual enlightenment. In the fields of education and art the cultural pull of Italy was overwhelming. In Italy were located some of the finest and most respected universities of the mediaeval world. In the fields of civil law, Bologna, Padua and Pisa stood at the pinnacle of European eminence, a fact reflected in the polyglot character of their teeming student body. The customary division of mediaeval universities into student 'nations' allows one to sample both the variety and the sheer numbers of foreign students enrolled in the Italian universities. In Bologna the Germans were especially numerous (and specially privileged in the university's constitution) but there were also considerable numbers of students from France, England and Spain, as well as smaller groups of Poles and Hungarians. By the beginning of the sixteenth century Padua was outstripping Bologna as the favoured university of English students abroad, and also attracting considerable numbers from Germany and eastern Europe.

The undoubted Italian roots of the new intellectual movement of Humanism assured Italian teachers of a leading role in the intellectual formation of the new generation of university-trained lay people throughout Europe. Students from other parts of the continent continued to colonize Italian universities deep into the sixteenth century, notwithstanding the growing confessional divisions that might have been expected to act as a disincentive.[1]

Italian cultural supremacy was even more profound in the field of the arts. At the dawn of the sixteenth century the Italian Renaissance was reaching the peak of its achievement. In Rome in 1500 Perugino was at the height of his powers, and Raphael just beginning to make his reputation. Michelangelo was also at the beginning of his long and spectacular career. The Florence school of Lippi had found its contemporary genius in Leonardo da Vinci, painter and polymath, the most variously talented artist of the Renaissance. In a long peripatetic career, the influence of da Vinci's work was spread from Milan, Florence and Rome, before in 1516 he became the most celebrated prize of Francis I's endeavour to draw to his court in France the best of the Italian artists.

In the world of the visual arts Italian supremacy was a universally accepted fact, and no northern artist could aspire to true mastery without the obligatory study trip to the peninsula. This was an assumption still as valid in the age of Rubens and van Dyck as it had been for the young Albrecht Dürer. Through the work of men such as Dürer – in his careful observation of nature the true disciple of da Vinci – the technical advances of the Renaissance were absorbed into northern art.

Thus visitors to Italy came for the most part to learn, trade or worship; overwhelmingly to learn. If it had remained thus Italy might had continued to enjoy its established economic and cultural leadership. But it was Italy's tragedy that by the beginning of the new century the most powerful visitors from northern Europe came as predators, to fight and conquer. These new circumstances would reveal the fatal weaknesses that lay at the heart of Italian civilization.

Peninsula Politics

An explanation of the complex and fragmented distribution of political power within the peninsula is best attempted by conceiving of three blocks of territory, of roughly equal size, running diagonally from north to south. These were respectively the kingdom of Naples, incorporating the islands of Sicily and Sardinia; the Papal States; and the city states of the northern plain. It is best to deal briefly with each in turn.

For much of the fifteenth century the kingdom of Naples, together with Sicily and Sardinia, was ruled by the royal house of Aragon. However, on the death of Alfonso V (1458) succession passed to his illegitimate son Ferrante, while the islands and Aragon itself were ruled by Alfonso's brother John. Matters were further complicated by the claim of a cadet branch of the French royal house, dating from the conquest of the southern kingdom in the thirteenth century by Charles of Anjou, brother of Louis IX. Although French control was seldom uncontested, Naples itself remained in French hands until the death of Queen Joanna II in 1435. When the Aragonese asserted control, the French were driven out, but the French claim was maintained and in 1481 devolved into the hands of the king, Louis XI. Most immediately Louis contented himself with investing Provence, the other portion of this inheritance, but the Italian rights remained, to be asserted in time of need. The Aragonese claim, meanwhile, would in due course devolve upon the warlike and ambitious Ferdinand, and later still his grandson Charles V. With two such powerful external forces determined to assert their rights, a contest became almost inevitable with the death of Duke Ferrante in 1494.

To fend off such a prospect Ferrante's successor, Alfonso II, formerly Duke of Calabria, would have required the assistance of other Italian powers; but relations between the Italian states were frequently troubled and complex. To the immediate north of the Neapolitan territories lay the long land frontier with the Papal States, the temporal possessions of the pope. For the Papal States the fifteenth century was a period of recovery after the disasters of the Schism and the long contests over papal authority. The years of exile at Avignon were particularly disruptive for papal authority in their temporal lands. The local nobilities inevitably used the opportunity to reassert a large measure of independence, and even in Rome itself the popes were often regarded as a foreign and alien presence. The return of a single, universally recognized pope to Rome following the election of Martin V in 1420 was therefore only the beginning of a long campaign to restore authority over the Papal States. Despite temporary reverses (as when Eugenius IV was chased out of the city following an unsuccessful attempt to bring down the overmighty Colonna clan), dogged persistence in due course succeeded in restoring a degree of control over the outlying provinces: the March of Ancona, Spoleto and the Romagna.

Map 3 Italy in 1492.

In these endeavours any apparent contradiction in the concept of the pope as temporal lord (never disputed) proved less of a handicap than an inevitable lack of dynastic continuity. Each new pope brought a new retinue of retainers and relatives to be rewarded with lands and titles. That said, successive popes pursued with remarkable tenacity two central strands of policy: to restore authority in the central states, and to prevent one foreign power dominating the peninsula to north and south. In these endeavours the heirs of St Peter were not afraid to play off one Italian power against another, or to make full use of their spiritual authority. Sixtus IV (1471–84) intervened aggressively to destabilize the Medici regime in Florence, and both Florence and Venice spent some portion of the latter part of the fifteenth century under papal interdict.

The concern for the papal patrimony was easily understandable. The lands of the marches provided the cornerstone of the papal income, particularly after the discovery of high quality alum (an essential fixing agent in the dyeing of cloth) on papal lands at Tolfa in 1464. The limits of papal expansion were reached with the successful campaigns of Cesare Borgia, nephew of Alexander VI, at the end of this century, and of Julius II, the 'warrior pope', in the early years of the next. Meanwhile the most energetic incumbents also applied themselves to the restoration of their now recovered capital. The decay of Rome during the years of tribulation is sometimes exaggerated. Nevertheless, with a population of around 80,000 in 1500 (and this would decline precipitously in the first three decades of the sixteenth century) it was far from being Italy's largest or wealthiest city. Negligible commercially, it lived to a large extent from the papal administration and religious tourism: the restless search for indulgences that brought countless pilgrims to visit its numerous shrines and monuments. Successive popes now applied themselves to the restoration and rebuilding of major public buildings; a campaign that would over the course of more than a century lead to a transformation of the city's public face.

North of the Papal States lay the ancient kingdom of Italy, formally still part of the Holy Roman Empire. In practice it was a patchwork of small independent principalities and city republics.[2] As in Germany there were considerable differences between the smaller lordships and larger powers, differences that tended to become accentuated during the course of the fifteenth century. By the end of this era the politics of northern Italy were increasingly dominated by the concerns of the four largest states: Florence, Milan, Venice and Piedmont-Savoy. The preceding period, for all its bewildering variety had seen the emergence of

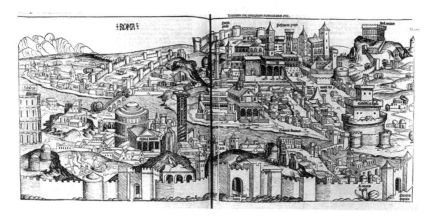

Figure 7   Renaissance Rome, from Hartman Schedel, *Historia Mundi*, Nuremberg, 1493. Courtesy St Andrews University Library.

two discernible trends: the progressive encroachment of the larger, more powerful states on weaker, smaller neighbours, and a failure to secure a lasting basis for co-operation between the larger powers that might have prevented foreign encroachment. In this last lay the seeds of destruction.

Of the four larger states two were arguably not wholly Italian, either in their territorial scope or political preoccupations. The duchy of Piedmont-Savoy sprawled over a large expanse of territory on both sides of the Alps. Bounded on one side by France and the other by Milan, the territories of the states of Savoy lay across the hugely strategic entry to the northern plains. But for much of the fifteenth century, particularly during the long regency of Iolanda, widow of Amadeo IX, Savoy struggled to assert itself in the company of more aggressive and predatory neighbours such as Burgundy, France and the Swiss Confederation. Early in the sixteenth century the long reign of Duke Carlo II (1504–53) established some dynastic security and made Savoy once again a force to be reckoned with. But that was for the future; for the moment the most tantalizing prize in the north remained the great northern city territory of Milan. Milan attracted the admiration of all who beheld it. According to the Spanish cosmographer Enciso it was without doubt 'the greatest in Italy and mightily inhabited and rich'.[3] In the first half of the fifteenth century Milan was ruled by the Visconti. The agricultural and commercial resources, not only of Milan but also the plains of Lombardy, allowed them to build a formidable collection of lordships. Inevitably this accumulation of land brought Milan into competition with other ambitious regional powers, most notably Venice. After Filippo Maria Visconti died in 1447 with no direct heir, in 1450 the city was forced to accept the lordship of Francesco Sforza, the most formidable *condottiere* general of his day. But the Sforza grip on power proved tenuous. In periods of prosperity Milan could aspire to a greater empire, such as lordship over Genoa. In other times they were themselves prey to other predators, particularly with the assertion of the French claim in 1494. By the early sixteenth century the Sforza dukes had become a pawn in the larger conflicts of the era, deposed or reinstated almost at will, until the death of the last of the line in 1535 brought Milan finally into the Habsburg orbit.

Of all the Italian city states it was Florence that did most to form the image of the peninsula; in its public image it was the epitome of civic patriotism and the epicentre of Renaissance culture. In truth the reality of Florentine government was more paradoxical. Behind a façade of wide public participation in the citizen assembly, the *parlamento*, real power became increasingly concentrated in the hands of a smaller number of dominant, and often feuding families. From the mid-fifteenth century the ascendency of the Medici threatened to put an end to Florentine republicanism. But in fact the Medici maintained their power only by assiduous attention to the wider political community – through the manipulation of patronage and the propagation of their own power through artistic propaganda. The Medici ascendency was secured only by persistent effort and the extraordinary charisma of one of the most gifted political figures of the age, Lorenzo the Magnificent, and even he could not provide for an orderly succession. When the direct line failed, Florentine politics reverted to a more normal mode. When, following the death of Lorenzo (1492), Florence was swept up in the general crisis of Italy, the Medici endured two substantial periods of exile (1494–1512, 1527–30).

For Venice the fifteenth century had witnessed a substantial reordering of priorities. The basis of Venetian wealth and power remained possessions outside Italy, in the Adriatic and Eastern Mediterranean. But the early part of the century saw a steady expansion of Venetian mainland territory, with the incorporation into the Venetian *terrafirma* of Vicenze, Verona and Padua, Brescia and Bergamo. The city's conduct in the government of these lands was regularly contrasted by enemies of Venice with its lofty self-promotion as a cradle of Republican values. For its mainland subjects, Venice was the 'city of three thousand tyrants'. These subject towns were not inconsiderable communities in their own right – Verona was a town of some 42,000 inhabitants – but claims to political autonomy fell on deaf ears. In Venice itself the range of the politically enfranchised was broad, but actual power was largely devolved on smaller councils and committees, most notably the executive Council of Ten. The presiding genius was the Doge, an elective office held for life, and consequently much sought after by the leading families of the city.

Despite the expansion of the *terrafirma*, Venice remained the most outward looking of the city republics, used by long experience to the conduct of international diplomacy and accustomed to treading the European stage as an equal party with Europe's nation states. Many a historian of sixteenth-century history has had reason to be grateful for the detatched, informed observation of Venetian ambassadors, whose regular and detailed despatches were posted back from many of Europe's capitals and carefully filed for the enlightenment of Venice's rulers and later generations. The success of Venice in surviving as a free state through all the vicissitudes of the sixteenth-century conflicts, despite the persistent hostility of greater powers, invested it with a special prestige, even if the principles of Venetian republicanism were more admired than imitated.

Alongside these larger states the smaller lordships were far from negligible, and certainly could not be ignored in the shifting patterns of power and diplomacy. Genoa, by dint of its extensive overseas trade interests, was both a force to be reckoned with and a coveted prize. Both France and the kings of Naples had designs against its independence. Other smaller lordships provided a base for ambitious warrior lords who sold their services in the quarrels of their larger neighbours, and intruding foreign powers. Many of these *condottieri*, such as the Gonzala of Mantua and the Este of Ferrara, built an enduring place in the political constellation; others, such as Cesare Borgia, burned brightly but left no enduring monument. The warrior bands raised by the *condottieri* terrified Italians partly because they recruited largely from the impoverished country areas, the *contado*. For all that urban Italians despised the 'men of the mountains', the vulnerability of the cities in time of conflict was a reminder of the fragility of their social peace.

The constant feuding, encroachment and jurisdictional conflicts between the Italian states brought an inevitable danger of escalation and foreign encroachment. In the middle of the fifteenth century the states came together in what was a potentially visionary attempt to avoid such a disaster, the Peace of Lodi (1454). The peace aimed to secure the recent resolution of the Sforza coup in Milan and Alfonso's claim to Naples, but also to provide against future foreign intervention in Italy's quarrels. By the terms of the peace none of the contracting parties was singly to wage war or enter conflicting alliances. They further undertook to support each other in the event of attack. The Peace of Lodi bought Italy 30 years of relative security before it broke down irrevocably in the face of the French invasion of 1494. This was a traumatic event, but Italians themselves sowed the seeds of catastrophe. In the last resort local Italian powers could not resist the temptation to summon external aid to secure advantage in their local quarrels. Exiled members of defeated factions in Milan and Naples stimulated intrigues abroad and particularly at the French court. Most damagingly, in 1494 Guiliano della Rovere, the future Julius II, fled to France to pursue his vendetta against his arch-enemy Alexander VI, and became a passionate advocate of a French invasion. As the French prepared their invasion, loans were advanced by Genoese bankers and Ludovico Sforza of Milan. The destabilizing character of these internecine feuds was greatly exacerbated by the availability of large bands of *condottieri* troops of no strongly fixed loyalties. They made up the majority of the mercenary armies that in the next 30 years would wreak such destruction in the peninsula.

The Italian Wars

In September 1494 Charles VIII of France entered Italy at the head of a large army. This was a decisive moment in the history of the peninsula, but also of Europe, inaugurating as it did 70 years of destructive warfare. In the first phase the wars were dominated by the ambitions of the French. Later, when the Aragonese claim was absorbed into the greater Habsburg Empire, the wars became a clash of two leading European powers, and were only finally resolved by the general settlement of the treaty of Cateau-Cambrésis in 1559.

The French invasion was not uncontroversial, even in France. In one sense Charles's expedition represented a renewal of a French interest that had never really been abandoned. France dominated Genoa sporadically through the fifteenth century; Italy's freedom from French interference since then had less to do with diminished interest than with more pressing preoccupations elsewhere, notably the conflicts with Burgundy and England. Even now, with these northern conflicts decisively resolved in France's favour, there were those who urged restraint. In the short term Charles VIII's triumphant progress down the peninsula seemed to lay such doubts to rest. Potential opponents melted before the French advance. By December the French had reached Rome, and in February 1495 they invested Naples. Faced by overwhelming military force the overmatched Angevin king, Alfonso II, abdicated, and Charles contemptuously brushed aside his designated heir, his son Ferrandino.

Subsequent events are highly instructive, because they suggest a qualitative difference between the French claims in northern and southern Italy – in strategic purpose if not in law. For France, the assimilation of Milan or Genoa would have been a valuable extension of French power in the Mediterranean. The recent incorporation of Provence and Burgundy had effected a substantial shift in the centre of gravity of French interests southwards. It was now not impossible to postulate a formidable transalpine bloc of territory, particularly if the weak, unstable conglomeration of lands that made up Piedmont-Savoy could be brought permanently into the French orbit.

In contrast, the French claim to Naples made little strategic sense. It has been suggested that Charles VIII was keen to assert his claim to Naples as a launching pad for a crusade against the Ottoman Empire. If so, he soon received a lesson in higher realities, as Aragon, Venice and Milan joined with the pope in a new diplomatic combination designed to match the overmighty intruder. With his lines of communication impossibly extended Charles had little choice but to begin the long march back to French territory. On the way, he met and parried the forces of his enemies at Fornova, a battle in which the French successfully cleared their passage out of the peninsula at the cost of surrendering their baggage train, containing much of the plunder of Naples. In the following year the French garrisons were systematically cleared out of Naples as Ferrentino made good his right as king.

On the death of Charles VIII in 1498 war was quickly resumed. To the established French claim to Naples the new king, Louis XII, brought his own claim of right to Milan as the Orléanist heir of the Visconti inheritance. Given that Louis also harboured a deep hatred of Ludovico Sforza, whose change of sides in the first war had so compromised the French, Milan now became the focus of his attention. An energetic campaign of diplomacy to isolate Sforza diplomatically was followed by a French invasion. Once again success was immediate. Sforza abandoned Milan, and a client administration was also established in Genoa, and although the Milanese soon tired of French rule

and briefly readmitted Sforza, the battle of Novara (April 1500)
proved decisive. Sforza was captured and taken to France a broken
man. When French forces assisted their ally Florence in subduing
nearby Pisa, the French had established an unmistakable supremacy
as the arbiters of Italy.

Flushed with this success, Louis now turned to the recovery of
Naples. Once again, Louis more than matched his royal forebear,
though only at the cost of an opportunistic treaty that provided that
Ferrandino's lands should be partitioned between the two most
powerful claimants, Louis and Ferdinand of Aragon. Louis was much
criticized by contemporary commentators (not least Machiavelli) for
the Treaty of Granada; for while it secured an easy restoration of the
French kingdom it also opened the way for the arrival of a powerful
competitor. By 1502 the tensions between the French and Spanish
garrisons led to open warfare; the following year the Spanish victory at
Cerignola gave them a decisive advantage. In 1504, despite a costly
new French expedition of relief, the remaining French forces were
forced into a humiliating withdrawal.

These first two wars, together with Louis XII's further sorties into
Italy in 1507 (to subdue Genoa) and 1509 (the War of the League of
Cambrai) firmly established one principle of the wars: that the French
presence in Italy would be both brutalizing and destructive. Captured
towns were put to the sword, or huge tributes demanded. The presence of large contending armies inevitably stripped the countryside
bare of food, and brought epidemic disease in their wake. In the last
years of his life Louis XII met his match in the warrior pope Julius II.
With the formation of the Holy League in 1511 France was for the
first time isolated diplomatically. When the only viable French army in
northern Italy was forced into retreat, French power collapsed like a
house of cards: Genoa rebelled and the Sforza were once more restored in Milan.

At the time of his death in 1515 Louis XII was scheming to overcome these reverses, and the cause was inevitably taken up by the new
king, Francis I. The customary round of preparatory diplomacy did
not on this occasion succeed in isolating Milan. Although Francis
secured the help of Venice and Genoa, Milan could rely on the support
of the emperor Maximilian, Ferdinand of Aragon and the pope; a
formidable league for the defence of Italy, and a sign of how wholly,
at this juncture, Italy had become the cockpit of Europe. Making
light of these opponents Francis moved swiftly into Piedmont,
and here, at Marignano (now Melegnano) French forces achieved a

crushing victory. Milan capitulated and another Sforza was removed to France.

The French victory set off a whirlwind of diplomacy, though the search for real peace was inhibited by a steady attrition of the leading personnel and consequent reconfigurations of the balance of power. The death of Ferdinand of Aragon (1516) passed the Aragonese claim to the young Charles V, a contemporary and inevitable rival for Francis; the death of Maximillian (1519) negated the painfully negotiated first peace of Cambrai, and brought the two rivals into direct competition for the imperial crown. Thwarted here, Francis looked for revenge, but imperial forces gained the upper hand in Italy. While Francis and his troops were tied up with conflicts on the northern border with the Netherlands, the imperialists ousted the French garrison from Milan. When French troops were then defeated at La Bicocca, Francis had no alternative but to return to Italy in person. A complex campaign was resolved by the shattering defeat at Pavia (24 February 1525). Francis was captured and removed to Spain; French pretensions in Italy seemed irretrievably damaged.

In fact, Pavia did not immediately secure the imperial ascendancy. Forced to accept humiliating terms for his freedom in the Treaty of Madrid (including the restoration to Charles of Ducal Burgundy), Francis was equally obliged, on his return to France, to repudiate the treaty on the basis that it was extracted under duress. An irredeemable personal animosity now clouded future relations between Charles and Francis. Others of Europe's ruling powers proved more understanding of Francis's behaviour. Few could feel comfortable with the extent of the emperor's victory: soon a new coalition, comprising France, Venice, Pope Clement and Francesco Sforza (since the emperor had occupied Milan, now a French client), had been assembled. The League of Cognac put a temporary check on Charles's plan to have himself crowned emperor, but at a terrible cost. In May 1527, cold, hungry and unpaid, the imperial army descended on Rome. Deprived of its commander, Charles of Bourbon, who was killed in the first assault, it proceeded, leaderless, to the sack of the city. After days of murder, rape and plunder, the imperial forces settled down to enjoy the fruits of their victory. Only after ten interminable months were they finally bribed into departure.

The sack of Rome horrified Christendom and temporarily deprived Charles of the moral advantage gained by Francis's earlier breach of trust. A hastily constructed alliance with England gave France enough support to negotiate an amelioration of the harsh terms of the Treaty of Madrid. In the Treaty of Cambrai (1529) Burgundy was retained, but at the cost of a huge ransom, and the abandonment of all French claims in Italy.

The Peace of Cambrai, coming so soon after the sack of Rome, proved an important watershed. Although Italy continued to feature in French schemes to subvert imperial power for another generation, until the Peace of Cateau-Cambrésis (1559), in Italy the die had been cast. Charles would face temporary reverses, but the imperial ascendancy in the peninsula was never seriously challenged, and the main theatre of the Franco-Habsburg conflict moved elsewhere. In 1536 reciprocal French and imperial invasions of Savoy and Provence brought general devastation but no recovery of French control in Milan. In due course, on the death of the last Sforza, the duchy was invested in the hands of the emperor's son and heir, Philip.

Renaissance Monarchy

The cost of the Italian wars, particularly for the peninsula itself, had been terrible. Two generations of repeated foreign invasions, encouraging in turn opportunist lawlessness on the part of native mercenary armies, had taken a heavy toll: both politically, and in terms of life and property. For the rest of the sixteenth century Italy would be essentially a political dependency. Venice continued to exercise an independent political role, particularly with respect to its particular sphere of influence in the eastern Mediterranean, and the papacy in Rome had a continuing, indeed increasing role in the religious and political controversies of the second half of the century. But of the other major Italian powers Florence was a mere shadow, and Naples and Milan largely passive units of the greater Habsburg Empire, into which they were now permanently absorbed.

For the rest of Europe the legacy of the Italian wars was more mixed. The fact that for 40 years Italy had been at the centre of the diplomatic calculations of almost all the major rulers of western Europe makes nonsense of a textbook tendency to regard these conflicts as peripheral to the events of the 'real' sixteenth century, a mere remnant of unfinished business from the mediaeval period. In fact, Italy continued to dominate the thought world of Europe's powers long after they had ceased actively to contest Italian territory. The prolonged contest for supremacy in the peninsula had left a substantial legacy in the Italianization of considerable parts of European political culture.

The wars in Italy had seen the deployment of what were, for their day, exceptionally large armies, and the constant war-making required a commensurate effort of tax gathering. For the campaign of 1494 Charles VIII raised a surcharge on the *taille* and several new sales taxes; new subsidies were inevitably required for the wars of Louis XII and Francis I. During the 30 years of the reign of Francis I (1515–47) his income from taxation almost doubled: from 5 million to 9 million livres. A similar upward trend inevitably occurred among Francis's principal competitors, Henry VIII of England (1509–47) and the emperor Charles V.

This expansion of the fiscal base in Europe's most aggressive, expansive kingdoms was a fundamental building block of what is often described as new or Renaissance monarchy. The two terms have subtly different implications: 'new' monarchy lays stress on administrative reform, an increase in bureaucracy, record-keeping, and the numbers employed in administration; Renaissance monarchy focuses on the mechanisms of cultural display, an expression of power through the visual symbols of majesty. In fact, the two were closely connected, and both mirrored earlier developments in the city states of Italy. The Italian states, as we have seen, were precocious in the sophistication of their bureaucratic development. Florence and Venice witnessed a multiplication in the already considerable numbers of their public offices; both kept highly efficient central archives for the mountains of paper generated by state affairs. In the emerging northern states the new bureaucracies created the context for some of the most spectacular careers of the age, the rise of Wolsey and du Prat, of Thomas Cromwell and Gattinara. Such careers sent an important signal to other aspiring youths, that a flair for administration was a possible alternative route to advancement alongside skills in the tiltyard or courtly flattery. Court society, of course, had room for both; there lay a large part of its danger and fascination.

The new court cultures of Europe differed from each other in significant ways; local circumstances inevitably dictated that one or other element of Renaissance monarchy would be more or less pronounced. Institutional innovation was most spectacular in England, where the movement of property following the dissolution of the monasteries was as important a stimulus to administrative development as the king's military adventures. In France the bureaucracy was expanded without fundamental changes in structure. The empire of Charles V presented its own special problems. Here the ambitious schemes for institutional change proposed by the (Italian) Gattinara ultimately came to little.

What all monarchies shared was a desire to express power through display, and here most of all they looked to Italy for inspiration and example. The French kings, in particular, did whatever they could to introduce the culture of Italy into their native lands. Francis I most famously recruited Leonardo da Vinci, Andrea del Sarto and Giovanni Battista Rosso. What Leonardo did in France is uncertain. Arriving in France at the age of 65, he was more than content with a pension, a château, and the obligation of discursive conversation with his eager royal patron. He died in France in 1519. Del Sarto was a disappointment, but Rosso undertook the interior decoration of the royal palace at Fontainebleau. Another notable later visitor was the sculptor and designer Benvenuto Cellini.

Francis was the most famous enthusiast for Italian culture, but his predecessors were far from negligible patrons. Louis XII brought back paintings from Italy but no artists. Perhaps the most enduring monument to his Italian cultural education was a new silver coin, the *teston*, the first French coin to have on it a head of the royal monarch. In this way the influence of Renaissance medal culture became generalized through the population. The most tangible Italian influence was in the field of architecture. Here the experience of classical models in Italy came at a profoundly opportune moment, since with the end of the Hundred Years' War the defensive military features that had dominated the country houses of the nobility became obsolete. In Italy the French were fascinated by the columns, pediments and decorated façades of buildings built on radically different principles, for display, leisure and beauty. The remodelling of domestic living space in France began under Charles VIII and Louis, and reached its zenith with the great rebuilding works of Francis I. The great Loire châteaux at Blois, Amboise, Fontainebleau and Chambord became the most visible expression of an architectural style that reflected both the supreme self-confidence of the regime and a conscious search for radical innovation. Inevitably the king's bold example found its imitators among the nobility and urban bourgeoisie, and soon the Renaissance style began to impact on domestic urban architecture. Here the influence was perhaps most profound in Germany, reflecting the close connections between the banking and merchant elites on both sides of the Alps.

Figure 8 The Chateau of Azay-le-Rideau. Photo Bridgeman Art Library, London. The fruits of government. There were fortunes to be made in the service of Renaissance monarchs. This Loire chateau was the (perhaps too opulent) creation of a banker and tax-farmer at the court of Francis I.

In these various ways the influence of Italy cut deep, even as the affairs of the peninsula receded from the forefront of political concerns. If, after 1530, Europe's rulers no longer looked to Italy as the cockpit of their most vital strategic concerns, the culture of the peninsula remained deeply admired. True, as the sixteenth century wore on, this applied far more to Italian art than political philosophy. The culture of Humanism and the Renaissance became too widely generalized to seem specifically Italian; and with the decline of the city republics, Italian models of government seemed far less relevant. It would need the religious convulsions that followed the Reformation, and Catholic reform, to return to Italy – and in this case, specifically the papacy – an important leadership role in the affairs of the continent as a whole.

4

The Winds of Change

Traditionally, histories of the sixteenth century have been what one might call progress orientated: they concentrate on features of sixteenth-century society which hold within them the seeds of modernity; often at the price of overemphasizing these precocious and rather fragile first blooms. So it is as well to begin by recalling, as repeatedly stated in chapter 1, that many of the basic structures of life underwent no fundamental transformation in the sixteenth century. There were no startling breakthroughs in the fields of nutrition, healthcare or public sanitation. Life for the vast majority of Europe's inhabitants remained harsh and bounded by the constraints of the physical environment. There was no fundamental change in methods of land transportation. Moving goods by land remained expensive and risky, putting a clear ceiling on the development of a consumer society. The same constraints applied in the field of information. With the introduction of post horses, about 1400, the natural limit had already been established to the acceleration of time. Sixteenth-century postal service could improve the density, sophistication or efficiency of such communication. But they could do little to cut the minimum time required to ride between Paris and Florence.

If we bear all this in mind it is clear that the important technological changes in sixteenth century society would be essentially incremental. There was no industrial revolution in the sixteenth century; no new sources of power and energy would transform the conditions of life. But the application of patient ingenuity did produce several significant improvements to existing technologies that would have far-reaching importance for the conditions of human life.

Power and Imagination

Let us consider some of these issues in relation to the two most abundant sources of natural energy available in the period: wind and water. The relationship between people and the natural elements in the pre-modern era was complex. Water was in one sense the lifeblood of existence; but it was also one of the greatest killers.

Water was crucial to the functioning of the sixteenth century in more than the obvious sense that drinking was necessary for life. In fact, at least in the cities, water was seldom drunk: with no reliable sources of clean water in urban areas, to drink water would have been far too hazardous. In sixteenth-century Europe other forms of liquid refreshment were thus essential parts of the diet of even the poorest classes: in rural areas milk, in northern Europe 'small' (that is weak) beer. Mediterranean societies drank wine. In the case of both beer and wine the process of fermentation helped destroy bacteria; it was also, of course, a necessary preservative, making possible storage and transportation. A regular supply of water was nevertheless regarded as essential in cities, for washing clothes, primitive sanitation, and for most of the industrial processes transported into or close to urban areas: fulling and dyeing of cloth, tanning, paper-making. Such trades required abundant supplies of fresh water, but they also rendered it filthy.

Waterways also provided the only economically viable method of bulk transportation. Much of Europe's trade thus flowed along the rivers of the continent; in many respects the patchwork of natural waterways was the real road system of the period. Large-scale trade flowed down the mighty rivers of central Europe – the Rhine, Danube, Seine, Elbe and Rhône – which between them mapped out the major merchant routes of international trade. The geography of river trade made possible some unlikely connections. Float a barge downstream from Prague and in 300 miles you will arrive in Hamburg. Not surprisingly, along the banks of the great rivers were situated many of Europe's most prosperous conurbations. Narrow draught boats, and the relative infrequency of bridges, meant that many of Europe's rivers were navigable for seagoing vessels for many miles inland: York in England, Orléans in France, and Seville in Castile were all examples of prospering inland ports. The sixteenth century also spurred a lively coastal trade, linking hundreds of small port towns that grew up in almost every available natural harbour. The coastal trade from northern to southern England, for instance, made possible the supply of coal from Newcastle to the growing metropolis of London; an increasing necessity as the city gradually eroded the stocks of locally available wood for domestic fuel.

For many of Europe's citizens, the sea was a vital link in the chain of everyday existence. Many drew their livelihood from the sea; others trusted themselves to occasional journeys over its powerful expanses; but all treated it with respect. Even today the sea retains its power to awe and destroy, but in the sixteenth century it was quite untamed. Coastal communities lived from the sea, but few of the families that harvested its then abundant fish would emerge unscathed. Most would lose loved ones from drowning or shipwreck at some stage of a harsh and difficult life. And coastal communities lived in constant fear of inundation. The great St Elizabeth's Day flood of 18–19 November 1421 was a catastrophe that left deep scars in the Dutch landscape and memory. On this occasion 500 square kilometres of land in Zeeland and Flanders was permanently reclaimed by the sea. Serious floods were recorded in this low-lying region throughout the sixteenth century, culminating in the great All Saints' flood of 1570. Around 4,000 people lost their lives, and so severe was its effects that it was possible to sail a boat over the flooded fields from Amsterdam to Leiden.[1] The Netherlands was notoriously prone to flood, but in other parts of Europe coastal erosion, or the silting up of harbours, could change the landscape quite drastically in the space of two generations.

So sixteenth-century people gave a lot of care and ingenuity to managing their relationship with the elements. On both land and sea, the patient application of craft skills and human ingenuity led to significant advance in the technologies of harnessing power. None were so dramatic and sudden as to rate mention among the great inventions of the period. But over the course of generations they would have a significant impact.

On land, European society registered a gradual improvement in the quality and efficiency of power mills. Water-powered mills had been known and used in the milling of grain for many centuries. In the later Middle Ages their use was gradually extended to various industrial products: the production of iron, paper-making, sawmills. In the process there was a gradual increase in the possible size and consequent power of the wheel: from 3.5 m in diameter in the thirteenth century to 10 m by the seventeenth century. Projectors also gave their ingenuity to the harnessing of wind power. Though the diffusion of this invention was severely restricted by climate, by 1578 the windmill was being used in Amsterdam for the throwing of silk, manufacturing cloth, extraction of oil, and rolling copper plate.

The most dramatic steps forward are visible in the ceaseless struggle to master the elements at sea. By the fifteenth century great strides had been made in the development of astronomical navigation. By the end of this century the best Portuguese navigators could calculate their position at sea fairly accurately by a combination of observed latitude and dead reckoning. The same process of trial and error brought notable steps forward in ship design and rigging. Following the introduction of the square-rigged sail on the mainmast in the thirteenth century, sailors gradually evolved the full-rigged ship of three masts. The large bulging mainsail was divided into several smaller square sails hanging on separate yards on the same mast, a change that made the sail stand flatter and the ship better able to beat to windward. A triangular sail on the mizzen-mast (at the rear)

Figure 9   Oceanic sailing vessel, from Johannes Lerius, *Navigatio in Brasilium*, Frankfurt, 1592. Courtesy St Andrews University Library.

made sailing closer to the wind possible, and allowed the ship to take a greater press of sail on the fore and mainmasts. All of this permitted a gradual increase in the size of vessels. At the beginning of the four-teenth century the normal size of a Hanseatic ship was about 68 tonnes. By the sixteenth century 360 tonnes had become a normal size for most cogs, and there were numerous Venetian carracks of 540 to 630 tonnes. Ships in Europe did not grow much above this size until after 1800.

Not all areas of seafaring showed such striking development. The science of cartography made little progress before the sixteenth century; indeed, it is probably only the vagueness of the primitive maps then available (particularly with regard to the size of the oceans) that em-boldened the first transatlantic explorers to undertake their missions. In fact, ideas of geography were formed as much by prose writings as by visual representations in the forms of maps. These writings ranged from the scientific, or pseudo-scientific, to the exotic and fanciful.

We can see this most clearly if we examine the thought world of the famous Christopher Columbus.[2] Fundamental to Columbus's world-view was Ptolemy's *Geography*, the second-century classic rediscovered and popularized in the early fifteenth century. From this Columbus and his contemporaries learned that the earth was a perfect sphere (an inaccurate observation, but universally believed at the time), and that the inhabited world extended in a continuous land mass from Europe to the easternmost limit of Asia. Sailing west across the ocean therefore offered a plausible route to Asia's riches. This was particularly alluring since it was widely believed (again following Ptolemy) that the Indian Ocean was enclosed to the south and India could not be reached by sailing around Africa. But if Columbus was emboldened by Ptolemy he was inspired by other books that explored in more colourful ways the exotic glories of the East, such as the travels of Marco Polo and the fictitious John de Mandeville, a hugely popular travelogue later revealed as a complete fabrication.

Ignorance and misunderstanding thus played as critical a role in stimulating voyages of exploration as true knowledge and techno-logical progress. The story of seagoing discovery is one that mixes courage, luck and seamanship in almost equal measure. Particularly the changes in ship design were the result of painstaking trial and error over many generations. The little fleet that Columbus assembled for his first voyage consisted of three carracks whose combined tonnage was only around 200 tons. But Columbus had discerned enough of the likely demand of long-distance ocean sailing to have the good sense to re-rig the smallest vessel, the Niña, from triangular lateen sails to a square rig. The little ship triumphantly stood the test of the voyage.

Incremental change of the sort described here is impossible to identify with a particular date or period. Its consequences are subtle and not always immediately apparent. There would be reverses along the way: Columbus, for all his pride in his cartographical skills, proved singularly inept at measuring latitude, and the solution to the problem of longitude lay two centuries in the future. But cumulatively, such steady application to the problems of seafaring, and change through observation and experience, made possible the great oceangoing voyages of discovery of the fifteenth and sixteenth centuries.

The Growth of Urban Culture

Much of what has been said in the first part of this chapter holds good when we turn to consider what was destined to be one of the most dynamic elements of European economic and intellectual life: the cities. Towns had, of course, played a crucial role in European commerce and culture throughout the high Middle Ages. The cities of Italy, France and the Netherlands had grown rich as centres of trade and government. Europe's universities were all without exception situated in cities. The mediaeval period had also established the institutions and traditions of their political power, and, in the case of the cities of Italy and southern Germany, of their independence. These centuries had also seen the development of the organizational structures, the rules of citizenship, guild membership and city government that lay at the heart of urban life.

When cities were surrounded by walls, these too were a mediaeval legacy. These proud symbols of separation and independence often enclosed considerable amounts of open space as well as the built-up area: this was one reason why in the sixteenth century cities could absorb considerable population growth without urban sprawl. The city wall was, along with the cathedral or principal parish church (another mediaeval legacy), the city's dominant architectural feature, and also of great psychological importance to the community's self-understanding. Its massive physical presence, and carefully regulated access through gates closely guarded by day and closed at night, gave the city community a sense of identity and separation that was, in reality, scarcely justified by the steady interchange of goods and people between the city and its rural hinterland. In this way the city always remained closely connected with the surrounding countryside, over which it sometimes exercised a degree of political control.

Nevertheless the sixteenth century was a period of rapid change for Europe's urban centres. Many towns and cities experienced a marked increase in population during the century. Whereas in 1500 only 154 cities had populations of 10,000 or more, by 1600 this number had growth by a third, to 220 (table 4.1). These bare figures of course mask great variations. Some cities fell in population during the sixteenth century. As late as the 1560s the English Privy Council was seeking solutions to the problem of urban decay. To some extent the growth of cities was a reflection of general population increase: the proportion of the whole population of Europe who lived in large cities rose only gradually (see table 4.2). But here the statistics probably do little justice to the contemporary impact of cities on sixteenth-century life. Many of Europe's largest and richest cities experienced quite spectacular growth during the course of the century. The trading metropolis of Antwerp, with an estimated population of 50,000 in 1500, doubled in size in the next 60 years. Rome experienced a similar growth between 1526 and 1600, and Paris, already one of Europe's largest cities with a population of 100,000 in 1500, had reached 200,000 by 1600. London experienced particularly dynamic growth: a city of some 60,000 inhabitants in 1500, it reached 100,000 by 1550, and 200,000 by the end of the century.

Table 4.1 Number of cities in Europe with over 10,000 inhabitants, by region

Year	1500	1550	1600
British Isles	6	5	7
Scandinavia	1	1	2
Low Countries	23	24	31
France	32	34	43
Germany	23	27	30
Switzerland	1	1	2
Austria/Bohemia	3	3	3
Poland	0	1	1
Italy	44	46	59
Spain and Portugal	21	31	42
Totals	154	173	220

Source: Adapted from Jan de Vries, *European Urbanization* (London, 1984), p. 29

Table 4.2 Percentage of total population of each region living in cities of over 10,000 inhabitants

Year	1500	1550	1600
British Isles	2.1	2.4	4.2
Scandinavia	0.9	0.8	1.4
Low Countries	18.5	19.5	21.5
France	4.2	4.3	5.9
Germany	3.2	3.8	4.1
Switzerland	1.5	1.5	2.5
Austria/ Bohemia	1.7	1.9	2.1
Poland	0	0.3	0.4
Italy	12.4	13.1	15.1
Spain and Portugal	5.7	9.0	11.7

Source: Adapted from Jan de Vries, *European Urbanization* (London, 1984), p. 39

What lies behind this extraordinarily rapid, even transforming growth? Such rises in population cannot be accounted for by natural population growth. Indeed, as was pointed out in chapter 2, cities tended to have above-average mortality, and a particular proneness to epidemic disease. These population rises occur in spite of considerable natural obstacles. In the sixteenth century people gravitated to towns because they were performing more and more important social and economic functions. This diversity of economic function is indeed what lies at the heart of what makes a town, and this is equally true of smaller towns as well as the largest. The 154 largest cities identified by Jan de Vries in his pioneering statistical survey are the apex of a pyramid of some 3,000 to 4,000 places that were vested with city rights of one form or another.[3] In the sixteenth century sparsely populated Norway had only ten towns, some of which had fewer than 500 inhabitants. These performed for their rural hinterland functions that mirrored the local economic role of the greatest European cities. However, the largest cities stood out as the centres of a sophisticated life, a magnet to the ambitious, and ultimately, real motors of social change.

The lifeblood of urban life remained, as it had always been, trade and commerce. Cities were characterized by a variety of economic functions, and a highly developed artisan life. A large majority of their productive inhabitants remained, as they had always been, involved in traditional artisan trades, concerned either with the production of

Table 4.3 Total population of Europe in millions, by region

Year	1500	1550	1600
British Isles	4.4	5.2	6.8
Scandinavia	1.5	1.7	2.0
Low Countries	2.35	2.9	3.1
France	16.4	19.0	19.0
Germany	12.0	14.0	16.0
Switzerland	0.65	0.8	1.0
Austria/ Bohemia	3.5	3.6	4.3
Poland	2.5	3.0	3.4
Italy	10.5	11.4	13.1
Spain and Portugal	7.8	8.6	9.2
Totals	61.6	70.2	77.9

Source: Adapted from Jan de Vries, *European Urbanization* (London, 1984), p. 36

clothes (weavers, shoemakers and the like) or food production (coopers, tanners, butchers and bakers). But in the upper echelons of urban society merchant life became steadily more sophisticated. Long-distance trade, previously the preserve of the celebrated mediaeval fairs, became the cornerstone of business for an increasing number of merchant families. The mechanisms of economic exchange became steadily more sophisticated, and routine. The effective monopoly on the international money markets enjoyed by the great Italian trading families in the fifteenth century had by the sixteenth been eroded by the French and the Germans. By the end of the sixteenth century most countries in western Europe had developed a functioning money market. In a development symbolic of the shift of economic power from Italy to the growing economies of northern Europe, by 1545 the Fuggers of Augsburg were Europe's largest bankers, presiding over an awesome range and diversity of economic interest. In 1519 Jakob Fugger was able to pledge Charles V a loan of 543,000 florins to underwrite his campaign for the imperial crown; this single transaction was six times the capital of the Medici bank in 1451.

As modes of communication became more reliable, merchants could become more sedentary, even as their economic ventures became more ambitious. The Fugger family owned mines in Tyrol and Silesia, and effectively controlled the production of Hungarian copper. Younger members of the family would be sent to serve an apprenticeship in distant mines, before returning to settle into the family business at home. The growth of capital brought with it a growth in associated branches of business: insurance, for instance, and the bonds of exchange that facilitated the transfer of assets without the physical movement of money. Europe's merchants sought constantly for business mechanisms that would facilitate the raising of capital, the movement of money, and the spreading of risk. Such motives were at the root of the growth of partnership or joint-stock ventures that became particularly associated with overseas trading ventures as the century wore on.

Trade created great wealth. A surviving tax assessment for sixteenth-century Nuremberg reveals that 416 burghers possessed taxable wealth of over 5,000 gulden; more than half of these exceeded 10,000 gulden. These wealthy citizens made up a sizeable 6–8 per cent of the city's households.[4] The sheer diversity of the city's economy is also strikingly revealed in these figures: Nuremberg's artisans were busily occupied in over 277 different trades, producing everything from playing cards to tobacco.

In these city societies where even the more prosperous journeymen had the prospect of cash surpluses from the necessities of life, we see the germ of a precocious consumer society. But this occurred without any fundamental reorganization of the means of production. Output of manufactured goods remained regulated by a guild structure that jealously guarded the privileges of the master craftsmen, who usually completed a long and arduous apprenticeship before receiving the rights to practise their art. This system was characterized by an instinctive conservatism that was not particularly friendly to innovation or diversification. Incomers were scarcely welcomed, particularly when they threatened the livelihoods of established practitioners.

Thus to the extent that this was an age characterized by innovation in manufacture or industrial production this often occurred away from cities, outside the regulation of the guilds. Industrial production is a term that in any case has little sense in the sixteenth century, except perhaps with respect to extractive trades such as mining. Mining was of course necessarily a rural industry: the precious seams near enough the surface to be worked by the primitive technologies then available were inevitably concentrated in mountainous regions such as the Tyrol, Bohemia and Hungary. But it is also true that other proto-industrial technologies such as iron- and glass-making often took place in the countryside, the choice of location being dictated by the need for plentiful local supplies of wood and running water. The major functions of cities with respect to industrial production were as reservoirs of capital, and as markets for the finished products. Even the manufacture of cloth and textiles – far and away the most important employer outside farming and food production – was to a surprising extent a rural practice. The raw cloths were often worked up close to the regions where the sheep were reared, and then taken to the cities to be finished and customized for the market.

a

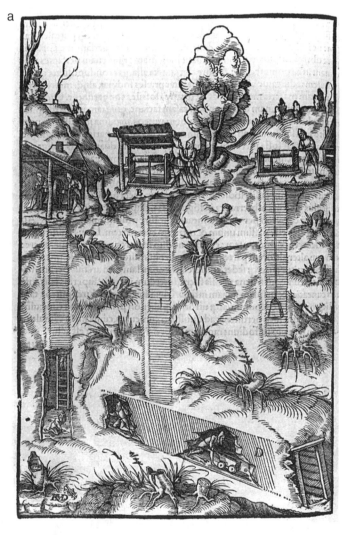

Figure 10a Mining, from George Agricola, *De re metallica*. Courtesy St Andrews University Library.

Figure 10b Windmills, from George Agricola, *De re metallica*. Courtesy St Andrews University Library.

It was thus in the domain of trade, rather than industry, that the sixteenth-century city established its supremacy – a crucial distinction between the sixteenth century and the modern industrial economy. But trade, nevertheless, lay at the heart of the city's function and existence, and the cornerstone on which all else was built. Here lay the origins of the city's function as centres of information exchange, culture and education. And in these domains the sixteenth century witnessed some of the most spectacular growth.

Trade required communication; communication required education. Cities were great centres of the education industry. Later in the sixteenth century there would be a great increase in the number of universities in Europe, spawned in part by the religious divisions of the Reformation. These created reluctance on the part of Protestants and Catholics alike to send their youths to be educated in universities across the confessional divide. But already the period had witnessed a vast increase in the number of educational institutions, particularly at

the level of secondary schooling. By the middle of the century virtually
every town of any size had its Latin or grammar school, usually
underpinned by a dense network of more humble establishments
teaching basic literacy skills. Antwerp in the Netherlands reputedly
had over 150 schools by the middle of the century, neighbouring
Ghent over 40; the smaller town of Veere, with a population of only
2,000, already had three.[5] This was admittedly in a region of unusually
high literacy, but in most parts of Europe urban elites had invested
heavily in their schools. In consequence, these became the focus of a
great deal of civic pride; often more so than the universities which, by
virtue of their charters and greater antiquity, were far more difficult to
control.

The building of a schoolhouse or hiring of a schoolmaster was often
stimulated by dissatisfaction with the existing clerical schools, often the
outgrowth of a cathedral chapter and tending purely to the training
required by clerics. In their place, the city fathers hastened to found
new public schools, often assisted by the provision of a substantial
founding bequest from a well-disposed local citizen. According to one
careful study, France witnessed an extraordinary proliferation of such
new foundations in the sixteenth century: perhaps as many as several
hundred.[6] City governments gave enormous pains to the management, curriculum and resourcing of such *collèges*, and of course to
providing the best teachers. The recruitment of a scholar of the reputation of Mathurin Cordier (who taught successively at the *collèges* of
Nevers and Bordeaux) burnished the prestige of the city as a whole.

The French experience was replicated all over Europe. The foundation of at least 410 new schools can be documented in England
between 1480 and 1600, and in reality the figures was probably
much higher. The German territory of Württemberg had 50 schools
in 1534 and 270 by 1581. Twenty new colleges were founded in
Portuguese cities in the 20 years between 1530 and 1550.[7] Together
such developments helped to foster the vast increase in literacy that is
one of the principal features that differentiate the sixteenth century
from those that preceded it.

The drive by city fathers to bring schools and education under their
control was one aspect of a more general trend evident during this
period: what one might call the laicization of urban space. This was a
major consequence of the Reformation, but the impetus also preceded
it. In several areas of city life that had once been almost the exclusive
preserve of the church the civil powers now increasingly sought to take
control: schools were one notable example, but the same could also be

said of hospitals and poor relief. In the process a great deal of property previously owned by church institutions was gradually transferred to lay ownership: a development obviously given a huge push forward by confiscations of church and monastic property in Protestant cities around the time of the Reformation.

But the increasingly lay control of urban space should not be confused with an impulse towards greater democracy. As city governments became more confident and assertive, they also became increasingly oligarchical. Even in cities that provided for a wide social representation in their government, the distance between the theoretical constitutional forms and the realities of power became more pronounced as the century wore on. Wealth, power and the defeat of competing jurisdictions prepared the way for the emergence of true urban aristocracies: the age of oligarchy.

The World of the Mind

The growth in urban literacy was greatly facilitated by (and indeed was partly responsible for) the rise of the printed book. This was the beginning of a long and distinguished history. In the four centuries that followed the invention of printing, the new technology would have a profound and transforming effect on many aspects of European life. It would come (precisely when is an interesting question) to play a dominant role in the process of information exchange and social interaction, only really challenged by the new technologies of the last half of the twentieth century.

So it is only fair to point out that printing was – in a purely technical sense – the crowning achievement of mediaeval technological ingenuity. The technical vision was in its day breathtaking, involving as it did the casting in metal of many thousands of individual letters, of uniform size and style, then used to ink an impression on paper or vellum,[8] before these could be dried, printed on the reverse, gathered and folded to form a book. It was an extraordinarily complex, expensive and daring endeavour, and it is to mediaeval guild society that we owe all the skills and technologies that made this possible: casting in metal, paper-making, the mixing of ink; not least, the design of the handpress (patterned closely on the sturdy wooden loom familiar from textile manufacture) and the capitalization of such an ambitious project.

It was also mediaeval society that had created the demand for books, for nothing else would have justified the almost reckless fervour with which the technical problems that beset the inventors were pursued to a successful conclusion. Fifteenth-century Europe had a huge appetite for books. Even in the manuscript age, universities had spawned a massive copying industry for learned texts and schoolbooks. It is no surprise therefore that the first printed books are carefully patterned on their manuscript forebears, and often, like manuscripts, individually hand-coloured and decorated.

In the first years fortunes were lost amid acrimonious quarrels between inventor and investors. But the book soon outgrew its tentative beginnings, and became a confident independent artefact in its own right. The first printed books appeared in Mainz, Germany, around 1450, yet within 30 years the new technology was generalized around much of western Europe. By 1480 printing had been established in at least 30 cities: in Germany and the empire at Strasbourg (1458), Cologne (1465), Augsburg (1468), Nuremberg (1470), in Italy at Rome (1464) and Venice (1469). In France and the Low Countries the two most important centres of printing were at Paris (established 1470) and Antwerp (1481). By the first years of the sixteenth century there were presses in over 100 locations, and certain European cities, such as Venice, Paris, Rome and Antwerp, had already established a reputation as major centres of book production.

By this time the book, until recently the most experimental of technologies, was also attaining its mature form. Certain basic techniques and practices, such as the practice of marking-up individual gatherings of leaves to aid correct ordering of the finished artefact, and the publication of the printer's address on the title-page or end of the book (colophon), had become generalized through the industry. In the larger, better-financed houses printers had successfully experimented with the use of more sophisticated specialized types such as Hebrew and Greek fonts. The initial slavish imitation of the appearance of manuscript through a uniform body of text in one font size had given way to more ambitious compositions, using varying types, marginalia, decorative initial letters and, in the most sophisticated books, woodcut text illustrations. As the publishing industry became established in this way, there sprung up around it a range of associated specialist trades: the bookbinder, type-founder, and merchants who specialized exclusively in the distribution and sale of books. The vastly increased demand for paper had spawned a huge increase in the number and quality of local paper mills. Most of all, printers had by now mastered the techniques for producing reliable texts at relatively modest prices, and this in turn had begun to transform the market for books. Books now seemed less wholly elite objects. Though they remained outside the reach of more plebeian households, in the houses of the upper strata of urban society it was possible to consider a book as a casual purchase rather than merely a professional tool.

For the book was at this stage overwhelmingly the province of urban society: this is true whether one talks of the market for books, their readership or authors. This had much to do with the fact that the skill of reading, literacy, was much more common in towns. By the beginning of the sixteenth century it is fair to say that literacy was no longer the professional monopoly of the clerical estate that it had been for much of the high Middle Ages. In cities a high proportion of the adult males possessed some rudimentary reading ability. In some parts of Europe this might have reached as high as 50 per cent. Rural areas naturally lagged far behind. In many villages the local priest might have been the only reader; sometimes even the priest had not entirely mastered the art. Even among the highest social classes of rural society literacy had not achieved the same status as in the towns. In the households of the nobility reading to some extent continued to be regarded as a technical service skill. Magnates required literate and numerate staff, but to the limited extent that reading formed part of their entertainment culture, they often still preferred to be read to rather than indulge in private, solitary reading. Indeed, the extent to which reading was a private activity more generally in European society is a debated and important question. Would people read to themselves, or aloud in groups? It is a question of some importance when we come to contemplate the relationship between literacy and social change.

In truth the sixteenth century witnessed such a boom in book culture that there was probably a growth in all types of reading, private and communal. The ubiquity and affordability of the book had a transforming effect on sixteenth-century education and ultimately on the whole intellectual culture of the age. The first impact was inevitably on the education industry, which even in the manuscript age had been the dominant consumer of books. Simple economics, which had so inhibited the invention, now worked brilliantly in favour of the printed book. Once a book had been set up in type, 1,000 uniform copies could be run off in a matter of days or weeks (depending on the length). Compared to the manuscript this represented both an enormous saving of labour, and a great improvement of accuracy. It was quickly apparent that the printed book could play a vital role in meeting one of the principal demands of Renaissance scholarship: textual accuracy.

The thirst for an accurate text was at the heart of the educational revolution that we know as Humanism. Humanism is a term so charged with meaning that it has become difficult to re-anchor it in its sixteenth-century context. But in truth, even in its own time Humanism was a multifaceted phenomenon: an intellectual movement, an aspiration of educational renewal, and at a much more humdrum level, an educational curriculum.[9] At its most basic, Humanism was the pursuit of a classical education, the study of the literature and languages of the classical world, Latin and Greek. This was already an advance on the mediaeval educational tradition precisely in that it added Greek to the standard curriculum; but in so doing, of course, it made it more the preserve of an educational elite.

The study of the classics had a particular end in mind: Humanists were convinced of the relevance of classical learning to modern life, and the Renaissance desire to retrieve the achievement of classical culture was partly aimed at recovering the glories of that most admired age. Of course, the classics were hardly despised in the Middle Ages. But Humanism was imbued with a sense that the classical heritage had been allowed to wither away, that it needed to be rediscovered, purged of corruptions, and presented in a new purity. The core activity of the Renaissance scholar was the hunt for classical texts and, when they were discovered, the discernment of an authentic text by critical comparison of surviving manuscripts. This movement went through several stages. The trawling of monastic libraries through the fourteenth and fifteenth centuries unearthed some notable discoveries; serious scholarly examination was made possible by the growth of large private libraries, again a fifteenth-century phenomenon; the sixteenth century contributed the diffusion of these texts in print. This in turn fostered developments of the techniques of textual criticism, which were among the enduring achievements of the Renaissance. As Richard Rex points out, the landmarks of Humanist scholarship in the early phase were the discoveries of manuscripts; in the later period, the publication of critical editions.

Beyond this, the achievement of Humanism was greatly inflated by some self-serving rhetoric. Rhetoric, in a technical sense, was at the core of the Humanist project, but an increasing quantity was also directed at self-congratulatory exaltation of the new learning, and denigration of the obscurantism of what had come before. Humanists had no time for the scholasticism of the mediaeval academic method, nor indeed were they inclined greatly to value the scholarly achievement of their forebears. Much of this criticism was unfair; we have already noted how in this, as in so much else, the sixteenth century built on solid foundations. Nevertheless by directing their fire at those who questioned the new intellectual agenda – or indeed its consequences – Humanists inaugurated a tradition of the elevation of the new that went very much against contemporary values. By and large the sixteenth-century mind found affirmation in continuities with the past. Change had always to be justified in terms of congruence and continuity: 'novelty' was deplored and feared. Here then Humanism, in its tone as much as its scholarly practice, offered something truly radical.

Humanism was also a community. An important achievement was to create a bond of fellowship between scholars spread through many parts of Europe, many of whom, without ever meeting, would nevertheless feel a part of the same shared endeavour. These connections were meaningful even when in reality they were extremely tenuous. When a young scholar wrote to Erasmus from distant parts, in the hope of eliciting some gracious response from the great man, this was more than merely a primitive form of autograph hunting. The younger man was expressing, and seeking affirmation for, his sense of a shared intellectual purpose, a comradeship of scholarship. Erasmus clearly sensed this. Even though as his fame grew he was increasingly badgered by such requests he did his level best to reply. He maintained a lively correspondence, for instance, with several parts of eastern Europe. At least by keeping a copy of the outgoing letter he could make sure he had full value for his time by publishing it in part of the collected editions of his correspondence which, like most of his writings, proved reliable best-sellers.

This sense of sharing and community did not predetermine choices individuals would make in the large questions of the day. While many men of Humanist learning would support the Reformation, others would remain securely anchored in the Catholic Church. Yet in the wider reformist community (which would include many who did not leave the Old Church) Christian Humanism was a powerful force, not least for its role in placing a critical examination of sacred texts on the educational agenda. The inference that sacred truths, or at least the received text of Scripture, could be subjected to the same process of critical enquiry as other historic writings was indeed an important and deeply unsettling development. Here the milestone event was the publication of Erasmus's *Novum Instrumentum* (1516), an edition of the Greek text of the New Testament with Erasmus's own Latin translation in parallel. Erasmus's text was not in fact particularly

Figure 11   Erasmus, from Theodore de Bry, *Icones Quinquaginta virorum illustrium*, Frankfurt, 1597. Courtesy St Andrews University Library.

radical, but for some any departure from the received text of the Latin Vulgate (the accepted common version of sacred writ since the fourth century) was already too dangerous a departure. Erasmus's publication encountered a hail of criticism, but at this stage Erasmus was able to ride out the storm. He had been shrewd enough to dedicate his new work to the pope, Leo X, who proved to be as susceptible to the flattery of the great Dutch scholar as were many of Europe's crowned heads. It was only in retrospect, when others took up the scholarly agenda for more radical purposes, that the full implications of Erasmus's work became clear. These were the days when Erasmus and

Humanism were most fully in vogue. Works like the famous *Epistolae obscurorum virorum*, which employed biting satire to lampoon opponents of the new scholarship, set the tone for a movement that derived much of its sense of moral supremacy through the mastery of wit and

Figure 12 Erasmus, *Moriae Encomium*, Basle, 1522. Courtesy St Andrews University Library.

ridicule. Erasmus himself was a master of the new world of print, riding the wave of his own popularity with a torrent of writings to suit the tastes of all possible readers. While princes cultivated the prince of Humanists, Erasmus cultivated publishers, for his impoverished early years had given him a strong sense of the value of money. His assiduous care not to lose control of his most valuable commodity – his writing – rewarded Erasmus with being the first author in the history of the printed book to make a fortune by writing.

Was the sixteenth century an age of fundamental intellectual change? Enraptured by the vision of the literary princes of Humanism, modern authors have made bold claims on behalf of an age that did see notable achievement in the field of literature and philosophy. But before we are carried away by the undoubted charm of the new learning, it is necessary to enter some sobering caveats. Throughout the sixteenth century there can be little doubt that the vast majority of Europe's inhabitants remained in comfortable and familiar thought worlds. This was true at both ends of the social spectrum and all points between. If the illiterate peasant could hardly have been expected to rise to speculative thinking, then a man like Charles V was also hardly in his caste of thought, precociously modern. The landed nobility too, remained largely wedded to traditional patterns of thought and action. Even as they embraced new techniques of land management and warfare, their values remained resolutely traditional, reflecting established concepts of caste, honour and inheritance. We have already seen in chapter 1 how far patterns of thought that we might think of as antiquated and backward-looking – such as belief in the power of the Devil – were actively promoted by educated groups in society.

There are plausible reasons why as scholars and historians we are likely to overvalue the real importance of an intellectual movement such as Humanism. It is hardly surprising that modern commentators should concentrate on the features in another age that we ourselves value highly in the modern world, and in our professional lives, and this goes both for systematic thought and the printed word. And of course, there is a pressing problem of evidential bias, for the book dominates surviving evidence to a quite disproportionate extent. We have to remind ourselves that in the sixteenth century print was but one means of forming minds, and impacted on a relatively narrow stratum of society. The whole world of verbal culture – song, ridicule, conversation and crowd action – is much harder to recover, and much easier to overlook.

The real long-term significance of Humanism was essentially two-fold. Firstly, it made possible great forward strides in technical scholarship. The sixteenth century was an age that concerned itself as none before with the establishment of precise text, with enduring consequences in several branches of scholarship. On a broader social front the moral, one might say psychological, impact of Humanism was that it emancipated the low-born to think speculatively. This was in some respects not without a certain irony, for humanists as a caste were great flatterers of the rich and powerful. Many humanists, their reputations established, ensured a comfortable living in sycophantic political philosophy, turning out comfortable texts in favour of the prevailing political orthodoxy. Nor was the Humanist *sodalitas* exactly a socially inclusive institution. Nevertheless with Humanism the range of voices that could be heard in debate was significantly widened. The real significance of Erasmus was more as a cultural totem, the illegitimate son who had risen through the power of his mind to a position of such eminence that crowned heads courted *him*. It was the symbolism of Erasmus's career that was ultimately of importance, more than any one of his large body of writings, for all their contemporary appeal and enduring charm.

5

The Reformation

Students of the Reformation are confronted by two bald questions: why Germany? And why Martin Luther? After all, there had been reform movements before. The whole history of the late mediaeval church had been dominated by disputes over the role and authority of the papacy, and mediaeval Europe had its share of heretics. In Bohemia, a hundred years before the German movement, the Czech reformer Jan Hus had in effect led this significant province out of the western church. Yet none could deny that the German evangelical movement was of a different order, eventually fracturing western Christendom into two irreconcilable factions. Nor can one really avoid the personal responsibility of Martin Luther. Thirty years ago there was a brief fashion for attempting to write a history of the Reformation in which Luther played a rather peripheral role. The democratization of the past, as one might call it, left less room for the great men of history. But this will not work. Luther's part in these events was so massive, and so instrumental, that it is impossible to imagine the movement without his personal part.

The key to understanding the Reformation lies in recognizing the potency of the peculiar cocktail presented by Martin Luther's own personal search for meaning in his religious life, played out in the particular context of sixteenth-century Germany. For while in many parts of Europe in the late Middle Ages the church was in rude good health, in Germany there were tensions and structural problems which the mediaeval movements of reform had signally failed to address. Indeed, the long struggle between the papacy and its critics during the Conciliarist dispute would only have concentrated minds on the fact that the problems of the church in the German lands were very much peripheral to the concerns of Rome. The call for local German solutions thus found a strong resonance, and it was Luther's genius that he could incorporate this patriotic agenda into what was in its origins a deeply, and narrowly, theological movement. But the particularity of these German issues also helps explain why Lutheranism achieved so little lasting success elsewhere in Europe. For all the initial interest in Luther and his protest, by the time of his death in 1546 the limits of what could be achieved under the banner of his church had been fully revealed.

The Church before the Reformation

The influence of the church in European society in the late fifteenth century was all-pervasive. Leading figures in the church hierarchy could have reflected on an institution with an unchallenged position at the heart of the community: robust, intellectually vigorous, and assured of a role in almost every aspect of human existence. In some parts of Europe up to 10 per cent of the population were members of the institutional church; collectively the church was Europe's biggest landowner. The clergy played a vital role in the lives of all late mediaeval communities, as dispensers of sacraments, managers of hospitals and schools, and providers of vital services such as writing and literacy. No European ruler could ignore the church in their political calculations; the pope was a major political force in his own right and a constant fixture in the strategic alliances of the day.

The Reformation, in this respect, was a movement of many paradoxes. In its first intention a movement of renewal and reform, the division of western Christendom was a wholly accidental and unforeseen consequence. And although it would result in the withdrawal of up to one third of Europe's population from obedience to Catholicism, the Reformation was in no respect a consequence of religious indifference. On the contrary, the church on the eve of the Reformation gave every sign of being an institution commanding general support. Indeed, it is now argued that the century before the Reformation was characterized by a degree of engagement in matters of worship and theology, especially on the part of the laity, unprecedented in mediaeval Christianity.

This was an age of church-building and religious enthusiasm. In Suffolk, England, during the fifteenth century, something approaching

50 per cent of parish churches were substantially remodelled, as citizens poured the new wealth generated by a successful wool trade into their religious lives. This was an age of great religious art, stimulated by the growth of the cult of saints. Increasingly during this period, popular mediaeval saints were adopted and invoked as guardians and protectors, and honoured for their benevolent interventions in the lives of those who invoked them in sculpture, painting and shrines. The collection of relics, small mementos of saints' lives or preserved parts of their bodies, became almost a cult in its own right. Some aristocratic collectors amassed monster collections, each carefully and often magnificently housed in custom-made reliquaries, and each carrying a documented remission from the torments of purgatory for those who gazed upon them. Albrecht of Brandenburg, Renaissance prince and patron of artists, amassed a collection of such magnificence that the assiduous visitor could accumulate a remission of some six million days. One of his greatest rivals as a collector in central Europe was, ironically enough, the Elector of Saxony, Frederick the Wise, later Martin Luther's patron and protector.

This was an age of pilgrimages and ostentatious public devotions; nor was the crusading urge entirely dead. More than one Renaissance prince aspired to lead a new Christian expedition against the Turks when more immediate European conflicts were settled. And this was an age in which the individual's ceaseless search for a sense of the divine was manifested in ever more elaborate devotional practice, and the pious expenditure of much hard-earned wealth. The commitment of the laity received tangible expression in a financial investment of unprecedented proportions: in the provision of funeral masses, voluntary offices and sermons, and the purchase of indulgences.

What then was required to move people out of this deep, and for the most part unquestioning, commitment, in many cases to turn them furiously against institutions to which they had given so much, in both emotional and financial terms? To such a question there can be no simple answer, and it is worth remembering that the sixteenth-century call for reform would elicit a very different response in different parts of Europe. But for historians with the benefit of hindsight there were sufficient indications even in the robust good health of the late mediaeval church of why, when a climate of criticism emerged in the 1520s, it achieved such a popular resonance.

In the first place, the evidence of Christian laymen's ever-increasing support for the church was itself slightly double edged. With the increasing investment of their wealth and time went rising expectations. The fifteenth century witnessed a great expansion of lay literacy and education. University education was no longer a clerical monopoly; in urban communities and princely courts it was no longer necessary to rely on clerics to act as clerks, scribes and schoolmasters, as had been the almost exclusive tradition of the early Middle Ages. And many of the religious institutions newly popular in the fifteenth century, such as confraternities, represented not only lay commitment to the church, but a desire on the part of the laity to take greater control over their religious lives. Confraternities were associations of pious laymen, often based around a trade craft and guild, who paid subscriptions for the purpose of having a priest say masses on behalf of their deceased members. It followed that the priest so employed was in effect their employee, and in the fifteenth century an increasing proportion of the clerical estate relied on such positions for their livelihood. The German city of Hamburg had no fewer than 99 confraternities in 1517; most urban communities of any size had a variety of such institutions.[1] In some parts of the church, such as England, even the parochial clergy were increasingly dependent for their salaries on voluntary financial donations, raised by the churchwardens on behalf of the parish. Not surprisingly, laypeople in return felt able to insist on a high standard of service in those they employed.

The capacity of the clergy to respond to these increased expectations varied greatly in the different parts of Europe, and even in different parts of the clerical estate. In England, for instance, the parish clergy seem to have enjoyed a high level of confidence among the population at large. Reasonably adequately trained and well disciplined, English priests seem to have given little cause for scandal. In this they were given an exemplary lead by their bishops, few of whom gave any cause for complaint through their moral conduct (Cardinal Wolsey, who acknowledged a bastard son, was a great exception among the English bishops). Most English bishops also played an active role in the administration of their diocese.

Pious, conscientious bishops were to be found in most parts of Europe, but in some countries they were clearly very much the exception. In France, most bishops were either non-resident royal officials, or the younger sons of the local nobility. In the Netherlands the structure of the church was so archaic that a growing population of over two million was served by only four bishops. But it was in the German Empire that the condition of the church gave most cause for concern. Germany teemed with clergy, many of them ill-educated and penniless indigents with no hope of a position. At the other end of the scale Germany's bishops were often great princes of the church, ruling over an independent princely state, their appointment jealously guarded by the pope and often the subject of an intensely political negotiation (not to mention the payment of a substantial fee). The prelates, for their part, often exploited the resources of their office with a ruthlessness that differed little from that of secular landlords, except in so far as through their spiritual office they enjoyed access to opportunities to raise funds denied to temporal lords. Clerical privileges often included the right to sell produce gathered on their lands in neighbouring urban markets without paying the usual duties, an exemption fiercely resented in these communities. Meanwhile a regular and substantial sum might be generated by the tax bishops collected from the more humble clerics of their diocese who wished to keep a wife. This tax was paid by up to 60 per cent of the clergy in some dioceses, such as Basle. Clerical and monastic landlords also played their full part in the reimposition of serfdom with which landlords secured their workforce in the wake of the Black Death. Less immediately resented was the exploitation of spiritual benefits such as the trade in indulgences, a relatively accessible and highly popular means of seeking some assurance of favour in the afterlife among Germany's Christian population at this date.

The great disparities of wealth, status and education were a source of considerable tension within the clerical estate. Prominent reformers within the clergy, such as Dean Colet in his famous Convocation sermon of 1510, made frequent and passionate calls for a renovation of the quality of religious life, to begin with the clergy themselves. But it was increasingly doubtful whether the traditional institutions of the church were themselves sufficient to create the momentum for a wide-ranging movement of reform. The history of mediaeval reform movements was in this respect salutory. The agenda of reform ostensibly lay at the heart of the Conciliar movement of the fourteenth and fifteenth centuries, but increasingly became subsumed in a political struggle for control of the papacy. Prominent individuals who allowed their call for reform to stray into overt criticism of a politicized and often corrupt papacy, such as the Bohemian Jan Hus or the Florentine prophet Savonarola, were condemned as heretics and destroyed.

The conflict of authority that lay at the heart of Conciliarism was eventually resolved in favour of the papacy, but the legacy in terms of practical reform was modest. Prominent laypeople interested in reform

could legitimately doubt whether the institutional church could provide the leadership for the wholesale renovation of the Christian life
that many saw as necessary. Some of this scepticism was seen in the
movements of popular devotion that posed an increasing challenge to
the more traditional piety of the monastic orders, in any case under
threat from the increased vitality of parish religion. In England pious
donations to religious houses had declined steeply even while parish-
based religious institutions were generously supported. Many religious
houses were in difficulties long before the Reformation, with criticisms
of the sincerity of vocations and a serious shortage of personnel. The
need for reform was widely recognized in parts of the religious orders
themselves.

The agenda of change was of obvious relevance to the new intellectual movement known as Humanism. Humanism was not in its wider
sense primarily concerned with church reform: the rediscovery and
celebration of classical civilizations, which lay at the heart of the
Renaissance, was a development of far wider application, in the
world of education, scholarship and the visual arts. But an intellectual
movement of such force could not leave the church untouched. To the
extent that the Humanism of the Renaissance celebrated the capacities
of people to govern their own destiny, it proposed a worldview fundamentally at varience with that of the church. At the same time, Humanists celebrated and acknowledged the growing self-confidence of a
newly articulate Christian laity. Such sentiments explain the huge
popularity of Erasmus's *Enchiridion militis christiani* (The 'Handbook
of the Christian Soldier'), and the author became a figure of European
renown with the publication of this vision of the active Christian
vocation. Erasmus was one of a growing number of writers who
employed wit and satire to decry the failings of the institutional
church, criticism that would provide a corrosive background to the
more frontal attack of Protestantism in the sixteenth century.

All of this was important but the greatest contribution of Humanist
scholarship was in its championing of new standards of critical scholarship in the fields of theology and the classics. Humanism promoted a
remarkable renaissance in the study of Greek and the ancient civilizations of the Middle East: significantly also the original languages of the
biblical canon. The rigorous scholarship that restored the uncorrupted
text of many Greek and Latin authors could also be applied to testing
the received text of Scripture (principally the fourth-century Latin
translation of St Jerome known as the Vulgate), against original
texts. This process set the new scholarship on a potential collision

with a church hierarchy that gave great weight to the accrued authority of church tradition, and that regarded the Vulgate as hallowed and sacred. The potential dangers of the new scholarship in this regard were demonstrated when Erasmus's celebrated new translation of the New Testament seemed to challenge the scriptural basis for the doctrine of penance.

The techniques of the new scholarship were eagerly embraced by many in the expanding university world, including those, like the young Martin Luther, not instinctively drawn to the implicit secularity of the Humanist project. But left to itself, Humanism posed no particular danger to the established church. The danger would arise if the theological scepticism of the intellectual critics of the church could be articulated in such a way as to tap into the broader seams of dissatisfaction that existed among the laity. It was precisely this combination that, emerging from an obscure quarrel among religious professionals in the 1520s, would shake the western church to its foundations.

Martin Luther

Luther's role as a catalyst of change was in many ways ironic. For until his criticisms of indulgence-selling brought him into conflict with the church hierarchy, with such fateful results, Luther's career had been conventional, indeed notably successful. Luther was a Catholic success story; an example of just what was possible within the unreformed pre-Reformation church. Born the son of a successful mine-owner in Saxony, Luther reaped the benefit of the educational revolution of the late Middle Ages, attending successively the cathedral school at Magdeburg and the university of Erfurt. The decision to enter the Augustinian monastery at Erfurt, taken against his father's will, was a turning point, but once achieved Luther rose steadily through the ranks of his order. A lecturer at the university of Wittenberg in 1507, Luther represented his order on business in Rome in 1510. By 1512 he was Doctor of Theology, and a rising force in the local university, recognized in Wittenberg as a powerful and effective preacher.

It was also during these years that Luther began to formulate the new theological understandings that would later underpin his theology. Luther was prone to depression throughout his life, and this may have been the background to a fundamental reordering of his thought with relation to judgement and salvation. Like many of his contemporaries, Luther found the concept of God as judge almost unbearably oppressive. The breakthrough came from a reading of Romans 1:17: 'For therein is the righteousness of God revealed from faith to faith, as it is written. The just shall live by faith.' Luther came to see that this could offer the prospect of mercy, not the damnation he saw as the inevitable consequence of his fallen state. Far from being judged, the suffering Christian was in fact rescued by God's free gift and Christ's sacrifice on the cross.

There was no sudden revelation, and Luther's concept of Justification by Faith built on a solid body of doctrine within the Catholic Church. But it did mean that when Luther later became embroiled with his own superiors, he had to hand the conceptual framework for a radical disavowal of the traditional framework of authority: a reordering of the theological order that would prove powerfully incendiary in the circumstances of the German Empire.

For all that, the issue that made Luther into a public figure was prosaic enough. Indulgence-selling was already a much criticized aspect of late mediaeval devotional practice. The offering of pious donations against the hope of mercy in the afterlife was obviously prone to abuse, pandering as it did to the most basic fears of ordinary Christians; and the manner in which the St Peter's indulgence was preached would have offended many less tender consciences than Luther's. The organization of fund-raising through this indulgence in northern Germany was in fact a highly sophisticated piece of Renaissance finance. In 1514 Albrecht of Brandenburg had been raised to the archdiocese of Mainz, but since he intended not to surrender his previous diocese of Magdeburg, and was in addition under the canonical age to be a bishop, the pope was able to insist on a considerable fee. He agreed in return that 50 per cent of the monies raised from the preaching of the indulgence in Albrecht's two dioceses could be set against this sum. The whole transaction was underwritten by the Fuggers of Augsburg, Germany's principal banking house.

It was a shoddy enough deal, made more offensive by the vigour and lack of sophistication with which the indulgence was preached around Magdeburg by Albrecht's agent, the Dominican friar Tetzel. Reports of Tetzel's activities spurred Luther to action. In October 1517 he published his 95 theses against indulgences, a call for academic debate wholly justified by Luther's position as a university professor. What Luther could not have anticipated was the widespread public interest that followed. Electoral Saxony was some way from the commercial heart of the empire, and despite the growing prestige of its new university, Wittenberg was at this stage not one of Germany's established intellectual centres. Yet within months Luther's theses had circulated widely, being reprinted in Leipzig and Nuremberg, and in the great international printing metropolis of Basle. Soon news of Luther's controversial writing was spreading among the intellectual community around Europe: by early 1518 Erasmus in the Netherlands had heard, and approved of Luther's protest against abuse within the Church. Luther and the debate over indulgences soon became a fashionable cause among Humanists and churchmen who had themselves been critical of abuse within the Church in the preceding years.

Public reaction was critical to Luther's fate; so too was the fact that the church hierarchy was slow to perceive the wider implications of his call for reform. In part this was a result of political circumstances that relegated Luther to the margins of a complicated agenda. The emperor Maximilian died on 12 January 1519, and it would be a full six months before his grandson Charles had secured the succession. In the meantime those concerned with the future direction of imperial policy were fully engaged, and critically Luther's patron, the Elector of Saxony, Frederick the Wise, had to be courted as a vital influence in the forthcoming imperial election. In consequence Frederick, a devout Catholic but fiercely proud of his new university and its suddenly famous local professor, had to be indulged in the perverse sponsorship of his turbulent friar. It was not until June 1520 that Luther's theses were formally condemned at Rome, in the papal bull, *Exsurge Domine*.

Luther made full use of the interval afforded by the slow processes of papal justice. His first big test was the meeting of the Augustinian chapter at Heidelberg in April 1518. Luther spoke well and effectively; hereafter members of his own order would be his most resolute early supporters. The following year, 1519, Luther confronted in debate one of the most effective of his growing army of Catholic critics, the Ingolstadt theologian Johannes Eck. Eck forced from Luther some damaging concessions. Rather than accept the orthodox judgement first pronounced by the legate Cajetan at Augsburg the previous autumn, Luther now claimed that the pope himself did not have the final authority to interpret Scripture. The ultimate authority was Scripture itself; this was the *sola scriptura* principle that became, together with Justification by Faith Alone, an intellectual cornerstone of the Reformation.

Through all of this Luther was writing feverishly, a torrent of writings in Latin and German, which simultaneously widened the scope of his criticisms of the church and brought them to a wider public. As it became clear that his own church would ultimately disavow his criticisms without the debate he sought, Luther moved to an ever more pessimistic and apocalyptic understanding of the role of the church hierarchy. Even before Leo X had agreed to condemn Luther, Luther had written off the pope as an agent of Antichrist. This was radical indeed, and it may be asked why so many Germans were prepared to honour Luther as a prophet and leader despite the increasing violence of his language. Essentially Luther's gift as a writer saved him from isolation and destruction. Culminating in his three great tracts of 1520, *The Babylonian Captivity of the Church, On the Freedom of a Christian Man*, and *To the Christian Nobility of the German Nation*, Luther developed in numerous tracts and pamphlets a complete manifesto of reform, a call for the radical renovation of the German church and the life of the Christian man. It touched a sensitive nerve both with Christians struggling, like Luther, with their own relationship with an apparently vengeful God, and secular powers resentful of the power of the church in the lives of the German cities and princely states. It was a powerful cocktail of resentments, and one largely unique to Germany.

Thus by the time the new emperor Charles V came to meet the diet of the German princes at Worms in April 1521 Luther was already a major public figure, his image familiar from an increasing flood of pamphlets and illustrated broadsheets. The emperor, a devout Catholic, had no wish to meet Luther, and intended at first merely to proclaim the pope's recent condemnation of his views. The German princes, however, insisted that Luther be heard; an ominous indication of the shifting balance of power within Germany. Luther therefore appeared personally to answer the charge of heresy. In a famous scene he refused to recant his views; more crucially, his safe conduct was honoured, and Luther was permitted to leave unharmed. Although Charles now proclaimed the imperial ban against him, he had lost his last best chance to snuff out the movement.

Luther was now dependent again on his loyal and supportive protector, Frederick the Wise. For a year after the Diet of Worms he remained incarcerated in the Wartburg Castle, held there for his own protection by the anxious Frederick. He occupied himself with writing and study, most constructively by beginning the new German translation of the Bible that would be his greatest and most enduring literary achievement. But even in his absence the movement continued to grow. In Wittenberg his university colleague Andreas Karlstadt ensured that the momentum of reform was not dissipated, introducing into the local liturgy a new German Mass. A similar pattern was established in many towns across Germany, as sympathetic laymen and clergy took up the call for the renovation of church life.

In many respects this was the crucial moment, as the call for reform finally outgrew the scandal and turbulence raised by the drama of the 'Luther affair'. It now became clear that in pursuing his own increasingly violent quarrel with the church hierarchy, Luther had tapped into a broad seam of resentment about the German church, which spoke to the concerns of many of his fellow citizens. In the pamphlet war of 1519–22 Luther certainly pursued his own theological agenda, but he was also careful to embrace a wide agenda of long-held grievances about the church: the provision of clerical services (and the widely resented fees clerics charged for sacramental offices), tithes, clerical immunities. Thus although Luther's central theological message, Justification by Faith Alone, was a real inspiration to many, what really struck a chord was his call for a return to pure scriptural teaching, with its implicit criticism of scholastic theology and a clerical ethos which left laymen excluded and disadvantaged. The preaching of the pure Gospel, *Rein Evangelium*, became the slogan of those who followed Luther in his call for a total renovation of church life.

This was most clearly expressed in the German towns. Germany in the sixteenth century was a land of towns; the landscape of the empire was densely packed with cities, many of them like Nuremberg and Augsburg centres of both a highly developed trade and cultural life. Some 65 were free imperial cities, self-governing territories that enjoyed a wide measure of political independence and separate representation in the imperial diet. In the years after 1521 most of the cities experienced evangelical agitation from priests and laymen sympathetic to Luther. By 1525 several, led by Strasbourg and Nuremberg, were prepared to follow the example of Wittenberg and proclaim the introduction of a new German service and the abolition of the Mass.

By now the movement had clearly outgrown the theological concerns of its founder. Luther returned to Wittenberg in 1522 and continued to write and preach, a torrent of new writings that scarcely abated, and largely drowned out his Catholic critics. Reprinted freely across Germany, these writings, and the works of Luther's supporters, seized and shaped the reform agenda. An authoritative estimate suggests that something in the region of 10,000 pamphlet editions issued from the presses of German-speaking lands between 1520 and 1530. Of these almost three-quarters appeared between 1520 and 1526, the high point of the pamphlet exchanges stimulated by Luther's reform movement. Overwhelmingly they were dominated by voices sympathetic to Luther's movement; the Wittenberg reformer was alone responsible for some 20 per cent of the overall total.[2]

Luther's productivity as an author was as astonishing as his mastery of so many divergent 'voices': the pastoral sermon, the serious work of systematic theological exposition; the biting, ribald satire. Yet,

Figure 13 Martin Luther, *Der CX Psalm Dixit Dominus*, Wittenberg, 1539. Courtesy St Andrews University Library.

ultimately, none of Luther's many hundreds of pamphlets would be as important to him, or as influential, as his new Bible translation. Begun during the year of enforced leisure in the Wartburg, the whole project was gradually brought to completion. The first editions of the New Testament were published in 1522, the whole text of the Bible, for which Luther had enlisted the help of Melanchthon and other fine scholars, was rendered into German finally by 1530. The book was a publishing sensation; by the time of the reformer's death in 1546 the printing houses of Germany had turned out a total of over 450 editions of the New Testament, the whole Bible, or its parts. On a very conservative estimation of edition size this suggests that at least half a million copies of Luther's text of the vernacular Bible had been put into circulation by the time of his death.[3]

But for all Luther's towering presence, a movement of this complexity could hardly remain under the direction of one man. Inevitably, the call for reform unleashed a vast and unruly surge of emotions, only imperfectly channelled by Luther's own reforming agenda. Not all those inspired by Luther would share his ultimate goals, or his innate social conservatism. Luther had a first inkling of this on his return from the Wartburg in 1522. In his absence Wittenberg had been convulsed by a group of self-appointed lay apostles, the so-called Zwickau prophets, who, supported by Karlstadt, had preached a much more radical reform than was acceptable to either Luther or the Electoral Court. Luther's return nipped this in the bud, but his influence could hardly be felt with the same force elsewhere in Germany.

The most damaging manifestation of this untamed energy was the Peasants' War of 1525. Although Luther's teaching found its most immediate resonance in the German cities, it also found many admirers among Germany's rural population. Here Luther's teaching of the social gospel, the equality of Christians before God, had a particular appeal, especially when applied to long held grievances about the harsh conditions of rural life. In many parts of rural Germany the church was deeply unpopular. The clergy were resented as harsh and oppressive landlords, not least for the reimposition of serfdom and the harsh terms of labour services, extracted as a traditional due in addition to rent. In 1525 many parts of Germany rose in revolt. Such peasant unrest was far from unprecedented: a similar series of risings, known as the *Bundschuh*, had smouldered along the Rhine basin for the previous 20 years. But now, ominously, the peasant leaders clothed their traditional grievances in the new language of evangelical justice: 'Third. It has until now been the custom of the Lords to own us as their property. This is deplorable, because Christ redeemed and bought us with his precious blood, the lowliest shepherd as well as the greatest lord.'[4]

To those who had denounced Luther as a social revolutionary, the Peasants' War appeared the final vindication. Luther himself, terrified that his movement would now be abandoned by the socially respectable, denounced the peasants and called for their suppression. By 1526, after a series of bloody engagements culminating in the wholesale slaughter of the Battle of Frankenhausen, the revolt had been put down, but at considerable cost. The destruction of the peasant army at Frankenhausen left 6,000 of the insurgents dead on the field, and many others were summarily executed in the brutal reckoning that followed. Thomas Müntzer, captured as he fled the field, was shown no mercy: tortured into a confession he was then brought to the camp of the victorious George of Saxony and beheaded.

In the brutal aftermath of the Peasants' War those who had spoken out against them were inevitably seen as complicit in the repression. Luther's own reputation was permanently damaged by the frantic violence of his polemic against the peasants. In his *Against the Murdering Hordes of Peasants* of 1525 he proclaimed, infamously, that anyone who killed a peasant did God a service. This would not be forgotten, and there is evidence that Luther himself bitterly regretted the intemperate language that his anxieties for the success of the Reform had induced. These were perhaps the most testing times Luther ever faced. In 1525 he had followed the example of several of his followers and taken a wife, Katharina von Bora. The union would ultimately bring him great happiness, but the marriage of a former monk and a former nun was a propaganda gift for his enemies. Then in 1525 also the great humanist Erasmus finally bowed to sustained pressure, and wrote against Luther. Luther replied in kind, and the breach was final. Many of the younger humanists kept faith with Luther, but the pyschological impact of Erasmus's criticism was profound. The mood of optimism that had accompanied the early crusading years of the evangelical movement in Germany was shattered beyond repair.

The Peasants' War and its aftermath was a fundamental turning point for the Reformation. By rejecting the aspirations of the countrymen, Luther and his magisterial supporters had made clear the boundaries beyond which reform could not be extended. In Germany's free cities, and in those states where the prince acted as sponsor, reform would proceed, a process that in the long term inevitably led to the

Figure 14 Lucas Cranach, portraits of Martin Luther and Katharina von Bora. Courtesy Oeffentliche Kunstsammlung Basel, Kunstmuseum, Photo Martin Bühler. These paired portraits show some of the tension of what was for both Luther and his movement the crisis point of the Reformation (1525–6). Later the couple would become an icon for the new model Protestant family.

increase in the power of the secular authorities at the expense of the church. But those who had interpreted Luther's call for reform as an opportunity for social levelling were driven out of the movement. Increasingly they were confined to the wilder fringes of evangelism, sustained by self-styled prophets and preachers of little theological training. The defeated and disappointed victims of the Peasants' War were the first adherents of the unofficial Reformation which found its most powerful manifestation in Anabaptism.

The shock of 1525–6 proved only a temporary setback. In the years immediately following, more of the imperial cities adopted the evangelical agenda, joined now by the first of the princes who officially adopted the movement in their lands. By 1529 they were sufficiently strong to band together to defy the emperor Charles V, who continued to insist that his condemnation of Luther, proclaimed at Worms in 1521, be enforced. The evangelical 'Protestation' against this decision in 1529 (the origin of the word Protestant), was followed in 1530 by the adoption of a common declaration of faith, the Confession of Augsburg, now in effect the credal statement of a new church. In the following decades the new movement consolidated its hold in the German lands. Luther himself, now securely established as patriarch of the new movement, accommodated himself to these developments. Mellowed by experience, the apocalyptic energy of his early preaching was replaced by the more practical work of church building, to which

Luther contributed a new genre of instructional literature, his German catechism. In this aspect of his work he was ably assisted by other talented men: Johannes Bugenhagen, who wrote church orders for many of the first Lutheran lands, and Philip Melanchthon, the quiet intellectual who contributed the first systematic exposition of the Lutheran faith, the *Loci Communes*. By his death in 1546 Luther's church had transformed the landscape of religious life in Germany for ever.

The Reformation outside Germany

Outside Germany Luther's movement never achieved the same impact. The circumstances that permitted the rapid dissemination of Luther's message were too particular to his homeland. This was partly because of the empire's unique political and social make-up, a highly urbanized society where the central political institutions were exceptionally weak. Also, Luther himself was a quintessentially German figure. Alongside an intensely serious and personal theological message, Luther also contrived to speak directly to the immediate concerns of his fellow countrymen, their frustrations with their religious life, their resentment of foreign interference in the German church. Little of this would have the same force outside the empire; outside Germany, too, those who took up Luther's call for reform often met with far more determined opposition than was the case in the empire. Here, papal condemnation of Luther's teachings tended to carry more weight, and those who espoused Luther's doctrines did so at the hazard of their lives. The first Lutherans to die for their faith were two Augustinian monks from the Netherlands, Hendrik Vos and Jan van der Eschen, executed in Brussels in 1523 as Charles V clamped down savagely on local manifestations of the German heresy.

Yet in the years immediately following the outbreak of the German controversies, the impact of German events was certainly felt across wide parts of Europe. Luther's writings were known and read in most parts of Europe: individual admirers of his works can be identified as far away as Sweden and Scotland in the north, and in Spain and Italy in the south. But the call for reform seldom provoked the same turbulence, or inspired the degree of popular support, as had been the case in Germany. Where Protestant churches were ultimately established it was generally through the agency of a sympathetic state power, as was the case in Scandinavia or England.

Outside Germany it was not surprising that the Reformation should have its most immediate impact in *Switzerland*. The Swiss Confederation was in its social and political structure not dissimilar to the empire, well provided with proud, independent cities, grouped around an inner core of rugged mountain cantons. The Confederation had won independence from its Habsburg overlords in 1499, at the end of the Swabian Wars, at which point it was effectively separated from the Holy Roman Empire. The close relationship between Swiss German and High German meant that there was no significant language barrier for evangelical writings to overcome. Most of all, the Swiss Reformation had its own inspirational leader in Ulrich Zwingli. Appointed to the prestigious post of *Leutpriester* (people's priest) in Zurich in 1518, Zwingli pursued a clear-minded agenda of reform which had much in common with that of the German cities. Zwingli had read and admired Luther, but there is no reason to doubt that reform in Zurich proceeded to an independent agenda, and Zwingli was able to call on considerable support from within Zurich's ruling elite. Spurred on by Zwingli, in 1525 the Zurich town council formally abolished the Mass, giving Zwingli and his colleagues a free hand to complete the work of reform.

The Zurich Reformation, so swiftly concluded, became a magnet and inspiration both within and beyond the Swiss Confederation. Many, both in the German cities and elsewhere in Europe, would in due course prefer the more radical Zurich model of reform to Luther's more conservative version. But within the Confederation, the response was more ambiguous. Zurich was one of the biggest and most powerful of the Swiss cantons, and its zeal to spread the evangelical message could easily be interpreted by its less powerful neighbours as a pretext for asserting Zurich influence over the Confederation as a whole. Thus whereas the German urban cantons most equal in size and self-confidence, Berne and Basle, swiftly followed Zurich into the evangelical camp, the smaller inner mountain cantons resisted, a resistance prompted in equal measure by their antipathy to Zurich and their loyalty to Catholicism. Towards the end of the decade, goaded by interference from Zurich, the Catholic cantons went to war twice to defend their independence, in the second war inflicting on Zurich a crushing defeat that also cost the life of Zurich's inspirational leader (Battle of Kappel, 11 October 1531).

Zwingli's death at Kappel put a decisive break on the development of the Zurich Reformation. Within Germany the eclipse of Zurich tilted the balance decisively back towards Wittenberg, much to the relief of Luther, whose antipathy towards Zwingli's theological writings had already provoked unseemly and damaging polemicizing between the two men. Within the Confederation, the Catholic cantons had effectively sustained their right to independent religious choice. On the Protestant side too the fronts were drawn. From this point on the most significant development would be the extension of Berne's influence into the French-speaking territories at the western end of the Confederation, which in 1532 encouraged the small city of Geneva to throw off the rule of its prince-bishop and declare for the Reformation. Four years later John Calvin, a young French exile, arrived to assist the process of consolidating the new evangelical order. It was hardly to be anticipated that this was in fact the beginning of the emergence of a new order that would in due course eclipse Zurich as the leading force within the Swiss Reformation.

In other parts of Europe the influence of Luther's movement often travelled in the footsteps of German immigrants and merchants. In both Scandinavia and *Eastern Europe* it was the small German communities who first read and disseminated Luther's doctrines, enthusiastically seconded by students who had studied in Wittenberg before returning to their homeland to spread the word. The lands of eastern Europe proved, in fact, surprisingly fertile ground for the Reformation, a circumstance now disguised for posterity by the later success of the Counter-Reformation in reclaiming Bohemia, Hungary and Poland. But in the decades following the German Reformation Luther's movement made a profound impact. Bohemia (now the Czech Republic), and Hungary, in particular, were well integrated into the the central European economic system, with strong trading links and communication links with Germany. The precious metals of the Czech lands were mined by an international community that included many German settlers from across the border in Saxony. The Bohemians, too, had their own reasons for welcoming Luther's reform, not least its apparent endorsement of their own religious revolt against Rome as followers of the fifteenth-century heretic and martyr Jan Hus. After initial suspicion the Hussites eagerly embraced Luther (and vice versa). Their strong tradition of political independence, established in a brutal war in the 30 years following Hus's execution (1415), meant that they could easily resist Habsburg attempts to call them to order. Secure in their knowledge that the new Habsburg monarchy (rulers in Hungary and Bohemia since the death of King Louis Jagiello in the defeat at Mohács in 1526) could hardly rule these lands without the co-operation of their powerful Estates, the

Bohemian and Hungarian nobles extracted a high price for their support. That included the toleration of Protestantism. The ironic result was that the Habsburg emperors, elsewhere the most resolute opponents of the evangelical movement, were forced to accept in these lands well-organized and robust Protestant churches, which became the dominant religious culture in these lands. The restoration of Catholic hegemony was forced to await the Habsburg victory in the early phase of the Thirty Years' War.

The kingdoms of *Scandinavia*, too, became strongholds of the new religion, though here the introduction of a robust and orthodox Lutheranism had less to do with local enthusiasm than the determin-ation of two strong-minded and opportunist kings. Whereas in the case of Christian IV of Denmark conviction possibly outweighed pol-itical considerations, with Gustavus Vasa of Sweden the opposite was certainly the case. Whatever the motive, the result was to build royal power at the expense of both the nobility and the clergy. In the case of Denmark it is possible to talk of an alliance between the king, who had already introduced reform in his German lands of Schleswig-Holstein before succeeding to the throne, and the towns, for both Malmø and Copenhagen showed a considerable propensity to reform. It required a brief but decisive civil war (1533–4) to overcome the entrenched opposition of the Catholic landed nobility to Christian's succession on the death of his uncle, the more cautious Frederik I. But after this the conversion of Denmark into a Protestant state proceeded apace; in 1537 the new king signed a Church Order, drawn up by Luther's closest lieutenant, Johannes Bugenhagen, who also on this visit ordained the first seven Lutheran superintendents. A Lutheran state church had been established only a decade after the Reformation had first begun to make an impact.

Sweden pursued a somewhat different course, partly because, in the case of Gustavus Vasa, there is little evidence of any disposition to favour Protestantism for its own sake. Rather, perhaps profiting from the example of the German princes who had adopted the Reformation, Gustavus clearly discerned the potential of the new evangelical teach-ing to assist his attack on the wealth and influence of the church in Sweden. The Reformation would experience several setbacks before a parliament in 1539 granted the king full control over the Swedish church; even so, the country would wait a further 30 years before the promulgation of a Protestant Church Order (1571). The very different character of the Scandinavian Reformation is underlined by the relative scarcity of vernacular religious literature to promote the new doctrines.

This was hardly surprising; neither country had the population to sustain a printing industry of any size, nor the critical mass of town dwellers to provide a market. In Sweden and Denmark the task of inculcating the new beliefs would necessarily follow the acts of state that won both lands to Protestantism.

Circumstances were very different in the three prosperous lands of western Europe where the fate of the Reformation was initially most uncertain: France, England and the Netherlands. *England* in this period was a land of contrasts. Much less urbanized than either Germany or the Netherlands, it nevertheless possessed a thriving international trade centre in London, and in Oxford and Cambridge two universities of established reputation. Both, in fact, would play a significant role in the early campaigns against Luther as Henry VIII turned to their finest theologians for the arguments that allowed him to enter the lists against the growing threat of Lutheran heresy. In 1521 Henry had published under his name a systematic defence of tradition doctrine against Lutheran heresy, the *Assertio Septem Sacramentorum*, an initiative that would earn for him the coveted title Defender of the Faith from a grateful pope. This comparative harmony could not however survive the strain caused by Henry's increasing desperation to secure release from his marriage to Catherine of Aragon, a step that a new pope, Clement VII, was in no position to sanction. The progress of the Reformation in England was thus closely bound up with Henry's personal affairs, as his tangled and frustrated international diplomacy forced him to contemplate radical steps that went very much against the grain of his own instinctive theological conservatism. In this respect the Reformation in England would follow a model much closer to that of Scandinavia than Germany or Switzerland. Although England, like Bohemia, had its own indigenous mediaeval heresy in Lollardy, Luther's attack on the church produced little resonance in England outside the colony of the German merchants resident in London. Indeed, although Luther's works were clearly imported into England at an early stage this may often have been for the convenience of conservative theologians who bought them to refute them, such as Bishop John Fisher and Sir Thomas More.

All of this changed when Henry made the fateful decision that only drastic action could extricate him from a marriage that, in the absence of a male heir, now threatened the future of his dynasty. In rapid succession from 1532, legislation was passed through Parliament curbing the influence of the papacy in England, and appointing the king Supreme Head of the Church. This and the divorce once achieved, the king moved to take control of much of the church's property through the dissolution of the monasteries. The political nation was, for the most part, obediently compliant rather than enthusiastic. There is no evidence of any great hostility towards the church and its institutions before the Reformation; on the contrary, both the English episcopate and parish clergy seem to have been by the standards of other European lands both well trained and living without scandal. On the other hand few were prepared to defy the king to defend the threatened institutions of the old church, and the king was to discover that, largely inadvertently, his own actions had stimulated support for the heresy he had so virulently condemned in his youthful writings. This was predictable enough. In the campaign against the church Henry and his faithful agent Thomas Cromwell made use of those who had the necessary polemical armory, and this was most conveniently supplied by continental Protestantism. Several open advocates of the new beliefs, such as the new Archbishop of Canterbury, Thomas Cranmer, and the preacher Hugh Latimer, attained positions of influence as a result.

As Henry's health failed in the last years of his life it became clear that his own actions had encouraged the growth of a powerful evangelical party at court. On his death in 1547 they moved quickly to establish their supremacy in the regency government necessitated by the youth of the new king, Edward VI. Thus the short reign of Edward VI saw the determined attempt to introduce a full Protestant Church polity into England, modelled on that of the Swiss and German Reformed churches, and driven on by a powerful alliance of Archbishop Cranmer and the Lord Protector, the Duke of Somerset. In the five years of the king's life much was achieved: two evangelical Prayer Books, a new English order of service, the stripping of the remaining Catholic paraphernalia from the churches. But time was too short to put down roots; on Edward's death in 1553, the religious changes introduced by his government were easily reversed by his Catholic half-sister, Mary. Only Mary's devotion to the papacy (which threatened the continued possession of former monastic property in the hands of those who had purchased it from the crown), and her determination to marry her cousin, Philip of Spain, provoked a half-hearted reaction. English Protestantism was reduced once again to a persecuted remnant, many of its most able figures taking refuge abroad, to avoid the martyrdom that was the fate of those who remained behind.

English Protestantism at least had its first brief moment of success (and Edward's reign would prove an important benchmark later when

Elizabeth's accession allowed a renewed return to Protestantism). The same could not be said of either France or the Netherlands. In both these countries those sympathetic to reform had to suffer cruel disappointment after the evangelical doctrines had made early inroads.

Perhaps nowhere was this disappointment more acute than in *France*, where political circumstances had seemed for a time to be uniquely favourable to reform. France had its own strongly rooted Humanist movement, led by the towering figure of the renowned New Testament scholar, Jacques Lefèvre d'Etaples. Equally important was France's strongly developed tradition of independence from Rome, which dated from the time when the mediaeval French monarchy was the leading force in Conciliarism and the sponsor of the schismatic Avignon papacy. This breach had been healed, but the price extracted by the French crown was a substantial degree of control over high ecclesiastical appointments in France, a privilege confirmed by the Concordat of Bologna in 1516. The architect of this agreement was the new king, Francis I, a monarch with strong Humanistic leanings who seemed inclined to endorse much of the reform agenda. His sponsorship of fashionable Humanist scholarship sent out signals that could not but alarm conservative forces in France, led by the Parlement of Paris and the theology faculty of the University of Paris, the Sorbonne. So from an early stage the battle-lines were drawn. The reform minded, led by Lefèvre and Briçonnet, the evangelical Bishop of Meaux, sought to pursue an agenda of evangelical renewal while remaining loyal to the highly independent French church. Conservatives, meanwhile, tried at every turn to tarnish these initiatives by association with the German heresy.

For a decade the reformers seemed to have the upper hand, secure in the protection of the king, and his sister, Margaret d'Angoulême. The turning point came in 1534, when a small group of radical emigré evangelicals contrived to exhibit in Paris posters denouncing the Mass in language of a ferocity previously unknown in polite evangelical circles. The king was outraged, and now more easily convinced of the dangers that lay behind the speculative preaching of the Parisian Humanists. In the persecution that followed this 'Affair of the Placards', Paris evangelism suffered a setback from which it never recovered, as many of its leading figures, Calvin among them, were forced to take flight abroad. In the years that followed, persecution abated, but French evangelism was reduced to a string of diffuse and essentially leaderless cells until the emergence of Calvinism in the second half of the century breathed new life into the shattered movement.

In the case of the *Netherlands*, the hostility of the state power was never in doubt. The provinces of the Low Countries formed part of the Burgundian patrimony of the new emperor, Charles V, whose hostility to Luther was intense and personal. Freed of the constraints that bound him in Germany, in the Netherlands he took rapid and decisive action to inhibit the spread of the new doctrines. This was all the more necessary since there was no doubt that the Netherlands would otherwise have proved fertile ground for the German heresies. The rich provinces of Flanders, Brabant and Holland formed one of the most urbanized regions of Europe. The prosperous cities of Bruges, Ghent and Antwerp enjoyed both a buoyant international trade and a proud educational tradition: this region was the cradle of northern Humanism, famed both for its high degree of literacy among the general population and the distinction of its Latin schools. It might have been expected in these circumstances that Luther's teachings would find an eager audience in the Low Countries, and leaders of the German movement were not disappointed. In the first two decades of the Reformation there were more translations of Luther's works into Dutch than any other European vernacular. The poorly structured and ill-led Netherlandish church was ill equipped to resist the appeal of the new doctrines, and Luther's teachings quickly found a deep resonance among the urban population. 'If there be three men that speak', wrote Cardinal Wolsey's envoy, Sir John Hackett, in 1527, 'the twain [that is, two of them] keep Luther's opinions';[5] a pardonable exaggeration that nevertheless conveys something of the extent of popular interest in the new teachings.

But even so robust a movement could make little headway in the face of so determined an opponent as Charles V. Luther's teachings were proscribed in the Netherlands even before his appearance at Worms in 1521, and this official condemnation was soon backed by an apparatus of persecution to match any in Europe. A series of proclamations made first the preaching or printing, later even the possession, of Lutheran books a capital crime. The first victims of the edicts were prominent local preachers who had dared to support Luther's call for reform; soon most had either been executed, forced to recant, or driven into exile in Germany.

The elimination of this first generation of Lutheran leadership had a profound effect on the Reformation in the Netherlands. Deprived of their theological guidance, Dutch evangelicals turned increasingly to visionaries and prophets whose rejection by the leaders of the evangelical mainstream found expression in a doctrine of violence and apocalyptic despair. This movement, the first, decisive phase of *Anabaptism*, reached its apogee in 1534 with the seizure of the German imperial city of Münster, just across the border from the eastern Netherlands. The proclamation of the Münsterite kingdom had a profound resonance in the Netherlands, particularly in the northern provinces and Holland, then suffering from a profound economic recession. Although an attempted insurrection that would have made Amsterdam a second Münster failed, thousands from the Dutch provinces flocked to the German New Jerusalem. When Münster was finally suppressed in 1535, many in the Netherlands were caught up in the bloody repression that followed. But Dutch Anabaptism proved a resilient plant; re-formed in the 1540s by the Friesland priest Menno Simons, and shorn of its more violent rhetoric, Dutch Anabaptism would survive to mount a plausible challenge to Calvinism in the second half of the sixteenth century.

In his other dominions Luther's movement would not cause Charles V the same problems. *Spain* was always likely to prove unfertile territory for Protestantism, since this was a land where memories of the struggle to reclaim the Spanish mainland from the Moors were still fresh. The conquest of Granada, completed in 1492, was heralded in the peninsula as the Catholic monarch's greatest victory, and undoubtedly helped to create a strong sense of identification between the Catholic Church and the developing self-identify of the new Spanish kingdom. Another important legacy of that period was the Spanish Inquisition, created as a means of testing the sincerity of those of other religions, Moors or Jews, who had converted to Christianity in order to stay in Spain after the Reconquest. In the new circumstances of the sixteenth century it could conveniently be turned against the rare individuals who showed signs of sympathy for the new heresies.

A more interesting case was that of the *Italian* peninsula. Here a robust response to Luther's call for reform might well have been expected. The proud city states of northern Italy were not much different from the German imperial cities in their traditions of political independence, and over much of the peninsula relations with the papacy were extremely tense. Many Italian churchmen were prepared to speak out at the slow pace of papally sponsored reform, and the cynical exploitation of papal power for political ends that had characterized much of the fifteenth century. It was probably also in Italy that theologians engaged most directly with Luther's doctrine of Justification by Faith Alone, since his reformulation of the doctrine of salvation commended itself to several leading figures on the reform wing of Italian Catholicism. Right up until the first session of the Council of

Trent men such as Reginald Pole and Gasparo Contarini hoped to persuade their colleagues that agreement on this central Protestant doctrine offered the basis of possible reconciliation between the two churches.

But Italian evangelism failed to live up to these promising beginnings. Nowhere, apparently, did Luther's call for reform produce the same popular resonance as in parts of northern Europe. Italian evangelism remained an elite movement, and those church leaders who favoured doctrinal engagement with Lutheranism were too bound up with the institutional church to follow the Germans into a repudiation of papal authority. Perhaps also cultural snobbery played its part: living in the cradle of Humanism and the Renaissance, Italians were reluctant to concede that the reform of the church could proceed according to an intellectual agenda emanating from the barbarous north. However this was, the polite evangelism of Italy made little progress against the entrenched forces of the church hierarchy. The decisive moment came in 1542, when two prominent leaders of Italian reform, Bernardino Ochino and Pietro Martyr Vermigli, abandoned their charges and fled abroad. Henceforth Italians would, like Ochino and Vermigli, make their most substantial contribution to evangelical reform from outside the peninsula, many of them attaining notoriety as freethinkers and dissidents on the very margins of the mainstream Protestant churches.

A survey of the progress of the Reformation outside Germany for Luther's lifetime thus leaves a much more mixed and troubled impression than one would sometimes gather from existing surveys. In many lands of Europe, like Italy, the 1540s was a decade of retreat for Protestantism. After the optimistic evangelism of the 1520s, followed by a decade of consolidation, the movement suffered substantial reverses in the middle years of the century. In France, Italy and the Netherlands, promising beginnings had now given way to repression, which forced all of those who wished openly to espouse the evangelical doctrines to seek safer climes elsewhere. Many chose the safer course of conformity. Even in Germany the situation was far from rosy. Luther's death in 1546 was followed by a determined effort to subdue German Protestantism by force, as the emperor Charles V finally took to arms to enforce the prohibition of evangelical heresy that had now eluded him for two decades. The Schmalkaldic War was a triumph for the imperial forces, and a smashing defeat for the Protestant princes. With the leaders of the Schmalkaldic League his prisoners and the Protestant army in disarray, it seemed even fleetingly possible that the emperor would be able to enforce the restoration of Catholicism, and thus reverse two decades of systematic church-building in the German princely states.

In the event the final victory would prove beyond Charles. New military reverses ultimately forced the concession of a treaty that guaranteed the freedom to worship according to the evangelical manner in the Lutheran states (the Peace of Augsburg, 1555). But the years of uncertainty had left the leaders of German Protestantism with a clear sense of the political limits of reform. Even before this, many even of the reformers had begun to question how far these German churches had progressed with the fundamental renovation of the Christian life that had been at the heart of Luther's call for reform. The Reformation, it seemed, was badly in need of a second wind.

6

Charles V and the Defence of Catholic Europe

In many respects the crucial moment in Charles V's long and varied career came very early – perhaps too early for him quite to measure up to the magnitude of the occasion. On 17 April 1521 the newly crowned emperor faced Martin Luther at the Diet of Worms, in front of the assembled dignitaries of the Holy Roman Empire. It was, by any account a curious encounter: the apostate monk and the 21 year old who ruled over half the western world. The path that had led Luther to this confrontation is familiar, if extraordinary. But in truth the combination of circumstances that had piled kingdoms and territories into the lap of the young Charles of Ghent was no less improbable. Now to him fell the judgement of a complex theological struggle that had somehow become the most pressing political issue in his German lands.

At the Diet of Worms it certainly lay within Charles's power to finish with Luther, if not the Reformation. Luther had arrived at Worms under safe conduct, but such safe conducts were not always honoured; there was a strong body of opinion that suggested that promises given to heretics were not binding. A precedent was supplied by the fate of Jan Hus, who a century before had arrived at the Council of Constance under a papal protection, which had then been rescinded: Hus was arrested, condemned and burned. Many, perhaps even Luther himself, expected that Luther would not leave Worms alive. Those who wished him well had Hus in mind when they begged him not to risk appearing at the diet; and there were certainly those among Charles's advisors prepared to suggest that his duty to his church lay in finishing with Luther, once and for all.

In the end Charles decided to honour Luther's safe passage, and a vastly relieved reformer was allowed to depart for Saxony and safety. The last best chance to snuff out the Reformation was gone.

The might-have-beens of history are fascinating if ultimately imponderable.[1] But if we cannot know what would have been the fate of the Reformation had Luther died a martyr's death in 1521, we can still ask why Charles did not move against him. The benefits of destroying Luther were obvious, the case against hinged on two

Figure 15 Barend van Orley, *The Young Charles V.* Courtesy the Budapest Museum of Fine Arts.

considerations. One was a fear that the death of Luther might have caused such an explosion of anger in Germany that the empire would have been ungovernable. This was certainly plausible; the consequence of Hus's martyrdom had been a revolt in his native Bohemia that had never been fully extinguished. Luther alive was already a patriotic cause, and the young emperor had had little chance to take the temperature of his German lands or win their loyalty. His progress to the imperial crown had been difficult enough and necessitated the expenditure of vast sums to ensure the loyalty of the seven electors. Charles was very conscious that he was regarded here as a foreign presence.

The political equation was well balanced; in the last resort what may have tipped the scales was Charles's innate sense of honour. The whole span of his career – ambitious, energetic, often quixotic – suggests that the breach of faith involved in such an act of *realpolitik* would have been deeply out of character, perhaps even beyond him. It may ultimately be to this that Luther owed his life and the future of his movement.

If Worms introduced Charles on to the public stage, it was but one of the many moments of grand theatre that punctuated his public career. Some such occasions came Charles's way by dint of his unique position, but others he seems deliberately to have courted. Few even of the crowned heads of Europe would have risked their dignity by challenging their adversary (in this case Francis I of France) to settle their quarrel by single combat. But Charles seems to have been in deadly earnest. He made such an offer at least twice (in 1528 and 1536), and even on one occasion embarked on detailed public negotiations with this end in view. Francis became so irritated that he had the imperial emissary locked up. This chivalric code helps give shape and consistency to a career that was otherwise so crowded and beset by crisis that it is easy to lose sight of the larger goals. For Charles was the accidental ruler of an empire so large that at one point he seemed seriously to aspire to the reunification of the whole of western Christendom in his own person.

Securing the Inheritance

The young Charles of Ghent was born in 1500, the son of Philip the Fair, Duke of Burgundy, and his wife, Juana of Castile. This was already an auspicious beginning; for although Burgundy was much reduced since it had challenged France in the fifteenth century, the residual possessions, Flanders and the Franche-Comté, still contained some of the richest, most sophisticated parts of Europe. However, the key to his eventual prodigious inheritance lay in the generation of his grandparents, for neither parent would ultimately derive much benefit from the dynastic chain of which they formed part. Philip of Burgundy was the only son of Maximilian of Habsburg. As such he would expect the reversion of the imperial crown, as well as the patrimonial lands in Burgundy and the Netherlands. Juana was the daughter of Ferdinand of Aragon and Isabella of Castile, and with the death of her elder sister and infant son, their nearest heir.

In 1506 Charles in effect lost both parents. His father, the energetic Philip died in this year, shortly after arriving in Spain to take on the regency of Castile (Isabella had died in 1504 and Ferdinand, by the terms of her will, did not succeed). But the death of her husband so afflicted Juana that she was soon patently unfit to govern. Ferdinand was left with little choice but to resume the regency, this time on behalf of the young Charles; his deranged mother was removed to strict confinement in the castle of Tordesillas (where she would live on until 1555). Charles, probably only dimly aware of these dark events in far-away Spain, was raised in the congenial atmosphere of the Burgundian Court at Mechelen. His emergence on to the larger stage occurred only with the death of Ferdinand in 1516, which, through his inheritance of the combined crowns of Aragon and Castile, raised him to the status of one of Europe's leading monarchs.

With his mother alive, if incarcerated, it was urgently necessary that Charles should hasten to take possession of his Hispanic lands. The time he took to do so illustrated graphically the hazards of sixteenth-century travel, even for the powerful. All through the summer of 1517 Charles waited at Vlissingen (Flushing) for favourable winds to bear him south. No sooner had they finally embarked than one vessel caught fire: all on board – 160 crew and passengers, and all the king's horses – perished. Blown off course by unfavourable winds, the battered fleet sighted land at Asturias, several hundred miles from the intended landfall of Santander. It was an inauspicious beginning to a difficult period of Charles's career.

Castile awaited its young ruler with some misgivings. There were concerns about the influence of Charles's Flemish advisors, and the peremptory demotion of the aged Cardinal Cisneros did nothing to calm these fears. A meeting of the Cortes of Castile was forthright to the point of insolence; but Charles had little time to address their concerns since the death in January 1519 of his other grandfather, the emperor Maximillian, now plunged him into another critical contest. Although Maximilian had attempted to secure the succession for Charles, he faced a formidable challenge from the King of France, a more experienced ruler who enjoyed good relations with several of the electors. A whirlwind diplomatic effort, together with bribes and promises of favour, secured the votes of the electors, and Charles prepared to depart to claim his prize. At this, the grievances of the Spanish kingdoms burst to the surface. It did not help that Charles, for the convenience of his travel itinerary, had summoned the Cortes of Castile to Santiago, in Galicia. Only after repeated votes, and then only barely, could a majority of the towns be found to approve the new subsidy that Charles had requested to underwrite his travels. By the time he set sail, this time via England, Castile was in open revolt.

The *comuneros* (literally, the revolt of the common people) was the most serious challenge Charles would face in his sovereign dominions. At first, discontent at the policies of the new regime was felt across a broad social spectrum. Delegates in the Cortes were outraged at the high-handed treatment they had received. Meanwhile the grandee nobles were deeply disenchanted by the favour shown to intimates from outside Spain; a grievance compounded by Charles's decision to appoint his old tutor, Adrian of Utrecht, regent in his absence. It was only when the *comuneros* began to espouse more radical goals that the grandees had second thoughts, and gave their reluctant allegiance to the king. In the summer of 1520, however, Charles's authority was under serious threat. In September delegates of 13 towns gathered in Tordesillas and proclaimed their right to govern the kingdom. More alarmingly than mere words, they also secured the castle and seized the person of the king's mother, Juana. What if they discovered that she was not as mad as was supposed?

Charles now did the sensible thing. Two leading representatives of the Castilian nobility were promoted alongside Adrian of Utrecht, and tax concessions proposed for loyal towns. As the *comunero* cause was taken up with enthusiasm by the peasantry and the social radicalism of the leadership became clear, it became easier to reattach the loyalty of the nobility. Nevertheless it required a pitched battle (at Villalar, 23 April 1521) to disperse the rebel army and bring the uprising to an end.

The Imperial Vision

The revolt of the *comuneros* convinced Charles of the need to return to Spain. In May 1521 he confirmed the condemnation of Luther and ended the Diet of Worms, and began the slow journey back to the peninsula via the Netherlands. The dispositions he now made for ruling his other imperial territories at least showed some recognition of the limits to the personal control one man could exercise over such vast dominions. In February 1522 he confirmed his brother Ferdinand as his heir in the Austrian Habsburg lands. This made Ferdinand *de facto* ruler of the central European Habsburg possessions, although this also left him the difficult problem of enforcing the Edict of Worms. The double marriage, in July 1521, between Louis, King of Hungary, and Charles's sister Mary, while Ferdinand married Louis's sister, was a further reinforcement of the family's influence in this region; though few could know the long term significance of this double union. The Netherlands, meanwhile, would be left in the reliable hands of Charles's aunt, Margaret of Austria.

Thus when in July 1522 Charles V arrived back on Spanish soil, he could view his prospects with far greater optimism than when he left three years previously. After a frenzy of activity to establish his authority, Charles now had at least the prospect of being able to shape the agenda. And in his new Imperial Chancellor, Mercurino de Gattinara, he had someone prepared to give shape and form to his most ambitious visions for the future.

Gattinara, a Piedmontese lawyer, had in 1518 replaced Jean Sauvage as 'Grand Chancellor of all the realms and kingdoms of the King'. Coming from one of the smallest territories in the imperial possessions, he could articulate a vision of the future without seeming to favour either Burgundy or Spain. He was prepared to do this in visionary, messianic language that seems to have chimed with Charles's own sense of manifest destiny. 'God has set you on a path towards world monarchy', Gattinara boldly declared to his young ruler in 1519. It was Gattinara's contention that the imperial title gave Charles authority over the whole world, for it was 'ordained by God himself, foretold by the prophets, preached by the apostles, and approved by the birth, life and death of our redeemer Christ'. Among the tangible recommendations that followed from this bold claim, was Gattinara's desire that Charles should follow in the footsteps of the emperor

Justinian and embark on a general reform of the legal system, 'so that it would be possible to say that there was one Emperor and one universal law'.

How seriously should this rhetoric be taken? To regard such language, as it must have appeared to Europe's other crowned heads, as little more than a cynical cover for dynastic opportunism, would be to risk missing some essential kernel of truth. Charles was greatly concerned with the defence of Christendom; and he believed that his imperial crown, and his enormous possessions gave him both a unique opportunity and a clear obligation to take this in hand. His earnest endeavours to confront the Turkish threat, and to prod successive popes towards convening a General Council, should leave little doubt how seriously he took these obligations. What is far more doubtful is whether Gattinara's musings created anything approaching a policy agenda. If Charles V in 1521 could look out on possessions in which his authority was now reasonably secure, his restless energy had hardly ensured him an interval of peace. Events crowded in relentlessly, giving Charles far less freedom to form policy than one might assume from his dominant position in European affairs. Charles's victory in the imperial election had sparked a predictably hostile reaction from France, and a French invasion of Navarre to exploit the turmoil caused by the *comuneros*. This had been comfortably repelled, and in 1522 Charles turned the tables with a treaty of alliance with England (the Treaty of Windsor) anticipating a joint invasion of France. Fighting resumed in 1524 with an imperial campaign against Marseilles. The complete failure of this venture, though embarrassing for the emperor was swiftly balanced by the crushing Spanish victory at Pavia (1525). With Francis a prisoner in his hands, Charles faced crucial decisions: if a new world order were to be created, it would have to be forged through magnanimity. The opportunity of a lasting peace lay at hand if Charles could forgo dynastic revenge and waive the claim to the ancestral Burgundian lands. In this context it is interesting that a cynical counter-proposal, to annex Languedoc and Provence and in effect partition the 'most Christian Kingdom' of France with England and Savoy, emanated from the Chancellor, Gattinara.

Gattinara's imperial vision was not then a coherent policy agenda. Even his cherished reform of imperial institutions fell easy prey to the exigencies of the moment. The Chancellor's visionary plan for a general Imperial Treasury came to nothing, and throughout the reign Charles would continue to raise funds from the separate constituent parts of his dominions essentially on an *ad hoc* basis. On Gattinara's death in 1530 even the office of Imperial Chancellor disappeared. Henceforth the administration of the Empire would rely on two distinct apparatuses: a Spanish secretariat, headed by Francisco de Los Cobos, and a Franco-Burgundian administration for northern Europe, headed by Nicolas Perrenot, seigneur de Granvelle. Both were men of great capacities, but essentially bureaucrats, not policy-makers.

In asking too much of Francis in the negotiations following his capture, Charles destroyed the prospect of peace. Immediately following his release after signing the treaty of Madrid, Francis set about creating a new alliance to oppose his tormentor; and he quickly found new allies concerned at Charles's apparently overwhelming position. A new campaign in Italy led to the capture of Rome by imperial troops, who now, starved and unpaid, proceeded to pillage the Eternal City. The sack of Rome scandalized Europe, and stripped the last shred of credibility from the rhetoric of Gattinara's Christian universalism. The settlement that finally ended this bitter and intense phase of the conflict with France, negotiated by those two pragmatic veterans, Margaret of Austria, regent of the Netherlands, and Louise of Savoy (mother of Francis I), was a sober and pragmatic acknowledgement of the dynastic balance of power. In this the Peace of Cambrai, or Ladies Peace (1529) represented a significant moment. By finally abandoning the claim to the patrimonial lands in Burgundy, Charles in effect acknowledged that his political conduct would continue to be governed by the constraints of real politics, rather than a rhetorical programme of unattainable goals. And although the peace hardly marginalized Italy, it drew an end to the period when Italy was the primary focus of policy. Charles was now free to turn his attention to the other pressing issues that crowded in upon him.

The Turkish Threat

A curious feature of Charles's early career was that, despite all the sound and chivalric fury, Charles was never on hand at the crucial moments of military success. He was still in Germany, at the imperial diet, when the *comuneros* were put down at Villalar. The victory at Pavia took place while the emperor was in Spain. The thirst for military glory was still unassuaged.

In the middle years of Charles's long reign the opportunity finally arrived to vanquish the enemies of Christendom personally. The

Ottoman Empire, long a needling presence on Europe's eastern and southern flank, now seemed poised to threaten the very heart of the Habsburg Empire. Ever since the fall of Constantinople in 1453, the Ottoman advance had been steady and inexorable. Northern Serbia was invaded by the Turk in 1459, Bosnia in 1463–6. In 1470 the Venetians lost Negroponte, and in 1468 Albania fell. Meanwhile a surrogate of the Sultan, the corsair Barbarossa, dominated the North African coast. Finally, and most urgently, in 1526 the Ottoman host had achieved a crushing victory over the army of King Louis of Hungary at Mohács. Louis was lost on the field of battle, along with most of the Hungarian nobility. His kingdom lay at the mercy of the invader.

The King of Hungary had died childless and the succession was uncertain. Ferdinand of Austria, by dint of the double dynastic marriage of 1521, had at least a plausible claim; the fact that only he, supported by the emperor, could effectively halt the Ottoman advance, clinched the issue. So Charles had dynastic as well as more altruistic motives for putting himself at the head of the campaign to turn back the Turkish threat, which in 1532 threatened Vienna. When he heard that the Sultan would be leading the Turkish host, Charles resolved to lead the Christian army in person. By combining the armies of Italy and Austria, together with a substantial contingent provided by the German Lutherans, a formidable force was put in the field. The emperor led the relieving forces into Vienna on 23 September: Suleiman was forced to retreat. For all that much of Hungary remained in Turkish hands, it was a signal and significant victory.

The focus of campaigning now switched to the western Mediterranean. In 1534 the corsair Barbarossa had raided southern Italy, a Habsburg heartland, before occupying Tunis. With Algiers already in his hands, Barbarossa now had a formidable base to prey on Spanish shipping across the vulnerable sea lanes linking Spain and Italy. Charles resolved to dislodge him. In June 1535 a large expeditionary force, the largest part supplied by his Castilian lands, descended on the Tunisian coast, near the fortified strong point of La Goleta. The fort was seized by frontal assault, and shortly thereafter Tunis itself. Barbarossa made his escape as best he could.

The conqueror of Tunis permitted himself a triumphant parade through Rome before, less productively, the war with France was renewed. But as soon as peace could be obtained, Charles turned his attention back to the Turkish threat. In February 1538 agreement was signed between Charles, Ferdinand, Rome and Venice for a joint effort against Suleiman, but Castile was unconvinced and the Cortes proved extremely reluctant to vote supply. The Holy League yielded little apart from the capture of Castelnuevo on the Dalmatian coast. As the promised offensive failed to materialize, the garrison was abandoned to its fate: all 4,000 perished when Suleiman's forces retook the port. Charles learned a hard lesson: if the war against the Ottomans was to rest on the financial strength of Castile, it was necessary that the campaign be concentrated where Spanish interests were most directly engaged, in the eastern Mediterranean. In 1541 a new expeditionary force was gathered, this time with Algiers as its goal. But it was late in the year (October) before the fleet set sail, and Algiers was well fortified; a severe storm severely damaged the fleet shortly after its arrival off the African coast. Retreat seemed the only option, and this was accomplished, albeit at the cost of abandoning the horses and artillery. The emperor congratulated himself that 'among the missing or dead, there was not one man of substance'; but there had been 4,000 more plebeian casualties, and an enormous expenditure had yielded nothing. The expedition of 1541 would be Charles's last major effort to effect a radical change in the balance of forces between Christian and Turk in the Mediterranean. If the decisive victory had proved elusive, the apparently inexorable Turkish advance had at least been halted. It would be left to Philip II to take up the baton, and to try to adapt the crusading concept of the Holy League to the new circumstances of sixteenth-century rivalries between the Christian states.

Lutheranism in the Empire

In the years since 1521 Habsburg authority had paid a heavy price for the failure to strangle the Lutheran heresy in its infancy. Emboldened by the emperor's absence, and the evident reluctance of Ferdinand to take firm action, the 1520s had seen the emergence of a group of Lutheran cities and princely states prepared to defy imperial authority and let the popular movement for evangelical reform have its head. This movement achieved its definitive form at the two imperial Diets of Speyer in 1526 and 1529. The diet of 1526 ended without decisive action against the evangelical delegates. In 1529 the Catholic majority voted to enforce the Edict of Worms, but the Protestant minority had sufficient self-confidence to enter a formal Protestation against this decision: this was the origin of the term 'Protestant'. So when in 1530

Charles V finally turned his attention back to the problem of Germany at the Diet of Augsburg, he faced a far more coherent body of opinion than had been the case at Worms nine years before. Charles's room for manoeuvre was further constrained by the evident need for the support of the Protestant princes in the forthcoming campaign against the Turks. Charles had to content himself with securing the consent of the princes to nominate Ferdinand as King of the Romans (in effect, securing the succession); but the problem of heresy was not addressed.

It would be a further decade or more before Charles would once again be able to give the problems of Germany his full attention, and the Lutheran states made good use of the intervening years. This was a period of church-building and consolidation. At Augsburg the Protestant states had presented a Confession of Faith (the Confession of Augsurg, 1530) which became the foundational doctrinal statement of their church. The following year, 1531, the princes joined together in a formal military alliance pledged to defend the new church by armed force if necessary (the Schmalkaldic League). In 1536 the League achieved a signal military victory, enforcing the reinstatement of the deposed Ulrich of Württemberg; Ulrich promptly converted this crucial state situated in the strategic south-western corner of the empire to Lutheranism.

The emperor could only watch helplessly as the religious divisions within the empire became ever deeper; the final realistic effort to achieve reconciliation between the confessions, the Colloquy of Regensburg of 1541, achieved little. With the failure of Regensburg Charles seems to have recognized that only military victory could halt the spread of Lutheranism. In 1544 he once again made peace with France (the Peace of Crespy) and began gathering military forces for the decisive confrontation. Charles embarked on this campaign knowing that there was no assurance of victory. Establishing himself at Regensburg, Charles summoned the armies of Italy and Hungary. When their juncture was effected, this amounted to an army of 65,000 men. The Schmalkaldic League, meanwhile, had an even greater force under arms: some 80,000 soldiers, supported by formidable artillery. But Charles proved more resolute in a difficult winter campaign, and the army of the princes was already much reduced by the time the two forces met at Mühlberg, on the banks of the Elbe (April 1547). The result was a shattering victory for the imperial forces. A few days later Charles rode into Wittenberg, now a conquered city. For a population still mourning the death of Luther just a few months before, this must indeed have appeared the end of all that the great reformer had achieved. If Charles was tempted to execute the long-delayed sentence against Luther, then his corpse, if not his living body, now lay to hand: buried in the parish church that he had dominated with his preaching for almost 40 years. A reliable tradition had Charles visiting the parish church to gaze at the reformer's grave. Once again, Charles held his hand, forgoing the satisfaction of a symbolic vengeance at a time when the pacification of Germany lay within his grasp.

Given the overwhelming nature of his military victory, the emperor's proposed resolution of the German religious question – the Augsburg Interim – offered the beaten Lutherans far more than might have been expected. Pending a more general settlement of church affairs, Lutherans were to be permitted to keep their married clergy, and communion in both kinds; this was to be the only remnant of their suspended Lutheran church orders in a new dispensation that was otherwise largely Catholic in tone. When Philip Melanchthon, after Luther's death the leading intellectual force in the church, intimated a reluctant willingness to accept the Interim, the kernel of a final settlement seemed to be at hand.

Ultimately, such optimistic hopes would be dashed. The Augsburg Interim quickly revealed itself as unenforceable. Although some cities, such as Strasbourg, introduced the new order, most Lutheran ministers spoke out strongly against it. Riots in the northern German states were an ominous sign of troubles ahead. Resistance focused on the important city of Magdeburg, which had refused point blank to accept the Interim; it now became a magnet for ministers expelled from other more compliant towns. It gradually became clear to Charles that only new military action would consolidate the fruits of the Schmalkaldic war. But as so often in his long career, new problems would emerge to prevent him pursuing the matter to a conclusion. For the first time, however, these emanated from the heart of his own family.

Dynastic Decisions

All through his career Charles had, in the Habsburg manner, made good use of his family. The loyalty of the Netherlands had been maintained through long absences by capable regents: his aunt, Margaret of Austria; and after her death, his sister, Mary of Hungary.

Meanwhile, after the warning of the *comuneros*, Charles had given the clearest possible indication of his duty to his Spanish dominions by repeatedly linking his family in marriage to the ruling house of Portugal. In 1526 Charles married Isabella, daughter of King Manuel; 17 years later the first fruit of this union, the young heir Philip, would be given in marriage to another Portuguese bride, Maria Manuella.

These were happy and judicious decisions. Charles had the greatest affection and respect for his wife, who proved a capable regent in his long absences from the peninsula. It was through these connections too that Philip would in due course inherit the claim to the Portuguese throne that allowed him in 1580 to unite the Iberian kingdoms. But dynastic duty could also be hard, and Charles did not spare his family. In 1533 he gave his niece, Christina of Denmark, to the much older Francesco Sforza, Duke of Milan, over the desperate pleading of Margaret of Austria, who was devoted to the young child. His one concession to sentiment was to allow his favourite sister, Mary, a widow at twenty-one on the death of Louis of Hungary, not to take another husband.

Dynastic diplomacy also played a large part in his response to German problems. In 1518 he had despatched his brother Ferdinand to Germany largely to get him out of Spain. But Ferdinand proved a loyal and capable representative, and Charles was more than happy to leave to his brother the compromises with the Lutheran states necessary to secure their military support against the Turks. In 1530 he had fulfilled his pledge to Ferdinand to have him named King of the Romans, with the clear implication that Ferdinand would follow Charles as emperor. Now, in 1548, having personally as it seemed vanquished the Lutherans of the empire, Charles began to rethink his future dispositions. Perhaps, after all, the security of his dominions could only be maintained under one controlling hand – and that of course would be his own son Philip. If Ferdinand, deeply respected through the empire and firmly entrenched, could not be dislodged, a possible way forward was to have Ferdinand name Philip as his successor, ahead of his own son Maximillian.

The suggestion brought Ferdinand close to open rebellion. Not even the good offices of Mary of Hungary, shuttling back and forth from the Netherlands, could smooth the troubled waters. Ferdinand's disenchantment was too total to be concealed, and strains over strategy spilled over into the imperial Diet of Augsburg of November 1550. Seeking support for his desire to crush Magdeburg, Charles found Ferdinand advocating giving priority to renewing the

Figure 16 Titian, *Charles V*, 1548. Courtesy Bayerische Staatsgemalde-sammlungen, Alte Pinakothek, Munich.

war with the Turks. The breach in the family compact could only give comfort to Charles's enemies. The French king, Henry II (who had succeeded Francis I in 1547), began the search for allies. Meanwhile Maurice of Saxony, the Lutheran prince whose defection to Charles had doomed the Schmalkaldic League, began plotting a new shift of loyalties. Although Ferdinand finally bowed to family pressure and in March 1551 accepted the alternating succession, his alienation was near complete. In the crisis that now overwhelmed Charles he would offer little assistance.

In the spring of 1552 the trap was ready. Maurice of Saxony, having reduced Magdeburg ostensibly as the loyal agent of the emperor, now marched his army south as the ally of the King of France. The unprotected Charles barely escaped capture by abandoning Innsbruck and a dangerous, uncomfortable passage across the Brenner Pass. But Charles was nothing if not resilient. Detaching Maurice from the French alliance by the promise of a future settlement of the religious question in Germany, the emperor set about gathering another army to reclaim from France the imperial city of Metz (occupied by Henry along with Toul and Verdun as the price of his support for the German Lutherans). The siege of Metz began as winter approached. The privations of the trenches and the freezing weather finally broke the emperor's army, and even his resolve. The defeat at Metz began a long process of disengagement that would end with his abdication and retirement.

Germany received the shortest shrift. Sensing that the German Lutherans could not now be broken, Charles formally resigned responsibility for a final settlement to Ferdinand. The terms of the treaty had been clearly intimated by the settlement with Maurice in 1552, but it was left to Ferdinand to make a concession that Charles could not bring himself to acknowledge; the formal acceptance of Lutheranism in the empire. The Peace of Augsburg in fact provided a historic, groundbreaking solution to the religious divisions within the empire, in effect allowing the ruler of each separate state or free city to determine the religion of their people (the principle known as *cuius regio eius religio*). There were safeguards to prevent ecclesiastical lands being secularized and converted (a necessary provision to guarantee a Catholic majority in imperial elections) and no provision for any other Protestant confession than Lutheranism. This would cause problems when Calvin's influence made itself felt in Germany in subsequent decades. But the Peace, both hard-headed and in its way visionary, was sufficiently sound to spare Germany the horrors of the religious wars that engulfed much of northern Europe in the following half century; at least until the climactic struggle of the Thirty Years' War.

The intractable problems of heresy and authority had left Charles with little affection for his German lands. Despite over 30 years wrestling with the problems of the empire, Charles had never troubled to learn German, a significant omission given his facility with languages (Charles spoke Dutch, Spanish, Italian and French). But Charles had a real affinity with the Netherlands, the lands of his first patrimony, and it was here that he chose to end his active political life. The last years in fact saw a steady brightening of political prospects. The marriage of his son Philip to Queen Mary of England in 1554 had threatened to tilt the strategic balance in northern Europe firmly away from France. The furious reaction of Henry II provoked one of the most brutal and destructive bursts of fighting of the long Franco-Habsburg conflict. This campaign, to which Charles was carried in a litter, would be his last. On 25 October 1555 he gathered around him in Brussels his family, counsellors and nobles, for a solemn act of abdication, the first of three such ceremonies that transferred to Philip the responsibility for his great empire: The Netherlands, Spain, Naples and the Americas.[2] As befitted Charles, it was a carefully choreographed event. Arriving on a mule at the very place where 40 years before he had begun his political life, the aged emperor reviewed for his audience his life and travels. He had visited Germany nine times, and Spain six; he had been in France four times, twice in Africa and twice in England. His voyages had taken him three times into Atlantic waters, and eight into the Mediterranean. Now he sought peace. Asking forgiveness for his errors, he exhorted Philip to be true to his heritage. Many present, including Charles himself, were overcome by the emotion of the occasion.

The lateness of the season discouraged a hazardous winter passage, and Charles lingered an uncomfortable year in Brussels before setting out for his chosen place of retirement in Castile. A fleet of over fifty ships had been assembled to escort Charles to Spain, but his arrival was a brutal reminder of how closely the appearance of affection is connected to the reality of power. Disembarking at Santander Charles found none of Spain's nobility waiting to greet him. He was forced to set out for Yuste with little ceremony and a meagre retinue. Gifts of fruit and delicacies along the way (which Charles, as ever, devoured greedily) revived his spirits, and he settled to his retirement with every sign of contentment. With his maps, clocks, books and family portraits this was not a particularly ascetic existence – the more so since Charles had obtained papal dispensation to devour breakfast before hearing Mass. Nor could Charles totally disengage from politics. The affairs of the peninsula, particularly the perilous state of the Portuguese crown, absorbed his energies, and couriers and despatches from Philip kept him in touch with the wider affairs of the empire. He died of malaria on 21 September 1558. It was a quiet end to a great and memorable life.

7

The Age of Religious War

The Reformation was from its very beginning a violent and destructive movement. In the first decade of the evangelical agitation armies marched under the banner of the Gospel in Switzerland and (more misguidedly) the German Peasants' War. In 1535 a joint army assembled by the Lutheran and Catholic powers of northern Germany would put down in violence the Anabaptist kingdom of Münster. But, by and large, in the first generation of reform, victims of the violence were largely low born. Zwingli died at the head of armed troops but, this apart, none of the leading protagonists needed to be unduly concerned that the conflict would touch them in their person. When Charles V captured the leading Lutheran German princes after the Battle of Mühlberg (1547), the punishment for their rebellion was a brief and honourable imprisonment. Neither John Frederick of Saxony nor Philip of Hesse feared the ultimate penalty; neither, it must be said did Martin Luther have much cause to fear for his personal safety as he hurried through the streets of Wittenberg. Fundamental issues were debated, as between Luther and Eck at Leipzig, or at the Colloquy of Regensburg (1541), in an atmosphere of reasonable civility. If a personal guarantee of safety was sought, as by Luther at Worms, it was generally honoured.

For some reason the conflicts of the second half of the century unleashed altogether more murderous passions. Violence was on a much larger scale, and altogether more deadly. Whereas Luther's generation turned their fury on statues and images, now the butchery encompassed priests and ministers, men, women and children. The age of religious warfare produced some notorious atrocities, and hundreds, sometimes thousands of victims. In England the 300 victims of the Marian burnings would be balanced by a similar number of Catholic priests who in the reign of Elizabeth suffered the agonies of hanging, drawing and quartering. In France the St Bartholomew's Day massacre, in the Netherlands the sack of Zutphen and Haarlem, claimed thousands of lives. And much of this violence was perpetrated not by soldiers on the field of battle, but by ordinary people, often against neighbours, members of their own community, former friends. Religious fanaticism gave the 'rites of violence' an altogether more deadly tinge.[1]

Nor could Europe's rulers stand above the conflict. For this was the Age of Assassination: for the first time since the Reformation Europe's crowned heads and other leaders of the contending churches had to fear the assassin's knife or the concealed gunman. In France the careers of an astonishing number of the leading figures of the Wars of Religion were ended by assassination: Francis and Henry, Dukes of Guise; Admiral Coligny; King Henry III; and King Henry IV. Not all were the victims of lone fanatics inspired by a vision of immortality. For the first time in the Reformation century political assassination also became an instrument of policy. Philip II sanctioned successive plots against the life of Elizabeth of England, and conferred a patent of nobility on the family of the man who shot William of Orange on the steps of his own house in Delft. Henry III of France plotted the destruction of Henry of Guise, as his brother Charles IX had ordered the elimination of Coligny.

In many respects, it seems, the conflicts of the second half of the century were marked by a murderous intensity lacking in Luther's lifetime. They culminated in a climactic struggle that saw the nation states of Europe locked in a fight for survival. These conflicts were both prolonged and fitfully intense. In place of the brief campaigns that marked the first generation of reform evangelism (the Swiss Kappel war lasted only a few weeks) we now contemplate religious wars that lasted over a generation. The French Wars of Religion stretched for 40 years, the Dutch Revolt even longer. None of the protagonists in the first stages of these conflicts would live to see their conclusion.

What was afoot here? The very different tone of the latter half of the sixteenth century can plausibly be traced to a combination of changes in the nature of both religion and society at large. The second half of the century saw the emergence of powerful religious forces in direct conflict: a revitalized Catholicism on the one side, Calvinism on the other. The violent collision between the two also coincided with changes in the nature of warfare that made wars more difficult to end. The result was two generations of fighting of a new and murderous intensity.

Catholic Renewal

It would be wrong to suggest that in the first generation of Luther's movement the Old Church went entirely undefended. From the first days the teachings of Luther and his allies were vehemently opposed, often with skill and courage. But it took some years for the church itself to marshal its defenders. Many of those who defected to Protestantism were themselves clerics, and this was sufficiently disorientating for the Catholic church. In Germany at least it was not easy for opposing voices to be heard.[2]

In the first decades the more effective defence of Catholicism thus came from those who had been the leading stakeholders in the pre-Reformation church: Europe's Catholic rulers. Enough set their face against the new movement to ensure that the Reformation outside Germany would suffer some notable reverses. Charles V's executions of members of the Augustinian order in Antwerp (1523) and the destruction in France of Louis de Berquin (1529) and Etienne Dolet (1546), were salutary reminders of the dangers of misjudging the ruler's intentions. However, the defence of the faith by these methods had distinct limitations. Even within the church not all agreed that terror and executions were an adequate response to theological criticism. And in relying on the secular arm, the church was always vulnerable to a personal volte-face on the part of the monarch, or a change of ruler. The same Henry VIII who burned John Lambert and Robert Barnes also decided that theological conservatism could be consistent with repudiation of the pope.

Most of all, it remained uncertain precisely what was being defended. In France, the question of how far Catholicism could accommodate reform – and what reform – was hotly debated for over two decades. Men like Berquin might have been over-optimistic, or foolhardy, but others in places of influence in France certainly hoped for a state-sponsored national movement of reform. Even in Germany conferences between Protestants and Catholics aimed at the reconciliation of theological differences between the dividing faiths, continued with some hopes of success until 1541 (the Colloquy of Regensburg).

Even after this, powerful forces within the Catholic establishment in Italy (the so-called *spirituali*) continued to explore theological formulations that were by no means incompatible with the Protestant understanding of Justification by Faith. When this failed, there were further high profile defections to Protestantism. The effect on morale can well be imagined.

It is in this context that one can understand why the Council of Trent (1545–63) was such a milestone event for the struggle against Protestantism. The deliberations of Trent decisively, and finally, set the limits of acceptable theological belief. The Council had been a long time in preparation, and the negotiations over location and agenda were subject to precisely the sort of base political pressures that Protestants had satirized so mercilessly. The Emperor Charles V favoured a meeting under his influence in Germany, successive popes were determined on an Italian location: Trent (now Trento), within the borders of the Empire, but in the Italian-speaking enclave south of the Alps, eventually satisfied both parties.

This difficult birth was certainly in the minds of those who assembled to confront the formidable agenda that lay before them. The pomp of the solemn opening procession on 13 December 1545 only barely disguised a disappointing turnout. At this point the overwhelming proportion of delegates were Italian: the Italian cardinals were supported by only two Spanish bishops, one French, one English and one German. It was a lopsided, unrepresentative presentation of the universal church. But the assembled fathers persevered, through long discussions and at times heated argument. By the time the Council closed some 20 years later (after three substantial periods of activity, 1545–8, 1551–2, 1562–3) they had achieved that comprehensive definition of Catholic belief that the church so badly needed.

The pattern of their deliberations was established early. The first substantive decision of the Council was to affirm the validity of the Latin Vulgate: a peremptory repudiation of years of Protestant (and Humanist) criticism of the venerable received text of the Bible. The following year the Council adopted a decree on Justification equally unequivocal in its forthright rejection of Luther's perception of Justification by Faith alone, and went on to affirm the canonicity of the seven sacraments (Protestants recognized only two). The fathers also affirmed the continuing validity of tradition alongside the authority of Scripture. The second period, 1551–2, produced a landmark declaration affirming transubstantiation.

The theological priorities established by this agenda were clear. By and large the Council discussed only such dogma as had been challenged by Protestantism. Each decision was an uncompromising repudiation of the Protestant position – and by implication the party within their own church which favoured accommodation. Even the rhetorical form of the decrees of the Council gave force to this determination: each declaration was posed as if repulsing the challenge of the enemy:

> Canon 12. If anyone says that the sinner is justified by faith alone, meaning that nothing else is required in order to obtain the grace of justification, and that it is not in any way necessary that he be prepared and disposed by the action of his own free will, let him be anathema.

> Canon 32. If anyone should say that the good works of a justified man are so exclusively the gifts of God that they are not also the good merits of the man himself; or that the justified man, by the good works that he does through the grace of God and the merits of Jesus Christ (whose living member he is), does not truly merit an increase of grace and eternal life ... let him be anathema.[3]

These theological debates were the core of the Council's work – perhaps rather against initial expectation. In the first discussions on procedure and agenda in December 1545 a majority of the bishops had voted in favour of giving precedence to discussing reform. This was unacceptable to the pope, who vetoed even a compromise proposal for parallel discussion of dogma and reform. Consequently only in the last sessions of 1562–3 were the bishops finally able to conclude the decrees on church reform that would shape the church's approach to internal renewal over the following centuries. In 1563 the Council agreed a long debated statement on episcopal residence, and, in an initiative of lasting significance, made provision for the establishment of diocesan seminaries for the training of priests. The last days of the Council saw a further raft of reforms, strengthening the authority of bishops over chapters and colleges, ordering episcopal visitations, reform of religious orders and clerical discipline. This flurry of activity allowed the fathers – by this time reinforced by substantial delegations from the other Catholic nations of Europe – to close the Council in December 1563 in remarkably good spirits.

The achievement of the Council was substantial, and of lasting importance for the Catholic recovery that now began to take shape in many parts of Europe. But the precise reason why this work was so important is not always clearly expressed. There is no doubt that in the short and medium term the importance of the canons that provided for the reform of church institutions can be greatly overplayed. The Council of Trent envisaged a thoroughly hierarchical model of reform, initiated by a reformed papacy, and pursued by reforming bishops. But what was to be the fate of the church in dioceses and provinces where bishops did not provide such leadership?

This, indeed, was the fate of the church in all too many parts of Europe. Examples of reforming bishops are well known, but they are well known precisely because they stood out. Elsewhere old established patterns of patronage and habits of conduct did not change quickly. Detailed studies of the impact of the Counter-Reformation in different parts of Europe have now made plain that it would be a matter of long generations, even centuries, before the impact of the Council's decrees was felt at a parochial level. By this time the decisive struggle with Protestantism was long settled. It is questionable indeed whether we can regard this aspect of Catholic renewal as a sixteenth-century phenomenon in any meaningful sense at all.

The most immediate achievement of Trent – and it was a considerable one – was through the clarity of its determinations of doctrine. The thinking that underpinned the work of the Council in this regard was well expressed by a confidant of Cardinal Morone, its guiding spirit in the last sessions, on the eve of the resumption of deliberations in 1562. 'It is the opinion of His Holiness', explained the Bishop of Ischia to the Duke of Savoy, 'that if one cannot heal the sickness in France and Germany, one would have to take care that the still healthy in Italy and Spain are not infected.'[4] The pope was too pessimistic with regard to France, but the point still holds. The church was to be defended by drawing up the battle-lines that would give it the unity and coherence to face a resurgent Protestantism.

Yet who were to be the troops to man the ramparts? It is not to denigrate what was eventually achieved by Counter-Reformation Catholicism to recognize that in the first generation – the vital generation in turning back the Protestant tide – the heart and soul of Catholic revival lay outside the conventional structures of the institutional church. In the history of the Counter-Reformation a special place is always reserved for the new religious orders, and first and foremost, the Jesuits. The vision that lay behind the foundation of the Jesuits was that of a Basque nobleman, Iñigo (better known as Ignatius) of Loyola. Invalided out of military service by a serious leg injury, Loyola had dedicated his life to the church, evolving through meditation and readings on the saints a life of profound asceticism and self-denial. When, in 1528, he settled in Paris to pursue his theological studies, he soon collected around him a small company of like-minded individuals, among them his fellow Basque, Francis Xavier. Together the group practised the rigorous programme of worship and self-examination devised by Ignatius, that later found fame as his *Spiritual Exercises*.

Ordained priests in 1537, in 1540 Ignatius and his followers were formally constituted as the Society of Jesus, dedicated to an active life of preaching and ministry and acknowledging absolute and direct obedience to the pope.

The principles embodied by Loyola – meticulous preparation and training, unwavering obedience, and a religious life of active service outside the cloister – proved an inspiration and lifeline to an embattled church. Loyola's fame ensured a steady stream of new adepts. By the time of his death in 1556 the original band of ten members had grown to 1,500, and this number would increase tenfold by the end of the century. The growth of the Society required the elaboration of a more complex administration, but this was achieved without compromising the principle of firm central direction. Each province of the Society had a superior or principal who answered directly to Loyola and his successors as General; each house established by the Society would have a rector responsible to the provincial. By 1556 there were 12 established provinces, including 3 outside Europe: Brazil, India and Ethiopia.

All novices who joined the order would be required to follow the full course of the *Spiritual Exercises*. The training was hard and many did not last the course. But those who did emerged fully committed to the order's primary goals of preaching, teaching and conversion. Jesuits eschewed the parochial ministry for service in schools, hospitals and the mission field, and also at court, for the order soon counted a number of Europe's crowned heads among their most fervent admirers.

It was undoubtedly in the field of education that the Jesuits left their most profound mark. The first Jesuit school was opened at Messina (Sicily) in 1548. The following year Ignatius assigned three Jesuits to teach theology at the University of Ingolstadt in Bavaria. However, it was not in the universities but in the Jesuit colleges, founded near a university to train future members of the order, that the Society found its most distinct role. The colleges date from the first days of the order. There were seven in existence by 1544, and very soon they began to attract students from outside the ranks of those training as Jesuits.

Senior members of the order, if initially surprised, soon began to recognize this as a most effective form of evangelization. The Jesuit colleges spread very quickly through Europe. By 1556 there were 35, some with very large numbers of enrolled students (900 at Coimbra in Portugal). By 1565 there were 30 colleges in Italy alone and new foundations were carrying the Jesuit message towards places like Prague and Poland.

It is undoubtedly true that the Jesuits opened a new era for Catholic education.[5] In the next two centuries the order created a remarkable network of educational institutions, at all levels: in all some eight hundred schools and colleges. From the beginning Jesuits manifested a notable commitment to the teaching of small children, based on both formal schooling and catechesis: some of the most effective early use of the printed book for Catholic renewal was in the catechisms of Peter Canisius and Emond Auger.

The effect of educational work was profound, but gradual. In the first generation the most important role of the new religious orders was providing a model of inspirational service – of sacrifice, if necessary unto death – that seemed beyond the institutional church. To Europe's Catholics, desperate for clear guidance in a world where the familiar was under threat, the new orders offered patient certainties and unflinching resistance to the church's foes. It was no wonder, for instance, that when the bewildered Catholic majority of Lyon in France were faced by a Protestant takeover of civic institutions at the beginning of the religious wars, that it was to a Jesuit, Emond Auger, that they turned for leadership.[6] The example could be repeated many times over, in many parts of Europe. Further afield, inspiration was provided by men like Francis Xavier, who in 1542 embarked on the first of his spectacular missions to the non-Christian world: in India, from where he established Goa as a base for Jesuit operations in Asia, and latterly in Japan. When Xavier left Japan in 1551 he could boast several thousand converts, and this and subsequent missionary successes provided a sort of compensation for the losses suffered to Protestantism nearer to home. The Jesuits also provided their fair share of martyrs: in the new mission fields overseas, but also within Europe with men like Edmund Campion, executed in England in 1581 for his part in attempting to reclaim England for the old faith.

The efforts of the Jesuits were seconded by other new orders that emerged from this era of turbulence and self-examination within Catholicism. The Capuchins began as an offshoot of the Italian

Figure 17 Jan van Scorel, *Members of the Jerusalem Brotherhood of Utrecht.*
Courtesy the Centraal Museum, Utrecht, inv. 2376. Societies of pious laymen
formed the backbone of Catholic resistance to the Reformation before the
provisions of the Council of Trent had had time to take effect.

Observant movement, and spread rapidly through the peninsula during
the 1530s. The new order benefited greatly from frustration among
Observants at a lack of reform within their own ranks. It made its name
in works of charity and in preaching. The Theatines, founded at Rome
in 1524, dedicated themselves to ministry and liturgical reform. The re-
examination of the vocation of the female religious life also led to
significant new initiatives, notably the foundation in 1535 of the Company of St Ursula (the Ursulines). The Ursulines' active life of charity
saved them from the enclosure that was the general fate of female
religious orders after Trent. It is significant that so many of these new
initiatives (and indeed, a large proportion of the Jesuits' recruits) emanated from Italy, and there can be little doubt that this active revivalism
played an important role in deflecting the movement of evangelical
reform within the peninsula from a more constructive engagement
with Protestantism. Even so, the new reforming orders had to suffer
some high profile defections, such as the spectacular apostasy of the
General of the Capuchins, Bernardino Ochino, who in 1542 abandoned his post and fled to Geneva.

Despite such occasional reverses, the new religious orders undoubtedly played a vital role as a new focus of Catholic endeavour in a world
turned upside down by heresy and discord. But it is important to
recognize that their emergence was in one respect merely the most
visible sign of a wider sense of revulsion and outrage among many of
Europe's Christians at the indignities heaped on their church by the

Protestant preachers. In a sense Catholicism survived the challenge of Protestantism because the practices and beliefs denounced by evangelical were devoutly loved and revered by many ordinary church members and parish priests, who were simply not prepared to give them up. They were often appalled by the damage done by Protestants to the fabric of traditional religion in their communities, and perplexed that these assaults were not more vigorously punished.

In many parts of Europe this commitment to the traditional ways far outweighed interest in evangelical criticism.[7] Church members looked only for a signal from the church's natural leaders. When it came they provided the willing foot soldiers in the battle against those who would destroy their way of worship: even when these were men and women who were often their neighbours, kin, or formerly, friends.

Calvinism

It is worth reminding ourselves that as the leaders of the Catholic hierarchy grappled with the problems of reform and renewal, Protestantism faced its own mid-century crisis. By the time of Luther's death in 1546 much of the early optimism of the movement had evaporated. Beyond the borders of the empire evangelical progress had become badly stalled: in France, the Netherlands and England, Catholic monarchs had clamped down ruthlessly on evangelical action, causing any who wished openly to espouse evangelical doctrines to seek safety elsewhere. Even in Germany itself, Lutheranism had been badly compromised by the bigamy of Philip of Hesse in 1540 (rashly approved by Luther and Melanchthon), and Charles V would shortly compound their problems when he took up arms in the Schmalkaldic War. The result was such a smashing defeat for the Protestant princes that it seemed as if Charles V might be able to insist on a forced restoration of Catholicism, reversing at a stroke two decades of systematic church building. The moment soon passed, but even so, it was clear that all was not well with the evangelical cause. Even before Luther's death, many of the reformers had begun to question how far the new churches had progressed towards the fundamental renovation of the Christian life that had been at the heart of Luther's call for reform. The Reformation, it seemed, was badly in need of a second wind.

The salvation of Protestantism came from what might at first sight have seemed an unlikely source. Geneva was at this point a small French-speaking enclave surrounded by three powerful neighbours: to the north and west, France and Savoy, to the east the Swiss Confederation. A latecomer to the Reformation, the city's population converted to Protestantism in consequence of a citizen rebellion intended to free itself from the control of its local bishop. For a decade or more the small city remained very much in the shadow of the larger Swiss Protestant powers, Berne, its heavy-handed protector and sponsor of the revolution of 1532, and Zurich, beacon of evangelical reform both within and beyond the Confederation. Its transformation from this lowly and essentially provincial status owed everything to the clear-minded vision of John Calvin, a French refugee who first came to Geneva intending nothing more than a rapid passage on to a more substantial centre of evangelical scholarship. By chance he remained to transform the city and its international influence.

John Calvin was by any reckoning a remarkable man. Born in Noyon, Picardy, in 1509, he was very much a figure of the second generation, graduating through a conventional education to the Humanist circle that flirted with evangelism in Paris in the early 1530s. Calvin was one of those forced to leave France by the persecution that erupted in the wake of the Affair of the Placards (1534). He now turned his considerable intellectual skills to a justification of French evangelism, which Francis I was attempting to demonize to justify his recent harsh repression. The result was the first version of his *Institutes of the Christian Religion*, an exposition of the new evangelical faith remarkable for its clarity and lucidity of expression. It was the spreading reputation of this book that persuaded Guillaume Farel, the first reformer of Geneva, to detain Calvin to assist him with the work of reformation, when Calvin passed through the city in 1536.

This first ministry was not a success. A stranger to the Swiss Confederation and to Geneva's Byzantine factional politics, Calvin was in 1538 outmanoeuvred and expelled, though he quickly found new employment as minister to the small French congregation in Martin Bucer's Strasbourg. Calvin profited greatly from this interlude, taking the opportunity to clarify his ideas of church organization in one of the greatest of the German Protestant cities. When he returned to Geneva in 1541 he did so, very much on his own terms, as the undisputed master of the Genevan reform.

Figure 18 John Calvin. From a private collection.

Calvin's recall gave him the opportunity to create in the city his own vision of the reformed church community. Not without opposition but with the steely determination that would characterize all his enterprises, Calvin introduced the best of what he had observed in Germany and his own small French church in Strasbourg. This included regular preaching and catechismal instruction for children and adults alike, combined with close regulation of the business and moral life of the community. The cornerstone of the enterprise was the co-operation of a close band of like-minded ministerial colleagues, all of them like himself exiles from France. Together they created the consistory, a new institution made up of equal numbers of magistrates (sitting as elders) and ministers who met on a regular basis to supervise the morals and religious life of the community.

The values of Calvin's Geneva were not intrinsically different from those of other early modern European urban societies. All societies deplored (and punished) drunkenness and adultery, and Geneva's penal code was not notably more severe than that of other cities of similar size. Its peculiarity lay in the care and determination with which rules were enforced, and the close co-operation that existed between the ministers, operating through the consistory, and the civil magistrates. For many around Europe, Geneva's growing reputation as a community living out the principles of reform, combined with Calvin's own reputation as a preacher and theologian, made it a beacon of hope in an unruly world. In the famous formulation of the Scottish reformer John Knox, it was 'the most perfect school of Christ that ever was on the earth since the days of the Apostles'.

Calvin's reputation today rests on his theological writings and his contribution to church organization, so it is good to remind ourselves that in his own day he was most famous as a preacher. He preached five times a fortnight, in what were virtuoso performances of impromptu exegesis, moving systematically through the books of the Old and New Testament. Occasionally he would break off to lambast the audience with their own deficiencies, for Calvin, like the prophets of old, had little good to say of the Genevan society so admired by outsiders. It was clearly a spellbinding performance. The Catholic chronicler Florimond de Raemond tells a revealing story of a French Catholic gentleman, returning from the wars, who decided to go home via Geneva to view the famous preacher. Imagine his surprise when elsewhere in the congregation he saw his wife and daughter, whom he had fondly imagined to be waiting for him at home. A fracas ensued which had to be resolved by the patient Calvin at the end of the service.[8]

Calvin's success in Geneva and growing reputation made the city a natural magnet for any other French evangelicals forced to contemplate flight or temporary exile. Through the 1540s and 1550s they were a growing number; indeed, so many settled in Geneva that local inhabitants began to feel that they would be swamped.[9] But the newcomers brought with them skills and capital, and Geneva prospered. Soon it was a major centre of Protestant publishing: like Wittenberg before it, Calvin's city grew rich on the reputation of its famous adopted son, for Calvin was also an indefatigable writer, turning out a steady stream of exegetical works, polemical tracts, sermons, commentaries and manifestos. The quantity was astonishing: at the high point of Calvin's activity as a writer his published output reached a quarter of a million words a year.[10] Much of this was in French, and directed to his former homeland, for Calvin never lost sight of the ultimate goal of bringing the Gospel back to France. By 1551 the French authorities were sufficiently worried to forbid any contact with the city of Geneva. So now Geneva opened up a second front. In addition to books, over the next ten years Genevan-trained ministers returned to France to nurture and lead the small congregations that were springing up in the image of Calvin's own.

By 1559 the political climate began to turn decisively in the Calvinists' favour. In July of this year the persecuting king, Henry II, died, the victim of a freak jousting accident that Calvinists were not slow to interpret as an example of the providential favour that seemed increasingly to shine on their movement. These were, indeed, years of hope and exultation for Protestants all over northern Europe. In England the accession of Elizabeth in November 1558 brought an end to the Catholic regime of her half-sister Mary, and promised a significant shift in the religious balance of power in north-western Europe. This in itself was sufficient to encourage sections of the Scottish nobility who had been keen to challenge the power of the French-dominated regency government of Mary of Guise. In 1559, stimulated by the impending return of the widowed queen Mary from France, they rose in revolt. Military aid from England tipped the balance in favour of the rebels; a short campaign, encouraged by religious demonstrations orchestrated by John Knox, led in 1560 to the establishment in Scotland of a Calvinist regime.

It is easy to see why Protestants across Europe took new hope from these events. After a decade of retreat, new life seemed to have been breathed into the Protestant movement. The effect was inspirational, even intoxicating. All Christians in the sixteenth century shared a perception of God as an active force in everyday events, but this sense of providential activism seems to have been particularly developed in Calvinism. 'God's Providence governs all' wrote Calvin in his *Institutes*. 'For he is deemed omnipotent, not because he can indeed act, yet sometimes ceases and sits in idleness... but because, governing heaven and earth by his providence, he so regulates all things that nothing takes place without his deliberation.'[11] This sense of God's active direction of events could easily be applied to the unfolding drama in France. 'Did you ever read or hear anything more opportune than the death of the King?' was Calvin's reaction to the death of Francis II in December 1560. 'He who pierced the eye of the father has now struck the ear of the son.'[12]

It is important to appreciate the atmosphere of the day if one is to comprehend how the triumphalism and defiance of French Calvinists drove France on towards religious confrontation. After two decades of retreat, Protestantism was once more on the march – in France, the British Isles, the Low Countries. If Catholics were prepared to defend their cherished heritage, then religious war was the inevitable consequence.

Sixteenth-Century Warfare

The sixteenth century, like all periods of human existence, is crammed with battles. Yet it is hard to think that anything much was ever settled on the battlefield. Even the most crushing victory – the battle of Pavia, for instance, which left Francis I a prisoner in the hands of Charles V, or Philip II's victory at St Quentin in 1557 – seemed to lead to nothing very much. When in 1571 the forces of the Christian Holy League annihilated the Turkish fleet at Lepanto, bells rang out all over Europe. The reaction of the sultan, when brought the terrible news, was admirably calm. 'The infidel only singed my beard; it will grow again' was reputedly the laconic response, and, ultimately, he was right. By 1573 Venice had been forced out of the Holy League and the great sea battle had achieved no decisive shift in the balance of power in the eastern Mediterranean.

The contrast with the previous generation is quite illuminating. In England, during the Wars of the Roses, relatively small forces could achieve significant results. The crown of England changed hands several times as a result of relatively small engagements: finally, and decisively, at Bosworth, where Henry VII emerged the victor of an engagement that ranged a mere 7,000 or 8,000 men against each other on either side. In the sixteenth century armies became ever larger, and wars ever longer, as commanders sought in vain for the killer blow. Wars became a struggle to outlast an equally exhausted opponent: victories were plotted in the royal treasury rather than in the field.

Does this shift in the nature of warfare amount to a 'Military Revolution'? And if so, what were the crucial revolutionary elements?

The concept of a military revolution has been so much debated in recent years that it becomes difficult to catch its essential essence.[13] What are the essential technological changes that are alleged to have been revolutionary? Most expositions focus foremost on the introduction of gunpowder, or battlefield firearms; but artillery had become fully a part of siege warfare in the thirteenth century, and firearms had played their part in battles since a century before. Larger armies? Armies were certainly larger in the sixteenth century, but the truly enormous growth comes a century later, with the fully professional armies of the late seventeenth and eighteenth centuries. The sixteenth century did not witness a fundamental change in methods of recruitment and payment, and this put an effective ceiling on the size of armies that could be raised, or the length of time they could be kept in the field. The noble affinity, or the county levy, remained a fundamental building block of armies throughout Europe, and they could only be kept in the field for a limited time. When Elizabeth of England addressed the assembled host at Tilbury in 1588 as the Armada sailed up the Channel the Queen roused herself for one of the most memorable acts of theatre of her reign. But this should not disguise the fact that Elizabeth's eager auditors were an ill-equipped ragbag of part-time amateur soldiers. Her rhetoric might have appeared in a harsher light had this force ever had to match up against the Spanish *tercios*.

Was there even a change in battlefield tactics (the heart of the original case for a military revolution postulated by Michael Roberts)? In fairness to Roberts one must acknowledge that the core of his argument related to the battles of the Thirty Years' War. Sixteenth-century battles were not marked by any profound change in strategic vision from the wars in Italy in the fifteenth century. Armies still consisted of much the same mix of noble hosts and mercenaries, cavalry and foot soldiers, pikemen and cannons. And they still fought in much the same way, in close engagement, pitting their personal courage and resolution against that of the enemy.

The difficulty for historians is that revolutions are far easier to identify when they involve the cutting off of heads or the storming of palaces. When we are dealing with a process of change stretching over many centuries the concept is of much less obvious value. And that, ultimately, is the fate of the 'Military Revolution'. Its technological changes stretch over so long a period, and are so difficult to place precisely, that the concept of 'revolution' becomes diluted beyond meaning.

Yet that said, with all of these reservations the sixteenth century does seem to witness significant change in two important respects in the way in which warfare operated. Firstly, during the course of the century Europe's naval powers adapted artillery to shipboard use.[14] The main consequence of this, however, would not be felt in Europe but as an instrument of domination in the non-European world, particularly the Indies. Here we have the essential explanation of how small bands of men could subjugate other numerous peoples and harness their wealth to European use (see chapter 12). Of more immediate relevance to European land warfare was a perceptible shift in the balance of advantage between offence and defence. This had been some time in preparation. The development of new type of defensive fortifications, the so-called *trace italienne* reflected a growing perception in the fourteenth and fifteenth centuries that the high stone walls of mediaeval cities were fundamentally vulnerable to artillery bombardment. The new fortifications were lower and more subtle, usually consisting of low sloping earthworks that would absorb metal shot, built to a zigzagging pattern to allow defenders to turn on attacking forces a murderous raking fire.

The new technology certainly caught the imagination, and during the course of the sixteenth and seventeenth centuries many new forts were built to the new fashion. Some cities even eventually took down their old high walls and replaced them with a bastion formation. But one must not be deflected by the charm of these new technologies from a recognition that the shift in the balance of power was at a more fundamental level than this. Most of the epic sieges of the sixteenth century – Metz in 1552, La Rochelle in 1573, Sancerre in 1573, Leiden in 1574 – occurred in places where the new bastions had not yet replaced more traditional defences. And siege warfare was only a part of it. Even the successful conclusion of such an action often brought little tangible benefit. The problem of sixteenth-century warfare was the inability to pursue any action to a decisive conclusion. Those who raised armies did so with clear goals in mind, but the real enemy was often not the perceived opponent. Sixteenth century armies lost far more men to desertion and disease than ever on the field of battle. Large conglomerations of men in temporary accommodation were magnets for disease; armies were impossibly difficult to keep fed and clothed, and the presence of even a passing army would often strip the region bare of provisions within weeks. The problems of siege warfare only magnified these problems, as sedentary forces had to be supplied over ever-increasing distances along quite inadequate roads. The larger the army, the more extreme the problems. A canny commander, such as the Duke of Alva in the Netherlands, would realize that far more damage could be inflicted on an under-resourced opponent by avoiding battle, than by allowing him a desperate chance of victory. Unpaid troops would often drift away leaving an embarrassed general little alternative but to withdraw.

The difficulty came where, as in the Wars of Religion, the legitimate power was attempting to enforce its authority on rebellious subjects given desperate courage by their faith. When the Spanish authorities turned their attention to the rebellious towns of Holland in 1573 the tables were suddenly turned. Here, all the advantages lay with the insurgents, particularly as when (as was the case with the revolts both in Holland and the Huguenot cause in the south of France) their main strongholds lay far from the crown's natural centre of operations. The problem was compounded by the fact that both sets of rebels could draw on funds and manpower provided by their co-religionists at home and abroad, a new and powerful form of military resource that is much underrated in general studies of sixteenth-century warfare.[15] So ultimately it mattered little that when they ventured on to the offensive, the rebel forces were every bit as woefully inept as their royal opponents. These were wars fought as much for the heart as on the field of battle. The royal and noble mind struggled in vain to find the military solution to new problems in an age when the physical environment and the available technologies were simply not yet capable of total war.

8

The French Wars of Religion

Occasionally in the life of a professional historian, one is privileged to experience something so unusual, so extraordinary, that it takes the breath away. In the small village of Dénezé-sous-Doué, close to Angers and the châteaux of the Loire, there is a small and little-visited system of caves. In the sixteenth century this was an area of quarrying, and the opportunities for work in the great houses of the river valley attracted some capable stonemasons. Yet some, at least, must have had time on their hands, for the masons of the village found time to carve in this small underground space an extraordinary group of over 100 figures. Most are in contemporary dress, and they include representations of many of the leading figures of the French court. The masons of Dénezé-sous-Doué kept well abreast of contemporary events. Among the figures they included an indigenous American, complete with feathered headdress, but what moved them most were events closer to home. For the central group in the tableau is a highly critical representation of the leading figures of the French Court.

These sculptures are not flattering, and they recall one of the most bitterly divisive moments of the early years of the conflict that consumed France for the second half of the sixteenth century. In 1560 a group of Protestant noblemen made a foolish attempt to seize the young king, Francis II, and wrest control of the government from the king's uncle, the Duke of Guise, and his mother, Catherine of Medici. The plot was thwarted and the plotters executed, and for this service the pope dispatched to Catherine a congratulatory gift: a sketch by Michelangelo for his Pietà. By the time it reached Paris, however, the gift had been tampered with. Someone had imposed their own harsh political comment on the drawing. The half-naked Mary now had Catherine's features, 'Jesus' was the sickly boy-king, and 'Joseph' the Duke of Guise, holding the axe with which it was said he ruled France. Catherine had the picture destroyed, but not before the story had been widely circulated. It was known to the Protestant author Nicolas Barnaud, who records it in his *Reveille-matin des François* (1574) and clearly also to the stonemasons of Dénezé-sous-Doué, who reproduced the group precisely as it is described by Barnaud.

This extraordinary artefact is scarcely known to historians. On the day I visited, my family were alone in the caves, and it is mentioned in no French textbooks on the Wars of Religion known to me. It raises many tantalizing questions. Who was responsible: a local trade confraternity, or an obsessed individual? What motivated this silent, tangible protest against the religious convulsions then tearing apart one of Europe's greatest states? What does it tell us about what France's people felt about the conflicts that raged around them, which they were apparently powerless to prevent?

The Road to War

The tribulation that engulfed France in the second half of the sixteenth century interrupted a steady progress towards a dominant position on the European stage. France had emerged from the long era of conflict between Francis I and Charles V as one of the most potent and powerful states of Europe. The provinces absorbed in the first half of the century had consolidated a formidable territory; with abundant agricultural wealth, rich and numerous towns, and a teeming population of some 16 million, France seemed destined for great things. The confidence of the nation was reflected in its monarch. Under Francis I the Renaissance monarchy reached its apogee, its opulent and impressive cultural legacy a metaphor for authority confidently proclaimed and exercised. When this authority passed from one adult king to another, with the accession of Henry II in 1547, the new king continued his father's policies. Despite many reverses along the way, the half century of warfare was brought to a triumphant conclusion with the recovery of Calais, the last English outpost on French soil, in 1558. Small wonder that the Treaty of Cateau-Cambrésis, which finally rung down the curtain on these

Figure 19 The sculptures of Dénéze-sous-Doué. The central group shows Catherine of Medici as the Virgin, with the young Francis as the Christ child and Mary Queen of Scots (wife of Francis). The Duke of Guise stands by with an axe.

decades of war by resolving long-standing territorial issues relating to Italy and the Burgundian inheritance, was greeted with a great outpouring of enthusiasm from France's well-tuned court poets. France, it seemed, could finally embark on a golden age of peace.

Unfortunately pressing issues lurked in the shadows to cloud this golden prospect. The first was the perennial issue of the crown's indebtedness. France, like many of Europe's states, had in fact succeeded quite well in ratcheting up tax income during the first half of the century. The *taille*, the tax raised on landed income, and the bedrock of the crown's regular income, rose from around 2.4 million livres in 1515 to 6.7 million in 1558. The total annual tax burden under Henry II amounted to 13.5 million livres, a 250 per cent increase over the course of 40 years. Yet this growth was always more than matched by growth in expenditure, as the French kings raised ever larger armies for their campaigns against Charles V. When Francis I died in 1547 he owed the bankers of Lyon almost 7 million livres, equivalent to almost his whole income for the following year. The situation only worsened during the reign of Henry II.

The level of taxation necessary to meet these obligations was unsustainable, as the king and his advisors knew only too well. To some extent the Peace of Cateau-Cambrésis was forced on the protagonists by mutual financial exhaustion (Philip II of Spain was forced to declare state bankruptcy, something France at least avoided). But Henry II also required an interval of calm to confront other pressing internal problems. In particular, there were signs that religious dissent, apparently vanquished, was beginning once more to be a serious threat. The highly orthodox Henry had little truck with dissidence of any stamp, and the early part of his reign had seen an intensification of pressures on French evangelicals. In 1547 the powers of the secular and ecclesiastical authorities to deal with heresy were consolidated in a new committee of the Parlement of Paris, the notorious Chambre Ardente. In the three years of its operation the Chambre examined and punished several hundred suspected heretics. In 1551 previous legislation against dissent was consolidated in a comprehensive and detailed decree, the Edict of Châteaubriand. This prescribed strict regulation of the book trade and inhibited any contact with centres of heresy abroad.

These measures were in part a recognition that the nature of heresy was changing during these years. The previously unorganized and rather diffuse individuals and groups against which the Parlement of Paris and the Sorbonne had agitated in the 1520s and 1530s would in the middle years of the century be replaced by something altogether more formidable. This change was made possible by the establishment of a recognized centre of emigré French Protestantism in Geneva. Even as he struggled to assert his personality over the recalcitrant citizens of the small Swiss city, John Calvin never forgot his native land. From the first days of his ministry until his death in 1564 much of his efforts, and many of his writings, were directed towards the conversion of France. From the publication in 1541 of the first French edition of the *Institutes of the Christian Religion* his influence over French evangelism grew steadily more discernible. The Edict of Châteaubriand, which specifically mentioned Geneva 11 times, was official acknowledgement that by 1551 Geneva had established a powerful influence over the movement, and during the following years the pace of events quickened further. The Genevan consistory responded to a steady stream of appeals to send pastors to lead small congregations of believers that were springing up within France itself. A secret Calvinist church was established at Orléans in 1554, in Paris in 1555, in Angers in 1556. In 1557 a group of ministers gathered together at Poitiers to discuss common organizational concerns, a prelude to the first national synod of the French Calvinist church at Paris in 1559. This adopted a version of the Genevan Confession of Faith and Catechism as the official credal statements of the French church.

The steadily more systematic organization of the French church was matched by an increasing self-confidence, manifested by growing defiance of the apparatus of repression. Not only were Calvinists growing more numerous; they were also for the first time beginning to win support in the higher echelons of society. When, in 1557, a hostile mob discovered a section of the Parisian congregation at prayer in a house on the Rue Saint-Jacques, it caused considerable disquiet that a high proportion of those detained were of gentle rank. Yet despite the stern example made of those arrested on this occasion, the following year the Paris church risked a further show of strength. A crowd of between four and five thousand gathered in the Pré-aux-Clercs, a meadow on the south bank of the Seine, singing psalms in full view of the royal palace at the Louvre. The demonstration, which lasted several days, was attended on at least one occasion by Anthony of Navarre, first Prince of the Blood, whom the Huguenots were most anxious to recruit. Also in their sights were the nephews of the Constable, Montmorency: Francis d'Andelot, who had gone as far as to introduce Reformed services on his estates in Britanny; and the Admiral, Coligny. Heresy had also infiltrated the Parlement of Paris, where a number of death sentences for religious offences had been commuted, and where in the spring of 1559 a young magistrate, Anne du Bourg, had launched an outspoken attack on royal policy. Why, he asked, should people die whose only crime had been to call on Christ's name, when adulterers and murderers escaped punishment? Taking the reference to adultery personally, Henry ordered the arrest of du Bourg and seven other councillors.

Having made peace with Spain, Henry now intended to take the problem posed by the new religious dissent in hand. But at a tournament staged to celebrate the Peace, disaster struck. The king insisted on taking part personally in the contests, and on the final joust of the day the lance of his opponent, the Count of Montgomery, shattered into his face. Splinters entered his brain just above the eye, and on 10 July the king died. Henry's death completely changed the political landscape. Although the new king, Francis II, was at 15 technically competent to rule, inevitably he would do so under the influence of more mature statesmen, and real power now lay in the hands of the king's two uncles, the Duke of Guise and the Cardinal of Lorraine.[1] Guise was an enthusiastic exponent of the late king's policies, so the new reign brought no respite for the Calvinists. The unrepentant Anne du Bourg was condemned and publicly burned, an event that, as was the case when a high-born victim suffered so horrifying a death, sent a shudder through the whole political community. But crucially the policy of repression no longer seemed to have the same moral legitimacy under the Guise regime as it had when backed by the personal authority of a mature king. Those who opposed the Guise monopoly of power now found the call for religious toleration a convenient rallying cry. When in 1560 a group of minor Protestant nobles made their ill-starred attempt to wrest the king from Guise control in the Conspiracy of Amboise, Louis de Condé, Prince of the Blood and brother of Anthony of Navarre, was among those implicated. Condé was arrested and, in a remarkable display of Guise confidence, condemned to death. But before he could be executed the fates again took a decisive hand when Francis II died suddenly of an ear infection.

The accession of the 10-year-old Charles IX required a formal regency, and opponents of the Guise were determined not to be outmanoeuvered for a second time. The young king's mother, Catherine of Medici, now emerged to a dominant role in government, a role that continued until her death in 1589. Catherine of Medici has not fared well at the hands of history. Her relatively plebian, Italian birth, made her an easy target for contemporary critics, and her reputation would never recover from her complicity in the decisions that led to the St Bartholomew's Day massacre in 1572. But at this juncture she embarked on a remarkable attempt to reconcile France's increasingly intransigent religious factions. Condé was released from prison, and restored to favour. He and the Guise were obliged to reconcile, in public at least. Most crucially Catherine explored every possible avenue for the resolution of the growing religious crisis. Her pursuit of a compromise culminated in the Colloquy of Poissy, an unprecedented conference between the leaders of the French Catholic Church and the Calvinist insurgency, led by Theodore Beza, Calvin's principal lieutenant and ultimate successor. Although the Colloquy produced no real resolution of basic theological differences, in January 1562 Catherine of Medici nevertheless went ahead and proclaimed a limited freedom of religion. For the first time Protestants in France were to be permitted to worship openly, and within the law.

Catherine's bold hopes of peace were soon dashed. Horrified Catholics, for whom the Duke of Guise was now the unquestioned spokesman, could never accept such a compromise of France's Catholic identity, and the January peace was soon undermined by flagrant violations on both sides. For, in truth, there is little evidence that at this stage French Protestants would have contented themselves with a victory half-won. Taking advantage of the power struggle at court, French Calvinism had since 1560 experienced a period of exceptionally rapid growth. From a handful of congregations in 1558 the church had grown by 1562 to a mighty body of over 1,500 congregations and 2 million members, at least according to the optimistic calculation of Admiral Coligny, now an openly avowed member of the congregation. More important than the statistics was the spirit of the movement. Inspired by the deaths of two persecuting kings, Calvinists saw clear proof of divine favour in such a propitious turn of events. All the evidence suggests that at this moment they felt that the conversion of France lay within their grasp. In towns across France the congregations moved from discretion, to insolence, to outright provocation. Congregations which two years before had been content with private gatherings in barns and private houses, now met quite openly, often marching the streets to chant the metrical psalms that were their trademark. As outraged Catholics attempted to take back the streets with their own shows of strength, confrontation was the inevitable result: the important provincial city of Rouen, in Normandy, witnessed nine such religious riots in the two years before the outbreak of war. In many cities the Protestants went as far as to commandeer churches for their own use, in the process invariably clearing them of Catholic statues and paintings, often with violence.

Thus when in March 1562 forces commanded by the Duke of Guise set upon a Calvinist congregation they had discovered worshipping in a barn at Vassy, Champagne, Catholic France was loud in its approval. Guise received a hero's reception in Paris, and Protestant members of the king's council withdrew to plot resistance. In truth, the speed with which they then raised an army against Guise indicates the extent to which planning for war had already taken place. The Calvinist congregations proved highly effective in raising manpower and money to buttress the noble affinities that flocked to Condé's standard. For all that, the first war was a military disaster for the Huguenots. They lacked a clear strategic vision once an attempt to seize the king had again been thwarted, and in Guise they faced one of the great military commanders of the age. While the Huguenot nobility quickly secured important areas of provincial France (such as Languedoc and Upper Normandy) for the cause, the one major set-piece battle of the war, at Dreux in December 1562, ended in victory for the Catholics. This victory was however subsequently negated by the assassination of the Duke of Guise by a lone Protestant adventurer, Jean de Poltrot. The fortunate removal from the scene of most of the rest of the leading protagonists either through death (Anthony of Navarre was killed at the siege of Rouen), or capture (Montmorency and Condé) allowed Catherine of Medici to force a negotiated settlement, the Peace of Amboise (March 1563).

The Failure of Peace

This might, indeed, have been the end of France's Wars of Religion. The Peace of Amboise provided what were, in view of their evident military weakness after Dreux, generous terms for Calvinist worship. Calvinist congregations were to be allowed to meet in one place in every local administrative unit (*baillage*) throughout France, and in addition on the land of every noble with rights of high justice who wished it so. An exception was made for Paris, since the capital had shown itself irreconcilably opposed to any concession to heresy. To ensure the treaty's acceptance Catherine embarked on a two-year tour of France to introduce the young King Charles to his people, and place his personal authority behind the call for religious reconciliation. But within a year of their return to the capital the fighting had resumed. The last, best hope of true reconciliation was lost for a generation.

In fact, for all the brave hopes expressed by Catherine and the small army of pamphleteers orchestrated on her behalf by the Chancellor, Michel de L'Hôpital, the Treaty of Amboise had solved very little. The treaty was a great disappointment to the leadership of the Calvinist churches, who felt that Condé had sold out their interests in return for the privileges accorded the nobility. There was a great deal of truth in this. Before the war the greatest concentration of Calvinist strength had been in the towns, but the future of the urban congregations was now highly uncertain. True, a place of worship was to be provided in each *baillage*, but in cities where the Catholics had succeeded in wresting back control by the end of the war, this was certain to be as far distant from the city as was possible. The sheer imprecision in the provisions of the peace thus carried within it the seeds of many bitter local disputes, appeals to the court, and flagrant violations. The Genevan reformers were bitter in their denunciation of Condé, and with good cause. The Peace of Amboise, by setting a clear limit to their rights of worship, broke the momentum of a growth that had been exponential in the years immediately before the war. Calvinism in France had in fact reached its high water mark, and in many parts of France the congregations were in decline before the massacre of St Bartholomew's Day dealt them the final blow.

The Peace also brought no reconciliation between the warring grandees. When brought news of the murder of the Duke of Guise, Admiral Coligny, the unchallenged leader of the Huguenot movement after Condé's capture, had expressed an unguarded satisfaction. For grieving Guise retainers this was sufficient reason to hold him personally responsible, a suspicion apparently confirmed when, despite Coligny's denials, the assassin Poltrot confirmed Coligny's knowledge of the plot under torture. Poltrot subsequently retracted this confession, but the damage was done. Avenging Coligny's involvement in Guise's death now became a principal objective for Catholics unreconciled to Catherine's peace. Indeed, this vendetta became a principal means to undermine efforts to make permanent a settlement that had compromised the Catholic identity of France in a way that many found simply unacceptable. A number of Guise followers actually signed a formal contract vowing never to cease the pursuit of vengeance against Coligny:

> I the undersigned promise and swear by the living God to keep and maintain the association made with the captains, lords and knights of the order to avenge the death of Monseigneur the Duke of Guise, rendering service and fidelity to Messieurs his brothers, Madame his wife and Monsieur his son, as I had promised to the said late Duke of Guise, whom God absolve, for the recovery of the rights he had claimed without exception or reserve. I promise also to use all my strength up to my last breath to expel from this kingdom or kill those who have made peace without punishing the murder, and to inflict a shameful death on

those who shared in the homicide, and I swear also to use all my strength in exterminating those of the new religion.[2]

Thus although the admiral was officially received back at Court, and formally absolved of complicity in the assassination, the enmity of the Guise was an assured part of the political landscape. The Protestant magnates could never really feel secure, particularly as when, in a famous incident in 1564, the Cardinal of Lorraine approached Paris with a large armed retinue, only to be turned back by the city's governor. Fears for their own safety were a part of the reason that caused the Huguenot magnates to resort to arms once more in 1567, in a renewed, and once again unsuccessful attempt to secure the person of the king.

With this 'Escapade of Meaux' a new element enters the equation, and one that would increasingly come to dominate the highly charged court politics of the years before the St Bartholomew's Day massacre. For now, in addition to their own domestic problems, the French Council were forced to keep an increasingly wary eye on events in the Netherlands. The dissident nobilities of France and the Low Countries were closely linked by ties of kinship and affinity, and the two conflicts became increasingly intertwined. When, in 1565, Catherine of Medici brought her tour of France to a climax at a meeting with her daughter Elizabeth at Bayonne (Elizabeth had left France in 1559 to marry King Philip of Spain), the sinister presence of the Duke of Alva led to the wildest rumours of what had been discussed. Among Protestants it was widely believed that the conference between Catherine and Philip's representative had sealed a pact to expedite the destruction of the new faith throughout Europe. These suspicions seemed to be confirmed when, in 1567, Alva began to move a considerable army from Italy to the Netherlands along France's eastern border. Although self-evidently intended for the suppression of resistance in the Low Countries, the proximity of so large a force set off panic among France's Protestants.

The brief outburst of fighting in 1567 ended in an inconclusive truce, and the conflict burst back into life in 1568. It was only with the Treaty of Saint-Germain, following renewed Protestant defeats on the field of battle (including, at Jarnac, the loss of their leader Louis de Condé) that the search for peace could be renewed. With both sides militarily exhausted, and the principal exponent of a hardline policy, the Cardinal of Lorraine, temporarily banished from Court, Catherine of Medici sensed a real opportunity of reconciliation. Once again, however, the complexities of the international scene threatened to frustrate her. After the failure of his feeble attempt to oppose Alva in 1568, the Dutch rebel leader William of Orange had little choice but to seek help abroad. Throwing in his lot with the Huguenots, he had fought in France with Condé; now, in the interval of peace, he sought French aid to revive the rebel cause in the Netherlands. He found an eager advocate in Admiral Coligny, now the unchallenged head of the Huguenot movement, who had also begun to exercise considerable personal influence over the young king, Charles IX. Coligny became the principal exponent of a bold attempt to reunite France's warring factions, by joining together in a new initiative against the traditional enemy, Spain. His proposal was for a military campaign to assist William of Orange as he slowly gathered together the forces to renew the war against Alva in the Netherlands.

Catholics at the French court recoiled in horror. To assist heretical rebels, even against the old enemy Spain, was to them anathema. The Spanish ambassador Zúñiga ratcheted up the pressure by emphasizing that any military aid to the Dutch rebels would be treated as a declaration of war. Through the long hot summer of 1572 the matter was debated back and forth in increasingly heated sessions of the Council. The marriage of young Henry of Navarre to the king's sister Margaret, intended to seal the new climate of reconciliation, in fact only added to the air of crisis, since it brought to the capital most of the leading figures of the Huguenot nobility. On 22 August a concealed gunman shot and seriously wounded the admiral as he walked back to his lodging from the royal palace, the Louvre. Who ordered this attack is a question that has never clearly been resolved. Catherine of Medici was widely blamed, both then and since, and it is indeed plausible that the Queen Mother had concluded that the only way to break Coligny's hold on her son, and avert the threatened foreign policy debacle in the Netherlands, was a surgical strike against its principal advocate. But Coligny survived, and with the Huguenot nobility baying loudly for the culprits to be named and punished, a panicking king was persuaded to order the destruction of Coligny and his principal lieutenants. The young Henry of Guise, son of the murdered Francis, personally led the attack on Coligny's quarters: the old man was knifed to death and his body thrown to the cheering crowd below.

Yet if what was intended was a quick and limited strike against the Huguenot leadership, nothing prepared the king and his ministers for the enthusiasm with which the Paris population now took up the murderous work. Long pent-up resentments against the Huguenot minority in their midst burst to the surface. In a three-day orgy of killing, Paris's population turned on their heretical neighbours. Some 2,000 lost their lives, including many of the Huguenot nobles so unluckily caught in the capital. News of the massacre set off a sympathetic wave of murders in many of France's provincial cities: at Rouen, Lyon, Troyes and Orléans in the north, Bordeaux and Toulouse in the south.

The Huguenot Struggle for Survival

The massacre of St Bartholomew's Day sent a collective shudder around Protestant Europe. The English ambassador in Paris, Sir Thomas Walsingham, actually witnessed the massacre at first hand. The experience left him with a settled hatred of Catholicism that continued until the end of his career. In Scotland the General Assembly of the Kirk proclaimed a public fast, 'to mitigate the wrath and indignation of God', and 'to provide remedy against the treasonable cruelty of the papists, and to resist the same'.

At first it must have seemed as if the French Protestant movement had suffered a terminal blow. It was not so much the scale of the killing, though that was horrifying enough: the Huguenot congregation in Paris was in any case only a shadow of its former size by 1572, and many of the victims in the capital were visiting dignitaries. Yet for all that the massacre hit disproportionately at the movement's leadership, the more significant impact was through the consequence of the psychological shock caused by such a terrible and unexpected reverse. French Calvinism had, in its early years, taken heart from the turns of events easily interpreted as conspicuous examples of divine favour. Now God seemed to have deserted them. Even Beza in Geneva seemed temporarily to have caught the mood of the moment, lamenting in his correspondence that God could have afflicted his elect in this way. The result was what amounted to a collective collapse of confidence. In many of the French cities, where the Huguenots were already an embattled minority, the local massacres were followed by mass abjurations, as thousands hastened to be reconciled into the Catholic faith of their vengeful neighbours. The mood of the day was aptly caught by the minister Hugues Sureau, who also abjured his faith at this time. In his testimony he made it plain that he considered the massacre to be a sign of God's displeasure with the movement. 'I began to consider it to be an expression of God's indignation,' he wrote, 'as though he had declared by this means that he detested and condemned the profession and exercise of our Religion.'[3]

Yet French Calvinism did survive; indeed, the massacre of St Bartholomew's Day ultimately proved to be far less of a turning point than it seemed at the time. The reasons for this are complex, and have not always been clearly discerned by historians for whom the events of 1572 have always been a convenient pivot on which to turn a discussion of the rise and fall of the French Huguenot movement. In fact, in most of the cities of northern France where the massacres had their most significant impact, the Huguenot movement had been in long-term decline before 1572, and often only constituted a small minority of the population by this date. The Catholic majority used this opportunity to eradicate a remnant, but the heart of the movement already lay elsewhere. By 1572 the Huguenot congregations were most securely entrenched in the south of France, and these provinces were largely unaffected by the massacre. Indeed, if anything the churches in this region grew as a result of an influx of refugees from the north. The cities of Montauban, Nîmes, Montpellier, and in the west at La Rochelle, now formed a beacon for resistance, giving their cue to a regional nobility that had also largely embraced the new religion.

For the French crown, the St Bartholomew's Day massacre was ultimately a gamble that failed. For if the Huguenot movement would not crumble away of its own accord, then the crown certainly did not have the resources to achieve victory by force. Here the realities of sixteenth-century warfare came to the rescue of the embattled minority. Secure in fortified places far distant from the crown's principal areas of strength, it required a sustained military effort to reduce them to obedience, and this was beyond a crown in ever more serious financial difficulties. An expedition against the nearest of the Huguenot strongholds, La Rochelle, in 1573, achieved little. Rather, the evidence of the crown's impotence revealed cracks in the façade of Catholic unity. St Bartholomew had in effect committed the crown to a policy of no compromise with dissent, and there were many who resented the restoration of Guise domination of government that such a policy implied. Between 1574 and 1576 this sentiment found expression in the emergence of a new grouping at Court, the so-called *politiques*, who by urging a new accommodation with the Huguenot minority also reinforced their own influence. The death of Charles IX in 1574 gave them their opportunity, since the throne now passed to his brother Henry III, who had unluckily accepted the throne of Poland barely a year before. His languid progress

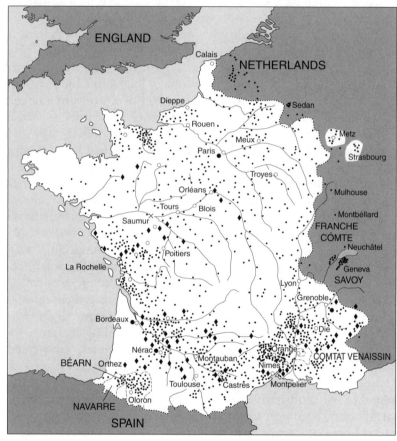

- · Established church
- ○ Church with more than one pastor
- × Protestant Academy
- ● Bi-partisan Chamber in a Parlement
- ♦ Place de Sûreté

Map 4   The Reformed churches of sixteenth-century France.

back to France only accentuated the sense of drift at the heart of government. On his return the dissident nobles forced on Henry a humiliating new religious peace (the Edict of Beaulieu) which gave the Huguenots freedoms as generous as they had enjoyed in their years of strength.

The years after the 'Peace of Monsieur' (as it became known in deference to the part played by the king's brother, Francis of Anjou, as spokesman of the *politique* nobles) marked the nadir of French Kingship. The new king lacked the character to reassert his authority, or seize the initiative. In truth, an empty treasury, and an exhausted nation, gave him little room for manoeuvre, but Henry did not help his cause by wild oscillations between extravagant expenditure on a bloated court, and equally extravagant displays of religious humility. A meeting of the Estates General, at Blois in 1576, voiced criticisms more outspoken than any king had been forced to accept, and repudiated the latest settlement with the Huguenots. The Protestant provinces of the south, meanwhile, largely ignored the king's wishes or instructions. In the wake of St Bartholomew, a number of voices raised the question of a total repudiation of royal authority. These monarchomach tracts, as they are known, represent the radical end point of Huguenot political thought. They articulated a wide range of theoretical justifications for subjects to cast off a tyrannical power. The best known were Theodore Beza's *Droit des Magistrats*, the *Francogallia* of the jurist François Hotman, and the anonymous *Vindiciae contra Tyrannos*.

These writings have been much admired by modern students of political science, who saw in them a precociously modern political spirit. But in the contemporary political context they were something of an irrelevance. Secure in their control of the traditional levers of power in their own localities, the leaders of southern Protestantism had little interest in overturning customary forms of authority. In their own time these writings were little more than a passing curiosity, a product of a bleak moment, the passing of which made their earnest theorizing seem irrelevant and embarrassing. This was even more the case when, with the death of Henry III's last brother in 1584, the very traditional process of dynastic succession seemed poised to give the Huguenots the prize that had eluded them by other means.

The Triumph of Henry IV

The long and tortuous road that led Henry of Navarre to the throne began with his flight from the royal Court in February 1576. Henry had survived the St Bartholomew's Day massacre, but at the price of his abjuration of Protestantism and abdication of leadership of the Huguenot movement. Henry abandoned his faith, and the ministers abandoned Henry; the events of 1572–6 left a legacy of bitterness and distrust that was not easily dispelled, particularly since Henry gave every indication of sincerity in his conversion to Catholicism. Thus Henry's acceptance back into the Protestant fold after his flight was only the beginning of an extended campaign to rebuild relations with the Huguenot nobility and restore his authority in the south. But Henry was a man of considerable natural political gifts, and he could count on a dense network of family connections among the nobility of Guyenne and Languedoc. The process had substantially been achieved when the death of Francis of Anjou in 1584 transformed his prospects.

Francis of Anjou did not cut an impressive figure, and history has not treated him kindly. But his death was a cataclysmic event for the French kingdom. For with his removal from the scene the heir to the throne was the nearest collateral relative, Henry of Navarre, a Huguenot. The defence of Catholic France, so earnestly pursued in arms and polemic, seemed destined to be undone by the failure of any of Henry II's four sons to produce a legitimate heir. This prospect provoked an upsurge of popular anger that destroyed the last vestige of Henry III's waning authority. This anger found expression in the revival of the Catholic League, a vehicle for Guisard sentiment in the 1570s that Henry had at first been able to neutralize by adroitly placing himself at the League's head. Now revived, the League became the cornerstone of a determined campaign to secure Navarre's exclusion from the succession. In 1584 this campaign was ominously reinforced by the conclusion of a treaty between the Catholic nobility and Spain (the Treaty of Joinville) promising Spanish military aid to secure this end. This monstrous meddling in the internal affairs of France demonstrated how low the crown had sunk in the esteem of its leading subjects. But Henry III had no real alternative but to bow before the wind, and he concluded a treaty with the League promising to exclude Navarre.

Henry of Navarre now took up arms against the League in a skirmishing campaign known rather comically as 'The War of the Three Henries' (after Navarre, the king, and Henry of Guise). In truth, the key to the resolution of these French conflicts now lay elsewhere. For Philip of Spain the alliance with Guise was part of his grand design to isolate Protestant England preparatory to the despatch of his army of invasion in 1588. When this Armada expedition failed so spectacularly, scattered by the unpredictable winds of the North Sea, the power of the Guise was perceptibly weakened. Henry III determined on one final effort to free himself from an association that was increasingly intolerable to him. In December 1588 he summoned Henry of Guise to his palace at Blois, and there had him assassinated. The following day the Cardinal of Guise, brother of the Duke, was put to death in the palace dungeons.

The treacherous murder of their hero and champion cut the last band of loyalty that bound Henry III to his Catholic subjects. Paris rose in revolt; in a furious torrent of pamphlets Leaguer authors denounced the treacherous king and his perfidious dynasty. The more intemperate called for Henry to be deposed, in an uncanny echo of the Huguenot radicalism that had briefly flourished in the wake of St Bartholomew. With such of his army as remained loyal Henry now laid siege to his capital, and it was in the camp before Paris that a Leaguer fanatic stabbed him to death.

Henry of Navarre was now in theory king, but of a kingdom most of which was disinclined to recognize his authority. It required six years, and all of his formidable political skills, to make this theoretical kingship a reality. The obstacles that lay in his path were, by any calculation, daunting. Much of the French nobility, and many of the kingdom's principal cities, were utterly determined not to accept him. Paris, Lyon, Rouen and Toulouse all rallied to the Duke of Mayenne, surviving brother of the murdered Guise, and now effectively the head of the League. Henry could look for little help abroad. Both the pope and Philip II were utterly committed to opposing his succession, and Philip when necessary would commit troops to assist the League. Even his erstwhile Huguenot allies viewed Henry with a wary distrust, aware that a new transfer of religious allegiance might well appeal to him as the only way to secure the kingdom.

To set against these formidable obstacles Henry had two major advantages. The first was his personality. From the beginning he looked and behaved like a king, exuding an optimistic authority that made light of obstacles largely by refusing to acknowledge them. He moved quickly to secure the loyalty of the commanders in the former royal army; these, along with loyal friends in the Huguenot high command created the basis of the force with which he plunged into the task of reducing his kingdom to obedience. His second, and critical, card was the failure of his League adversaries to produce a credible alternative king. At first the League proclaimed Henry's uncle, the Cardinal of Bourbon, as King Charles X. But as an aging cleric he obviously offered no long-term solution, and he was in any case a prisoner of Henry. After his death in 1590 the search for a new

POVRTRAICT ET DESCRIPTION
DV MASSACRE PRODITOIREMENT
COMMIS AV CABINET ET PAR L'AVCTORITE
DV ROY, PENDANT LES ESTATS A BLOIS EN LA
perſonne de Henry de Lorraine Magnanime Duc
de Guiſe, Protecteur & Deſſenſeur de l'E-
gliſe Catholique, & du Royau-
me de France.

LES Seruices que Henry de Lorraine, Magnanime Duc de Guiſe Protecteur & Deſſenſeur de l'Egliſe Catholique, & du Royaume de France imitât les vertus à admirer de feu de tres-louable & per- peti-elle memoire, François de Lorreyne ſon pere, ne meritoyent la re- compence que vous voyez, Chretiens Catholiques. On ſçait que Fran- çois de Lorraine, au recouurement de Bologne, fut bleſſé d'vn coup de lance en la teſte, & laiſſé pour mort en la place. Qu'il a depuis courageu- ſement deffendu Metz. A Renty il retira le Roy d'vn grand peril de ſa perſonne. Il a remis le Pape Paul 4. en liberté : Et comme il fut mandé reuenir d'Italie, la France eſtant reduite en grande perplexité, apres la priſe du Conneſtable, l'expugnatiô de S. Quentin, Ham & le Chaſtelet, Il commença à faire retirer l'audace des Ennemis, chaſſant le Baron de Polleuille de Breſſe. Et qui plus eſt, durant l'extreme rigueur de l'yuer, il bannit l'Anglois de France, reconqueſtant ſur luy Calays, & toute la Côté d'Oye. Peu apres il força Thionuille. Et apres la mort du tres-chre- ſtien Roy Henry, Pendant le peu du regne de François 2. Il s'oppoſa Ca- tholiquement aux Heretiques, Deſcouurit, & meaſtrit leur conſpiraſion à Amboiſe. Et encores depuis regnant Charles 9, il ſe moſtra touſiours conſtant à reſiſter tous les ennemis de l'Egliſe. Voires loſques à pluſtoſt quietter la Court, que d'eſtre conſentant à l'Edict de ſauoir. Mais quand il veit Paris en grande oppreſſe par le Prince de Condé, qui s'eſforçoit y planter la Religion nouuelle, il retourna à la Ville, contraignit ce Prince à en ſortir, La defend par armes, & les fauxbourgs, contre ſon Armée. Eſtant dreſſé ſon Camp, il coſtoya l'ennemy vers Orleans, & de là vint forcer & remettre Rouan en l'obeiſſance du Roy. Puis il retourna apres à pourſuyure l'ennemy, qui côme il euſt rompu la bataille de l'armée Ca- tholique pres Dreux, conduite par le Conneſtable, qu'y fut fait priſonnier Il attaqua le Prince de Condé tellement, qu'il fut prins auſſi, & les Catho- liques demeurerét les maiſtres. De là il s'approcha d'Orleans, & Paya reduite en grande extremité, l'Admiral auec les Miniſtres Huguenots, ſuſciterent vn Poltrot, qui traiſtreuſement le tira d'vne piſtole par derriere, dont il mourut, Penſans que quand ils auroyent fait mourir ce Prince tres- catholique, que Dieu euſt puis apres laiſſé les ſiens.

Mais Henry de Lorraine magnanime Duc de Guyſe, & ſes Freres tres-genereux, ont voulu encores ſupporter l'egliſe de Dieu, & embraſſer ce qui touche au repos du pauure peuple. Il contraignit les Huguenots, d'eux departir du ſiege qu'ils entreprenoyent deuant Sens, & s'oppoſa à la deſcente des Reiſtres pour les Huguenots. Et apres la taille de Iar-

nac, il deffendit Poitiers contre les forces de l'Admiral. A Moncôtour on le veit au milieu de la bataille des ennemis, là où il fut bleſſé. Au ſiege de S. Iean d'Angeli ſeruit de beaucoup. A la Rochelle il y fit de tant grands exploits, que rien plus : Et ſi on l'euſt voulu croire, les Rochelois fuſſent maintenat Catholiques. Et apres la mort du Roy Charles, il a tant fidelement aidé à conſeruer la Couronne au Roy, qu'il n'y a miſe entre les mains à ſon retour de Poulongne. Dauantage tout ſous en l'enemy de l'here 3, ſachant que Thoré amenoit des forces d' Allemagne en France, il luy alla au deuant, & à Baccara il le defit, & ren- uoya ceſt eſtourdi s'en venoit. Mais il y fut griefuement bleſſé en la ioüe ſe- neſtre. Depuis perceuant qu'on vouloit amortir l'Egliſe Catholique, en France, & y ruiner le pauure peuple, il aduiſe qu'il eſtoit bon & ſalu- taire, de liguer les Catholiques, afin de s'oppoſer à vng deſſeing tant mal- heureux. Il aduertit le Roy, que les Princes François Heretiques ſoyent amas de Gens en Allemaigne, & comme les aduertiſſemens que de long temps il faiſoit, vinſſent à paroiſtre, & leſquels on ſaignoit ne vouloit croire, Voicy tombé ſur les bras du Roy & des Catholiques, à l'im- pourueu vne armée de plus que quarante mille hommes, laquelle apres pluſieurs ſecouſſes il a deffait & mis en route à Auneau.

Par apres il ſe trouue tout ſeul incpinément à Paris, lors qu'on vouloit executer à mortiers Principaux Catholiques : Par la prouidence de Dieu, ſa preſence ſeulement cauſa, qu'il n'y aduint aucun ſcandale. Le Roy ſaignant vouloit tenir ſes eſtaz à Blois, luy mande l'aller trouuer, ce qu'il fit. Et comme par la cloſture d'iceux il fut aduerty, que ſa Ma- jeſté luy vouloit mal, d'autant qu'il ſouſtenoit & l'Egliſe & le Peuple, il ne le luy vouloit diſimuler. Et la Veille de S. Thomas Iſle luy declaré. Le Roy luy reſpond, qu'il n'auoit l'ame ſi meſchante, faiſant pluſieurs ſer- mens, Meſmes prenant à reſmoing le Sainct Sacrement, qu'il deuoit reco- uoir le lendemain : Ce qu'il fit. Qu'il n'y auoit homme au môde que plus il aymaſt que luy, pour les ſeruices ſignalez qu'il luy auoit faits, & qu'il ne le reſcompenſeroit bien. La reſcôpenſe a eſté telle que vous la voyez. Dans vn Cabinet de Roy, qui le premier a violé en lieu de ſeur acces & ſeureté, maintenant prophane, voire en pleine aſſemblée des Eſtats.

Or donc ques ſi la Foy eſtoit malade, encores dis-ie morte, en quiſe- roit-ce qu'on la reſuſciteroit ? Ceue ſeroit à Henry de Valois, que ſes peuples de France & Poulongne auroyent recours pour la faire reuiure. Pource, que les Catholiques y prennent bien garde.

Figure 20 'The Assassination of the Duke and Cardinal of Guise' (in French). Copyright Royal Library of Belgium, Brussels. (a) Pourtraict et description du massacre . . . de Henry de Lorraine . . . [Brussels: Rutg. Velpius, s.d.]. Broadside. VB9. 744 VI 2b.

CRVÁVTE PLVS QVE BARBARE
INFIDELEMENT PERPETREE PAR
HENRY DE VALOIS, EN LA PERSONNE DE
MONSIEVR L'ILLVSTRISSIME CARDINAL DE
Guife, Archeuefque, Duc de Reims, dedié
& confacré à Dieu.

Apres que Henry de Valois euft fait cruellemét affaffiner Môfieur le Duc de Guife, Prince de rare & incomparable valeur, pour les bons feruices faits, & par fes predeceffeurs, luy & les fiens à l'Eglife Catholique & au repos & foulagement de la France : s'oppofans toufiours heureufement aux ennemis d'icelle.

Non content de ce, fa cruauté toufiours alteree, entre autres Princes il feit auffi arrefter prifonnier Monfieur l'Illuftrifime & Reuerendifime Cardinal de Guife (Loys de Lorraine) Archeuefque, Duc de Reims.

Et le l'endemain 24. de Decembre, Vigile du fainct iour de Noël, il feit plus que le tyran Herodes : car parauant la Natiuité de noftre Sauueur, il voulut preuenir le iour des Innocens, en ce que luy ayant fait figner vn blanc, fur les 9. heures du matin, il feit le maffacrer par des bourreaux, de la compagnie du Capitaine Gad, à coups de hallebardes) qu'amene Clermont d'Antragues, pendant qu'il alloit à la Meffe, voila veritablement bien ouyr Meffe : Cruauté fentant pluftoft fon infidele que Roy tres-Chreftien, attentant fur vn perfonnage facré & dedié a Dieu, Mais i veut peut eftre qu'on ne l'efpargne non plus, veu qu'à l'exemple & faits d'vn Roy le peuple fe conforme ordinairement : neantmoins les Catholiques n'enfraignent les Ordonnances diuines, croyans que Dieu tout bon punit vn mefchant par vn autre. Qui pourra aduenir lors que bien toft il delibere fe ioindre auec le Roy de Nauarre, & l'Anglois s'il peut. O mort falutaire & proffitable à vous feul, & a voftre inuincible Frere, Piliers de l'eglife militante : Martyrs, car ainfi vous peut-on bien appeller, pour autant que les Catholiques croyent affeurément, que vous eftes efleuez aux fieges bien heureux de ceux qui nous ont baillé la foy confermee par letr fang, pour laquelle vous & plufieurs de vos deuanciers auez efté outrageufement maffacrez. Mort dis-ie falutaire, pour vous d'autant qu'elle tefmoigne voz magnanimitez inuincibles, & la perfidie & lafcheté de l'Ennemy de l'Eglife, lequel Dieu ne permettra viure long temps : Car ô vous, Monfieur le Cardinal, eftant preft a receuoir le Martyre, dites ces mots : ie prie à Dieu que celuy qui me fait meurtier, vienne bien toft, en fa prefence, rendre raifon de cefte tyrannie.

Veritablement pour vn Roy, fe difant tres-Chreftien, c'eft trop attenté que de s'attaquer aux Protecteurs & Deffenfeurs de la Religion Catholique : l'Eglife de Dieu eftant inuincible, & lors que fes ennemis penfent l'auoir affligée, Elle eft la Palme mefme, qui côtre fa force fe réd toufiours la maiftreffe : Et les ennemis d'icelle fe trouuent ruynez en moins d'vn clein dœil, tefmoing Iulien l'Apoftat, qui fe fentant frappé, comme par vn remords de confcience, dit : Tu as vaincu, ô Galileen. Ainfi affeurement deuons nous croire qu'il en aduiendra a ceux qui, comme luy, fe bandent contre Dieu.

(b) Cruaute plus que barbare ... perpetree par Henry de Valois ... [Brussels: Rutg. Velpius, s.d.]. Broadside. VB 9.744 VI 2b. These two very rare surviving broadsheets are examples of the torrent of literature that poured from the Paris press after the assassinations, and further inflamed a hostile public opinion against the king.

figurehead led the movement into disagreement and conflict. One suggestion was a daughter of the king of Spain, but a Spanish Infanta would have implied the greater evil of domination by the ancient enemy. In the face of Henry's evident determination to rule, and increasingly broad hints of his willingness to abjure his Protestant faith once more, Catholic resistance began to weaken. The tensions within the League were finally exposed when diehard members of the radical wing of the movement seized control of Paris, executing a number of more moderate magistrates. Although Mayenne swiftly reasserted control, the whiff of social revolution made new converts for Henry's cause. In 1593 the moment for which Henry had carefully prepared, and Mayenne and Philip of Spain dreaded, arrived: the king solemnly abjured his Huguenot beliefs, and was received back in to the Catholic fold. The following year he triumphantly took possession of his capital, Paris.

Henry's recovery was not yet complete. In the years that followed there were further negotiations with magnates and cities that held out for the League. The continuing weakness of the king's position was revealed in the vast sums of money he was prepared to promise to win back their allegiance: 900,000 crowns to the Duke of Lorraine, 600,000 to Guise (son of the assassinated Duke), 700,000 to the city of Rouen, and so on. But even this sort of expenditure was a bargain compared to the cost of a military campaign, and perhaps these pledges would never have to be redeemed (for the most part, they were not). In 1595 Henry declared war on Spain, a patriotic war to replace civil war, but one that still had to be fought and paid for. All in all the last decade of the conflict was enormously destructive. For a time, as the Duke of Parma twice marched south at Philip's insistence to rescue his League allies (at Paris in 1590 and Rouen in 1592), and Elizabeth of England sent troops to assist Henry, France became the centre of the European conflict. And the reduction of Henry's Catholic enemies still left the issue of his former Calvinist friends.

The jilted Huguenots could hardly have been surprised when Henry adopted the religion of the vast majority of his people, but they could still extract a price for their co-operation. Long months of tense negotiation and brinkmanship eventually brought forth the Edict of Nantes, the final act of the conflict (1598). The Edict guaranteed the Huguenots freedom of worship in places of established strength; but they were not to proselytize, nor establish new churches or schools. The treaty secured the immediate future, while it held the seeds of a long term attrition of the movement. As he had with his Catholic opponents, Henry sweetened the pill with generous financial incentives: the congregations received a cash dividend, while the king also undertook to pay for the garrisons that would protect the Huguenots against future bad faith or a repetition of the St Bartholomew's Day massacre. The resolute ministers ensured that these sums were indeed paid.

The Wars of Religion were a disaster for France, and this had a significant impact on the rest of Europe. By effectively neutering Europe's most potent nation state, the wars delayed the emergence of a great power for half a century, and to this extent also artificially prolonged Spain's dominant role in contemporary European affairs. In the process France had been preserved for Catholicism, if at a cost. And it is worth emphasizing that this Catholic identity had been preserved not through the leadership of the 'most Catholic kings', as the French monarchs were styled, but by its people. Faced by a crown eager to find compromise with the Huguenot movement in the 1560s, and by a bench of bishops emasculated by a tradition of political time-serving, the defence of France's Catholic identity fell to an unlikely alliance of a military nobility, and foot soldiers in the middle ranks of the clergy and Catholic laity. It was these who from the beginning set their faces against the compromise implicit in the Edict of January 1562, and who prevented their Huguenot fellow citizens from enjoying the peaceful enjoyment of the privileges granted them by the Peace of Amboise, and subsequently frequently reaffirmed. The Huguenot minority protected by the Edict of Nantes was a shadow of the movement's former strength, as both sides knew well. If only the Catholic Church had been so resolutely defended elsewhere in Europe, Protestantism would not have secured much of a footing. Nowhere was this more obviously the case than in the lands immediately to the north, the 17 provinces of the Netherlands.

9

The Dutch Revolt

During the course of the sixteenth century, Europe's citizens could have witnessed some awesome spectacles. The Field of the Cloth of Gold or the Battle of Lepanto were each in their own way extraordinary and unforgettable, and no witness, or participant of the St Bartholomew's Day massacre would ever have erased it from the memory. But for its sheer shocking unpredictability little could compare with the awesome scenes that greeted the English financial agent Richard Clough when he entered the cathedral of Antwerp after a night of high drama on 20 August 1566. 'We have had this night past a marvellous stir', he reported to his employer, the financier Thomas Gresham, the following day, 'all the churches, chapels and houses of religion utterly defaced, and no kind of thing left whole within them, but broken and utterly destroyed.'[1] Clough had wandered down to the church late in the day; when he entered the church an astonishing sight greeted his disbelieving eyes.

> I went into the churches to see what stir there was there, and coming unto the church of Our Lady, it looked like a hell, where were above 10,000 torches burning, and such a noise as if heaven and earth had got together, with falling of images and beating down of costly works, such sort that the spoil was so great that a man could not well pass through the church. So that, in fine, I cannot write you in ten sheets of paper the strange sight I saw there, organs and all destroyed.

And what was most astonishing was the total absence of any attempt by the authorities to prevent the destruction. It was as if government was afflicted by a sudden but totally debilitating paralysis: so much so that even in places where the numbers of active church-breakers was small they went about their work totally undisturbed.

The outbreak of the Dutch Revolt in 1566 was for those who lived through it an astonishing and awe-inspiring event. For a few brief months in the summer of this year political authority seemed to have dissolved. The provinces of Flanders and Brabant were among the most prosperous and populous regions of Europe, but they now witnessed a rush of organized dissent of a type unprecedented in the Netherlands. First, there was the so-called hedge-preaching, where thousands gathered in orderly and disciplined crowds in the open air to sing and listen to sermons. Then, in a savage and appalling contrast, these same sober congregations turned in fury on their Catholic churches, which were swiftly and ruthlessly desecrated. In the space of a few weeks some of the richest churches in Europe were stripped of the artwork and ornamentation that had accumulated over centuries of pious giving.

Viewed from a historical perspective the unfolding of these events is puzzling for two reasons. Firstly, because the state apparatus in the Netherlands was both advanced and well organized; there certainly existed instruments of government that might have protected the churches. And secondly, this was a regime that had set its face more determinedly against the spread of heresy than any other in Europe. From the beginning of Luther's movement the spread of Protestantism in the Netherlands had been resisted with every weapon at the state's disposal, and with considerable success. Executions for heresy had begun in the Netherlands in the 1520s, and continued up until almost the eve of the outbreak of the revolt. To understand why this retarded and persecuted Reformation movement was able to erupt with such force and fury in 1566 requires some explanation; and for this one must look back some 40 years to the very beginnings of Dutch Protestantism.

The Origins of Dissent

It is now recognized that there were considerable obstacles to the successful exportation of Luther's movement out of his native Germany (see chapter 5). But in fact Luther's initial call for reform found a strong resonance in the provinces of the Low Countries. Like Germany, this was a highly urbanized region, with proud and prosperous urban communities eager to sponsor a renovation of religious life. This was not in fact yet the full 17 provinces of the later sixteenth century: the northern provinces of Friesland, Groningen, Overijssel, Gelderland and Utrecht would be incorporated only in the reign of Charles V (see map 5). But the core, the Burgundian inheritance, was the most prized: the provinces of Holland and Zeeland, Flanders, Brabant, and the Walloon (French-speaking) provinces of the south. It was here that the bulk of the population was concentrated, in the towns and ports of Holland, the industrialized cloth villages of the Flanders *Westkwartier*, and particularly the great cities of Bruges, Ghent, Antwerp, Brussels and Louvain. Their articulate, highly literate populations received with approval the printed literature of the Reformation, both local editions of Luther's own writings (quickly translated into Dutch in quantities not equalled in any other European language) and the Bible in their own language. Between 1520 and 1540 there were some eighty editions of Luther's works published in Dutch in the Netherlands (the comparative figure for England is 9). But for many the greatest impact of the new religious climate would have been seen in the proliferation of new editions of the vernacular Bible: a total of over 60 New Testaments and complete Bibles in the equivalent period, many of them lavishly illustrated. There was also much to criticize in the local church, including a governmental structure not altered since the high Middle Ages, and woefully inadequate to meet the needs of a population that had grown rapidly since those days. For the whole 17 provinces, with a population of over two million, there were only four bishops. So those who raised their voices in support of Luther's calls for reform found a ready response. By the mid-1520s Erasmus and other local commentators were reporting a flight from the monasteries, and the growth of a popular following for those who styled themselves Lutheran or evangelical.

Left to itself, there is little doubt that this groundswell of support, particularly among the educated and opinion-formers in the towns, might have made of the Netherlands a second stronghold of the Reformation movement. But the Netherlands was not Germany: in particular the Dutch towns were not free to follow their own independent political course. Specifically, the ruler of the Dutch provinces, the very same Charles V who had laboured so unsuccessfully to thwart Luther in the empire, was determined not to see his own Dutch patrimony fall victim to the German heresies. Almost from the beginning, in fact even before Luther was formally condemned in the empire, Charles began to marshal the agencies of repression against the

Map 5 The Netherlands under Charles V.

new beliefs. A decree of 1520 forbade the publication, sale or dissemination of any unauthorized religious works. By 1529 infringement of the proclamations (*placards*) on matters of religion was made punishable by death. In 1523 Charles underlined the seriousness of his purpose by ordering the execution of two prominent supporters of the evangelical doctrines. These were the first executions of Luther's supporters anywhere in Europe, and initiated a campaign of repression unrivalled for its sustained ferocity: in the next 40 years 1,200 men and women would be put to death in the Netherlands for their religious beliefs, and many more forced into exile.

This persecution served its purpose. By 1530 the leadership of the first generation of Netherlands evangelism had been effectively destroyed, most of its leading figures having been forced either to recant their views or take flight to Germany. The rise of Anabaptism in the following decade (which at its height, at the time of the Anabaptist kingdom of Münster, found many adherents in the Netherlands) only seemed in retrospect to have completed the social exclusion and marginalization of Dutch Protestantism. The discovery of small evangelical cells in several cities in the 1540s led to a new wave of executions and exile. At the time of Charles V's abdication in 1555 he could justly pride himself that he had preserved his northern kingdom for Catholicism, albeit at a considerable human cost.

But as events would prove, Dutch evangelism was not completely dead. The repressive measures undertaken by Charles may have retarded its development by a full generation, but the social conditions that had encouraged the first growth of Lutheranism were not fundamentally changed. In particular there had been no renovation of the Netherlandish church that might have equipped it to repulse a new movement of reform.

The Growth of Dutch Calvinism

In the middle years of the sixteenth century events conspired to make such an outcome possible. In effect, this change was made possible by a largely fortuitous coincidence of three developments: the growing influence of the new force of Calvinism in northern Europe, the accession of Elizabeth in England, and the outbreak of religious warfare in France.

Dutch Calvinism, ironically, was very largely a creation of the ruthless repression of Charles V's later years. Among those forced to flee abroad as a result of the persecutions of the 1540s were a number of educated men who had professed little more than a mild evangelism. Left to themselves they would probably have been little threat; but once settled abroad they had little choice but to band together with more determined opponents of the regime who now huddled together in small refugee communities. These exile churches soon fell into the intellectual orbit of Calvin and his new church at Geneva. Calvin, it should be recalled, had started his career as a minister to such a refugee congregation (at Strasbourg) and his Genevan church order offered a clear and appropriate model of church organization for such groups. Calvinism with its strong sense of discipline and providential destiny proved an ideal creed for groups existing in hazardous and difficult conditions. Within a few years the local authorities in the Netherlands found themselves faced with an embryonic Calvinist church in their own territories, small secret communities sustained and abetted by the exile congregations.

All of this might have come to little but for the marked shift in the geopolitical balance of northern Europe that followed the accession of Elizabeth I to the throne of England in November 1558. The death of the devout and unswervingly Catholic Mary meant that Philip II lost far more than a wife. With Mary's death England was transformed from a reliable Catholic client into a major irritant and, increasingly, a hostile adversary. One of the first intimations of the new cold climate in Anglo-Spanish relations was the easy welcome afforded by the Elizabethan regime to religious refugees from the Low Countries. Not only were they permitted to settle in England; they were also allowed to re-establish the foreign churches in London (which Mary had closed), and a number of new satellite churches in Essex and Kent, principally at Sandwich, Canterbury and Colchester. These became convenient bases for increasingly violent raids upon their homeland. Repeated representations on the part of successive Spanish ambassadors failed to persuade Elizabeth's ministers to restrict the exiles' freedom of movement, and the issue became a major cause of the final rupture between the two countries. For the exiles, the safe haven in England was a vital base of operations in the half-decade before the outbreak of the revolt.

This was troublesome enough, but a difficult strategic situation rapidly became yet more treacherous with the outbreak of the French Wars of Religion. In the years after 1559 the French monarchy was going through its own crisis of authority. Following the death of Henry II the authority of his young sons Francis II and Charles IX came under sustained attack. As in the Netherlands, the issue was partly constitutional – who should take the lead in government in the absence of a mature adult king – but antipathies among the leading counsellors were dramatically sharpened by differences over policy towards Protestant heresy. After 1559 French Calvinism embarked on a period of buoyant, and apparently uncontrollable growth. By 1562 the strains of containing the mounting antagonisms between the religious confessions proved too much, and France toppled into civil war.

In terms of scale, Netherlandish Calvinism was at this stage no more than a pale shadow of its French counterpart. As against 1,000 or more churches at the beginning of the 1560s, there were scarcely more than a handful in the Low Countries, and of these only the important Antwerp church seems to have enjoyed a near continuous existence. Other urban congregations in places like Bruges, Ghent, and in the Walloon (French-speaking) provinces at Valenciennes and Lille, scattered and reformed as opportunity arose or persecution dictated. Dutch evangelicals could still only wonder at the freedoms enjoyed by their French counterparts.

Nevertheless, the turbulence in France had a profound impact in the Netherlands for several reasons. In the sixteenth century all borders were much more porous and open than they would subsequently become in the modern era. This was particularly so of France's northern border with the provinces of the Netherlands, because this lowland area possessed no geographical feature to define or divide, in a region that in any case shared a common language. In consequence there was little to restrict the free movement of people, goods or ideas. The ruptions in France thus inevitably caused reverberations in the provinces in the Netherlands, particularly in the French-speaking or Walloon provinces that were directly adjacent to the French domain. Here Calvin's works could be read in their French original, and the government in Brussels could do little to prevent the circulation of huge quantities of such illicit literature.

But the growth of French Calvinism also had a profound impact on the nascent congregations in the Dutch-speaking areas. The leaders of Dutch Calvinism followed with close attention the stages in the growth of a national church in France. In 1561 one of their ministers, Guido de Brès, presented a draft of a national Confession of Faith, based wholly on the recently published French confession. Shortly hereafter the Netherlandish churches began to create a structure of church government, again based on the model of the French national synods. In the years following the outbreak of fighting in France, Dutch Calvinists also began to imitate the provocative and confrontational behaviour that had brought French evangelicals such a dividend. For the first time Dutch Calvinists shrugged off the secrecy that had previously clothed their activities, and staged defiant open services; sometimes, to make the provocation more extreme they preached in the churchyards of Catholic churches. In 1562, in a further ominous development, for the first time the minister preaching at one such service was protected by armed guards. When these dangerous activities resulted in the arrest of participants, evangelicals on occasions staged raids to free their condemned colleagues from prison.

Faced with this increased evidence of religious anarchy the authorities in the Netherlands could not but be concerned. But the rebirth of domestic heresy was not only a problem of order for the Dutch political classes; it also represented something of an opportunity. For the last, and by no means the most insignificant, impact of French events in the Netherlands was that they also gave the Dutch nobility an example of how political crisis could be turned to their own advantage.

Political opposition

In 1559 Philip had left the Netherlands, as it turned out, for ever. He did so at a moment when his relations with the governing classes in the Low Countries had turned unusually bleak. In the first years after the abdication of Charles V, the Netherlands was the nerve centre of the Spanish Empire. Philip had been present at the great ceremony of abdication in Brussels, and the Netherlands became the base from which he launched the last phase of the war against France, crowned by the victory at St Quentin in 1557. But by 1559 much had changed. His royal consort, Mary Queen of England, was dead, and Philip had been steadily more exasperated by the reluctance of the Netherlandish estates to grant him the military support that he required, and that he felt was his due. Pressing problems in Spain also required his personal attention, and in August of that year he departed for the Iberian peninsula.

He left behind as regent his half-sister, Margaret of Parma, the last in that sequence of capable Habsburg women who helped shape the history of the Netherlands in the sixteenth century. However, unlike Mary of Hungary, a capable regent in the 1530s, Margaret was not the sister of Charles V but his illegitimate daughter; in the status-conscious remnant of the Burgundian court over which she would preside, it was a telling distinction. Furthermore, her inner circle of advisors was dominated not by the grandee lords of the Order of the Golden Fleece, but by relatively low-born men, such as the highly capable chief secretary, Antoine Perrenot. For men like the Count of Egmont, Philip II's old companion in arms, this turn of events was perplexing. Equally feeling his exclusion from power was William of Nassau, Prince of Orange, a young favourite of Charles V who did not discern the same warmth in his relationship with the new king. William compounded his fall from grace by marrying the daughter of the Lutheran Elector of Saxony in 1561, a match that gave him a substantial power base among the German aristocracy, if little personal happiness.[2]

In 1563 William and his allies had their chance to register their impatience with their exclusion from real power, when Philip attempted to activate a long gestated plan to reorganize the structure of the Netherlandish church. The reform was long overdue and made good sense in terms of a renewal of religious life. In place of the four existing dioceses, there were to be 18, all occupied by men of sound learning. But in the process vested interests were bound to be disturbed. The incomes for the new bishops were to be diverted from abbeys and cathedral offices that had provided reliable incomes for the younger sons of the Netherlandish nobility; neither were they enamoured of the proposed educational qualifications, which would have further restricted their patronage opportunities. So the new plan was opposed by an opportunist coalition that made much of a fear that the new bishoprics would presage the introduction of the Spanish inquisition.[3] No matter that the apparatus already existing to control heresy in the Netherlands was more stringent than anything ever seen in Spain, the charge stuck. Opposition focused on the person of Perrenot, now promoted Cardinal Granvelle. Margaret was persuaded that his presence in the Council was no longer acceptable to the higher nobility. She wavered and then gave way. Granvelle was despatched back to his native Franche-Comté, and the opposition had claimed their first scalp.

The respite was short-lived. By 1564 the nobles were once more grumbling, and now the cause of the persecuted evangelicals was beginning to attract their attention. One must not assume that this was an entirely cynical concern. As governors of the various towns and provinces of the Low Countries, the Netherlands grandees had direct responsibility for the maintenance of public order, and could not but be alarmed at the evidence of a growing climate of disaffection. By 1563 and 1564 there was clear evidence of a crisis at hand in the management of heresy in the Netherlands. Emboldened by open insurrection in France, Dutch Calvinist communities were increasingly willing to force the issue by provocative gestures. There was a steady growth in reported attacks on the objects of Catholic veneration and even incidents of public preaching.

Most ominously, it was clear that the urban authorities, which inevitably bore the major burdens in the struggle against religious dissidence, had lost the stomach for salutary justice. In 1564 the Antwerp authorities attempted to put to death by burning a Calvinist minister who had fallen into their hands. The crowd that had gathered to witness the execution rioted in support of the condemned man, and an attempt to rescue him from the stake (and to lynch the executioner) was only barely averted. Such a challenge to their authority would have shaken the will of any urban government in the sixteenth century, for in an age before standing police forces any law required the implicit consent of the governed for the social values that underpinned justice. In the case of execution of respectable fellow citizens for differences on matters of conscience, this was manifestly no longer present. Hereafter the Antwerp authorities simply chose not to notice the evidence of the growing evangelical congregations in their midst. Elsewhere in the most populous parts of the Netherlands it was a similar story. Most of the towns of Holland had abandoned executions for heresy (often after similar incidents) as early as 1559, and by 1563 the three major towns of Flanders had embarked on legal action to prevent the provincial inquisitor, the industrious Titelmans, from operating within their jurisdiction.

So there was considerable justification for the claim made by the grandees on the Netherlands Council of State that the present policy against heresy could not be sustained. In 1564 the leading nobles despatched the greatest of their number, Count Egmont, to Spain to make the point to Philip II in person. Egmont was received with fair words, and on his return to the Netherlands he gave an encouraging account of his negotiations. So when, in November 1565, Philip made clear that his views had not been changed, and ordered that the heresy laws should continue to be enforced in all their severity, the leading Netherlandish nobles could justly feel that they had been betrayed. They took their revenge by ostentatiously withdrawing their support from the embattled regime of Margaret of Parma. There was even, in the case of one of their number, William, Prince of Orange, discreet contact with the growing number of the lesser nobility who had now associated themselves with the call for reform. It was these allies in the lesser nobility who now took up the initiative, gathering together a petition demanding an end to persecution; but the signal given by the grandees when they formally withdrew from the Council of State in January 1566 was also crucial. When in April 1566 the noble Confederates defied the regent's authority by appearing armed in her presence to present their demands, her powerlessness to resist was obvious.

Thus politics certainly played its part in the collapse of authority that ushered in the first Dutch revolt in 1566. Against this, nothing but the religious fervour that had been gradually building during these years of political persecution explains the intensity of the reaction to these events in 1566. The scale of the demonstrations of support for change clearly took both the regent and her noble opponents by surprise; the noble conspirators quickly discovered that they had called into existence a force beyond their power to control. In this respect the events of 1566 were crucial to the future evolution of Dutch Calvinism. At an early stage, and in crucial contrast to the movement in France, the Dutch Calvinist communities emancipated themselves from reliance on their noble patrons.

When in April 1566, and under the severest duress, Margaret of Parma ordered a temporary suspension of the heresy laws, this was widely interpreted, both in the Netherlands and elsewhere, as ushering in a permanent change in policy. Dutch Calvinists in exile hurried back to their homeland to take advantage of the new freedoms. Existing congregations began to meet with greater openness and others were swiftly formed. The summer of the hedge-preaching seemed a glorious celebration of the new freedoms: part religious service, part demonstration against a regime whose authority was swiftly ebbing away. Then in August came the iconoclasm. To contemporaries the apparently wanton destruction of church property was an enormous shock. For many of the Calvinists' allies in the nobility this was the final encouragement to abandon an alliance in which many of them had been frankly uneasy, and had now led to such dreadful consequences.

The iconoclasm was a traumatic and shocking event, but viewed in its contemporary context should not have been entirely unexpected. Throughout the Reformation century, occasions where Protestants seized the reins of power against the wishes of the local authorities tended to be accompanied by episodes of this nature. Numerous examples could be cited from Germany and Switzerland in the first generation of reform, such as the famous 'Bilderstreit' that established Protestant dominance in Basle in 1529, or even the violence and destruction in Wittenberg orchestrated by Karlstadt in Luther's absence at

Christmas 1521. Equally, during the recently unfolding events in France the Huguenot advance had been accompanied by widespread desecration of churches. Iconoclasm might take different forms, and serve subtly different purposes. In the first generation it had frequently been orchestrated as a polemical means of making a theological point: demonstrating the powerlessness of previously revered sacred objects as they were cast down and humiliated. In the cities of France it also undoubtedly served to force the hand of town governments reluctant to act to authorize Reformed worship without higher authority. This seems to have been the primary motive in the Netherlands, though examples of desecration rituals could also be cited.

In the short term the violence certainly achieved its objectives. In the days and weeks following the iconoclasm a badly shaken government conceded all the churches at this point desired: a new decree of September granted freedom of worship in places where Protestant congregations already in practice existed. In a series of local settlements with respective town councils and governors this was translated into permission to occupy suitable places of worship, or, where this would have proved too provocative (as in Antwerp), to erect their own church buildings. The exultant congregations set about their work with a will, gathering funds for their new churches and erecting the structures of congregational government that were the hallmark of a full Calvinist system. Each church now elected elders to assist the ministers in the government of the community, and the maintenance of congregational discipline. Deacons were appointed to supervise the provision of poor relief. By Christmas most cities in the Netherlands had a fully organized Calvinist church, and in cities such as Ghent and Antwerp the newly erected church buildings added a new and distinctive profile to the city skyline. The speed with which these churches were constructed was an ostentatious demonstration that those who adhered to the new congregations included many from among the cities' financial elite.

But even as the Calvinists celebrated their good fortune, the political tide was beginning to turn against them. In retrospect it appears that the iconoclasm, while achieving the immediate objectives of forcing the regent's hand, had dealt a fatal blow to the loose opposition coalition that bound together the reformed and their allies in the nobility. Many among the uncommitted had been appalled by the destructive force that accompanied the assault on the churches. To the nobility it was a powerful signal that the forces that they had unleashed posed a real threat to the established political order. So the regent, struggling to re-establish her authority in the autumn of 1566, found some surprising friends among former critics of the regime. By the end of the year she was ready to take the offensive, and the Calvinists were faced with the difficult choice of capitulation or outright military defiance; if they chose the latter, they would remove any last shred of credibility from their claim to be loyal subjects of the king. In the event, the Calvinist leadership fell uncomfortably between the two. In December 1566 Calvinist troops sent to relieve Valenciennes were defeated by the regent's forces at Wattrelos. The following March a motley force of irregulars raised by the Calvinist congregations was put to flight at Austruweel, just outside Antwerp, while members of the city's church watched impotently from the walls. With that, resistance was effectively ended, and in the spring of 1567 most who had compromised themselves through membership of the churches took flight.

Revolt renewed

The collapse of the revolt in 1567 and the subsequent retribution was obviously a dark hour for those who had greeted the events of the 'Wonderyear' with such optimism. Notwithstanding Margaret of Parma's eventual success in restoring order, Philip in Spain lost no time in despatching his most feared general the Duke of Alva to stamp out the last embers of opposition. His arrival in Brussels in August 1567 was swiftly followed by the establishment of the notorious Council of Troubles. In a four-year period the Council of Troubles condemned over 10,000 to death, concentrating especially on those known to have been involved in the iconoclasm, or those who had held office in the churches as elders or deacons. Although former leaders of the congregations writing from exile now tried to distance themselves from responsibility for the church-breaking, blaming the fickle crowds, or (more implausibly still) Catholic priests, the tribunals had a clear sense of where responsibility lay.

The nobles who had done so much to undermine the regent's authority also did not escape their share of responsibility. Those most directly implicated in the armed resistance – Brederode, Culembourg, Hoogstraten – took themselves off to Germany, where they were joined, after some initial hesitation, by William of Orange. This circumspection saved his life. William's co-conspirators in the noble opposition, Egmont and Hornes, were arrested within days of Alva's arrival. They were subsequently tried and, on 5 June 1568, beheaded in the Grand Place at Brussels. Orange was condemned in absentia, and his goods declared confiscated. This left him little alternative but to commit himself fully to the struggle against Alva; and with the death of Brederode, in Germany in February 1568, he was now the unchallenged leader of the exiled opposition.

In these new circumstances Orange had little choice but to forge a partnership with the Calvinist congregations. For Dutch Calvinism these were not altogether years of darkness and despair. The moment of religious freedom during the Wonderyear may have been fleeting but it had achieved a great deal of importance for the future. The fact that of the 10,000 who received the death sentence from the Council of Troubles, 90 per cent were tried in absentia, tells its own story: those who were most implicated in the events of 1566 had succeeded in taking themselves off to safety abroad. Most importantly, the brief period of optimism in the summer and autumn of 1566 had caused many who had previously held aloof to join the churches, and these were now compromised beyond return. In the face of Alva's relentless pursuit, they had little choice but to join the exile, most settling in England or Germany where they brought new vitality to the exile churches.

The huge growth in the numbers adhering to the exile churches in this period was a demonstration of a further critical consequence of the Wonderyear. For it became manifest that even at the cost of apparent defeat the Dutch Calvinist church had emerged as the dominant force among the competing evangelical groups in the Netherlands. Until this point diversity among Protestant opponents of the regime had been an inevitable legacy of the generation of persecution. It is quite possible that in simple numerical terms before 1566 Calvinists might have been outnumbered by Mennonites and other Anabaptist groups, particularly in Holland and the north where the Calvinist presence had been negligible. In Antwerp both groups competed with a substantial Lutheran community, which drew strength from its connections with Germany. The Wonderyear brought this competition to an end. The clear supremacy manifested by Calvinism during this year, both in terms of its internal organization and its prominence in the opposition, ensured that henceforth it would play overwhelmingly the dominant role in the religious opposition to the regime.

In the enforced period of exile after 1567 Dutch Calvinists set about consolidating this advantage. The speed of events during the Wonderyear had led inevitably to a degree of variation in the practice among the new churches that had sprung up in the Netherlands. The interval of the exile allowed the churches to review this experience and establish the total harmony of church order and liturgical practice to which they aspired. This was achieved at the synod of Emden in 1571, a milestone event for Dutch Calvinism conducted with a spirit of purpose and with a sense of measure not always evident in such gatherings. As well as confirming a common statement of beliefs and church order, the synod also established the putative organization of the Dutch church, ranging the individual congregations into colloquies and local synods. This organizational structure encompassed both the exile churches and churches back in the Netherlands temporarily in suspension. Given that in 1571 there was no real reason to expect that the opportunity would ever arise to re-establish these churches, the synod's decisions gives a valuable insight into the sort of unquenchable optimism that might result from the Calvinist sense of providential destiny.

The synod of Emden was also important for what it revealed of the Calvinist church's relationship with the erstwhile political opposition. In the years following the collapse of the first revolt, Calvinist exiles would forge a new and ultimately decisive alliance with the leading figure among the opposition grandees, William of Orange. However, this relationship was not without its difficulties. In the immediate aftermath of the Wonderyear, the Calvinist leadership had reason to treat William with great suspicion. His vacillating conduct during the rebellion was not forgotten; in particular they found it difficult to forgive his decision, as governor of Antwerp, to do nothing to prevent the slaughter of the Calvinist forces at Austruweel. When, in 1568, William declared war upon Alva to recover his confiscated lands and offices, the Calvinist churches did little to assist him. Drawing largely on his own resources and German connections, William assembled an army and advanced cautiously into Brabant. Alva cannily refused the engagement that was William's only chance of decisive victory, and his poorly paid force soon began to disintegrate. Meanwhile a second army, advancing into Friesland under the command of his brother Louis of Nassau, was intercepted and destroyed by Alva's troops at Jemmingen. The calamitous failure of this expedition taught William that unless he sank his own cause into that of the religious struggle his prospects were hopeless. The year 1569 saw William and his brother in open negotiation with the French Huguenot leadership, and it was at the head of a new expeditionary force sponsored by the French that William would return to the Netherlands in 1572.

Even so, this was an association in which the churches would function as an equal, if not senior partner. The synod of Emden ostentatiously refused to adopt William's political objectives as a formal part of their protocols, despite his clearly expressed wishes. It was a highly significant gesture. Henceforth the balance of power within the rebel association would always favour the goals of the congregations, rather than William's vision of an open, essentially nationalistic conflict against Spanish rule. Dutch Calvinism had successfully resisted the long-term subjugation to the interests of their partners in the nobility that had so decisively shaped French Calvinism, and arguably much to its disadvantage.

The Struggle for Survival

By the winter of 1571–2 William's feverish activity to revive the cause of resistance seemed at last poised to bear fruit. New troops had been painstakingly gathered, and the alliance with the French Huguenots offered at least the prospect of more reliable foreign backing. Most important of all, by lending his name to the activities of seafaring privateers waging war on Dutch shipping from the exile ports in Germany and England, William had at last found an effective means of carrying the fight to Alva. These 'Sea Beggars', as they were known, in reference to the original protest of the *Gueux* in 1566, were often lawless and difficult to command. But from safe havens in Emden and the Channel they were well placed to cause havoc among the shipping that was the lifeblood of Antwerp and the northern provinces. The third part of their booty levied by Orange's agents helped replenish his depleted coffers. Most significantly the Sea Beggar attacks had a most serious effect on the economy of the Provinces, already teetering on the brink of recession. Initially cowed by the brutality of Alva's repression, by 1572 the population was in an increasingly ugly mood. Few bothered to hide their indignation at the new taxes, including the notorious 'Tenth Penny', levied by Alva to meet the costs of the occupying troops. Thus Orange's troops entered the Netherlands in 1572 with fair hopes of a welcome from a population groaning under the burden of economic hardship. As ever, the strategic vision was ambitious. Two separate armies were to invade the south and central Netherlands. Meanwhile, in a development that would have unexpected significance, the Beggar fleet was to stage a landing on the Holland coast. On 1 April the Beggars seized the small

Figure 21 Holland, from Sebastian Münster, *Cosmographia Universalis*. Courtesy St Andrews University Library. This contemporary map catches well the difficulty of communications caused by coastal flooding and inland waterways. In the years after 1572 the Spanish troops crucially failed to overcome these logistical difficulties.

Holland port of Den Briel, and shortly thereafter Vlissingen (Flushing) in Zeeland. As Alva, preoccupied elsewhere, delayed reinforcements, the rebels were able gradually to infiltrate most of the cities of Holland. When the land campaign in the south swiftly turned against Orange,

Holland was left as the slightly improbable centre of resistance. In October William of Orange bowed to the inevitable and journeyed north to take charge of the northern revolt.

The years that followed were a brutal and desperate time for the Dutch revolt. The rising in the south extinguished, the royal administration (in which Alva was in 1573 succeeded by Don Luis de Requesens) was able to turn all its efforts to the subjugation of the handful of towns in rebel hands. The terrible fate of Zutphen, sacked by the Spanish army in 1572, and Haarlem, which fell in 1573, gave the rebels a clear indication of what they might expect if they surrendered. The Spaniards enjoyed overwhelming advantages, both in the number and quality of their troops, and in resources. But this was difficult terrain for campaigning, boggy and low lying, and criss-crossed with river systems and canals. The rebels made the most of these advantages; most of all, thanks to the Sea Beggars, they never lost control of the sea.

By 1574 the Holland campaign had resolved itself into a siege of Leiden, strategically placed at the heart of the province. The Spaniards already controlled Amsterdam and Haarlem: the fall of Leiden would leave the few remaining towns in rebel hands in the north and south of the province utterly isolated. For over a year Spanish forces invested the city; the population, cut off from supplies, endured terrible privations. But it was the besiegers whose resolve broke. On 3 October the emaciated garrison looked out to find the Spanish camp abandoned, and the siege at an end. This glorious moment in the city's history is still celebrated in a raucous annual carnival.

The revolt was saved, and in the moment of triumph William could not but acknowledge the part played by his Calvinist allies. They had provided much of the backbone of Leiden's resistance, and the exile communities abroad contributed precious funds, munitions and troops. But the churches extracted a high price for their commitment to the rebel cause. In the Holland towns that joined the rebellion in the summer of 1572 the Calvinist congregations lost little time in appropriating the principal churches for their worship. Where the municipal authorities proved slow to respond, they again used the time-honoured tactic of iconoclasm to secure their demands. Thus far William was prepared to accommodate his allies, but he balked at their next demand, that the Calvinist faith be the only form of worship permitted in the liberated towns. This demand completely cut across William's goal of an inclusive, tolerant autonomous state free of

Spanish troops. However, in the heated atmosphere of a desperate struggle for survival William had little choice but to give his allies what they demanded. In December 1573 William recognized the inevitable and finally joined the Calvinist church. The following year he did not intervene when the States of Holland formally banned the Catholic Mass.

This religious fanaticism would ultimately undermine much of what Orange had achieved through patient diplomacy. The years of warfare had taken a heavy toll, both on the Spanish treasury and the patience of the loyal provinces. The Sea Beggars' control of the sea destroyed trade; William, meanwhile, worked calmly to foment dissent. In 1576 he achieved his reward. In March of that year Requesens died, leaving the Spanish government effectively rudderless. In November, the Spanish troops, unpaid and mutinous, descended on Antwerp, and put the defenceless city to the sack. Several days of looting left 8,000 dead and 1,000 houses destroyed. The response was swift – on 8 November the States General signed the Pacification of Ghent, by which the previously loyal provinces made common cause with Holland and Zeeland to rid themselves of Spanish troops. The second revolt was at an end.

The Failure of Unity

The Pacification of Ghent fleetingly held out the prospect of a free Netherlandish state encompassing the whole 17 provinces, with William of Orange as its respected elder statesman. But this vision was as short-lived as it was appealing. Rivalries among the nobility and a new spirit of conciliation on the part of the Spanish administration soon eroded the apparent solidarity between the provinces. But the heaviest blows to hopes of an all-embracing free state were dealt by William's most stalwart allies, the Reformed congregations. Forbidden by the terms of the Pacification of Ghent to disturb the religious peace of the southern provinces, the Calvinists nevertheless pressed eagerly for the renewal of public worship in former urban strongholds such as Ghent and Antwerp. In 1578 they went further, staging a civic coup which overthrew the town government in both cities, and established a new radical Calvinist regime.

For many of the conservative nobility this was the last straw. In 1579 the Walloon provinces of the south formally reaffirmed their allegiance to Spanish rule, and readmitted foreign troops. The northern provinces responded with their own treaty, the Union of Utrecht, and the battle-lines were drawn. From this point on the borders between an independent northern state and a loyal Spanish satellite in the south would be determined by military action.

For this, the Spanish were at last well equipped. In 1577 Don John of Austria, Governor General in succession to the deceased Requesens, summoned to his side Alexander Farnese, Duke of Parma. When in October 1578 Don John succumbed to the plague, Parma succeeded him. Parma would prove to be outstanding both as a military commander and in the peacetime arts of government and diplomacy, and the fortunes of the crown began steadily to improve. It was his subtle and soothing spirit that had in 1578 succeeded in assuaging fears of the return of Spanish troops, and reattaching the Walloon provinces (though massive bribes to members of the Walloon nobility also helped). After the two alliances of 1579 indicated that the limits of diplomacy had probably been reached, Parma set about completing the recovery by military means. In successive campaigning seasons he moved inexorably through the plains of Flanders, forcing the capitulation of city after city: Oudenaarde in 1582, Nieuwport, Dunkirk, Axel and Hulst in 1583, Bruges and Ghent in 1584. Finally, in 1585 Antwerp, the jewel in the rebel crown, capitulated to his forces.

By this stage the rebel provinces could no longer maintain the illusion that their resistance was to the king's agents rather than Philip himself. On 22 July 1581 the States-General finally recognized the inevitable, and declared Philip II deposed. Who should be in his place proved an equally difficult question. The innate conservatism of the age is nowhere better revealed than in these troubled steps towards independence. It had taken 15 years formally to acknowledge the obvious fact that the revolt was a direct assault on Philip's sovereignty, and even now his deposition led to a prolonged search for an alternative head. At times this threatened to descend into farce. At first high hopes were vested in Francis of Anjou, brother of the French king, but Anjou proved politically ill equipped for the complex politics of the Netherlands, and in 1583 he withdrew in disarray. The assassination of William of Orange on 10 July 1584 was a further savage blow. The revolt had lost its most charismatic leader at a time when the military effort was in crisis. In desperation the rebels turned to Elizabeth of England. Finally, in 1585, the English queen offered grudging military support. It was too late to save Antwerp, but in the years that followed, enough to slow the Spanish advance.

The Road to Independence

The despatch of English troops to prop up the flagging rebel cause was hardly altruism on Elizabeth's part. Since 1572 her attitude to the revolt had been maddeningly fickle and inconsistent, but by 1585 it was obvious even to the cautious queen that the final subjugation of the rebels would be an inevitable prelude to a Spanish invasion of England. So English troops came, and although they scarcely excelled on the field of battle, they did enough to persuade Philip that the final resolution of the Dutch issue could only be achieved as part of a more general settlement of the complex of problems that faced him in northern Europe. In 1587–8, therefore, Parma's campaign was suspended while preparations went forward for the invasion of England (for which Parma was to supply the troops). After the defeat of the Armada expedition, Parma was again called away from his primary task to prop up Spain's allies in France, with two extended expeditions to save Paris (1590) and Rouen (1592) for the Catholic League.

With the military pressures thus relieved, the States General were finally able to mount some sort of military effort to recover territory lost in previous years. In 1591 the capture of Nijmegen, Deventer and Zutphen re-established Dutch control in the north-eastern provinces; in 1594 the surrender of Groningen ended Spanish presence in the far north. With that, the boundaries of the free northern state were effectively set, for all that the conflict would continue (admittedly at a far lower level of intensity) until the signing of the Twelve Year Truce in 1609. The military successes of these years owed a great deal to the generalship of Maurice of Nassau, second son of William of Orange, whose contribution to this final stage of the struggle for independence cemented the special role of the Orange dynasty in the emerging new state. Installed as hereditary *stadholders*, the family would enjoy a quasi-royal status, the only power capable of challenging the otherwise overwhelming influence of the province of Holland.

Following the loss of Flanders and Antwerp, Holland was inevitably the dominant power in the free state. The loss of Antwerp was a bitter blow, but not absolute, for much of what had made for Antwerp's sixteenth-century greatness was now appropriated by the new northern state. The Spanish reconquest was followed by a huge exodus of Protestants from the southern provinces: from Antwerp, which lost almost half its population in these years, but also from Bruges, Ghent, and the cloth-making towns of the industrial *Westkwartier*. Most of these settled in Holland, bringing with them their skills, and their capital. To the Flemish incomers the new state owed a large part of the exhuberant growth of the seventeenth-century Golden Age.

For the Calvinist church, which had contributed so largely to the struggle for independence, the result was more mixed. It was in the 1580s and 1590s, as the threat of reconquest gradually receded, and the northern provinces progressed tentatively towards an independent nationhood, that the distinctive character of Dutch Calvinism began to be fully manifest. Its role in the struggle for freedom had ensured the church of a central place in the life of the new state. In towns across the nation, the Reformed congregations now possessed the most prominent (in the case of smaller communities, the only) churches, now appropriately 'cleansed' and reordered in the austere Dutch manner familiar from countless paintings of the Dutch Golden Age. The churches' ministers enjoyed regular and reasonably generous salaries, paid by the state and guaranteed on the incomes of former church lands. Its services were usually numerously attended, at least in the major centres of population.

And yet, as the years rolled by, many among the Reformed *dominees* could not suppress the ungrateful thought that things might have been so much better. Prominent though their place was in the life of the new nation, there were many among their flocks who proved stubbornly resistant to the implementation of the ministers' visions of a fully reformed society. Although a large proportion of the population frequented their services, only a relatively small number became full members of the church, placing themselves under its discipline and attesting their faith through an examination of doctrine. Most painfully of all, in crucial areas where the ministers hoped to establish their influence, the town magistrates frequently withheld their co-operation. Poor relief and schooling, for instance, in a full Reformed system such as that operating in Geneva, very much the province of the church, remained firmly under magisterial control. Nor did the magistrates always live up to the ministers' demanding expectations in their pursuit of drunkenness, immorality or recreation culture, particularly those pastimes disapproved of by the godly, but much beloved of the city elite, such as dancing and the theatre. And while other competing churches were never fully authorized, the magistrates did little to prevent the numerous dissenting groups, notably the Mennonites, from gathering for worship. As the threat from Spain diminished, even Catholics were permitted to gather together virtually unhindered (and these were a surprisingly numerous residue, especially in the conquered Generality lands of North Brabant).

The ministers had not expected that the magistrates would prove such uncooperative partners in the building of a godly society, and on occasions frustration would spill over into bitter recrimination. But from the point of view of the magistrates, their position was understandable enough. Having embarked on a long and difficult struggle to free themselves from one form of Inquisition and intolerance, the magistrates had little intention of subjecting themselves voluntarily to another. And so the ministers were left to thunder their imprecations and warnings of retribution to appreciative, but not always dutiful congregations.

In this respect the seventeenth-century Dutch Republic would inherit what the Dutch ministers themselves would have recognized as only a very incomplete Reformation. But for all that it was an achievement that posterity would acknowledge as remarkable. Whereas in France the initially much more numerous Huguenot congregations were by now reduced to a stubborn rump in a Catholic state, the Reformed church in the Netherlands would never lose its claim to a central part in the life and cultural identity of the Dutch Republic. This much had been assured by the Calvinist role in the first critical years of the Revolt, the resistance to Alva, and the obdurate campaigns with William of Orange. By the convictions and sacrifices of this first generation, Calvinism was firmly embedded in the foundations of the free Dutch state.

10

The Making of Protestant Britain

For much of the sixteenth century the political classes of England and Scotland feuded with all the passion of estranged neighbours. Yet in 1603 a Scottish king would ascend the English throne with the connivance and general approval of the English ruling elite. This unlikely turn of events owed much to the eccentricities of the Welsh Tudor dynasty that had occupied the throne of England for almost precisely that century: the determination of the father, Henry VIII, to marry often, the equal determination of the daughter, Elizabeth, not to marry at all. But it also owed a great deal to Protestantism. There was little that bound together the English aristocracy and the Scottish king (for whom they soon developed a profound distaste) than a shared commitment to Protestantism. It was a determination to preserve England as a Protestant nation that gave James VI and I his opportunity;[1] and which would in the next century doom his son Charles when his actions threatened to undermine this cherished identity.

For all the glories of hindsight there are many ironies in this unlikely turn of events. For the prevailing mood among historians had been to regard the translation of England to Protestantism as largely accidental, and certainly grudging. If England became a Protestant country, it did so largely at the behest of its rulers, and against its better judgement.[2] If this was so, the transformation was indeed profound. For by the end of the century England and Scotland were rightly regarded as cornerstones of Protestant Europe. The faith would become so deeply ingrained that in the seventeenth century both nations would defend their religious affinity with a passion that verged on bigotry. And yet the adoption of Protestantism had been, by the standards of the turmoil that had gripped much of Europe in this period, remarkably smooth. There were no English Wars of Religion, and in Scotland the transition to Protestantism was achieved by a near bloodless revolution in a matter of months. In the light of the events described in the two previous chapters and in the poisoned climate of the age this was certainly a remarkable achievement, and one that requires explanation. To see why this should have been so it is useful to review the complex inheritance when, in 1558, Elizabeth emerged from the shadows to claim her crown.

Elizabeth and the Protestant Inheritance

When Elizabeth came to the throne in November 1558, her battered nation had been through three completely different religious settlements in the space of 12 years. The last years of the reign of Henry VIII had been characterized by a state of half-Reformation, in which theologically traditional elements mingled with a half-achieved evangelical agenda. Contemporaries found it baffling: so too have historians. But this was not 'Catholicism without the pope' as it has sometimes been described. The king's personal preference for conservative theology – the assertion of the Real Presence in the Eucharist, a ban on clerical marriage – should not disguise the real damage that had been done to the old Church. This went far beyond a simple repudiation of the authority of the pope. In the course of 15 years during which the evangelicals had sporadically been given their head, images had been removed from churches, shrines destroyed, pilgrimages and purgatory discredited. The whole structure of English monasticism had been swept away. An English Bible had been introduced, and reform-minded bishops and nobles advanced to positions of influence. This was not far short of what might have been expected of Lutheran states in Germany or Scandinavia; indeed, in the speed of change it was often in advance of those slow-moving Reformations.

When Henry VIII died in 1547 the evangelicals positioned at the heart of government seized control to finish the job. For six heady years the eyes of Protestant Europe were all on England as in the difficult years after Luther's death the island kingdom provided a rare beacon of evangelical progress. Significant figures from the European churches even journeyed to England to assist in the creation of a model Reformed church polity.

The early death of Edward VI and the accession of his resolutely orthodox sister Mary brought a new reversal. The legislative structure of the Protestant church was dismantled, and, after a tense interval while the temperature of the political nation was measured, the authority of the pope was restored. The English people resumed their old observances with every sign of enthusiasm. But Mary's government faced considerable problems in making good the destruction of 20 years of sustained attacks on the traditional structures of belief. While the priests resumed their Mass, they did so in churches and Cathedrals brought low by the ravaging of their accoutrements and assets: virtually none of the church property seized during the early Reformation and distributed among the political classes was restored. This was the price of their compliance, and it was a high one: even if Mary had lived for 30 years, the church would never have been restored to its pre-Reformation glories. This was in any case unlikely: Mary was 37 when she ascended the throne, and by 1556 it was obvious to everyone that the marriage with Philip II of Spain so optimistically entered into would bear no fruit in terms of children. Those not reconciled to the regime could ponder the preferences of her only surviving close kin, Elizabeth; and once the queen had declined the opportunity to rid herself of her sister when Elizabeth was peripherally implicated in Wyatt's rebellion, the reversionary interest grew ever stronger. The pressure was maintained by a steady stream of Protestant irreconcilables, who offered themselves up as martyr witnesses for their faith: over 300 were executed by burning during the reign, including the Archbishop, Cranmer, and 4 former bishops: Ridley, Latimer, Hooper and Ferrar. The horrors of public burning may have caused many to ponder whether this was what they intended when they welcomed back the old Church. Other remnants of the former Protestant establishment either took themselves off to the continent, or lurked in England in a state of nominal obedience. As Mary's Council struggled to resolve these persistent problems, the regime received a final psychological hammer blow. A principal cause of concern when Mary married Philip was that England would become a pawn in the Habsburgs wider political designs. Indeed, this was almost inevitable, as Spain's sworn enemy France could hardly see the union as anything other than a threat. In January 1558 French armies swooped to seize Calais, the last, symbolic and in fact well-defended outpost of English territory on the Continent. The humiliation felt in England was acute.

Thus when Mary died in November 1558 the welcome for her young heir seems to have been heartfelt; and not overly complicated by anxieties for what she might do to her sister's church settlement. Elizabeth in fact had a remarkably free hand, and she used it with a decisiveness that would not always characterize her actions as the cares of office took their toll. For those reading the signs the early months gave clear signals of the queen's intentions. She surrounded herself with figures who had prospered under the Protestant regime of Edward VI, and generally been eclipsed under Mary. Her first minister was William Cecil, secretary to the Privy Council in Edward's reign; her favourite Robert Dudley, son of the executed Duke of Northumberland. Her new Archbishop of Canterbury would be Matthew Parker, formerly chaplain to her mother, Ann Boleyn. The other major offices of church and state were largely distributed to returning Protestant exiles. This, it was clear enough, would be a Protestant regime.

These should have been difficult times for the fledgling government. The new queen, whose illegitimacy had once been confirmed by act of Parliament and whose claim to the succession rested upon uncertain foundations, was the last best hope of a failing dynasty. The queen, as councillors fretted in countless memoranda, had neither husband nor close kin; the nearest heir was Mary, Queen of Scots, wife of the French Dauphin and soon to be Queen of France. Had Elizabeth died early (as she nearly did in 1563, from smallpox), England too might have plunged into the same religious civil war convulsing neighboring lands on the continent.

Given this evident insecurity, the confidence with which Elizabeth and her advisors addressed the complicated problems of domestic and foreign policy arising from a new restoration of Protestantism, was remarkable. A Parliament gathered to settle religion in 1559 compliantly reinstated the Second Protestant Prayer Book of Edward VI, with some small refinements reflective of recent continental theological developments.[3] But Elizabeth balked at the introduction of the full Calvinist church order urged upon her by foreign theologians and some of the English exiles who, having withdrawn to the continent during Mary's reign, now returned to inaugurate the new era. Bishops were retained, and so too ecclesiastical vestments, which many of the hotter Protestants regarded as an unacceptable popish survival. When in 1566 Elizabeth insisted upon uniformity in clerical attire, a substantial proportion of the English clergy (up to 10 per cent in London), refused to submit, and were deprived. Further attempts to move the queen to a more perfect Reformation, whether by Parliamentary statute or subtle pressure through the bench of bishops, proved equally unavailing; the Church of England would remain, in the words of its Protestant critics, 'but halfly reformed'.

But that was for the future. In 1559 other, equally pressing, problems crowded in upon her.

Revolution and Reform in Scotland

Later, in her mature years, Elizabeth's approach to foreign policy initiatives was overwhelmingly cautious and circumspect. But in the early days of the regime, the queen and her advisors were capable of acts of great courage and boldness. Nothing illustrates this better than the intervention in Scotland, which played a decisive role in installing a friendly Protestant regime. By this single bold stroke Elizabeth achieved all that English foreign policy had unsuccessfully striven to achieve through the costly expeditions and bloody battles of the first half of the century. The result was the installation of a sympathetic political elite underpinning a decidedly Protestant settlement that, with only the briefest interval, dominated Scottish society for the rest of the century.

In Scotland, Calvinism had its most fortuitous victory, but in some senses also its most complete. Unlike in France and the Netherlands, one could not claim that the Calvinist church settlement was accompanied by a large groundswell of popular support; nor was it long in the preparation. For all the positive propaganda of John Knox – the Scottish Reformation's principal historian, as well as a leading protagonist – the Scottish Reformation was overwhelmingly a political event.

The Scottish church did not proceed in splendid isolation from the reforming currents on the continent, but in truth the impact of German evangelism in the first generation was slight. In 1528 Patrick Hamilton, a churchman who had studied in Wittenberg and tried to popularize Lutheran theology back in his native land, was burned at St Andrews. In 1546 a similar fate would befall George Wishart, a young man who had travelled in Switzerland and absorbed the theological precepts of Zwingli in Zurich. Returning in 1544 Wishart had embarked on a peripatetic ministry through Fife, Lothian and Ayrshire, encouraged by signs at court that the regent, Arran, was prepared to embrace a modest state-sponsored reform. In 1543 Parliament had approved the possession of vernacular Scripture, but the following year this concession was withdrawn, and Arran's 'godly flit' was over. The arrest and execution of Wishart in 1546 signalled that conservative forces, led by Cardinal Beaton, had prevailed, though Beaton himself would soon fall victim to the revenge of Wishart's supporters, who murdered him in St Andrews shortly after Wishart's execution. In a final reckless gesture of defiance the insurgents seized St Andrews castle. When, inevitably, they were forced to capitulate, a number (including John Knox) were despatched to the French galleys.

The incident at St Andrews demonstrated the extent to which the cause of reform had already become intertwined with larger political issues. To many Protestant evangelism was associated with the influence of England, and so largely discredited by the hostile turn of relations of Henry VIII's last years and the invasion of 1547 by the Duke of Somerset. The cause of Catholic reform, meanwhile, fell under the sponsorship of those who flourished through French influence. When James V had died shortly after the defeat at Solway Moss in 1542, he left an infant child, Mary, on whose shoulders fell the hopes of the future dynasty. In the struggle for influence James's widow, Mary of Guise, initially lost out to Arran, but following the collapse of Arran's pro-English regime Mary emerged from the shadows. Government now began to take on a distinctly French tinge. In 1548 Mary had been packed off to France and promised in marriage to the dauphin Francis; French troops were diverted to Scotland to help counteract the English threat. But not all welcomed the growth of French influence, and evangelism became increasingly their vehicle. In 1557 a faction of four noblemen and a reformist laird signed a bond undertaking to establish Protestant congregations and godly ministry. The bond was a traditional means of cementing ties of patronage and association in Scottish life, but here it was being put to a revolutionary purpose.

At first the 'Lords of the Congregation' gained few allies. Plenty of room had been left on the bond for additional signatures, but none came forward. Mary of Guise had been tolerant of religious dissent, and few could see the need for all-out confrontation. But now again politics took a hand. In November 1558 the death of Mary Tudor opened the prospect of a Protestant regime south of the border. Protestant exiles were encouraged to return to Scotland, and soon found an audience for their preaching. While John Willock preached to a gathering congregation in Edinburgh, in May 1559 John Knox returned to stir up passions in Perth, St Andrews and Dundee. The Regent was obliged to contemplate sterner action, but by this point the rallying cry of reform seemed increasingly like a patriotic war of liberation against French control. Still, by the end of 1559 French reinforcements seemed to have tipped the balance back towards the regent, and in November the Mass was restored in Edinburgh.

These events faced the English government with an increasingly stark choice: to assist the installation of a friendly Protestant regime dominated by the Lords of the Congregation, or to preserve a cautious neutrality that would allow the regent to re-establish Scotland as a reliable French satellite. Spurred by William Cecil, Elizabeth took the plunge. After months of more discreet financial aid to the rebel lords, in March 1560 English troops crossed the border. This intervention, and the death of Mary of Guise from illness on 11 June, tipped the balance in the insurgents' favour. The Treaty of Edinburgh arranged for the removal of French troops and for a meeting of Parliament to settle matters of religion. Here the Protestants triumphed. The Mass was abolished, and Parliament adopted a Confession of Faith drafted by Knox and his colleagues based closely on the French Reformed Confession.

Protestantism had won through, but the nature of the church that would emerge from these turbulent beginnings would only slowly become evident. The Calvinist church in Scotland was the child of a political revolution; it was not to any great extent underpinned by a broad basis of support in the population at large. The limits of support in the political nation were clearly indicated by the fate of further negotiations in the Scottish Parliament. While the Confession of Faith was formally endorsed, the second foundational document of the new church, the Book of Discipline, was not. This was a detailed blueprint of reform, based closely on the national church order established in France, but adapted to local circumstances. It made provision for a full Calvinist church structure of consistories and colloquies (the Kirk session and presbytery) and the exercise of consistorial discipline. But while Parliament was happy to prohibit the Mass, it had less desire to overturn the structures of an old church that had fully respected the interests of the leaders of Scottish society. This was particularly the case in the important matter of church lands. In the old Scottish church a high proportion of parish endowments had been appropriated by a lay patron or superior church body, and the lairds were not impressed by hints that these incomes should be made available to support the work of the new church. In 1562 a reluctant compromise was agreed – the Thirds of Benefices – which left two-thirds of purportedly clerical incomes in the hands of their previous possessors, and gave one third to the crown for the support of the Reformed clergy. But this was not the limit of the old church's tenacious hold. Monasteries had not been abolished, and surviving members of religious communities lived out their days in full possession of their property, if not their religious observances. While several bishops joined the new church others did not, and they too remained in office; so for a generation the Scottish church was ruled by curious parallel governments, with the old diocesan structure existing alongside the new system of presbyteries and superintendents. To a large extent the progress of the Reformation would depend on the work of an inner core of charismatic preachers, and the level of support they received from local magnates. By the mid 1570s leading towns such as Edinburgh, St Andrews, Stirling and Glasgow were quite effectively evangelized, whereas Aberdeen, in a region dominated by the conservative earls of Huntley, did not even have a kirk session until 1573. Meanwhile Highland society marched to an entirely different drum, confessional choice depending almost entirely on the personal preference of the clan head. Over the course of years Scotland's Calvinist ministers would prove themselves quite adept in accommodating the practices of the faith to Highland custom and belief; a measure of 'acculturization' of which the apparently rigid structures of Calvinism are not always thought capable.

Mary, Queen of Scots

In August 1561, when Mary, Queen of Scots returned to claim her kingdom, she was 18 years old. She had lived almost her entire life at the French court, first as the promised wife of the Dauphin, latterly, briefly, as Queen of France. None could have blamed her if she was now daunted by the prospect that faced her, a young widow entering a kingdom she scarcely knew, whose language was less familiar to her than French. Waiting to receive her was a political nation that had just repudiated both her religion, and the French alliance she embodied. Her prospects in France must have been gloomy indeed for this to have been more alluring.

In fact, on her return Mary accommodated herself to these difficult circumstances with considerable spirit. The religious settlement recently concluded was scrupulously honoured. Mary made no secret of her personal devotion to the Catholic faith, but also no real effort to proselytize. The first four years of her personal reign were remarkably successful. Even in England, where Elizabeth had no reason to forgive Mary's casual reassertion of her claim to the English throne (predicated on Elizabeth's illegitimacy), Scotland slipped down the political agenda.

Then, in a three-year period between 1565 and 1567, everything went horribly wrong. In March 1565 Mary married her cousin, Henry, Lord Darnley. Although the union was soon blessed with issue – a son, the future James VI, was born in June 1566 – the full political disadvantages of the marriage were quickly manifest. Elizabeth of England took a dim view of an alliance that further strengthened Mary's claim to her throne (Darnley was a great-grandson of Henry VII, a far from obscure relationship in a family blessed with so few close kin). Darnley's Catholicism, and his evident influence over his young bride, alienated the Scottish nobility, particularly the influential and respected Earl of Moray. Lastly, and most compellingly, Darnley's own faults of character were soon a political issue in their own right. Arrogant, volatile and dissolute, Darnley's erratic behaviour alienated both his wife and the Scottish nobility. In March 1566 his estrangement from Mary was sealed when he lent his aid to a mean-spirited conspiracy to murder the queen's Italian secretary, David Rizzio. Darnley's own elimination was not long to follow. In 1567 he was assassinated at Holyrood Palace at the climax of a bizarre and half-bungled conspiracy (the building was blown up, but Darnley's body found strangled outside). Mary's involvement was widely suspected, but not proved; the queen then squandered what remained of her limited political capital by marrying the leader of the regicides, the Earl of Bothwell. Mary and her new husband had little force to put against the now openly rebellious lords; returned to Edinburgh as a prisoner, she was swiftly transferred to prison in the remote island castle of Loch Leven. Although, after 11 months' captivity, she contrived to escape, the loyalists that returned to her side were easily defeated by the forces of Moray, now appointed regent for the infant James since her formal deposition. Mary had little alternative but to seek safety in flight, and for some reason she chose the long ride to England, rather than a boat to France. It was an unfathomable, and ultimately fatal, mistake.

Mary's arrival was a further complication for an English government toiling under the pressure of events in an increasingly hostile world. The heady optimism of the first years was now thoroughly dissipated. The foreign policy triumph in Scotland had been followed by a disastrous intervention in France on behalf of Huguenot allies who promptly abandoned the English force sent to assist them. The defeated English expedition brought back plague to London and harsh lessons for Elizabeth. Relations with Philip of Spain had also worsened since he had gallantly offered to make Elizabeth his bride in place of the deceased Mary. Trade wars between England and the Netherlands had led to a total embargo on the export of unfinished cloth to Antwerp (a trade vital to the English economy). Philip for his part was increasingly exasperated by the welcome afforded to Protestant refugees from the Low Countries. When, in 1566, returning exiles played a major role in fomenting the Dutch Revolt, his patience was exhausted. The arrival of Mary, Queen of Scots, still the focus of the hopes of those who dreamed of a Catholic succession, could hardly have come at a worse time. Instead of a triumphal progress to the English court, Mary was allowed to come no further south than Carlisle castle, as Elizabeth sought advice how to proceed.

With Mary in England a final fatal catalyst, the tensions building through the decade now threatened to overwhelm the Elizabethan regime. In 1569 the pent up hostility against the queen's Protestantism found voice in the rising of the Northern Earls. The following year the pope, Pius V, sent belated encouragement to the rebels by pronouncing Elizabeth's excommunication and deposition. In 1571 the Ridolphi plot, the first of a series of conspiracies aimed at the queen's assassination, was revealed and thwarted. The complicity or at least tacit approval of Philip II and the Pope was widely suspected.

Somehow, Elizabeth and Cecil weathered the storm; and then they began to fight back. In 1572 the Duke of Norfolk, first noble of England and a stalwart of the old faith, paid the ultimate penalty for permitting his name to be linked with that of Mary, Queen of Scots, at the head of an alternative Catholic regime. Despite the almost universal clamour that Mary should share his fate, Elizabeth preferred for the moment to leave her in the genteel captivity to which she had been consigned since the stage-managed 'trial' for complicity in Darnley's murder had shredded her reputation without finally resolving the question of her guilt. Elizabeth, in effect, was offering her royal prisoner a stark choice: either accept that her political life was at an end, or realize that any further meddling in England's affairs would have deadly consequences.

Elizabeth and her Parliaments

A striking feature of the crisis of these years is the extent to which the dramatic events surrounding Mary and Norfolk were played out with the full involvement of the political nation. The evidence of Norfolk's treason was presented not only to his trial, but to a meeting of peers in the Star Chamber, and of the citizens of London in the Guildhall, while pamphlets carried the news to the country at large. The parliamentary session of 1572 witnessed a carefully orchestrated campaign for new treason laws to protect the person of the queen. Various drastic measures were advanced, including the execution of Mary; in the event Elizabeth prorogued Parliament with the matter unresolved, but the debate had served its purpose. The political nation had been reminded of the extent to which the queen, in her person, embodied England's future security.

Elizabeth was not always so keen to hear the opinions of her loyal subjects. In the first months of the new reign the central business of the day, the establishment of the religious settlement, had almost been derailed in Parliament (though by the recalcitrance of the House of Lords, rather than by the enthusiasm of the Commons, as was once thought).[4] Those who regarded the religious settlement of 1559 as unfinished business consistently looked to Parliament to move the matter forward. Various unofficial measures of reform were pursued through the sessions of 1563 and 1566, climaxing in the great Puritan programme of 1571 and 1572. Bills advanced in these years would have taken action against absenteeism and non-preaching clergy, reformed the *Book of Common Prayer*, and, most radical of all, allowed parishes to abandon its use altogether in favour of the strictly Reformed liturgy of the Dutch and French churches in London.

The political nation also showed a prolonged, and to Elizabeth's view, insolent interest in the issue of her marriage. After encouraging petitions early in the reign, opinion turned full circle when, later in life, the queen seemed resolved to take as her husband Francis of Anjou, brother to the king of France. The prospect of this union was by now abhorrent to many, and the queen eventually backed away, contenting herself with exacting a cruel vengeance on the author and publisher of a famous pamphlet against the marriage, Stubbs's *A Gaping Gulf.*

A recapitulation of these famous confrontations – and the House of Commons witnessed further attempts at religious reform as late as 1584 – should not blind us to the largely consensual nature of the vast proportion of parliamentary activity. As far as the queen was concerned the principal function of Parliament was the granting of taxation, and would only be summoned when this became necessary. Parliament in fact met less frequently under Elizabeth than had been the case in the reigns of Edward and Mary: an average of once every three and a quarter years. But this was still, by European standards, remarkably frequent, and during the sixteenth century the English Parliament matured into a role in government unique among European assemblies in a sovereign nation state. The English Parliament was remarkable both for the range and extent of its legislation, and for the persistence of its voice in the affairs of the nation. The English Reformation, for instance, was a series of transformations effected and enacted entirely through Statute. This, and the fact that Henry VIII frittered away in military adventures the windfall income (from the dissolution of the monasteries) that might have given the monarchy a more permanent freedom of manoeuvre, earned it a permanent place in government. The crown accepted this because it was a relationship of mutual benefit. Only the crown could summon Parliament. And if it did so initially to secure taxation, this also offered the opportunity to explain royal policy, to orchestrate demonstrations of solidarity, and to take the temperature of the political nation.

In return, members of Parliament sought statutory regulation of an increasing range of issues and problems. For its members, meetings of Parliament were both an onerous obligation and an opportunity. The parliamentary session could be both expensive and uncomfortable, and many members would absent themselves before the end. But many had arrived with a legislative agenda of their own: seeking benefits for their local community, trade or commercial interests, or for themselves. Most bills introduced in Tudor parliaments were private measures of one sort or another, and the growth in the volume and complexity of legislation was mirrored by a growth in the House of Commons itself (343 members in 1547, rising to 462 in 1601). With so much at stake few boroughs of any size were content for their voice not to be heard. If the sixteenth century thus witnessed a vast increase of legislatory intervention in many different areas of life, this was largely at the behest of representatives themselves. Apart from the regulation of trade and manufacturing processes (a concern of mediaeval parliaments) Parliament now gave increasing attention to social issues. No fewer than 13 bills were presented to Elizabethan Parliaments to address the problems posed by drunkenness and taverns. The greatest monument to this fretful concern for good order and good morals was the Elizabethan Poor Law, which evolved out of a process of trial and error, and repeated legislative initiatives. The structures that emerged, for the care of the poor and indigent and discouragement of the 'sturdy beggar', would form the basis of the English Poor Law until the nineteenth century.

The Conflict with Spain

The crisis of 1568–72 placed international events at the heart of the government agenda. After these years Elizabeth and her councillors could hardly ignore the evidence that the most powerful forces ranged against Protestantism on the continent also wished England ill. As France and the Netherlands plunged repeatedly into conflict over the following decade, discerning England's true interests became ever more tortured and difficult.

For all that, it would be another 16 years before conflict with Spain was fully joined, with the despatch of the Spanish Armada in 1588. Whether this should be treated as a triumph of English foreign policy is a matter for debate. It is at least arguable that had England intervened much earlier to assist the Dutch in their rebellion – in 1572, for instance, or after the Pacification of Ghent in 1576 – she could have done so in far more advantageous circumstances. This was the course of action consistently urged on Elizabeth by a powerful faction among her advisors, including Sir Thomas Walsingham and the Earl of Leicester. These councillors were by this point fully convinced that the enmity of Spain was confirmed and unalterable. That they were right can now be documented from Philip's own private papers, which reveal that as early as 1574 he was fully determined on the destruction of the heretical regime in England.

Yet Elizabeth hesitated, blowing hot and cold with the Dutch. She would turn a blind eye to the Calvinist fugitives who used England as a base for their operations, yet stopped always one step short of open support. The queen was undoubtedly deeply influenced by the experience of 1562–3, when, flushed with success in Scotland, she had committed troops to assist the French Huguenots; only to have them make a separate peace and then join forces with the French royal army besieging the English expeditionary force in Le Havre. And it must be said that for much of the period the Dutch rebel cause looked so desperate as to render it a poor investment. Yet the result of Elizabeth's policy was that Philip was thoroughly alienated – for the Spanish ambassador in London was fully aware of the covert English aid to the Dutch refugees – without England having struck a serious blow at Spanish power. Elizabeth was finally forced to intervene when Dutch fortunes were at their lowest ebb, to prevent the rebels' total destruction. As a result England faced the Armada, three years later, with her military force stretched to capacity and the treasury virtually empty.

Figure 22 Roanoke, from Thomas Hariot, *Narratio Virginae*, Frankfurt, 1590. Courtesy St Andrews University Library.

The Netherlands was not the only source of irreconcilable tension between England and Spain. While England harboured Flemish rebels, Spain fomented discord in Ireland, with two small expeditionary forces in 1579 and 1580. But this was also a conflict that was no longer confined exclusively to the European theatre. For almost from the beginning of the reign English mariners had challenged Spain in that part of her empire that was most vital in underpinning the whole structure of its global economy: the New World.

In 1562 the well-connected West Country merchant adventurer John Hawkins had embarked on the first of a series of slave-trading expeditions, shipping Africans from West Africa to the Caribbean, where they were sold on to Spanish settlers. Both legs of this trade infringed a Spanish monopoly, and Hawkins's activities spurred furious Spanish protests. But a second expedition went ahead in 1564, this time with the financial backing of the queen. When a third fleet was trapped in the roadstead of Vera Cruz, San Juan de Ulúa, and badly mauled by the Spanish fleet, the full consequences of this enterprise were clear for all to see. Yet as relations with Spain deteriorated further in the 1570s, English encroachment became more serious and more openly confrontational. Between 1570 and 1577 at least 13 English expeditions to the Caribbean were mounted, all unofficial and all unlicensed. Some, like Drake's first voyages to the Isthmus of Panama in 1570 and 1571, were clearly more geared to plunder than trade. The third expedition of 1573 succeeded in waylaying a mule-train of bullion outside Nombre de Dios, and a small fortune found its way back to England.

In large measure these voyages were opportunistic, fuelled by greed and hopes of plunder; but they were also ideological. Many of the mariners came from West Country stock, men who nursed deep-seated hatreds against Spain and Catholicism. Francis Drake in particular was imbued with a passionate Protestant faith. A Spanish prisoner captured during one of his expeditions offers an arresting account of divine service on board his fleet. It began with prayer and an hour of Psalm-singing, after which Drake sent for the ship's copy of Foxe's *Book of Martyrs* and angrily harangued his startled prisoner on the illustrations.[5]

As relations with Spain deteriorated further, Drake's passion became an important instrument of state. In 1577 he set out with a new fleet, the costs of which had been underwritten by many of the leading

Figure 23 Drake's attack on Cartegena, from Hieronymi Bezoni, *Americae*, Frankfurt, 1599. Courtesy St Andrews University Library.

members of the Court. The destination was Peru, but having rounded
the Cape of Good Hope (the first English vessel to accomplish the
notorious southern passage) Drake sailed on to complete his famous
circumnavigation of the globe. In 1585 Sir Walter Raleigh's Virginia
expedition opened up a new front in Spanish territory with the
Roanoke venture. But with English troops about to embark for the
Netherlands, the focus of the conflict now switched back to Europe.
Drake's audacious raid on Cadiz in 1587 performed one last signal
service, mauling the assembled shipping sufficiently to delay the fleet a
full year. But by 1588 the Armada was ready to sail.

The Spanish Armada would fail, but the issue was in doubt until the
last moment: as indeed was its real strategic purpose. Was the Armada
indeed intended for the conquest of England, or merely to force a
chastened Elizabeth out of the Dutch war?[6] Whatever the intention,
the stakes were high and the forces formidable. When Medina Sidonia
set sail from Lisbon he commanded a fleet of over 130 vessels, including the cream of the Portuguese ocean fleet. They faced in the Channel
some 140 English vessels, including some 18 galleons of the queen's
fleet, with assorted barks and pinnaces. A fleet battle of this sort was
unprecedented in European history, and so, unsurprisingly, indecisive.
The Spanish Armada made its rendezvous with Parma off the Flanders
coast, and it was only here that a combination of English fireships and
Channel gales decided the conflict. The English fleet now commanded
the Channel, so the Armada had no choice but to make its way home
by the inhospitable northern route round the British Isles and Ireland.
Some 50 vessels were lost on these rocky shores before the remnant of
the fleet limped home.

It was a stupendous victory, though the consequences were felt
more in continental Europe than at sea. The defeat of the Armada
tipped the scales against Spain in the French and Dutch conflicts, but
the terms of the sea war were not radically altered. An attempt to carry
the war into the enemy camp by seizing Lisbon in 1589 ended in
confusion and farce. Hereafter English mariners sought in vain for the
killer blow that would humble Spanish power at sea a second time.
These years revealed the limitations of the public–private partnership
that was the characteristic creation of Elizabethan sea power. However
effective this was for the sort of predatory voyaging that had so
angered Spain in the early years of the reign, the active pursuit of
openly declared war required greater discipline and clearer lines of
command. An age of true naval greatness would await the development of a fully professional navy in the two centuries that followed.

The End of an Era

In truth, the last decade of the sixteenth century was a difficult time for Elizabethan England. The war in Europe consumed resources on a vast scale, and there were no other spectacular successes like the defeat of the Armada to raise spirits. In addition, the crown was obliged to wage war on a second front: a difficult, prolonged and apparently insoluble conflict in Ireland, which proved dirty, expensive and utterly demoralizing. Parliament, exasperated by repeated and escalating calls for funds, turned its fire on the court. A particular source of anger were the monopolies on the manufacture and distribution of new products, imported luxuries and even staple goods distributed by the crown to favoured courtiers in lieu of grants of land or pecuniary reward. By the end of the century such a system, which had once served to protect fledgling technologies, was largely discredited and the two Parliaments of 1597 and 1601 demanded action to rein them in. Sir Walter Raleigh, it was discovered, enjoyed monopolies on tin, playing cards and the licensing of taverns; it was hard to see how any of these had brought economic benefit to the commonwealth. Mutinous MPs wondered when the crown would grant some favoured courtier a monopoly on bread. Faced with such a torrent of criticism, the government was forced to curb the system's worst excesses.

These years were difficult for Elizabeth personally. The queen was now in her sixties, and all the art and science of the age – even the well-paid flattery of court painters – could not disguise a physical deterioration. One by one, her old trusted servants had pre-deceased her: Leicester in 1588, Walsingham in 1590, even the venerable Burghley finally in 1598. Although a perfectly capable new generation was on hand to take their place, Elizabeth was personally susceptible to active, handsome young men who by their physical presence reminded her of her glory days. Favourites of an earlier age, like Raleigh and Sir Christopher Hatton, were not without energy and merit, but her encouragement of the Earl of Essex was to prove a costly mistake. Essex tragically mistook favour for influence, and an unequal power struggle with the younger Cecil, Robert, now installed at the heart of government, led to a foolish rebellion, disgrace and execution. The brutal repudiation of her last protégé was a final reminder for Elizabeth of the loneliness of power. As she clung to the remnants of life, her loyal councillors discreetly prepared for the next reign.

Nevertheless, if the last years of the reign could not mask a certain sense of stagnation and decay at the heart of government, this was not an era devoid of achievement. The religious controversies that had beset the middle years of the reign had now receded. Most Protestants who remained within the church had now reconciled themselves to the imperfections of the Elizabethan settlement, freeing the bishops to harry those on the wilder fringes whose pursuit of godly utopias commanded little public or political support. Puritanism had given way to separatism. The effect of this change would be felt mostly in the new century, and in the New World. For Puritans the English church was increasingly something to be cherished and defended rather than importunately denounced. For the trials of the last three decades had secured England's Protestant identity. Through a generation of conflict in which the enemy had been foreign, Catholic and dangerous, English people had come to identify their church, their Protestantism, as a cornerstone of their identity; but this was not manifested necessarily in any profound grasp of the theological tenets of faith. While English readers seem to have been avid consumers of catechisms and other cheap volumes of religious instruction, their clergy, as elsewhere in Europe, continued to lament how shallow was their grasp of doctrine. But the identification could be more subtle and oblique, but still very real. The Catholic festival year, for instance, had been gradually superseded by a calendar of new, largely unofficial and profoundly Protestant patriotic festivals: the defeat of the Armada and 'Crownation' day, the date of Elizabeth's accession. In 1605 they would be joined by 5 November, the date of the discovery of the Gunpowder Plot, proof, if proof were needed, that Catholicism was still perfidious, deadly, and deeply un-English.[7]

This was also a golden age for the arts. For most of the sixteenth century England had lagged behind the continent. It was an accepted fact before the arrival of Hans Holbein that to have a decent portrait painted it was necessary to go abroad, and for all the gritty intellectualism of its two universities, in the 1560s England was still regarded as a cultural desert. When in 1563 the scholar Robert Ascham ventured to send greetings to Pierre Ramus in Paris, he was rewarded with a monumental put-down: 'Who in Britain', mused the philosopher, 'could possibly be such an admirer of me that he could take the trouble to forward good wishes across the very ocean and all the way to Paris?'[8]

The 40 years of Elizabeth's reign changed all this. In this time a talented generation of poets, painters and dramatists succeeded in moving English letters away from a tradition of servile imitation that had characterized the arts to this date. With Spenser, Marlowe and latterly Shakespeare, the English language had found its own distinctive voice. In assessing the significance of this phenomenon it is necessary to look beyond the enduring genius of Shakespeare to other less celebrated playwrights: to Kyd, whose *Spanish Tragedy* beguiled London audiences with a historical wish-fulfillment of the extinction of the hated crowns of Aragon and Castile; or Christopher Marlowe. An interesting case in point is Marlowe's *Massacre of St Bartholomew's Day*, not least for what it reveals of the divergent perspectives of the literary critic and the social historian. Literary specialists tend to dismiss the play because it is so bad. But in its own day (1591–2) its tale of Catholic perfidy and the triumph of Henry of Navarre enraptured London playgoers at a time when English troops were ready to embark for France to sustain Henry's cause. Other plays, more notable dramatically, addressed current political issues with more subtlety. Studies of weak kings (Edward II, Richard II) ventilated underlying insecurities for the future of the dynasty that had no place in open political debate. But most of all an expanding range of comedy, tragedy and historical pageant kept an eager audience entertained. The London theatre was revolutionary because it demonstrated that it was possible to write for profit: to make a living from paying customers rather than relying on the generosity of patrons.

A Scottish King

So it was that when Elizabeth expired in 1603 her designated successor would inherit a kingdom whose place in the European political and cultural firmament was now secure. For James VI and I this was a long-awaited apotheosis. But his had been a brutal initiation into power politics. An orphan (or in the case of his reviled and imprisoned mother, almost worse than an orphan) from the age of one, his progress to adulthood had been carefully overseen by magnates who had no wish to see him disturb their own hard won place of power. However, James did succeed in putting his stamp on Scottish government. The years preceding his assumption of personal power (1585) had been characterized by a bewildering series of political convulsions and enervating internecine conflict. In his infant years the 'king's party' faced a number of challenges. Both the Earl of Moray, regent from 1567 to 1570, and his successor Lennox, were murdered, and the eventual victor in this power struggle, the capable Morton, was himself deposed and executed in 1581. On his own assumption of power James had to face the difficult issue of Elizabeth's execution of his mother: filial protests and outrage had to be balanced against the need not to damage his hopes of the English succession.

It is not surprising that the personality that emerged from these trials was a mass of contradictions. Personable and disarmingly casual with his inner circle, James had nevertheless developed a very high view of this kingly office; whether this was in rebellion against the views espoused by his tutor, George Buchanan, or through observation of the political chaos that had preceded him, it is hard to tell. But conservative at heart, James had succeeded very well in keeping the peace among Scotland's magnates in the two decades of his mature kingship, partly because he did not look beyond its natural leaders for his intimate councillors. On the whole, the Scottish political nation wished him well when, in April 1603, he hurried south to claim his inheritance – if only in appreciation of the irony that three centuries of warfare and English bullying should have ended thus.

11

Philip II and the Resolution of the Reformation Conflict

In the second half of the sixteenth century the burden of defending Catholic Europe fell to a quite extraordinary degree on one man, Philip II of Spain. France, Europe's other main Catholic power, was too preoccupied with internal problems; the king's German Habsburg cousins were too immersed in the complex problems of the empire, and, in the case of the emperor Maximilian II, too compromised in their attitudes to Lutheranism. Popes came and went with too great rapidity to offer real leadership. The task of spearheading the Catholic counter-attack fell almost by default to the king of Spain.

Philip was equal to the task. Although he differed from his father, the emperor Charles V, in many aspects of personality, Philip shared with him an utter detestation of heresy. When after the emperor's abdication Philip returned for the first time to Spain, one of his first acts was to preside over a spectacular *auto de fe*. Rather improbably, alleged cells of Lutheran sympathizers had been discovered in Valladolid and other major Spanish cities; among the suspects rounded up by the Inquisition were a number of prominent individuals, men Philip knew well. The king showed them no mercy. As the condemned men were led to their death, one of the most prominent victims, the governor of Toro, Carlos de Seso, called out to the king, 'How could you permit this to happen?' Philip's reply was chilling: 'I would bring the wood to burn my own son, if he were as wicked as you.'[1]

This was a moment that to many seems to encapsulate Philip II: cold, unbending, fanatical. Such a perception has been the staple of historical writing. Few historical figures have been painted in so consistently unsympathetic a light. The denigration of Philip began very early. Even in his own lifetime Philip's alleged crimes and treachery were a staple of the Black Legend of Spanish tyranny, which linked together maltreatment of native populations in the New World, the brutality of Spanish troops, and treacherous Spanish diplomacy in a seamless web. At the centre was the figure of the king, cold and pitiless: a man who would break any promise for political ends, who would order the assassination of opponents, who would even, it was said, contrive the death of his deranged son.

To some extent this caricature is a tribute to Philip's pivotal importance in almost every aspect of the religious conflicts of his age, for the king of Spain was indeed tireless in his efforts to sustain the cause of Catholicism, and uphold his dominions. But in truth, even those who should have been his allies were sometimes uncertain of his motives. Philip characteristically took a high view of his own aims and intentions. 'You can assure his Holiness', he wrote in a letter of 1566 to Don Luis de Requesens, 'that rather than suffer the least injury to religion and the service of God, I would lose all my states and a hundred lives if I had them, for I do not intend to rule over heretics.' But the popes were not always reassured. They saw the Spanish imperialist rather than the Catholic crusader. Sixtus V, pope from 1585–90 and Philip's partner in the Enterprise of England took a more realistic view: 'The King of Spain as a temporal sovereign, is anxious above all to increase his dominions. The preservation of the Catholic religion, which is the principal aim of the Pope, is only a pretext for his Majesty whose principal aim is the security and aggrandizement of his dominions.'[2]

Even today it is by no means easy to separate myth and reality with such a complex and dominant personality. Recent studies of the king have taken sharply differing views of his motives, his personality, and his achievement.[3] The truth is that both Philip and his contemporary critics were right: utterly sincere in his commitment to his faith, Philip was also wholly committed to the defence and enhancement of his dynastic inheritance. In this he was no different from any other ruler of his day. It was because the inheritance was so large, and so powerful, that others of Europe's rulers were drawn inexorably into opposing his designs. For as with his father the emperor, the identification of a common purpose between the defence of the faith and the aggrandizement of his own power seemed more obvious to Philip than to Europe's other crowned heads.

Like the emperor too, Philip's actions were often based far less on long-term calculation than others supposed. Although Philip was well capable of the inexorable patience that contemporaries found so striking, policy-making was for him, like any sixteenth-century ruler, largely reactive: dealing with short-term crises as events crowded in from different parts of extensive and vulnerable dominions. If Philip scarcely enjoyed the luxury of long-term planning, it is nevertheless possible to identify shifting priorities. In broad terms the first full decade of his reign was dominated by the affairs of Spain and the Mediterranean. It was only after this conflict was resolved that Philip could turn the full might of his empire to the resolution of the Reformation conflict in northern Europe.

Return to Spain

For three years after the abdication of Charles V Philip made the Netherlands the centre of imperial government. It was here, in Brussels, that he received investiture of his vast dominions – Castile, Aragon, the Americas, Naples, Sicily and Milan, the Franche-Comté and the Netherlands – and it was here, for the moment, that the most pressing issues demanded his attention. The long conflict with France was reaching its last stages, but one intense burst of fighting (and the morale-boosting victory of St Quentin) lay between Philip and the peace of Cateau-Cambrésis. His marriage to Mary Tudor of England accentuated this northern orientation. Philip had to build this matrimonial alliance into an enduring union without alienating his English subjects, understandably wary at the prospect of being swallowed into the larger Habsburg dominions. He also needed to offer Mary sound counsel in her eager desire to eradicate Protestant heresy in the kingdom. Philip applied himself with characteristic duty to the concerns of these northern realms, but it was already obvious that he was a very different man from his cosmopolitan father. Born and brought up in Spain, he was, by background, thoroughly Hispanicized. A poor linguist, he spoke none of the languages of his other dominions, nor the French of international diplomacy.

It would be wrong, however, to characterize Philip as a reluctant prisoner in the Netherlands. The later Spanish orientation of his reign was one dictated by events rather than by self-indulgence. In his early years as king, Philip thoroughly enjoyed many aspects of the sophisticated life of the Netherlandish court. As a young man he partook eagerly of princely pursuits – dancing, hunting and womanizing – and he would take back with him to Spain many aspects of Netherlandish fashion, court etiquette, and style. But by 1559 the demands of Spain pressed ever more urgently. Much had changed to make his presence in the Netherlands less necessary. His wife Mary Tudor died in November 1558, and her successor Elizabeth politely refused Philip's half-hearted offer of marriage. The war with France was over. Spain, meanwhile, urgently needed its king. The discovery of heresy in the cities of the peninsula in 1557 was a shock that shook Castilian society profoundly, for Spain prided itself on having shown itself impervious to Lutheranism. The regent, Philip's sister Juana, insisted that Philip's presence was necessary if the evil were to be purged.

On his return to Spain Philip gave his full support to the campaign against the enemy within. There is plausible evidence that the threat from Lutheranism had been deliberately exaggerated by the Inquisitor General, Valdés, to shore up his own personal influence, that had previously been on the wane. In the hysteria generated by the revelations, he took the opportunity to move against some high-placed rivals. But Philip would countenance no doubts, even when Valdés sensationally contrived the arrest and imprisonment of Carranza, newly appointed Archbishop of Toledo, and the highest ranking churchman in the land. Several hundred suffered in the purge, and Carranza, despite strenuous protestations of orthodoxy, would remain imprisoned for 17 years.

By giving his full support to the punishment of dissent, Philip gave the clearest possible signal that any deviation from orthodoxy would not be tolerated. The campaign was a success: heresy was purged, and Philip could turn his attention to other serious concerns. These were indeed pressing. Years of warfare had left the treasury drained and state finances in disarray. The patience of the Castilian estates had been stretched to breaking point by constant demands for funds to pursue the war in the north. Philip had little option but to order suspension of payments to creditors, in effect declaring a state bankruptcy. This, the second such suspension in three years, was enormously damaging to the credit of the regime, and Philip was forced to promise prudent management of finances to secure resumption of normal flows of money.

In compromising with taxpayers and bankers Philip had little room for manoeuvre, for a new crisis soon loomed that threatened more than temporary financial embarrassment. In June 1559, before his return to Spain, Philip had given his approval to a Spanish-Italian expedition to carry the fight to the Turks in the Mediterranean. The goal was the capture of Tripoli, but the fleet moved slowly, and it was

March 1560 before the expedition effected the occupation of Djerba, on the North African coast. Here, in May, the Spanish fleet was surprised by the Turks – half the ships were lost, and 10,000 men left captive to be paraded in triumph through the streets of Constantinople. It was the greatest reverse ever suffered by Spanish arms.

The king responded with commendable resolve. Efforts were immediately put in hand both to rebuild a Mediterranean fleet, and to reform its administration. In the meantime the Turks ruled the seas, and Spanish prestige sank low. Philip, sensibly, concentrated his energies on what was within his power to influence. Through the powerful personality of Ruy Gómez (later Prince of Eboli) a firm hand was established on the administration of Castilian government. The king, meanwhile, found solace and domestic contentment in a happy marriage with his third wife, Elizabeth of Valois, promised to Philip as part of the general settlement of peace with France in 1559. An extended trip to Aragon in 1563 succeeded in assuring the loyalties of the fractious and independent Mediterranean kingdoms. Philip was demonstrating a talent for government, and a sensitivity to the needs of his Spanish kingdoms, that gave ample evidence of his maturity as a ruler. He would need all of this experience and resolve in the trials that lay ahead.

The Crisis of the Reign

The year 1565 brought further ill tidings in the Mediterranean. In the spring of that year the island of Malta was attacked by a strong Turkish fleet, and its custodians, the Knights of St John, were soon pushed back to a few isolated fortresses. The fall of this strategic outpost, which dominated the sea lanes between Spain and Italy, seemed imminent. Urgent action was required, and in September a Spanish fleet under Garcia de Toledo was able to relieve the beleaguered knights. Malta was saved and Philip rejoiced; the victory did much to restore his battered prestige. But the problems in the Mediterranean were certainly a preoccupation that prevented Philip from giving proper attention to the looming crisis in the Netherlands. In the early months of 1565 the fractious Netherlandish nobility had sent the most distinguished of their number, the Count of Egmont, to solicit Philip's support for a change of policy. Repression of the now rampant Protestant heresy had failed, and the Netherlandish grandees counselled conciliation. Egmont, the victor of St Quentin, was a personal

favourite of Philip and an old companion in arms. The king was at
pains to treat his representations with courtesy and consideration.
Egmont was led to believe that his embassy had been a success; so
when, after his departure, Philip gave instructions that the heresy laws
were to be rigorously enforced, the count felt betrayed and humiliated.
The grandees took their revenge, withdrew once more from the
Council, and left Margaret of Parma to deal with the rising religious
agitation. By the time Philip was persuaded of the need for limited
concessions, in July 1566, the provinces had already descended into
turmoil.

The horrors of the iconoclasm shook the nobility out of their
complacency and allowed Margaret of Parma to restore control. Philip,
freed of immediate cares in the Mediterranean, could apply his mind to
a permanent pacification. Many among his Spanish advisors urged him
to settle the north in person, and there is little doubt that this is the
course that his father, Charles V, would have followed without hesitation. But Philip hung back; he was resolved to travel north, but only
after pacification was complete. In February 1567 the Duke of Alva,
Spain's most renowned general, was despatched from Italy with
10,000 men to assist Margaret of Parma in this process.

Philip would have had no illusions that Alva, always an advocate of
severity and an uncompromising enemy of all dissent, would have
carried out his instructions with the utmost severity. Arrest began
within days of his arrival; a humiliated Margaret of Parma resigned
and left Alva to his gory task. Philip soon abandoned his stated
intention to follow Alva north. If he had ever truly intended to
renew his acquaintance with his turbulent northern subjects events at
home soon made this impossible. Most urgent of all was the health of
his son, Don Carlos. The prince's erratic behaviour had been the
subject of much gossip as he grew to adulthood, and by 1567 his
emotional instability was too obvious to be ignored. In January 1568
he was placed under confinement; six months later, having ruined his
health with self-inflicted privations, he died. Hostile opinion abroad
was quick to see the king's hand at work, but in truth Philip seems to
have been blameless in what was a terrible family tragedy born of his
son's insanity. Worse was to come. In October, Philip's much loved
young wife, Elizabeth of Valois, also died.

These were dreadful times. In 1568 Alva in the Netherlands was
forced to report an upsurge of resistance, as William of Orange attempted from Germany to restore his own position by force of arms.
Then at Christmas a revolt broke out in Spain itself, in the southern

Figure 24 *Don Carlos.* Courtesy Museo del Prado, Madrid.

Moorish province of Granada. Provoked by an ill-advised attempt to prohibit Moorish customs, language and dress in the province, the revolt could not have come at a worse time, with Turkish power once more looming in the Mediterranean.

A desperate king turned to his young half-brother, Don John of Austria. A brutal war, lasting a full year, finally brought the surrender of the Moors: reprisals continued through 1570. In November Philip decided on drastic measures to prevent the rebel provinces ever again providing a potential fifth column on the Spanish mainland. Eighty thousand inhabitants were expelled from Granada and dispersed through the peninsula.

With the ending of the war in Granada, Philip was ready once again to carry the fight to the enemy. The Turkish occupation of Cyprus in 1570 was enough to convince the Italians that action was necessary. A Holy League of Spain, Venice and the pope was formed to mount a joint naval expedition, again under Don John, to relieve the island. Don John caught up with the Turkish fleet in the Gulf of Lepanto, and here, in a stupendous naval battle between two galley fleets, the Turks were vanquished. The Turks lost 30,000 men and all but thirty of their 230 ships; the Christian losses were a mere 10 ships.

Christendom rejoiced and Philip enjoyed his finest hour. In retrospect, Lepanto would bring no fundamental readjustment of the balance of power in the Mediterranean. The Turkish fleet was quickly rebuilt, and in 1573 Venice would leave the League to make a separate peace. In September 1574 a massive Turkish fleet recaptured Tunis. The war between Spain and the Turk would settle into a cautious equilibrium, formalized in a truce of 1578, renewed annually thereafter. But the most urgent threat to the Spanish sphere of influence in the western Mediterranean had been repulsed, and the general disengagement from active warfare allowed Philip gradually to reorientate his priorities to the north. At home, too, the future seemed somewhat brighter. In December 1571 Philip's new young wife (he had married his niece Anna of Austria in November 1570) produced a male heir, Fernando.[4] The Netherlands appeared peaceful; the New World disgorged a spectacular harvest of silver. In retrospect 1571 must have seemed a rare interlude of optimism and success before the pressure of events began once more to take their toll.

War in the North

Although Alva's harsh regime in the Netherlands had inspired considerable criticism among Philip's Spanish advisors, the king does not seem to have shared their concerns. It was only when in 1572 Alva's heavy hand, and the taxes necessary to pay for the occupation, provoked a new revolt, that Philip began to consider an alternative policy. For a time events continued to play in his favour. The ambitious invasion plans of the irrepressible William of Orange seemed to have been terminally undermined by the destruction of his French allies in the St Bartholomew's Day massacre. When Philip heard news of the massacre he made no secret of his delight. When the French ambassador visited him the following day, the king 'began to laugh, with signs of extreme pleasure and satisfaction'. But a brutal winter of warfare did not succeed in snuffing out the last of the rebellion in Holland, and in 1573 Philip decided to replace Alva with his trusted confidant Don Luis de Requesens. Quite what Requesens was required to do was unclear: Philip seemed unable to decide whether a change of leadership should signal a change of policy. Distant from the Netherlands and bewildered by conflicting advice, the king would increasingly become a prisoner of events.

Indeed, even sympathetic historians of Philip's reign had some difficulty discerning what were, if any, the strategic priorities of these years. It is clear that in Philip's mind, at least, the old amity with England had been abandoned. In 1571 the Spanish ambassador to London became embroiled in a confused conspiracy to assassinate Elizabeth and install Mary, Queen of Scots, as queen (the Ridolphi plot). In 1572 Philip stated in a private despatch, 'What I want is that all the Christian Princes join together against England.' But in 1573 a treaty patched up trade relations with England, Elizabeth reduced aid to the Dutch rebels, and an uneasy peace was restored. In the Netherlands Philip continued to attempt to provide resources for the military subjugation of the rebels, while not discouraging Requesens's overtures for peace. Beset by conflicting advice, the king found solace in supervising a very particular private project: reuniting the bones of his ancestors in the specially constructed vault of his new palace/mausoleum at the Escorial. Through the course of the year a procession of corpses made their solemn way through Spain: his parents Charles V and Isabel from Yuste and Granada, his grandmother, Juana the mad, from Tordesillas. Aunts, former wives and infant brothers were roused

Figure 25   The Escorial. Photo AKG London

out of their final resting places from Granada to Valladolid. They were deposited under the high altar to await construction of the new family vault.

Meanwhile in the Netherlands affairs went from bad to worse. In 1575 the two indecisively pursued and inherently contradictory lines of policy began to unravel. In this year Castilian state finances, always teetering on the brink of calamity, collapsed completely under the weight of multiple commitments. Philip was forced to declare a state bankruptcy, a technical device intended to force creditors to restructure short-term, high interest debt as long term obligations at lower rates. But the immediate effect was to cut off the flow of cash to the army in the Netherlands, with disastrous effect. After a series of mutinies the Spanish troops attacked and sacked Antwerp. The whole of the Netherlands now united to rid the provinces of the foreign armies. Philip's northern policy lay in ruins.

The king was phlegmatic in the face of misfortune. Doggedly he set himself to the task of recapturing the initiative. In place of Don Luis de Requesens, who had died, exhausted, in March, Philip nominated the hero of Lepanto, Don John, to find peace in the Netherlands. To that end he was empowered to concede anything 'saving religion and my obedience'. Thus encouraged, Don John accepted on the king's behalf the terms of the Pacification of Ghent, before in his turn becoming enmired in the treacherous politics of the northern realms. Dispirited and bewildered, Don John resorted once more to arms, and in January 1578 his forces defeated the troops of the Estates at Gembloux. A few months later he died, to be rewarded ultimately with a berth in the family vault at the Escorial.

Don John's military prowess had given loyalists in the Netherlands a breathing space, at the same time that even more enticing opportunities were opening up nearer to home. In 1578 the young, and rather unstable king of Portugal, Sebastian, had led an army that included the cream of the Portuguese nobility in a crusading campaign against the Berbers of Morocco. There, at Alcazar-el-Kebir, his entire army was wiped out. The childless king was among the dead: after Sebastian's great uncle, the old and infirm Cardinal Henry, the next in line to the throne would be none other than Philip of Spain.

The unification of the Iberian crowns would be an enormous prize, and Philip was determined to achieve it. Jurists were sent to Portugal to argue the king's legal claim. Should these arguments fail, an army was mobilized to press the case more directly. When in January 1580 King Henry finally expired, Spanish armies quickly occupied Portugal in Philip's name. This was the final service of the Duke of Alva: in 1582 he died, still basking in the king's renewed favour. Alva's passing removed the last of the great servants whose rivalries had split the court in the first part of Philip's reign. Ruy Gómez, Prince of Eboli, had died in 1573, and his widow had shared the disgrace of Antonio Pérez in 1579. Now Philip was increasingly alone. His much loved fourth wife, Anna of Austria, had died in the influenza epidemic of 1580, and the king did not remarry. The direction of policy was now, more than ever, wholly in the king's hand.

The Armada

Shattered by repeated bereavement and concerned for the fate of his dynasty (the death of his third child, Diego, left only one little son, Philip) the king could hardly afford to retire into private grief. Indeed, the incorporation of the Portuguese crown gave him his best ever chance finally to resolve the problem of northern heresy. In the Netherlands, the military prospects brightened year by year as the Duke of Parma made steady progress with his campaign of reconquest. In 1585 Antwerp fell to his inexorable forces, which finally forced the hand of the reluctant Elizabeth. By the Treaty of Nonsuch English troops were finally committed to the defence of the Dutch revolt.

Historians have, on the whole, been inclined to praise the restraint that kept Spain and England from open conflict until the late 1580s. But all the evidence of Philip's private correspondence suggests that he had decided long before that the final solution of his problems in northern Europe required Elizabeth's eventual removal. As we have seen he expressed such a view as early as 1572, and again in 1574, and although the relationship oscillated back and forth thereafter, by the end of that decade English raids on Spanish possessions in the New World had finally destroyed any hope of peaceful reconciliation. Nevertheless the Treaty of Nonsuch was apparently critical, for it seems to have convinced Philip that the eradication of the English threat must now precede the final subjugation of the Dutch rebels. From that determination the Armada campaign was born.

Patiently as ever, Philip made his depositions. In 1586 he began the laborious task of assembling an invasion fleet. The deep sea galleons inherited from the Portuguese formed the core, and though preparations were interrupted in 1587 by Drake's famous raid on Cadiz, by the year's end a formidable fleet had been collected. The Cadiz raid cost the Armada a year, and its commander, for Santa Cruz died in February 1588, to be replaced by the Duke of Medina Sidonia, a capable military commander who nevertheless had no experience of naval command. Against this the intervening year had brought a further welcome political development with the assertion of Guise power in France. With northern France now effectively under the control of the Catholic League, Spain was assured that the Channel's southern shore would be in friendly hands. On 30 May the Armada left Lisbon, only to be forced into La Coruna by contrary winds. Nevertheless by late July it was underway once more, and on 6 August Medina Sidonia effected his landfall off Calais, ready to take on the expeditionary force to be provided by Parma's army of Flanders.

It was here that the plan began to fall apart. Parma's army was not ready to embark, nor could he easily bring the troops out to the fleet, anchored in deep water off the coast, for the Dutch rebels commanded the shallows between. This crucial stretch of shoaling water that lay between the Armada and the troops to be embarked held the key to the whole campaign – but the Armada, incredibly, had sailed with no coherent instructions as to how this difficulty was to be overcome. Taking advantage of the confusion, the English fleet attacked with fireships. The anchored galleons cut their cables and fled, precipitating a running battle with the English fleet that forced them far into the North Sea. With no chance of beating back to the rendezvous against contrary winds, Medina Sidonia had no alternative but to order his fleet to make their best way back to Spain around the British Isles. Half the fleet, and 15,000 men, were lost in the process.

The Last Years

The Armada expedition was a strategic disaster, and Philip could not evade responsibility. It was bad enough that the battle plan was itself crucially flawed, leaving the critical juncture of troops and fleet largely in the hands of fate. There is no evidence that Philip had even clearly considered what Parma's troops would do if they had safely achieved a bridgehead. The king took the news with his usual stoicism, but there was no doubt that the damage to Spanish prestige was enormous. The reverse left Philip diminished, both in the eyes of friends and enemies abroad, and of his own subjects. A replacement fleet was swiftly built, but for the moment the English seemed to command the seas. Philip's enemies took courage, and the defeat of the Armada led to a rapid deterioration of the general strategic situation in northern Europe. In France, Henry III's strike against the Guise (barely conceivable had the Armada not failed) and his own subsequent assassination brought to the throne Henry of Navarre, as sure an enemy of Spain as the Catholic League had been Philip's reliable ally. Philip was now obliged to commit military resources in a desperate attempt to prevent Henry securing his crown; this in turn further undermined Parma's situation in the Netherlands. Now at least Philip was prepared to entertain talk of conceding limited toleration for the rebellious provinces in the northern Netherlands, but it was too little, too late. Increasingly confident of their ability to match the Spanish troops in the field of war, the rebels had no need of concessions. When, in 1593, Henry announced his conversion and effectively thereby assured the pacification of France, Philip was powerless. Henry capped his triumph by declaring war on Spain.

These were also difficult and dispiriting years within Spain itself. The flight of the former state secretary Antonio Pérez, in captivity since his fall from grace in 1579, provoked a conflict in Aragon that soon turned into a fully fledged rebellion. Pérez, a native Aragonese, sought protection from the liberties of the kingdom, and he found support from local nobles inflamed by Philip's attempt to override local jurisdiction by inciting the Inquisition to pursue Pérez on a trumped up charge of heresy. The revolt was eventually suppressed with great pains and some brutality; even then Pérez evaded the fate of many of his supporters, finding sanctuary first in France and then in England. Even Castile, which had responded to the defeat of the Armada with a generous grant of taxation, was by now restive. In 1593 the Cortes of Castile granted new supply only on conditions that would almost have created a contractual constitutional relationship between king and assembly. Not surprisingly, this was the last time the Cortes was summoned during the reign.

These tribulations took a heavy toll on the king. For many years before he had suffered from poor health: gout, the scourge of the Habsburgs, had afflicted him since the mid 1560s, and the passing of the years added a litany of painful and debilitating conditions. Worn down by successive bereavements and calamities, Philip became increasingly reclusive. He returned from Aragon in 1593 scarcely able to conduct business or even to write. The cardinal Archduke Albert (later ruler of the southern Netherlands) was summoned from Lisbon, in effect as regent. In March 1594 Philip made his last will. Although he would linger on a further four years, it was as a virtual invalid. Power passed gradually to the son, Philip, who would succeed him. The king lived just long enough to see the conclusion of a peace with France, the Peace of Vervins, that many contemporaries regarded as the most humiliating acknowledgement of defeat ever conceded by such a proud people. It was, in effect, a total capitulation to a rampant Henry IV. The Netherlands, meanwhile, were made over to the government of Albert and Isabella (Philip's last daughter), who were to marry and rule as joint sovereigns. The proud empire that Philip had fought to hard to protect was crumbling as he lay dying.

12

New Worlds

In the longer term there would be no development more momentous for European society than the assertion of sovereignty over other continents, begun in this era. Yet if we confine ourselves narrowly to the period itself, the impact of voyages of discovery is less certain. For the ruling elites of Spain, Portugal and other places that enjoyed the riches of the new conquests, the impact was profound; in Europe as a whole, much less so.

For all the imaginative scholarship devoted to this subject, it is in fact extremely difficult to assess accurately how far the discovery of unknown lands beyond Europe would have impacted on the European consciousness during the sixteenth century. There are many reasons for this that go beyond the obvious limitations of the records, and a difficulty in discerning how fast or deeply knowledge spread. In fact, Europeans already had a highly developed consciousness of the lands beyond their own continent – unknown lands, nevertheless fully populated by the fabulous tales of Marco Polo and John de Mandeville. De Mandeville's immensely popular (fictitious) narratives peopled the worlds he discovered with headless men with eyes in their shoulders, monsters and voracious cannibals. Marco Polo was more careful, and perhaps one had to come from his own mercantile background to be truly fascinated by his endless computations of wealth and suspiciously precise computation of the tax revenues of far away empires (though such readers also knew enough to expose his frauds). In any case, there is no doubt which was the more popular: to judge by the surviving manuscripts of de Mandeville, of which over 300 survive from before the age of print.[1]

The fictions of the great travelogues were willingly perpetuated by the first cartographers, who filled the empty spaces of distant lands with monsters and prodigies. The deeps of the ocean were replete with sea monsters. Such perceptions were surprisingly tenacious. Guillaume Le Testu, author of the influential *Cosmographie Universelle*, had no hesitation in describing Africa as a continent populated with snakes 700 feet long, basilisks that could kill a man at a glance, satyrs, 'Blemmyae', that is men with no heads, and 'Cynocephalics', or dog-heads (note the pseudo-scientific terminology). And this work dates from 1556, long after the oceanic voyages had begun to open up the real wonders of distant continents. Here the imaginative author could

Figure 26 Monstrous peoples and serpents, from Sebastian Münster, *Cosmographia Universalis*. Courtesy St Andrews University Library.

draw on what Europe's peoples felt represented the outer reaches and dark places of their own world. Europe's citizens certainly would not have felt they needed to go far afield to experience the strange and terrifying. Their own backwoods – mountains and forests where most would scarcely dare tread – were filled with creatures and demons of terrifying, scarcely human shape.

Through the overland trade with the East, Europeans were already in contact with the wonders of far-away civilizations. They knew not to underestimate the sophistication of these distant societies, and they knew to value the precious goods that filtered through into European markets. The strange and the exotic were part of their appeal – and much prized when unusual artefacts could be brought back and displayed. Strange and exotic beasts from the East were a subject of great curiosity when they were brought to Europe, and eagerly studied and collected. Most of Europe's principal rulers maintained a menagerie, none of them better and more various than that of the kings of Portugal, with their privileged access to the great beasts of Africa and Asia. When King Manuel I was desirous to conciliate a new pope, Leo X, in 1514, he had the happy inspiration to send to Rome as a congratulatory gift a small elephant. The gift caught the imagination of a delighted pontiff, and indeed all who beheld him. The arrival of the elephant in Italy caused such a sensation that huge excited crowds gathered to view the animal as it plodded down the road to Rome. They so delayed the progress of the Portuguese embassy, thronging round the startled animal to gawk and clamour, that the ambassador began to fear for the elephant's safety.[2]

In some respects then Europeans already had a strong sense of the world beyond: a strange, incalculable mixture of the mythical, the fanciful and the dimly experienced. The first explorers had a difficult task making their experiences match up to these exaggerated expectations. Some of the first popular travel writers to experience the Indies and Americas pandered shamelessly to the appetite for the outlandish, in accounts of their discoveries that strayed far towards pure invention. Others, more scrupulous, were at pains to emphasize that the peoples they encountered were men like themselves, despite curiosities of dress, custom and demeanour. The debate around the humanity of the savage was one of the most crucial, and often far from disinterested, aspects of the European encounter with the New World.

Yet for all the prejudice, presuppositions and often downright cruelty that they brought to these New World encounters, it is hard not to admire the sheer courage of those who braved the endless, unknown deep waters in search of new lands. Dangerous voyages over mountainous seas in tiny vessels at the mercy of fickle winds – such enterprises required men of a rare stamp and reckless courage. It is perhaps unrealistic to expect of those who pursued such voyages, and the scarcely less terrifying journeys into the interior that conquered kingdoms, the sensitivities and curiosity of the cultural anthropologist.

Pioneering Voyages

In opening up worlds beyond the Atlantic coasts, the peoples of Europe would owe an incalculable debt to the seafarers of Portugal. The Iberian kingdom, with its rugged extended coastline and lush coastal habitat to a large extent already lived from the sea. The technical refinements that made possible longer voyages were the product largely of their hard-won experience. In the fifteenth century the Portuguese had made steady progress in expanding the coastal and island regions known to Europeans. In 1415 a Portuguese army captured Ceuta in Morocco, and with this embarked on a progressive discovery of the West African coast. Ships driven off this coast chanced upon the important Atlantic islands, and these were progressively explored and colonized: Madeira, the Azores and the Cape Verdes. By the 1460s the Portuguese had reached the Gulf of Africa and Sierra Leone. As they pressed south and into the interior they may have learned that the Indian Ocean was accessible from the sea: a momentous discovery that was then confirmed by the audacious voyage of Bartolomeu Dias, who in 1488 rounded the Cape of Good Hope. In the last years of the old century Vasco da Gama at last confirmed the hope of this optimistic name by pressing on around the Cape to reach India. A decade later the Portuguese were in China.

The rapid and astonishing success of these voyages reveals the intelligent sense of direction and purpose that lay behind them. The major expeditions were sponsored by the crown; their clear and unclouded intention to appropriate a large part of the rich eastern trade. With this end in view another brilliant seaman and royal servant, Afonso de Albuquerque, in the second decade of the century laid the basis of empire, taking Goa, in India (1510), the vital Malacca (1511) and Hormuz on the horn of Arabia (1515). These conquests set the tone for the Portuguese settlements, which would be a network of strategic trading ports rather than colonies. The Portuguese had neither the men, nor the resources to establish a colonial empire. They achieved what was an astonishing success for such a small kingdom because they were not deflected from the original intentions of the exploration by a surprisingly easy success. Whether they could make good the claim of right against other greedy and ambitious powers only time would tell.

In the last decade of the fifteenth century the lure of the East excited many others, including the Genoese seaman Christopher Columbus. Most likely he knew nothing of the important voyage of Bartolomeu Dias. Rather, his cartographical and cosmographical researches had inspired in him a conviction that a bold westward voyage across the empty ocean beyond the Azores would open up a new route to the east.

The son of a weaver, Columbus's obscure early years seem to have been consumed by a search for social respectability. His restless ambition led him towards two of the best possible routes for fame and social advancement: books and the sea. From seafaring he learned of the Portuguese discoveries of the Atlantic islands; from books he acquired enough learning to be able to support his projects for voyages of exploration with written authorities in his long and painful search for sponsors. The arguments he advanced were various and changing, and at first they fell on deaf ears. It was only in the euphoria generated by the conquest of Granada that his chosen royal patrons, Ferdinand and Isabella, were prepared to offer the financial backing that allowed Columbus to mount his first momentous voyage.

In August 1492 Columbus set sail from Palos with his tiny fleet: three small ships, two (the Pinta and the Niña) provided by the port in quittance of a fine owed to the royal treasury. Striking south to the Canaries (a choice crucial to his success, opening up the possibility of a following wind), the fleet struck out due west. After 33 days of anxious sailing his ships sighted land in the Bahamas. In three months of pleasant cruising round the islands, Columbus alighted on Hispaniola and, at last, found gold, before the loss of his flagship, the Santa María, necessitated a rapid return home.

On arrival in Spain Columbus hastened to the royal court at Barcelona, where his exhibits (natives and gold trinkets) were enough to convince his royal patrons that discoveries of significance had been made. Unfortunately an initial landfall at Lisbon had also alerted the shrewd Portuguese king, and with two major powers now committed to exploration the necessity of agreed lines of demarcation was apparent. The result was the Treaty of Tordesillas, agreed with the help of a complaisant Spanish pope, Alexander VI, and intended to separate a Portuguese zone of influence from Africa eastwards from the Spanish

Figure 27 Columbus. Courtesy St Andrews University Library.

westward explorations. At the last moment the Portuguese succeeded in pushing the line of demarcation 275 leagues westward, on the grounds that their ships were often forced to sail far out into the Atlantic to catch favourable winds for the southern voyage. Though they did not know it this would ultimately give them rights to the as yet undiscovered territories of Brazil.

In 1493 Columbus sailed again with a vastly larger fleet of 17 assorted caravels and pinnaces manned by some 1,200 men. This itself was sufficient proof of the prestige, and great hopes, invested in his discoveries. A swift voyage brought the fleet to Dominica and thence to Hispaniola, where Columbus established a settlement, Isabella. But as the scale of his ambitions increased, so his problems multiplied. Columbus was an explorer of genius and insight, but as a colonial governor his skills never matched his vaunting ambition. The settlement was poorly sited and badly led. By the time Columbus returned to Spain in 1496 it had effectively failed. Although there was nothing to show for their sizeable investment in this second voyage, Columbus still had enough credit with the Catholic monarchs to win support for a new expedition in 1498. Now at least he discovered the vast continent of South America; but the collapse of the colony of Hispaniola led to his removal and return to Spain in disgrace. A succession of tough minded agents of the crown now began the settlement of the Caribbean islands in earnest. New expeditions first consolidated the troubled Hispaniola (1502), then Jamaica (1509) and Cuba (1511). From these secure bases other Spanish voyagers discovered and prospected the isthmus of central America. In 1513 Vasco Núñez de Balboa led an expedition through the tropical forests of Panama to gaze, for the first time, on the Pacific.

The Conquest of America

Of all the great histories of European expansion, nothing is so extraordinary as the destruction of the great empires of Mexico and South America. The Mexican empire of the Aztecs and the Inca dominion of Peru were two of the world's great civilizations, as even those who destroyed them recognized: cultured and sophisticated, rich and socially intricate. From their base in the valley of Mexico, the Aztecs had by 1500 created a well-settled dominion that stretched from the Pacific to the Caribbean. A population of around 20 million was divided between prosperous villages and great cities such as the capital Tenochtitlán, a marvel that amazed all who saw it. Their carefully organized territories were unified by networks of roads and imperial institutions as sophisticated as anything then evident in Europe.

In retrospect historians have managed to explain, if not explain away, the Spanish triumph. They cite their use of horses and dogs (unknown to the local inhabitants), the co-operation of local enemies of the ruling power, the ravages of western diseases, even the pessimistic nature of Aztec religion. But none of this should detract from the sheer mind-numbing improbability of what was achieved by two tiny expeditionary forces, led by men whose ruthlessness was matched only by a level of greed and ambition that blinded them to the overwhelming likelihood of defeat. It is a truly extraordinary tale, both in its accomplishment, and in the magnitude of its consequences.

At the time of the expedition to Mexico its leader, Hernán Cortés, was a man of established reputation in the new settlements. He had taken part in the conquest of Cuba under Diego Velázquez, and risen

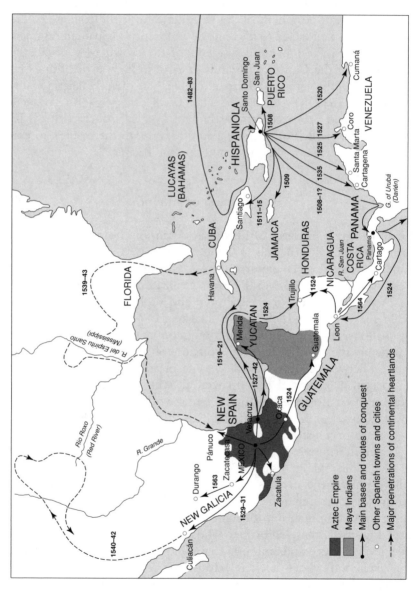

Map 6 The Spanish Conquests in North and Central America.

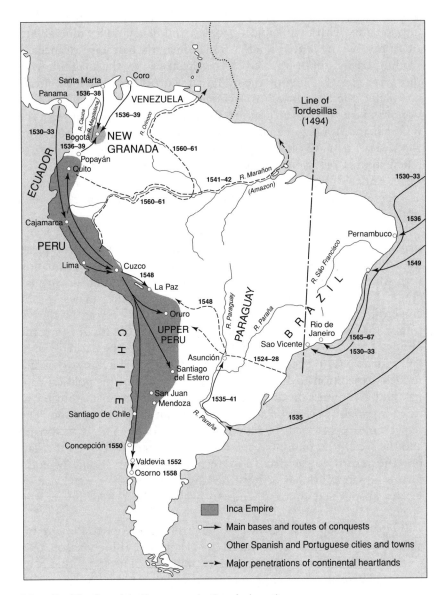

Map 7   The Spanish Conquests in South America.

to a position of responsibility in the local administration. When in 1518 Velázquez appointed him to lead a new expedition to the mainland, Cortés seized the opportunity. His force consisted of 11 ships, 600 men and some 16 horses. Advancing into the interior, Cortés quickly grasped the essential nature of the Aztec supremacy, their unpopularity with their subject peoples, and hence their vulnerability. Attempts by the Aztec king, Montezuma, to halt his advance by sending costly gifts only alerted the Spaniards to the magnitude of the prize that lay before them. When Cortés and his men finally completed the long march to Tenochtitlán (now Mexico City), they were received with great honour. Cortés acted decisively to seize the unfortunate Montezuma, and through him the city. Forced to return to the coast to stave off an expedition sent by the jealous Velázquez to relieve him, Cortés hurried back to find the Spanish garrison under siege. After a difficult and bloody retreat, Tenochtitlán was systematically conquered and reduced. Victory, in August 1521, marked the end of the Aztec Empire.

Cortés now faced the difficult task of justifying his conduct and making good his claim to suzerainty in the enormous new conquest. To do this it was necessary to answer the charges of insubordination with which a frantic Diego Velázquez was now besieging the Spanish court. Cortés made his case in five magisterial despatches to the emperor, Charles V, letters that have become not only an invaluable source for the events of the conquest, but a unique insight into the minds of the conquistadors.[3] Initially they achieved the desired result, and Cortés was named as Governor General. But a disastrous and reckless expedition to Honduras dissipated much of his political capital, and a commission of enquiry despatched from Spain threatened ruin. In 1528 Cortés returned to Spain to put his case in person. The remarkable impact made by his entourage (a troupe of native acrobats) and the wealth he poured at the feet of the emperor rescued the day, but the return to Mexico (now rechristened New Spain) brought further disappointment. After the appointment of a new viceroy Cortés abandoned his new lands to live out the rest of his days in Spain.

If Cortés was at least a man of some position, Francisco Pizarro was almost the archetypal adventurer, an illegitimate, illiterate son of a soldier. Like Cortés, Pizarro had committed himself to the New World at a relatively young age. By the time of the expedition to Peru he was the hardened veteran of several campaigns, and had carved out a position of wealth and influence in the newly founded town of Panama. His first southward exploration proved difficult and costly; to circumvent the opposition of the governor of Panama Pizarro determined on a direct appeal to the emperor. The fact that his journey to Spain coincided with the triumphant return of Cortés was a fortunate stroke. In the climate of euphoria Pizarro achieved appointment as viceroy of the kingdoms that he now undertook to conquer.

The expeditionary force gathered under his leadership was tiny: a mere 180 men and 27 horses. But his return to Peru coincided with the last stages of a debilitating civil war in the Inca kingdoms. Profiting from the confusion, Pizarro pressed inland to Cajamarca, where under cover of a parlay he treacherously apprehended the Inca king Atahualpa. Reinforced with a further 600 men, Pizarro was able to extract a huge ransom from Atahualpa, who was then not released but put to death. The Inca army melted away and the capital, Cuzco, surrendered without a struggle. Peru was conquered, and Pizarro and his companions settled down to enjoy the spoils.

Colonial Exploitation

The age of conquest was the opportunistic achievement of a very small body of men. The systematic exploitation of these vast new dominions would require skills of a different order and, it was already sufficiently clear, men of different character. The fate of Pizarro and his lieutenant Almagro, both of whom died a violent death after they quarrelled over the spoils of victory, brought home what was already sufficiently clear from the later career of Cortés in Mexico. The reckless boldness of the conqueror was not easily blended with the talents of a patient administrator.

The new conquests were undoubtedly, in the first generation, brutal, arbitrary, and exceptionally wasteful of human life. That they survived at all owed a great deal to the distant guiding hand of the emperor, and the men despatched to bring order to the quarrelling conquerors. The relationship between the local power and ultimate authority in Spain was always delicate. A great deal had necessarily to be left to the local power, particularly after the establishment of viceroys in Mexico (1535) and Peru (1543). These potentates presided over an increasingly large and complex administration, dedicated to maintaining Spanish authority, repelling interlopers, and supervising the extraction of wealth and its successful transfer back to the homeland.

To them too fell the task of adjudicating the conflicting claims of the many thousands who now descended on the New World in search of fortune. These new colonists found a life of considerable hardship, and few would grow rich. But they were surprisingly numerous. According to an informed estimate, something short of a quarter of a million people of European origin emigrated to the Spanish New World dominions in the first 80 years after Columbus. The vast majority were from Spain, and indeed from the kingdom of Castile, for the American enterprise was not one in which the Aragonese kingdoms significantly shared. The Spanish authorities exercised surprisingly close control over those who took part in the repopulation of the Indies. All emigrants were required to obtain licences from the *Casa de Contratación* (the Royal House of Trade), and a consistent attempt was made to limit the movement to Castilians of good character. Jews, Muslims, *moriscos* and heretics were absolutely forbidden to settle in the New World.

New settlers found a land in which the indigenous population was experiencing a catastrophic decline. Warfare, mistreatment, and harsh, unfamiliar labour all took a toll: most deadly of all were European diseases against which native peoples had no immunity. The figures make terrible reading. The indigenous population of central Mexico, estimated at 25 million in 1521, fell off to 16 million by 1532, 6.3 million by 1548, and to a pitiful 2.6 million in 1568. This represents a 90 per cent decline in 47 years. Comparable trends have been proposed for many of the island settlements and the rest of Central America. In Peru the decline was less severe, but still marked: from 3.3 million in 1520 to 1.3 million in 1570. In all regions, but particularly in the Caribbean islands, the maintenance of a functioning economy soon demanded the bringing in of large numbers of Africans as slave labour. This flourishing trade did as much as the vision of Spanish gold to excite the greedy interest of foreign interlopers.

Even among this much reduced native population, the new settlers were thinly spread. In a survey of 1570 they represented little more than 1 per cent of the total population of the Spanish colonies.[4] They huddled together for support and mutual protection in the new towns that rapidly sprung up around the Spanish colonies. Characteristically, Charles V gave detailed advice both on where these new settlements should be positioned, and how they should be built and governed. Towns, he advised, should be located in moderate altitudes, not subject to fogs, and with prevailing winds from north and south. If on a river they should be located so that the rising sun was shown first on the town, and not reflected from the water's surface into the eyes of the inhabitants. Even if, in reality, the new settlers necessarily made more *ad hoc*, practical decisions in the field, the emperor's strictures do reveal the extent to which the colonists recognized an opportunity to create entirely new, model communities, unconstrained by inherited municipal geography or stifling local custom. Much attention was given to the establishment of municipal government, division of land, and the creation of civic buildings. By the middle of the century, the largest communities could aspire to the attributes of mature westernized societies. In 1553 the Royal and Pontifical University of Mexico opened its doors. A similar foundation in Peru was authorized at the same time, though not in fact endowed and organized for another 25 years.

Away from the larger towns the settlement had a more brutal face. Here, the most important institution for transforming conquest into colonization was the *encomienda* system. The *encomienda* was not, as its sometimes assumed, an innovation specifically designed for the exploitation of the huge populations and spaces of the New World but, as in other instances, a Castilian institution adapted to new circumstances. An *encomienda* was a form of lordship consisting of towns and villages that the crown 'commended' into the charge of deserving persons for a specified time, allowing them to collect specified goods and services. As interpreted by the fortunate holders of these franchises, the *encomiendos*, it soon mutated into a form of forced labour close to slavery.

Encomiendas ranged enormously in size, from the huge domains granted the captains of the conquest to far more modest holdings. Cortés had 23 separate *encomiendas* totalling (according to his own reckoning) some 115,000 natives. Others, towards the bottom of the scale, obtained only a single village. Whereas settlers stoutly defended the system as the only means of forcing recalcitrant natives to the work necessary to sustain society, the crown always had misgivings. When these were fully articulated they caused the first great crisis of authority in the colonies.

In the mind of the crown the conquest of the Indies was never conceived solely in terms of sovereignty or economic gain. Rather an assertion of Spanish right was always intended as a means to win new populations to Christianity. There is no reason to doubt that this objective was sincerely, even passionately held. The early injunctions of Queen Isabella recognized the evangelical imperative as among the highest priorities for the settlement of the new lands. Each new town was to be provided with a church, and a chaplain who would baptize and instruct the Indians. The queen further instructed Governor Ovando to encourage intermarriage, 'so that both races will communicate with each other and the Indians be instructed in our sacred Catholic faith'. As this rather startling instruction perhaps makes clear, Spain, though a crusading nation, had no missionary tradition.

During the Reconquest the kings of Castile had generally allowed Moors and Jews to retain their faith as long as they accepted Christian rule. The techniques of conversion had to be learned and inevitably, given the magnitude of the task, and the shortage of personnel, early approaches were somewhat rudimentary.

The principal agents of evangelization were members of the religious orders. In 1524 Observant Franciscans arrived in Vera Cruz to begin the work of conversion. They were joined two years later by 12 Dominicans, and later a company of Augustinians. By 1559 Mexico was host to over 800 such missionary friars, organized in 160 houses. Their influence was felt widely, if not always at a very profound level. The roving friars adopted a very direct approach, breaking up native idols and temples, building churches, and performing mass baptisms. Martín de Valencia, the leader of the Franciscan apostles in 1524, boasted that his company had performed one million baptisms in a single year. The quality of such conversions is obviously greatly to be doubted. Certainly the Jesuits, arriving in the 1560s, viewed the work of their predecessors with great scepticism.

The emperor Charles, true to form, made his contribution in the establishment of due order and proper church government. In 1543 he obtained from the pope the right to establish episcopal jurisdictions in the Americas, fix their sees and define the limits of their territories. The first New World dioceses were suffragans of Seville, but from the 1540s archiepiscopal sees were erected independently. By 1564 Charles and Philip had erected a complete ecclesiastical organization comprising twenty-two dioceses and five archdioceses: in Santo Domingo, Mexico, Lima, Tegucigalpa and Santa Fe de Bogotá.

It is important not to view the evangelism of the Indies with cynicism. Whatever the quality of the conversions effected, the influence of the friars was powerful, not least in forming attitudes to the indigenous citizens. Here, from the beginning, there always existed a tension between the instincts of the first conquerors and settlers, and those who viewed issues of human rights through the spectacles of faith and legal jurisdictions. The first settlers had a low opinion of the rational powers of the native inhabitants. When Governor Ovando arrived in Hispaniola in 1501, he found natives who, as he reported, lived in primitive conditions, worshipped idols and devils, and preferred feasting and idleness to honest work. Those who gazed upon the civilizations of the Aztecs and Incas could hardly sustain such a charge, but the desire to put the conquered peoples to work created a strong imperative to treat them more as chattels than as citizens.

These perceptions were from the beginning not fully shared by those in authority in Spain. Queen Isabella accepted the establishment of the *encomienda* for practical reasons, but with grave reservations. The system, since it required the forced labour of Castilian subjects (for so the conquered peoples were now regarded) was of questionable legality, and doubts could only be confirmed by the evident brutality of its application. The most indefatigable and effective campaigner for the rights of the native peoples was the veteran Dominican Bartolomé de Las Casas. Las Casas, who spent most of his life in the Indies, had arrived first as a settler in Hispaniola, where he held a *repartimento* (allocation) of Indians and participated in the conquest of Cuba. Following the spiritual upheaval that led to him joining the Dominicans in 1514, he became an indefatigable campaigner for Indian rights. His passionate, utterly one-sided writings played an important part in turning the debate in Spain. Later his accounts of settler maltreatment of the native peoples would assure his books a second life in Protestant Europe as a staple of the developing Black Legend of Spanish cruelty.

In his own lifetime Las Casas carried the day. In 1537 Pope Paul settled the question of the natives' humanity with a ringing declaration: 'We consider that the Indians are truly men and that they are not only capable of understanding the Catholic faith, but, according to our information, they desire exceedingly to receive it.' Five years later the emperor promulgated the New Laws, which represented a wholesale assault on the abuses of the *encomienda* system. Slavery was outlawed and those taken illegally were ordered to be freed. Furthermore a drastic restriction of the *encomienda* envisaged the immediate suppression of those granted to official bodies (such as the church); the remainder were to be suppressed on the death of the present holder.

The New Laws created outrage in the colonies. The settlers threatened revolt, and here they had the sympathy of most local agents of the crown. In general, esteem for the indigenous peoples was highest among authorities in Europe with no first-hand experience of the Indies, lowest among those who had day-to-day dealings with the colonial system. Peru rose in revolt; a similar catastrophe was only barely averted in Mexico. In the event, the New Laws were recognized to be unenforceable. The shortfall in labour was met by the importation of increasing numbers of slaves from Africa. Concern for their human rights does not seem to have been so live an issue.

At much the time that these debates were at their height, a series of events occurred that would change the European perception of the

Figure 28 The Spanish exploitation of the Americas, from Hieronymi Bezoni, *Americae*, Frankfurt, 1595. Courtesy St Andrews University Library.

Indies very considerably. The search for precious metals, for gold and silver, had always been a critical part of the lure of the New World. A first torrent of booty from the great conquered civilizations further whetted the appetite, but mining for gold proved to be an unpredictable and frustrating business. Deposits were swiftly exhausted by the technologies then available, and there were few fortunes to be won. The evidence suggests that gold production in the Indies had already peaked between 1541 and 1560, though at what level is impossible to calculate.

Then from 1545 the Spaniards made a series of major strikes, all of silver: first at Potosí in Peru, then at Guanajuato and Pachuca in Mexico in the 1550s. Technological advances enhanced the value of these breakthroughs. In 1555 a Mexican miner, Bartolomé de Medina, devised a process for extracting silver through an amalgam of mercury.

Soon after the Spaniards chanced upon an enormous deposit of cinnebar, which produced quicksilver for Potosí.

Silver production was the most complex economic enterprise of the Indies, requiring multiple separate operations with advanced technology and a numerous labour force working in terrible conditions. The quality of the working environment may be judged from the fact that African slaves (who had to be purchased) were generally employed only for surface tasks. The deadly work underground was reserved for the unfortunate indigenous peoples. But Spain profited too massively for such issues to be of weight. In the 1530s, when Spain first began to exploit the mines of Mexico, silver registered in Seville was valued at three million pesos. By the 1570s the value of the silver extracted had reached 37 million pesos, a twelvefold increase.

The Spanish silver mines soon came to have an almost mythical place in the European consciousness. The Spanish government developed an elaborate administration to protect the *Carrera de Indias*, a convoy system that linked Spain and the Indies. No wonder, for it was not to be expected that other European powers would observe the extraordinary wealth that flowed from the Spanish and Portuguese overseas possessions without wishing to have their part.

Challenges

The assault on the Iberian monopoly of the New World began almost as soon as news of the New World discoveries began to circulate around the courts and seafaring communities of Europe. As early as 1504 French privateers began raiding Spanish transatlantic shipping on the final stages of the voyage towards home waters. In 1523 one Jean Fleury even succeeded in detaching two vessels bringing the wealth of the Mexican conquests back to Charles V. This spectacular treasure galvanized French seafarers to a concerted assault on Spanish shipping, a campaign legitimized by the sporadic state of war between Charles V and the French king. From the 1530s the French corsairs extended their marauding into the Caribbean.

It was only towards the end of the long Franco-Habsburg conflict, however, that the plan was conceived for a more substantial challenge to the Hispanic colonial monopoly, with two ill-fated French expeditions to Brazil and Florida. Both, significantly, avoided the main centres of Spanish power, and both involved the minority French Huguenot community, though the Brazil expedition certainly enjoyed a degree of official sanction. This notwithstanding, both were costly disasters. The discovery of Brazil had been an accidental consequence of the Portuguese search for favourable winds on the voyage to the Indies (1500). But the late adjustment of the terms of the Treaty of Tordesillas gave the Portuguese rights here that they were not prepared to relinquish, and in the 1530s the Portuguese crown took steps to promote permanent settlement. In 1530 an armed fleet under Martim de Sousa founded the first fixed townships, at São Vicente and Pernambuco. Nevertheless, by the standards of the Central American colonies the Brazilian settlement seemed rudimentary, and in 1555 a French expeditionary force was despatched under an experienced captain, Nicolas Durand de Villegagnon.

The French venture was from the beginning flawed and it did not take long for it to dissolve in acrimony and anarchy. Many of the settlers (including the minister and later chronicler, Jean de Léry) were Huguenots. Villegagnon was an acerbic and resolute Catholic, and the disintegration of co-operation soon led to the execution of three of de Léry's co-religionists. The rest fled and the remnant of the colony was soon picked off by the Portuguese. The sole thing of value to emerge from the fiasco was de Léry's *History of the Voyage to the Land of Brazil*, one of the great works of anthropological travel writing of the century. Suitably warned, the Portuguese now took steps to reinforce their hold on a colony that, for its excellent hardwoods and strategic placement on the route to the Indies, was increasingly valuable to them. The new captain general, Mem de Sá, took steps to found a new settlement near the site occupied by the evicted French – the origins of Rio de Janeiro.

The French incursion into Florida was, if anything, even more brutally dealt with. The large stretches to the north of Mexico had to this point hardly concerned the Spanish crown, until Philip was alerted to their value by French attempts to establish colonies first at Port Royal in present-day South Carolina (1562), then at Fort Caroline at the mouth of the St John river. The expedition was led by two experienced captains, Jean Ribault and René de Laudonnière, and had the enthusiastic backing of the admiral, Gaspard de Coligny. But the outbreak of the civil wars prevented the despatch of necessary reinforcements, and the colony was already failing before it was set upon and destroyed by a force sent for the purpose from Spain under the ferocious Pedro Menéndez de Avilés. Having executed the remnant of the garrison, Menéndez went on to found a new settlement, thus effectively claiming Florida for Spain.

The collapse of these early colonizing ventures, and the subsequent preoccupation of the French Wars of Religion, left the way open for a new, and ultimately more formidable interloper. English encroachment, always an irritant to the Spanish, grew ever more damaging, leading ultimately to a total rupture between the two nations. The English ventures flourished partly because the objectives of the voyages, left largely in the hands of hard-nosed seafaring captains, remained pragmatic and focused on critical economic objectives. John Hawkins had visited the French colony at Florida only days before its final destruction, and he had seen the pitiful rabble to which it had been reduced. It was a hard lesson that small, undercapitalized colonial missions had little chance of success. Rather, the English would flourish by forcing an entry into the Spanish monopoly at its most vulnerable point – the lucrative trade in African slaves – and, as tension grew into open hostility, by blatant assaults on Spanish cargos.

These expeditions, indignantly opposed by the Spanish authorities, and surreptitiously financed by the English elites, gradually brought relations between the two powers to the point of collapse. But the Spanish had little to gain by pushing relations to an open breach, as was demonstrated in the last decade of the reign, when English ships preyed unrestricted on Spanish settlements in the Indies, and on ships in transit. This was warfare at its most lucrative and cost effective. When English seafarers were seduced into more ambitious schemes the limits of their capacities became quickly apparent. This was true both of strategically ambitious attempts to strike a single crippling blow against the Spanish Empire (as by seizing the annual treasure fleet) or in attempts to establish English colonies. The dangers were there to see in the calamitous expeditions of Sir Humphrey Gilbert, who between 1578 and 1583 plotted a series of unfocused privateering and colonial expeditions, the last of which yielded a short-lived settlement in Newfoundland and the shipwreck and death of Gilbert himself. But others were not deterred and within two years capital had been raised for a new venture to the region that came to be called Virginia.

Under the charismatic leadership of Sir Walter Raleigh, a settlement was established on the river Roanoke. Determinedly and expensively reinforced from England it enjoyed a fitful existence until 1590, when the latest fleet found the fort abandoned and the colonists disappeared. Raleigh returned to privateering; the Virginia colony was not revived until 1607.

The last decade of the century witnessed an intensification of the sea war, and the first emergence of a power that would enjoy a great colonial future: the Dutch. The war against Spain had already taught the Dutch the profits to be made in preying on enemy shipping, and, indeed, that these profits were available without the hazards of long-distance voyages. From the collapse of the first Dutch revolt in 1567 the efforts of privateers licensed by William of Orange, the so-called Sea Beggars, were by far the most effective means of sustaining the war against Spain. Based in German, French and English ports, the Dutch commanded the busy sea lanes through the Channel and North Sea, effectively throttling the main artery of European trade from the Mediterranean and Iberian lands to the Baltic.

The emergence of a free northern state after 1585 set the Dutch on the road to more ambitious ventures. The Spanish recovery of the southern provinces, particularly the recovery of Antwerp, led to a considerable emigration, and a flight of capital, north to Holland. This capital required employment, and a more ambitious age of Dutch voyaging now entered the realm of possibility. The final crucial element in this new venturing was the incorporation, since 1580, of the Portuguese crown in the dominions of Philip II. In the short term this made available to Philip the formidable Portuguese oceangoing fleet for the Enterprise of England. The damaging long-term consequence was that Portuguese possessions were now a legitimate target for the enemies of Spain.

The Dutch were not slow to take advantage. The great expansion of Dutch enterprise in the last years of the century touched all theatres of Europe's most lucrative trading activities: the Baltic, Mediterranean and Levant, the Africa trade and the Caribbean. It was only in the final years of the century that the potential of the Indies trade was fully realized. At this point Dutch intervention came with the establishment of a *Compagnie van verre* in Amsterdam by a consortium of nine rich businessmen. They pooled a capital of 290,000 guilders, enough to buy the equivalent of 60 or 70 large houses in Amsterdam. The fleet they sent out returned in 1597, and though depleted and much diminished by the hardship of the voyage (and mismanagement) the success of the venture ignited the imagination of the Dutch mercantile world. Other companies were founded to exploit the new opportunities, and by the end of 1601 no fewer than 65 ships had sailed. The danger of competition between rivals spoiling the trade spurred the States of Holland to step in. In 1602, after months of negotiations, the United East India Company (VOC) was duly founded. By this time too, the English had realized the promise of the East. The English version of the East India Company was first constituted, with a list of

101 subscribing merchants, in 1599. One of the great rivalries of the first imperial age was set to begin.

Perspectives

What then was the impact on Europe of the first great age of colonial expansion? For none of the major protagonists can the fruits of their engagement ever be said to have matched their hopes. The attempts by English, Dutch and French seafarers to carry off the wealth of the Spanish gold and silver fleets never succeeded, for all the effort and ingenuity expended, in inflicting serious damage. Much more serious losses were inflicted on the Spanish economy by the less glamorous privateering in home waters. In this respect the Dutch Sea Beggars were some of the most cost-effective warriors of the sixteenth century. The greatest economic impact of the privateering effort in the Spanish Main was probably through the extra costs it forced on the Spanish authorities to protect their trade: these were considerable.

But against the emotional impact of the rivers of gold and silver flowing from the New World, such hard-headed realities seldom impacted. In purely monetary terms, the steadily rising trade in Eastern spices and fabrics funnelled through Lisbon probably had a far greater impact on the European economy and generated more wealth for the kingdom. But such wealth was never seen as threatening in the same way. The combination of Spain and precious metals had a place in the European imagination that nothing else could match.

If we chart the wider emotional impact of the New World economies it is possible to discern a sequence of evolving reactions. The initial discoveries produced a sense of wonder and excitement that was quickly superseded by more practical sentiments. First came a sense of opportunity, as the riches and extent of the new lands at first seemed quite boundless; even by the end of the century, decades of exploration had only succeeded in charting, still less settling, a tiny proportion of the new land mass. The unknown lands now ripe for exploration had expanded exponentially, a challenge for the increasingly modish science of cartography that would be relished, if not always reliably solved. But with a sense of opportunity came anxiety – first on the part of the colonial powers, a need to protect to their own exclusive use what had been won. This anxiety then transmitted itself to other European powers, with a growing sense that the riches of the New

World – always much multiplied in the imagination – would allow Spain to establish a new order of world domination. Here the strategic anxieties of competing powers, and the cupidity of their subjects, coincided to produce the first great age of European privateering.

These concerns and anxieties were naturally most acute among the rulers and advisors of Europe's states, and this leaves still unresolved how far disseminated among the population was a sense of the new non-European worlds. Cartographers and cosmographers played their part in expanding the horizons of the educated – and this was a great age of travel writing. At a time when Europeans were discovering, with the help of popular scientific literature, the marvels of their own natural world, this interest was easily extended to the exotica of distant continents. Here the skills of the woodcut artists and the printing press did much to domesticate the expansion. In this way, rather than through food and consumer luxuries, the experience of new worlds began to trickle into wider consciousness, for in the sixteenth century most of the products we associate with the colonial age (sugar, spices, dyes and silks) were well known in Europe already. The growth of a consumer society that would take as a matter of course the new delights that the East and New World had to offer (coffee, tea and tobacco) was a product of the next two centuries: Europe's true imperial age.

13

Eastern Europe

All history, it has been said, is contemporary history. What is meant by this is that our experience of the present, our modes of thought and cultural assumptions, inevitably colour the way in which we experience the past. Put at its most extreme this would imply that we are all such prisoners of our environment that there is no real avenue to a 'true' view of the past. Most historians would believe that as individuals we have enough sense of self at least to dilute the bleakest implications of such a thesis: though this may simply reflect the fact that bias or prejudice is always easier to spot in others, and in other ages, than in our own. Nevertheless we would all certainly accept that there is no such thing as an unadulterated historical reality.

The ways in which current events can impact directly on our perceptions of the past – even a past as distant as the sixteenth century – is perhaps most obvious if we consider the history of Eastern Europe. To most historians of my generation (I was born in 1957), the Eastern Europe of our youth was unknown territory. The post-war settlement after the Second World War sliced brutally through the political heart of the continent. Berlin and Vienna, great cultural centres of 'Central' Europe, were now isolated outposts of western culture in a hostile, and largely closed world. Lands such as Hungary, Czechoslovakia and Poland disappeared behind an 'Iron Curtain', as part of an Eastern bloc allied with or subject to Soviet Russia. They seemed, and for a time they were, impenetrably foreign. Nor was all of this expected to change. It was the commonly accepted wisdom of the day, even in the 1980s, that the Berlin Wall and Iron Curtain were permanent features of the political landscape. No-one then anticipated the collapse of

Communism – and this should be recorded before historians get round to explaining why its fall was inevitable.[1] These events are a humbling reminder of why history is an interpretative, rather than predictive science.

The culture of the Cold War inevitably had an effect on the way scholarship – even of much earlier periods – treated these countries. Part of the difficulty was practical. Cultural intercourse was almost completely suspended. Travel, even for tourism, was arduous and complicated, and always expensive: scholarly archives could be accessed only with the greatest difficulty. Nor were scholars in those lands free to choose the subject or intellectual direction of their work. Western historians in contact with scholars active in those lands were obliged to familiarize themselves with an alternative vocabulary that reflected the underlying presumptions of Marxist theory: what was to us the Reformation became 'the pre-Bourgeois Revolution'.

Beyond these practical experiences there was however also a more subtle impact. Because these societies were so foreign for us, it was more easily assumed that they must too have been distant and foreign in previous centuries. Without this ever having been very clearly stated, textbook studies of the sixteenth century largely reflected this contemporary sense of distance from lands such as Bohemia, Hungary and Poland. Twenty years on literally everything has changed. The Soviet bloc and with it this sense of 'Eastern Europe' is itself consigned to history. Places such as Hungary, the Czech Republic, Slovenia and Croatia welcome millions of western visitors. To those who take these tourist opportunities great cities such as Prague and Budapest seem as vital and fully a part of Europe as their German and Austrian neighbours.

The reintegration of these countries into contemporary European culture encourages a different perspective of how these lands might have been in the sixteenth century. And indeed, the situation we have now at the beginning of the twenty-first century comes much closer to that which would have pertained 500 years ago. For in that period the lands that were for much of the twentieth century closed to us formed an integral part of the economic, social and intellectual heart of Europe. In terms of the central European economy, the lands of Bohemia formed an essential unity with the German speaking lands to the north, south and west: Silesia, the Habsburg estates in Austria, and the city states of the southern empire. The mines of the Bohemian Erzgebirge were essentially colonized by immigrant German workers from Saxony and beyond; meanwhile the silver mines of Hungary

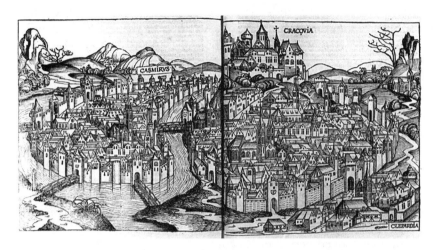

Figure 29   Cracow, from Hartmann Schedel, *Historia mundi*, Nuremberg, 1493. Courtesy St Andrews University Library.

functioned very largely thanks to the investment of German capital from such places as Augsburg and Nuremberg.

Cultural and intellectual connections were equally strong. Prague was one of the great universities of mediaeval Europe, drawing its student community and distinguished professors from all over Europe. Other notable centres of learning were situated at Wrocław (Breslau) in Silesia and at Cracow in Poland. The new artistic and intellectual movements of the period flourished in this environment. Particularly striking was the impact of Humanism. Poland, Bohemia and Hungary displayed an allegiance to the thought and teachings of Erasmus no less striking than his well-documented affinity with Spain. In the 1520s Erasmus was the most popular author of Cracow: the local printing presses published no fewer than forty editions of his works between 1518 and 1550.[2] In his own lifetime scholars and churchmen in these eastern lands eagerly pursued a connection with the great Dutchman, through letters, gifts or, where possible, personal visits. The collected correspondence of Erasmus bears eloquent testimony to the strength of these connections.[3] His friends in Poland included many of the most prominent members of the political and ecclesiastical hierarchy of that country. A Polish protégé, John a Lasco, would eventually even purchase Erasmus's library, providing the funds to comfort his later years. The career of a Lasco, later a prominent and notable convert to the Reformation, can serve as an example of the extent to which the elites of these eastern lands shared the common intellectual experience of European culture and education. A scion of a notable Polish family, a Lasco was educated at Vienna, Bologna and Padua, one of many thousands of students who flocked to Italy from eastern Europe. In 1524 he accompanied his brother on a diplomatic mission to the court of Francis I, and it was in the course of this expedition that he first met Erasmus in Basle.

Some of Erasmus's closest friends among eastern Europeans hailed from Bohemia, among them Sigismundus Gelenius and Caspar Ursinas Velius. The enthusiasm of Jan Slechta even extended to attempting to entice Erasmus to visit Prague, an opportunity the latter politely declined. In Hungary the establishment of a Humanist circle was largely the achievement of the great Conrad Celtis, who travelled to Hungary twice during the 1490s, the same decade during which he spent a prolonged period in Cracow.

As with Humanism, so also the Renaissance. The lands of eastern Europe embraced the Renaissance with remarkable enthusiasm, and at an early date: so much so, that art historians have argued that the Renaissance attained in Hungary its purest form outside the Italian peninsula. Here a seminal influence was the fifteenth century king Matthias Corvinus (1458–90) who consciously sought to reinforce the tenuous power of the crown by creating a glittering court and surrounding himself with scholars and artists. The most lasting monument to his activity was the famous Corvinian library, a collection, in its day, of some 500 texts, one of the greatest libraries of the age. From Hungary the influence of the Renaissance spread north and east. For three generations Italian artists were active in Poland, taking advantage of the enthusiastic patronage of the ruling Jagiello family. The influential King Sigismund I (1506–48), for instance, had been educated by Filippo Buonaccorsi, a Humanist associated with the circle of Pomponio Leto. The greatest memorial to Sigismund's artistic enthusiasm was the superb arcaded courtyard of Wawel Castle in Cracow: an outstanding example of the influence of Italianate artistic principles.

It is of course important to avoid the risk of allowing the pendulum to swing too far: to make of eastern Europe a mere reflection, however luminous, of the dominant western social and cultural currents of the day. There were distinctive features of eastern society not so strongly reflected further west. All the lands that have so far featured in this account had a highly developed estates tradition, a tradition of political representation that concentrated power especially in the hands of the landed nobility. This was in a sense also a shared western tradition, for such a feature of social organization was characteristic of the whole of mediaeval Latin Christendom. But whereas in western Europe the political institutions that gave constitutional expression to such power had tended to wither and fall into disuse, in eastern Europe they remained vibrant. Indeed, as the sixteenth century wore on the power of the estates was if anything increased *vis-à-vis* the ruling dynasty. In this respect the experience of western and eastern Europe diverged during the sixteenth century.

There were also great cultural differences between different parts of eastern Europe. The developments that have thus far been described, the influence of Humanism and the Renaissance, the economic and cultural connections that bound these societies to Germany and Italy, were largely confined to Bohemia, Hungary and Poland. This was one of three distinct zones. The lands to the north-east, the remainder of the kingdom of Poland/Lithuania, stretching away to Muscovy, were much more foreign and remote. They were far less connected, and had far less in common, with western Europe. Crucially, the kingdom of Poland overlapped the borders of Latin Christendom. While the western part of the kingdom, including Cracow, was firmly enmeshed with western culture, the new lands of the kingdom of Lithuania stretched away into the eastern steppes, lands where the influence of Russian Orthodoxy vied with the still more antique tradition of paganism. To the south and east lay a third zone, the remnant of Byzantium, now since the fifteenth century the trans-Balkan possessions of the Ottoman Empire. These lands were settled by a bewildering variety of peoples and ethnic groups, overlayed by two unifying but competing cultural influences: the established influence of the Greek Orthodox Church, and the recent political domination of the Turks.

At the beginning of the sixteenth century the governance of these diverse and varied lands was still in a state of considerable flux. After the death of Matthias Corvinus in 1490, Hungary had accepted as king the Jagiello ruler of the lands of the crown of Bohemia, Vladislav II. This represented in effect the reassertion of the power of the landed aristocracy, since Vladislav was recognized as a weak king. This, and the religious differences between Hussite Bohemia and Catholic Hungary ensured that the union remained more personal than institutional. The kingdom of Bohemia was itself at this time a somewhat loose amalgamation of territories, comprising the lands of Bohemia, Moravia, Silesia and Lusatia. While Bohemia and Moravia formed a close unit (analogous to the twentieth century unity of Czechoslovakia) Silesia was ruled directly by Hungary between

1469 and 1490, and rejoined Bohemia only on the death of Matthias Corvinus.

Poland was also at this time ruled by a branch of the Jagiello dynasty. The massive, sprawling state of Renaissance Poland was a creation, as so often, of a mediaeval dynastic union: the marriage in 1385 of Jadwiga, Queen of Poland, to Jagiello, Grand Duke of Lithuania. This alliance brought together two very different states – mediaeval Lithuania was the last pagan state in Europe, a vast sprawling land dominated by a powerful warrior nobility, the *boyars*. This closed society was now thrown open to western influences, creating, in due course, a state remarkable for its ethnic and cultural diversity. Poland had six official languages, and played host to a multiplicity of different ethnic groups, including Ruthenians, Armenians, Jews, Germans and Muslims, alongside the dominant Polish and Lithuanian castes. The Lithuanian inheritance also brought Poland into direct competition with Muscovy, another expanding and ambitious power at the beginning of the sixteenth century, but one whose cultural and social traditions had little in common with those of Latin Christendom.

This then, in outline, sketches the cultural and political map of eastern Europe at the dawn of the sixteenth century. The new era would bring huge changes, partly (as elsewhere in Europe) as a result of dynastic perturbations, partly through the impact of larger movements of social and religious change emanating in the lands to the west. Three, in particular would be of especial moment: the impact of the Reformation; the further advance of the Ottoman Empire towards the heart of Europe in the south east; and the (connected) extinction of the Jagiello dynasty and establishment of Habsburg power in the region. Together, these momentous events would shape eastern European society for centuries to come.

The Habsburg Inheritance

In the history of sixteenth century Eastern Europe the single most formative event undoubtedly took place on the bleak battlefield of Mohács on 29 August 1526. This in itself was unusual, for as has been pointed out before, battles seldom proved decisive in settling sixteenth-century conflicts. But Mohács certainly proved the exception, for here the consequences were truly far reaching. The young king of Bohemia and Hungary, Louis Jagiello, had led his troops into battle against what appeared to be a small contingent of Turks. But by the time battle was joined the Turkish advance guard had been joined by the main Turkish host, and the Christian army was annihilated. Among the dead were the king himself, the Archbishop of Esztergom, 28 magnates, 500 nobles and 16,000 men; a full three-quarters of the Hungarian army.

With the death of the king, the Jagiello dynasty was extinct. The crown was now claimed by the Habsburg, Ferdinand of Austria, brother of the emperor Charles V. Connections between the two families had been close for several decades, an alliance reinforced by a double dynastic marriage, which saw Ferdinand married to Anna, sister of Louis, and his sister Mary to the Hungarian king (the Treaty of Vienna, 1515). When Louis died without issue Ferdinand was thus able to claim the crowns of Hungary and Bohemia by right of inheritance and alliance. But his claim did not go uncontested. Even the urgent danger posed by the presence of the rampant Turkish host could not persuade the powerful Hungarian and Bohemian nobility to accept the protection of the Habsburgs, if the cost would be absorption of their kingdoms into the greater Habsburg Empire. In both Hungary and Bohemia the principle of elective monarchy was vigorously maintained and a section of the Hungarian nobility went so far as to elect John Zápolya, Count of Spiš, as their king. When the Turkish host pressed on to take Buda and Pest, the kingdom was in effect split into three: the Transylvanian kingdom of Zápolya, a central zone of Turkish influence, and the western remnant under Habsburg rule. Even in Bohemia, where Ferdinand was grudgingly accepted, the nobility used the current travails to reassert their influence in affairs of state. Ferdinand thus faced a bafflingly complex and discouraging situation in bringing these new lands under control; the exigencies of the current political situation would ensure that he was never, in fact, wholly successful.

To the new king, Bohemia might at first sight have seemed the larger prize. In the high Middle Ages Bohemia was certainly most closely integrated with the affairs of the German-speaking lands. Bohemia itself fell within the bounds of the empire, and indeed the heirs to the crown of St Stephen held one of the seven precious electoral votes that determined the holder of the imperial crown.

In the fifteenth century, however, the tumultuous events of the Hussite Revolution had set the kingdom of Bohemia on a different, divergent course, and one that had much to weaken connections with

Germany. The execution of Jan Hus at the Council of Constance (1415) had caused a patriotic explosion in his native land; since the ruling dynasty were implicated in his arrest they too shared in the obloquy. When a series of papally sponsored crusades designed to crush the insurgents by force met with humiliating failure, the battered king, Sigismund, had no choice but to make terms. The Hussite Utraquist Church became, in effect, a separated national church, protected by the nobility, who also profited greatly through the humiliation of the crown. The more radical militant branch of the movement, the heirs of the violent Taborites, became known as the Unity of Bohemian Brethren, a voluntary congregational church not accorded the same legal recognition, but also effectively protected by sympathetic nobles. The Catholic Church was reduced to the merest remnant, concentrated mostly in the outlying German-speaking lands. In Czech lands it was a hierarchy without a congregation.

In the years immediately before Mohács the connection with Germany had been partially rebuilt through the spreading influence of the Reformation. The affinity between the Hussite 'first' Reformation and Luther's movement was not immediately manifest, and it was only when Luther was driven into a defence of Hus's views by the able Catholic controversialist Johannes Eck at the Leipzig disputation (1519) that a process of constructive engagement began. In the first decades enthusiasm for Luther was most pronounced among the Unity of Bohemian Brethren and reformed Utraquists. Conservative Utraquists were at this point more inclined to pursue rapprochement with the Catholic Church. On his accession in 1526 Ferdinand I was initially able to exploit these differences quite successfully, at least to the extent of creating a loyal court party of Catholic and Utraquist royalists. Nevertheless, political and religious opposition grew steadily, culminating in 1539 in a formal demand for religious freedom. The campaign against Ferdinand also stimulated greater co-operation between Utraquists and the Bohemian Brethren, encouraged by the Lutheran pastors who had taken firm control of the formerly Catholic ethnic German mining towns.

A critical moment in Ferdinand's relations with his Bohemian lands was reached with the Schmalkaldic War of 1547. The majority of the Bohemian estates refused to obey the king's order to raise an army to fight against the German Protestant neighbours. The rebellion was short lived, and along with reprisals against the leading nobles implicated, Ferdinand ordered the suppression of the Bohemian Brethren. A considerable number took refuge in Poland.

As in Germany, however, the assertion of royal power could not be converted into a decisive settlement of the religious question. Although a synod of 1549 adopted articles intended to facilitate union with the Catholic Church, both the estates and leaders of the Utraquist Church repudiated the concessions. Throughout the 1550s and 1560s, nobles and cities through north and west Bohemia openly appointed Lutheran pastors. The evident failure of coercion prompted a change of policy. The king now ceased attempts to suppress the Protestant confessions, and adopted instead a policy of actively promoting Catholic renewal. In 1556 the Jesuits were summoned to Prague, and established the first of their many colleges. Their influence here, as elsewhere in eastern Europe, was profound, but Bohemia was still a fundamentally Protestant land right up until the point when the rebellion of the Bohemian Estates in 1618 unleashed the Thirty Years' War. The Habsburg victory at last enabled the wholesale reconstruction of the Bohemian nobility and with it the forced conversion of the Bohemian lands.

The problems that faced Ferdinand in Bohemia were of a type all too familiar to the Habsburgs from their German travails: obstreperous nobles and a population apparently unshakeably wedded to dissident religious confessions. But in Hungary Christian rule faced a struggle for survival. Even before Mohács, royal authority in the kingdom had been considerably eroded since the heady days of Matthias Corvinus. Vladislav, dubbed 'King OK' for the good-natured way in which he approved every request made to him, had allowed royal income to dwindle to a fraction of its former healthy yield. His son Louis, a warrior only in his own imagination, was intellectually and emotionally a child. Relations between the social orders, already tense, had sunk to a new low with the Peasants' Revolt of 1514, put down with great savagery by the vengeful nobles. When the defeat at Mohács cut a swathe through the ruling class, this fragile society seemed on the verge of disintegration. It hardly helped that for the next years the Christian leaders of Hungarian society were largely occupied with resolving the competing claims to the throne. Those who favoured a native born king elected John Zápolya, son-in-law of the King of Poland. Ferdinand swiftly assembled a counter faction to declare him king. An initial military campaign brought Ferdinand a victory of sorts, but Zápolya remained largely in control of Transylvania, the part of the kingdom most distant from Habsburg strength. In 1528 Zápolya entered into a formal alliance with the sultan.

In 1529 the Turkish army, which had retreated with its plunder after briefly occupying Buda in 1526, returned to the field. This year, it soon became clear, the intended target was Vienna. For Ferdinand, this moment of maximum Christian peril was in some respects a blessing, since it forced his brother, the emperor Charles, and the German princes, to recognize the urgency of the situation. But, the moment of danger once past, the emperor's priorities shifted elsewhere, and Ferdinand was again left to defend his frontier kingdom. For a time this seemed to be beyond him. A disastrous campaign in 1537 forced Ferdinand to recognize Zápolya, the Turkish client; then in 1541 new military disasters brought the final loss of Buda, and a subsequent almost total collapse of Ferdinand's authority among the Magyar nobility. The embattled king had little choice but to accept the limitations of his position. Henceforth Habsburg rule was in effect confined to the westernmost portion of the kingdom, with an independent Transylvania to the east, and a zone of Ottoman control between.

Though calamitous for royal authority, these were not in fact particularly difficult years for the Hungarian people as a whole. In particular, the travails of the crown provided a welcome respite for those who favoured the new doctrines of Protestantism. Hungary was a multi-ethnic state, with large colonies of ethnic Germans as well as Slovenes, Croats and Serbs alongside the majority Magyar population. The earliest inroads of the new doctrines were predictably among the Germans of the mining cities and Buda. And though the Hungarian diet approved a decree punishing Lutheran beliefs with death (1523), Mohács put an end to any prospect of enforcing it. In Upper Hungary and Transylvania most of the major cities installed evangelical preachers during the 1530s and 1540s.

In the middle decades of the century the Reformation made some progress among the non-German populations, but the most spectacular developments of the latter sixteenth century were reserved for other Protestant confessions, most notably Calvinism and Unitarianism. The influence of the Swiss Reformed churches made its first appearance in the 1540s. In this first generation Eastern Europe was a mission field of the Zurich reformer, Heinrich Bullinger, who in 1559 was the guiding hand behind the first ordinances of the Hungarian Reformed Church. But in later years the influence of Geneva became predominant, and Debrecen a true eastern capital of the Reformed faith (as it remains still). Moravia and Transylvania, meanwhile, provided a haven for dissident sectarians persecuted by all the mainstream churches. In

Transylvania Unitarians (who rejected the doctrine of the Trinity) flourished under the charismatic leadership of Ferenc Dávid, though the transition to a formal church exposed the weaknesses of the movement. When one takes into account the relative freedom from religious constraint in lands under Turkish control, eastern Europe can be seen to have well merited its growing reputation as a haven of religious toleration.

By this time the authority of the Habsburgs had passed into the amiable, undogmatic hands of Maximilian II (1564–76). By the time of his accession the authority of the Catholic Church in the eastern Habsburg lands had reached its lowest ebb. Even their own dynastic territories in Austria were by this time to all intents and purposes Protestant. Maximilian accepted this situation with a good humoured resignation that has led some to suspect that he himself harboured Protestant sympathies. Although he did not impede the beginnings of a Catholic mission to restore the faith in these lands, spearheaded by the Jesuits, he did little to encourage it. Maximilian's energies were devoted instead to the encouragement of a broad-minded and broad-ranging intellectual activity. The circle he patronized was cosmopolitan and eclectic, including humanist scholars, cartographers and legists. His patronage reconnected Prague to the intellectual world from which it had been divided by the Hussite revolt, while Protestantism played its part by expanding the range of institutes of learning to which Czech and Hungarian students now decamped in their thousands. For most Wittenberg was the first port of call, though many attended several academies. The Hungarian lexicographer Albert Szenci Molnár, to take one example, attended Wittenberg, Heidelberg, Strasbourg, Basle and Geneva, moved thence to Italy, back to Heidelberg, and finally sought work in Herborn and Altdorf.[4] From 1576 Maximilian's successor, Rudolph II, would put the final seal on this cultural Renaissance by moving the imperial capital from Vienna to Prague.

These cultural advances coincided with an era of economic prosperity, stimulated by the systematic exploitation of primarily mineral resources: Styrian iron, Tyrolean and Bohemian silver, Hungarian copper and gold. Agriculture flourished and wine, wheat and flax, beer and fish found their way on to German markets. In some respects this seems almost a golden age for these central European lands: certainly it could hardly have appeared otherwise, viewed from the perspective of the mid-seventeenth century, when the Bohemian revolt of 1618 had unleashed the carnage of war on to these Habsburg kingdoms.

Ottoman Europe

In considering the place of the Ottoman conquests in eastern Europe there are two aspects of this often little considered question that demand our attention. First there is the material issue of the lands themselves, a considerable portion of the European land mass by the end of the fifteenth century, and one steadily and apparently inexorably increasing. In this context the fall of Constantinople in 1453, though cataclysmic in its symbolism, in fact falls nearer the midpoint of the two centuries of steady Ottoman progress through the Balkans towards Latin Europe. In the hundred years before they took Constantinople the Ottomans had already invested and colonized much of the Byzantine hinterland, including Thrace, Bulgaria and Macedonia. With the successful conclusion of the siege the advance gathered pace once more. Two campaigns in 1454 and 1455 smashed the Serbs, in territorial terms the largest geographical buffer between the Turks and the west; the fall of Nova Brno also gave them control of its important silver and gold mines. In the following decade the Turkish advance enveloped the rest of the Greek peninsula (1458–61), followed by Herzogovina (absorbed 1483) and Albania (1468–78). Meanwhile Venice was progressively driven back in the struggle for the Aegean Islands and the Dalmatian (Adriatic) coast. In 1520 the Ottoman host seized Belgrade, the southern key to Hungary; the triumph of Mohács then allowed the progressive occupation of much of Hungary. This was not quite the high water mark of Ottoman success: Moldova was subdued in 1538, and later raids devastated Transylvania, and took the fight to Polish territory in the north, and through their client state in the Crimea, to the borders of Muscovy.

The Ottoman advance towards the heart of Christian Europe, and particularly the collapse of the kingdom of Hungary, had a profound impact on the European psyche. For Luther, the victory of the Turkish horde was a sure sign of the imminent end time – as well as a further indication of the bankruptcy of Christian leadership (the papacy). Luther was among a number of Lutheran scholars (they included Melanchthon and Justus Jonas) struck in 1529–30 by the relevance of the Turkish onslaught to apocalyptic prophecy, and he returned to the theme in his writings whenever the Turkish threat became urgent. In 1541 the final assault on Buda prompted his *Admonition to Prayer against the Turks*, in which Luther characteristically interpreted the present peril as a judgement on the German people for their sin. Two years later he wrote to the Saxon elector declining a personal exemption from the Turkish war tax. 'I want', he declared, 'to fight the Turk with my poor man's penny, alongside the next fellow; and who knows whether my little free-will offering, like the widow's mite, may not do more than all the rich compulsory taxes.'[5]

The hardening of fronts in the Balkans in the second half of the century did not diminish interest in the Turks as an alien and deeply threatening force in European life. A survey of books published in France between 1480 and 1609 records twice as many titles relating to the Turks as to the Americas. The Lyon publisher Benoist Rigaud, king of sensation literature, had a highly successful sideline in books relating to the wars against the Turks. For these he had procured a small stock of colourful woodcuts, featuring sinister looking Turks in turbans, and frenetic battle scenes, which he cannily reused for numerous different tracts. None of these little books was more than sixteen pages long.

One of the things that emerges from a perusal of this sensation literature is how little the western European public actually knew of life under the Turks. In particular, they had little sense of what Ottoman

Figure 30 The face of the Turk, from Sebastian Münster, *Cosmographia Universalis*. Courtesy St Andrews University Library.

rule must have meant for the approximately five million Christian peoples settled in the Turkish provinces within Europe. Fed a diet that harked repeatedly on the ruthless cruelty of the sultan and the pitiless ferocity of their soldiery, the realities of the situation might well have surprised them.

The Ottomans, for instance, never attempted any forced or large-scale Islamicization of the Balkans. One reason for this lay in the prescriptions of the Koran that Muslims should be liable to lower taxes than non-Muslims. Since the Ottomans relied greatly on their Christian subject peoples for revenue, too great a level of conversion would have been financially disadvantageous. To exploit the new lands the Turks continued most of the existing tax regime, overlaid with their own new system for the extraction of a steady tribute from agricultural areas. This involved leaving in place taxes that would seem to have no place in a well-ordered Islamic society, such as those on the trade in wine, or the slaughtering of pigs. Certain local taxes and dues were reserved to the sultan, others allocated to support the local administration of the appointed Turkish officials. The cornerstone of Ottoman rural administration was the *timar* system, grants of rights of exploitation to selected *sipahi*, originally trusted servants who had played their part in the conquest.[6] The terms of the grant were strict. The *sipahi* had no claim on ownership of the land itself, which remained the property of the sultan. Revenue was raised through a modest levy of peasant labour service (three days a year, much as had been customary under Christian rule) and a more substantial tithe on the annual harvest.

The Ottoman system also relied heavily on these captured Christian provinces for recruits to man their armies, which could then be deployed to face Muslim rivals in Anatolia (southern Turkey) and the Arab world. On the face of it, this was a brutal process. Christian children were forcibly removed from their homes to be brought up to barrack life: no further contact with their families was permitted. The youths were given new Muslim names and obliged to adopt the Islamic faith; those who refused faced death. The human toll on the Christian ethnic populations was enforced according to a strict quota, and families with young boys often adopted desperate measures to save them, through flight, hiding, or persuading a compliant priest to leave them off the parish list.

The human suffering that underpinned such a system is obvious, but for those who came through the strict training the life of a Janissary offered considerable career opportunities. A considerable number from the ethnic subject peoples in due course rose to become some of the most privileged and powerful soldier administrators in the empire. According to one authority, of the 49 Grand Viziers who served the sultan between 1453 and 1623, a clear majority were of Christian-European origin, including at least 11 Slavs, 11 Albanians and 6 Greeks; only five were of Turkish extraction.[7] It has been observed, with some justice, that the Ottoman Empire began its conquest of the Arab world only after it had absorbed these Balkan lands. The Balkan peoples were an essential agent of this conquest.

Most of all the conquerors made no attempt to suppress the Orthodox Church. On the fall of Constantinople in 1453 the Sultan Mehmed II personally selected a new Christian patriarch. His choice fell, not accidentally, on Gennadius, a popular monk who had orchestrated opposition to the terms for the reunification of the churches negotiated at the Council of Florence in 1439. For most Orthodox Christians life under Ottoman rule was infinitely preferable to the patronizing and unfavourable terms for reunion offered by Rome; and for their Ottoman masters the mutual antagonism between Latin and Orthodox Christianity offered a further bulwark against the possibility of a successful crusade. The Orthodox Church was therefore granted extremely favourable conditions, their synod being permitted total autonomy in matters of doctrine, and the clergy exempted from taxation. The church also retained extensive jurisdiction in civil and family matters such as marriage and inheritance, where Ottoman law was not easily applicable. In return the local clergy took a conspicuous role in local administration, even acting as assessors and collectors for taxes levied by the Ottoman state apparatus. In this they anticipated the role allocated to Protestant pastors in the confessional Lutheran state of the later sixteenth century.

The role of the Orthodox Church was not always respected by the subject peoples in the Balkans. By some the clergy were regarded as little better than collaborators. But by granting the church such power and autonomy the Ottomans were in large measure merely continuing the long-standing primacy of religion, rather than ethnicity, as the principal badge of identity in the Balkans. This was the basis of the *millet*, a system of social and religious segregation that gave to existing separations of social classes and religious groups the force of law. Historians have been critical of the *millet*, particularly those who have seen it as a form of enforced separate development akin to apartheid. But there is no evidence that the Ottomans deliberately restricted the educational or commercial opportunities of the Christian peoples. If we are to analyse reasons for the progressive retardation of Balkan culture *vis-à-vis* the rest of Europe, two separate factors may be of some importance. Firstly, the first century of Ottoman occupation brought a progressive drift of Christian populations from town to countryside, thus away from the centres that everywhere in Europe provided the greatest opportunities for education and social mobility. Secondly, the Orthodox Church remained an institution of stifling conservatism. As it had resisted the Renaissance and disdained the Reformation, so in later centuries it would provide fierce opposition to the march of science. Fundamentally, it was cultural divisions within Christianity, rather than Ottoman rule, that lay behind the progressive alienation of the Balkan lands from the European mainstream.

What then can be said, in summary, of the impact of the Ottoman Empire in Europe? Certainly there was a curiosity about Arabic culture, shared by even so trenchant a critic as Luther. In 1537 he published with a new preface an edition of a fifteenth-century account of captivity under the Turks. Five years later he published a free translation of the exposition on the Koran by the thirteenth-century Dominican Ricoldus. When the first tide of eschatological fear receded, there were many in western Europe who were prepared to recognize the Ottoman Empire for what it certainly was: an ordered society and a great civilization. But to the extent to which this perception advanced in western Europe during these years, it was based on the experience of merchants, and of diplomats at the Ottoman court, rather than any sense of what life entailed for the Christian peoples under Ottoman rule. Theirs was essentially a hidden experience.

What could certainly be said is that the Ottoman advance into eastern Europe revealed once and for all the bankruptcy of the crusading ideal. This was perhaps the final revelation of what was already an established fact, for all the continued prevalence of crusading rhetoric. After all, the most systematic crusading of the fifteenth century had been not against the infidel but against fellow Christians – the Hussites. Then when the Turks arrived, literally in the heart of Europe, for all the shrill pamphleteering and warnings of doom, many of Europe's ruling elites saw here as much opportunity as danger. This was true of the Hungarian nobility, who did not scruple to trade on the disaster of Mohács to enhance their own power; the very similar reaction of the German Protestant princes; and the prolonged cynical diplomacy of Francis I of France. Perhaps most of all this was a monument to the damage the Protestant rebellion had already done to the Catholic psyche. Even before the Turks exposed the military unpreparedness of the west, the trauma induced by Luther's movement had already made the notion of an undivided Christendom seem too remote to be worth defending.

Towards Muscovy

The kingdom of Poland/Lithuania was Europe's true borderland. In the sixteenth century it straddled an immense area of some 350,000 square miles. Even though much was sparsely settled, it embraced a population of some three million, divided among many races and ethnic groups.

The period ushered in by the marriage of Jadwiga and Jagiello was one of increasing stability. The Teutonic Knights, the other potential regional power, were subdued by the smashing Polish victory at Grunwald (1410). Other potential troublemakers, such as the Scandinavian nations, were too consumed by their own quarrels. Polish society took on an increasingly settled character, typified by the emergence of a clearly stratified society of estates. The five estates – clergy, nobility, burghers, Jews and peasantry – were each ordered according to prescribed rights and rules; mobility between estates was severely circumscribed. That this caused so little social tension may partly be

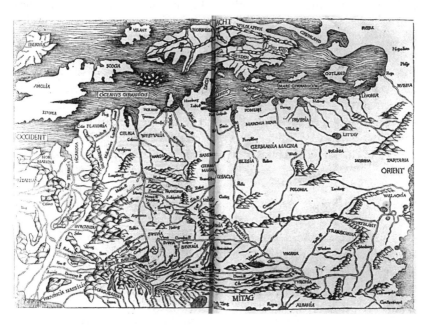

Figure 31 Northern Europe, from Hartmann Schedel, *Historia mundi*, Nuremberg, 1493. Courtesy St Andrews University Library.

attributed to the healthy state of the economy. For Polish agriculture, in particular, the fifteenth century was a period of rapid recovery after the fourteenth century crisis. Flourishing agrarian farming became the basis of a substantial surplus crop that was available for export. By the later sixteenth century this had become a cornerstone of the north European economy. It might defy all present expectations to regard Poland as the breadbasket of Europe, but so in this era it was. Other exports to western Europe included timber, livestock, hides, wool, flax and hemp. Substantial deposits of salt, silver and iron prepared the way for steady expansion of industrial production. By the early sixteenth century Poland had its own money market, and a flourishing urban merchant class.

Economic prosperity created a propitious climate for the consolidation of the Jagiello dynasty. The long reign of Kazimierz IV (1440–92) raised the status of the royal house, and held the ambitions of the powerful barons in check. His first son, Vladislav, succeeded to the thrones of Hugary and Bohemia; three others followed in turn on the throne of Poland. The last of these, Sigismund (1506–48), was a notable patron of the arts, architecture and music; but many of the Italians and Germans who came to Poland in search of commissions worked also for other active patrons in the towns and nobility. This was, in this era, a society with disposable wealth.

During the sixteenth century three major challenges would arise to threaten these generally favourable perspectives. Two were external, and one domestic. Those from without were the challenge of the Reformation from the west, and, from the east, the ambitions of the other major regional power, Muscovy. The perturbations caused by these incursions were then compounded by the failure, through natural causes, of the Jagiellonian dynasty. Sigismund's son, Sigismund-Augustus (1548–72), married three times, but had no male heir. Facing the incipient extinction of his line, and spurred by the ominous power of Muscovy, he decided on fundamental steps to weld together his disparate dominions. A formal union of the Polish and Lithuanian lands was imposed, despite stern resistance from the greatest Lithuanian magnates. Henceforth there was to be one 'Republic' of Poland, with a single assembly, the Sejm, a unified currency, and an elective monarchy.

In view of the hopes invested in this bold constitutional experiment, it was doubly unfortunate that so many of those on whom the crown of Poland/Lithuania was bestowed proved unequal to the responsibilities. The first was one of the worst: Henry of Valois, brother of Charles IX of France and a veteran of the St Bartholomew's Day massacre. He came in February 1573, protesting his devotion to his new lands, only to steal away, four months after the coronation, when the death of his brother presented him with a more enticing prize at home. Thus humiliated, the Polish nobility fell to acrimony and re-crimination, and the new constitution seemed on the verge of collapse. Matters were not helped by Henry's evident determination to retain his Polish kingdom after his return to France, and it required a formal (and time-consuming) process of deprivation before the search for a successor could begin. Yet from among the welter of hopeful candidates (including the predatory neighbour, Ivan the Terrible) emerged a king of unusual capacities, Stefan Batory, Prince of Transylvania. Having seen off his rivals and disciplined the rebellious, Batory embarked on a remarkable reforming career. The judiciary was revitalized and the royal army given a much-needed injection of discipline; the depleted royal treasury was restored. Most of all the apparently inexorable power of Muscovy was turned back. But the vagaries of elective monarchy ensured that much of the good work was undone by a successor, Sigismund III, who like Henry of Valois was more concerned with his homeland (in this case Sweden) than his new kingdom. The election of the scion of the house of Vasa inevitably drew Poland into the ambitious schemes of Scandinavia's most thrusting dynasty; a further complicating factor was Sigismund's Catholicism, which in due course made him even more unacceptable to the pious Swedes than to Poland. Having early in his reign considered abdication – or the ingenious recourse of selling the throne of Poland to the Habsburgs – the death of his father John III (1592) led to a long and ultimately fruitless struggle to make good his rightful claim to Sweden (he was formally deposed in 1599). His Scandinavian preoccupations inevitably alienated many of his previous Polish supporters. The Vasa kings of Poland (Sigismund was succeeded by two of his sons) enjoyed no high reputation.

The constitutional difficulties faced by the post-Jagiellonian kings were all the more trying as a result of the by now immensely complicated state of Polish religion. Poland was, in the mediaeval period, one of the most important and valuable provinces of the Roman Church. A bulwark against Orthodoxy and paganism to the East, in the fifteenth century it had remained largely undisturbed by the Hussite commotions in neighbouring Bohemia. Reflecting this constancy the Polish hierarchy was much cherished in Rome, and through their land holdings, veritable princes of the church. In 1512, for instance, the Archbishop of Gniezno possessed 292 villages and the Bishop of

Cracow 230 – this at a time when the greatest secular magnate possessed only 30 such properties. Such a powerful institution might have seemed well positioned to resist the lure of Protestantism, particularly since the king, Sigismund I, was of a conservative disposition. His strict edicts against Protestantism were initially continued by his son Sigismund Augustus, before the pressure for some relaxation became too intense.

As so often in eastern and northern Europe, the first conduit for Protestant influence was the ethnic German population. In their case Protestantism was eagerly embraced as a manifestation of an ethnic particularity that found little other expression in the Polish/Lithuanian state. The towns of Danzig (Gdańsk), Elbing and Thorn were soon strongholds of Lutheranism, and among the knights of the Teutonic order the pace of defections was so rapid that their Grand Master had little option but to follow their example. In 1525 Albrecht of Hohenzollen begged Sigismund to turn Prussia into a secular fiefdom, with himself as it hereditary duke. Sigismund obliged, and a new northern state was set on its long journey to European predominance. For the moment, however, Prussia remained a loyal Polish fief.

Among ethnic Poles the Reformation made slower progress. Against those who in 1534 promoted the publication of a Polish Bible, the defenders of Catholicism were largely successful in their attempts to paint Protestantism as an alien culture, antipathetic to the traditions of a Catholic faith so deeply embedded in the patriotic past. Thus the progressive amelioration of punitive laws in 1555 and 1557 was mostly of benefit to the German Lutherans of the cities and their few allies among the gentry. At this date the Polish Reformation was on the brink of an important and rather surprising step forward: the planting of a significant and increasingly powerful Calvinist church.

Calvinism found widespread support among the middling nobility, who resented both magnates and bishops, and saw a means to improve their own position. And indeed, Calvinism now made rapid progress, inspired by the charismatic leadership of Jan Laski (John a Lasco), who in 1556 returned to Poland to promote the evangelization of his native land. Two decades of steady pressure brought real political power, with the Calvinists at one point commanding the loyalty of an estimated 20 per cent of the nobility and a majority among lay members of the Sejm. Laski undoubtedly aspired to the conversion of the Polish state, an unrealistic aspiration particularly as shortly after his own death (1560) disagreements within the church led to permanent schism. In part Laski's own well-meaning attempts to promote a religious formula acceptable to all parties was responsible; the confession was rejected by Geneva and ultimately repudiated by the Polish church. Nevertheless the Calvinists remained a powerful lobby, one of several significant confessional groups who benefited from the Confederation of Warsaw of 1573. Enacted in the interregnum following the death of Sigismund II, the conversion was a declaration of the whole Sejm to maintain freedom of conscience as a cardinal principle of public life.

This notwithstanding, fundamental Polish allegiance to Catholicism was not seriously threatened. The Polish Catholic church in fact mounted a very successful defence against the double threat of Protestantism in the west, and Orthodoxy in the lands of Lithuania (a triple threat, if one takes into account the looming presence of Islam). Against the international reputation and connections of Laski Catholicism found its own powerful champion in the charismatic Stanislas Hosius. Hosius, the author of a celebrated Catholic Confession of Faith and many notable works of anti-Protestant polemic, went on to build a considerable international reputation, and was ultimately honoured with a presiding role at the Council of Trent. At home his influence was seconded by the arrival (at his behest) of the Jesuits in 1565. The new orders built on an intense, stubborn religiosity expressed particularly in devotion to the Virgin Mary.

In the second half of the sixteenth century Poland was host to a remarkable variety of Christian faiths, all of considerable vibrancy: Catholics, Calvinists, Lutherans; and among the sectarians, the Bohemian Brethren, Polish Brethren (heirs of the Calvinist schism of 1562), Arians, Antitrinitarians and Unitarians. That they coexisted at all was most unusual, and recognized as such by contemporary commentators. But in truth without some sort of accommodation Polish society could hardly have held together to oppose the greater threat that lurked in the east: the power of Muscovy.

The sprawling lands of Poland/Lithuania were bound to excite the interest of the emerging power of the eastern steppes. The grand princedom of Muscovy had been dramatically enlarged during the reigns of Ivan III (1462–1505) and his son Vasily III (1505–33), mostly at the expense of the declining Tartar power. Eastward expansion continued during the reign of Ivan IV (1533–84), aptly named the Terrible. But it was the tzars' westward ambitions that mostly concerned successive kings of Poland. The sixteenth century opened with a brutal campaign that brought defeat for the Lithuanians and devastating raids deep into Poland. The war continued at intervals until 1537, bringing further victories for Muscovy and territorial gains. The minority of Ivan the Terrible (who succeeded at the age of three) brought an interlude of uneasy calm, before the collapse of the Livonian state in the later 1550s provoked a multilateral conflict, involving Poles, Muscovy and the Scandinavian nations. In Muscovy many disapproved of Ivan's preoccupation with Livonia, and felt that richer pickings were to be had by pursuing expansion to the south and east. The Polish state, however, was not able to profit from these divided counsels, and the result was a malignant stalemate. Ivan returned to haunt the Poles at frequent intervals, proposing himself as king when the crown fell vacant in 1572, and taking advantage of Stefan Batory's internal preoccupations to pounce on Livonia. Christendom breathed a sign of relief when, on 18 March 1584 and exactly as predicted by his 60 astrologers, Ivan suddenly expired.[8]

The Poles knew enough about Muscovy to know that it was a very different society to their own. The tenuous authority of the tzars over the noble class had been built by sporadic outbreaks of murderous violence, episodes that encompassed many hundreds of victims and cruel and inventive methods of execution. Between 1564 and 1570 Ivan further reinforced his authority through the *Oprichnina* experiment, a reign of terror all the more complete since his chosen instruments, the *Oprichnina*, enjoyed complete legal immunity. In 1570, convinced that the city of Novgorod was plotting treachery, Ivan conducted a purge of its leading citizens that left the cultivated city a ransacked wreck. It was, even by contemporary standards, a brutal and arbitrary society.

For all that, Muscovy was increasingly engaging the interest of more than merely its harassed, frightened neighbours. In 1553 a misguided English expedition searching for a north-eastern passage to Asia was shipwrecked on the freezing northern coasts of the Russian Arctic. Its leader, Richard Chancellor, was conveyed to Moscow and to an interview with the tzar; he returned home with a charter granting English merchants rights of trade. The result was the formation of a Muscovy Company, and a sporadic, often strange episode in diplomacy and trade. English interest was confined to Muscovy goods, particularly furs, tar and flax. Ivan had more expansive aims, that extended at times to a possible refuge in England if he fell victim to real or imagined conspiracies, or an English bride. But the English venture was a rare exception, and for the most part Russia remained a largely closed society. The strong streak of insularity was aptly symbolized by the seventeenth-century tzar who kept a special ewer by him to wash his hands whenever he had been polluted by conversation with westerners.

Muscovy was an unusual and exceptional case, and should not unduly colour our perception of eastern Europe as a whole. Even in lands quite distant and remote from the centres of western European culture the events of the sixteenth century could impact in surprising and complex ways. A case in point is Moldavia, a remote kingdom on the borderlands of Russia and modern day Romania. In the sixteenth century it fell under the sway of the Turks and its population was largely Orthodox, but the mid-sixteenth century witnessed an extraordinary attempt to convert the kingdom to Protestantism.[9] This was the project of Jacob Basilicos Heraclides, known as Despot, who ruled the country between 1561 and 1563. Despot was a colourful character, who on early travels in Germany, Scandinavia and Poland had received an eclectic Protestant education. His own confessional position is obscure, though there is some evidence that he may ultimately have come to embrace the radical Reformation. On his accession in 1561 he moved swiftly to introduce Protestant pastors, and to institute a reform of morals based on Protestant principles. This included replacing the local relaxed attitude to divorce (freely available on payment of a fine) with a complete ban. But his disregard for Orthodox sensibilities in this and matters of ceremony – he moved, like Henry VIII, to confiscate sacred vessels made of precious metal – proved his undoing, and in 1563 he was assassinated by the Orthodox boyars.

Despot's short-lived experiment revealed the limits of engagement between the Protestant and Orthodox traditions. In the first decades of Protestant evangelism figures on both sides had been keen to explore the possibilities of co-operation, for which the mutual detestation of Roman Catholicism seemed to provide sufficient basis. But in the last resort the attitudes of the two churches towards the visual aspect of worship – the rich iconographic tradition of the Orthodox contrasting with the much more sceptical stance of Protestantism – created an unbridgeable gulf.

The engagement between the two traditions remained cautious, leaving a tangible monument only in the curious and arrestingly beautiful hybrid religious art that spread through part of the Polish kingdom: altarpieces that adapted features both of the Orthodox icon and the school of the Saxon court painter Lucas Cranach. These, though, are objects of more artistic beauty than theological coherence: a tangible reminder of the curious consequences that may result when different cultural value systems collide and mingle, but without achieving understanding.

14

Culture

The Social Purpose of Art

One of the most significant shifts in European cultural history over the past generation has been the rediscovery of 'popular' culture. Inspired by a seminal book by Peter Burke (published in 1978), the recognition that it is possible to reconstruct the entertainment culture of ordinary people has been both liberating and challenging.[1] It has demanded not only that historians examine a much wider range of cultural media – songs, ballads and proverbs, for instance, as well as plays and paintings – but also that they look at the familiar in a new way. A painting by Pieter Breughel becomes interesting not only for who painted or commissioned it, but also for what it tells us of the recreations of the ordinary: their clothes, dances, gestures and attitudes. A religious procession needs to be considered not only from the point of view of its participants, but also from that of its audience. The effect of these developments has been both to broaden and deepen the study of early modern culture, and to draw it into the mainstream of social history.

Thirty years on these new discoveries are themselves the object of re-evaluation. It is clear now that the term 'popular culture' is itself problematic, for any neat division between what was popular and what was elite has proved elusive. Certainly there were cultural manifestations that by dint of their location, sophistication or expense were exclusively the property of the elite: court masques, for example, or in the world of print, the emblem book. But it is increasingly clear that non-elite cultural forms had an appeal that spread right across the social spectrum. This applied in every area of cultural life. Popular, semi-pagan or superstitious religious practices had as deep a resonance with the aristocracy as in the community as a whole. In another sphere Carnival performed in urban cultures the cathartic role it did precisely because all social orders became involved. And throughout Europe Calvinist consistories found they had overreached themselves in their efforts to regulate the behaviour of the lower orders when they tried to ban dancing; for the magistrates, too, loved to dance.

This is not to say that early modern culture was essentially democratic, or that it conduced to breaking down cultural barriers. The same cultural manifestation could be experienced by citizens of different sorts or conditions in subtly different ways. The altarpiece, commissioned by one of the leading families in the city, would be experienced by the whole community, but each from their ordered place in the body of the church. A procession was in one sense a socially inclusive communal experience, as it wound through the streets; but there again, the position of all participants was carefully laid down to manifest and express publicly their place in the social hierarchy.

With these reflections in mind it probably now makes little sense to describe cultural media as 'elite' or 'popular'. We may learn more about the culture of the sixteenth century by exploring a variety of media in terms of their intention. Of course, none of these categories was hard and fast: the same activity, or artefact, would function differently to different members of the community. But such an approach does bring home that our early modern forebears did not spend precious resources, or their valuable recreational time, without a clear sense of purpose, or audience.

What then, was the social purpose of art? At the risk of inciting the indignation of art historians, for whom the beauty or quality of a work of art is its defining feature, I would propose that expenditure on art, performance or cultural ostentation was intended to perform one or more of the following functions. It was intended for entertainment, or display. It could serve to reinforce hierarchy or group solidarity. It could serve instruction or devotion; and last, and probably least, it could be intended purely for aesthetic pleasure.

First then, art was intended as entertainment. The sixteenth century was not a time when people had no time for recreation. Although work was often poorly paid and back-breakingly hard, it was also bounded: by custom, religious festivals, guild regulations, most of all by the availability of sufficient heat, light and power. Time, for leisure pursuits, was not therefore a particularly scarce resource. Far more circumscribed were the social groups who could spare precious financial resources for non-essential purposes.

Thus although all orders of society possessed a vigorous entertainment culture, expenditure on leisure was already a form of conspicuous consumption, and thus limited either to special occasions (such as a harvest feast) or the upper social orders. For these reasons more formal entertainments played the greatest part in the leisure culture of the court, the noble household, or the urban elites. In the court, access was likely to be restricted; in the cities a play or pageant might be put on as a self-conscious gift of the ruling magistracy to the community as a whole.

In these respects entertainment – recreation in its purest sense – spilt easily into display: an ostentatious exhibition by those with the power that came with surplus wealth. Display was important to sixteenth-century people: to defend or enhance reputation, to assert status or identity, to lay claim to a superior place in society. Sixteenth-century European societies differed in the extent to which wealth defined status, though the accumulation of wealth over a course of years, or generations, seldom went unrewarded in status terms. But only so much could be done through marriage alliances and purchase of nobility or office: many were tempted to accelerate the process through a bold assertion of right, through behaviour, conspicuous expenditure, or dress. Such claims might of course be contested, maligned or ridiculed. One of the most sensitive indicators of cultural belonging was – then as now – dress. Dress was not only one of the most affordable of status indicators; it was also one of the most flexible. If the aspiring found they had overreached themselves, by a doublet of extravagant material, or a hairstyle too elaborate, then these could be far more easily put away, or undone, than an altarpiece could be uncommissioned.

Because dress was such a volatile cultural form, and so susceptible to individual initiative, its implications for status and hierarchy were taken seriously. Many European societies forcibly applied themselves to maintaining social distinctions of dress, particularly to prevent members of inferior social orders adorning themselves in costly fabrics, or wearing a sword, the attribute of nobility. Where social pressure proved insufficient, they reached for legislation. The French crown, for instance, sponsored repeated edicts restricting the wearing of silk. The fact that they returned to the subject so often demonstrates the importance they attached to such regulation; but also, perhaps, how persistently the socially ambitious aspired to the respect that came with costly attire.

Dress could also play its part in the identification of group identity; but then so did many other forms of artistic display or performance. One of the most carefully orchestrated, and subtly layered of such occasions was the gracious entry, a formal meeting between an urban population and their ruler practised in many European cultures, often (though not always) at the beginning of a reign. The constitutional purpose was for the ruler formally to take possession of the city. The population attested their obedience, and the ruler in return promised gracious government consistent with inherited custom and established local privilege. But beneath the outpouring of praise for the new ruler, their dynasty and their qualities, was an unstated but unmistakable assertion of right. This was a right implied by the wealth of the city from which a gracious lord could expect every support – a less generous prince, less so. There was competition, then, both between the town and the prince, and more overtly between the different guilds and estates which vied to outdo each other with the ingenuity, erudition and opulence of their tableaux.

Generosity, duty and piety were all motives freely displayed in such choreographed occasions, as they were in processions, gifts of art or precious artefacts. But they were seldom the sole motive. A rich merchant family who contributed a new altar to the parish church may have been moved by genuine piety, though probably also by hope of benefit in the next world. More immediately they had already marked themselves out in this world as people of status and position. Before the Reformation such pieces would normally be commissioned as a triptych: a holy family or crucifixion in the centre panel, the donor family portrayed with saints in the side panels. The tradition proved a resilient one, even in lands where Protestantism took root. Although such places had no further use for saints, they often continued to cherish religious art, and in Lutheran Germany there emerged the strange hybrid form of the funeral picture. This was a single panel with a scene usually from the New Testament, and arrayed beneath (redeployed from the redundant side panels) the deceased and his kin. Here, in these stiff figures, menfolk to the left, wife and daughters to the right, lay the primitive origins of the family portrait. We see the continuation of this tradition in the funeral monuments of the English Anglican Church.

Thus was art, through its opulence, its quality, through the renown of the commissioned artist (which might or might not be the same thing) an essential tool in the reinforcement of social hierarchy. Commissioned art did not remain the preserve of the wealthy individual.

Groups such as guilds, fraternities and learned societies would also commission art, partly to signal their importance within the social nexus, partly as an expression of group solidarity. The guild altarpiece, or portrait of a patron saint, was the most common artistic expression of this in the period before the Reformation. Later, particularly in Protestant cultures, this gave way to the group portrait, in the first known examples usually stiff figures arrayed around an equally stiff and unappealing banquet. It would not be until the following century (particularly in the Dutch Republic, where the group portrait attained its greatest popularity) that artists would fully master the peculiar problems posed by the lifelike depiction of large numbers of figures.

Works of art could be didactic (as could buildings). Art could express a truly held personal piety, though the intensity of the feeling communicated would in this case owe as much to the skill of the artisan as the passion of the patron. But a purely aesthetic motivation was an indulgence for the very few. One can think of a few individuals for whom the pursuit of art for its own sake became a consuming passion, such as the emperor Rudolf, who in later years shut himself off with his burgeoning collection of curiosities in the castle at Prague. Meanwhile his dominions slid into discord and disarray. But such rare (and discouraging) examples rather make the point: the arts flourished in society precisely because those involved in the economy of culture understood their purpose. And this went for those who created such artefacts, as much as those who vied for their possession.

Court Culture

From all that has been said above it will be clear that the courts of Europe provided by far the greatest opportunities for cultural display. Europe's ruling houses disposed of the largest resources – if not necessarily in terms of cash, then implicitly through the income of their lands and taxes. What they could not always pay for they could often command. Their courts also represented permanent concentrations of influential people who must be awed, impressed and also diverted during the longeurs of court ceremony. Courts stimulated the most formal, but also the most elaborate of entertainments.

In court culture the border between business and pleasure was elided to extinction. Any gathering involving large numbers became the opportunity for negotiation and exchange of information. Any ordinary personal function involving the ruler became enmeshed in layers of formality and custom. In this respect the everyday bodily functions of the prince – eating, riding, hunting, devotions – became as important a part of court routine as the conduct of business. Princes sent important signals by how they conducted themselves on such occasions; and they eagerly imitated and adopted the protocol of the most fashionable courts.

For all this there was also a place for recreation, and many kings, nobles and bishops eagerly embraced the cultural opportunities that came to them by virtue of their wealth and status. Many commissioned or collected fine things: art, of course, but also tapestries, jewellery and books. Tapestries were a particular vogue in the sixteenth century, valued for their intricacy and workmanship, but also for their practical value to rulers or nobles who had many properties to furnish. When a lord moved around his dominions with his household, tapestries could be rolled up in the baggage to adorn a new set of draughty walls. Perhaps even more than paintings, in the sixteenth century tapestries were employed to laud the achievements or lineage of the ruling house: the proud monarch portrayed in some imaginary classical scene, or representations of one of their greatest victories. Jewellery and plate were also functional aspects of cultural display, for alongside their aesthetic and artistic merit they represented a portable reserve of wealth. Many a crowned head would *in extremis* turn such artefacts into liquid cash, whether by having them melted down, or preferably, leaving them in pawn with their bankers.

Books, though of less immediate utilitarian purpose, were no less eagerly collected. By the sixteenth century an extensive, costly library had become an almost indispensable badge of cultural belonging for Europe's major rulers. Some of these collections were huge: when Philip II moved the first instalment of his library to the Escorial this was already a collection of 4,000 volumes, and 30 years of collecting lay ahead. Royal collectors also invested largely in lavish and ornate bindings, and commissioned special copies printed on vellum rather than the usual paper. The greatest rulers, of course, also collected scholars, but whereas only one could have Erasmus (and none could reincarnate Cicero) all could proclaim the sophistication of their commitment to the liberal arts by buying, embellishing and displaying costly editions. When it came time to open their covers, then reading too could be a very public act. Those who could afford it would generally choose to be read to, and such a preference implied neither ignorance nor intellectual indifference (any more than employing a chauffeur implies anything about your driving skills). In an age when

Figure 32 Solomon receiving the Queen of Sheba, Flemish tapestry. Photo © CMN.

habits of oral communication trained the memory, learning could effectively be imbibed by such means. Rulers such as Henry VIII, Francis I and Philip II were regarded in their day as men of refinement and learning, and this was more than just conventional flattery. All took a keen interest in issues of the mind, and their encouragement gave the lead to others around them. Sixteenth-century courts were a perplexing mixture of high culture and the basest brutality.

Music played an exceptionally important role in the life of the court. Most of Europe's rulers employed a decent troupe of singers and instrumentalists; some were themselves highly accomplished musicians. Henry VIII was a skilful lutanist and a fair composer; though his continental contemporaries could not always match him for skill, they certainly shared his determination to create a sophisticated environment for performance. Francis I was one of a number who turned a blind eye to the dubious practices used to recruit for the choir of the chapel royal: several boys with beautiful voices were kidnapped, which was apparently not uncommon.[2] Collectors as they were, Europe's crowned heads vied for the best composers, the most beautiful voices. But the composers were not hard to persuade to attach themselves to one or other of Europe's major courts: here lay the best prospect of a decent living, as well as access to the best trained musicians to perform their works. In consequence, most of the great composers of the sixteenth century did their finest work at court: Vittoria at the court of Philip II, Thomas Tallis at successive English courts (seemingly indifferent to the changes of religion that spanned his long career).

Instrumental players had at this day a much lower status. As mere mechanicals, their life was often hard, since they were forced to attend the court when the prince went on progress, or even on campaign. They could expect inferior billets; when they were not playing they might even be expected to haul artillery, or perform other menial functions of camp life. In the long run, however, all those involved in the production and dissemination of music would profit from royal patronage of music printing. This was the age when the printers of Europe fully mastered the art of printing music from moveable type, first with single line notation, then in parts. The technology was comparatively intricate, and required considerable investment: it thus benefited greatly from the interest of Europe's rulers, and the protection, by way of monopolies, they gave to their favoured printers. With these printed part songs, music was ready to make an important leap out of the public domain and into the private home. By the end of the sixteenth century such parlour music was an important part of the entertainment culture of well-off burgher households.

During the course of the sixteenth century Europe's rulers also lavished huge resources on the setting of court life, on the internal and external architecture of their palaces and castles. The sixteenth century was a time of feverish building, remodelling and architectural innovation for crowned heads all over Europe. The best known, because the most striking and enduring examples of this architectural enterprise, are the Loire châteaux of Francis I, which have survived virtually unchanged from that day to this. Distant from the main cities, the Loire châteaux nevertheless made a striking polemical point, for this was indeed the first age in which kings of France could build or remodel their castles with concern only for beauty, rather than the need that they should be defensible. By their ostentatious lack of ramparts or features of conventional castle architecture they made a clear point about the unchallenged power of their royal occupant.

The French kings were by no means unusual either in their enthusiasm as builders, or in the resources they poured into their schemes. Henry VIII, partly through the dissolution of the religious houses, accumulated over 40 royal residences by the end of the reign, and considerable care was given to fitting out and rebuilding the most favoured. The Habsburgs, as one might expect, were assiduous and ambitious builders. When Ferdinand I took possession of Bohemia Italian artists and architects were soon summoned to his retinue. The Belvedere, a colonnaded interior garden created for the Prague castle, was a fine and at the time no doubt sensational example of the application of Italian principles.[3] Yet this was only the first of a number of ambitious architectural projects with which the Habsburgs changed the face of their central European cities. Nor were they alone. The architectural enthusiasms of the Jaglionian kings of Poland have already been mentioned, and the competition for precedence among Germany's princely houses had predicable consequences. When the Saxon electors renovated their castle of Torgau in the 1530s they added several modish features, including an exterior spiral staircase that would not be out of place at Amboise or Chenenceau. The rival branch of the Wettin family in Ducal Saxony was not to be outdone. When after the Schmalkaldic War the Electoral dignity passed into their hands, Maurice of Saxony celebrated his new dignity by building a new castle in Dresden, and began a significant transformation of the city. The greatest of the German prince-builders was Maximilian I, Duke of Bavaria. His patronage was an appropriately lavish celebration of a ruling house that had staked its position and reputation on an unswerving devotion to Catholicism. As their cause prospered with the progress of the Catholic Reformation, so their architectural manifestations became more triumphalist and baroque – as this implies, the greatest achievements of this rebuilding lay in the seventeenth century.

Most singular, and certainly the most doggedly pursued of all the royal building projects was Philip II's new palace at the Escorial. This formed part of a larger project to move the centre of Spanish administration from Toledo to Madrid: perhaps to avoid the damp climate of the city on the Tagus, perhaps to break free of a city associated for centuries with the power of the great magnates. With the court settled (somewhat unwillingly) in the new capital, Philip conceived for himself a new, more private family residence some way out of the city. The new San Lorenzo del Escorial reflected a variety of intentions. It was to be a monastic foundation, to celebrate Philip's great victory over the French at St Quentin, and to include a royal palace, the royal library, and a chapel with a family mausoleum. Begun in 1563, construction and refinement continued for much of the reign, but by 1568 the Escorial had already become a part of Philip's regular perambulation around the circuit of royal residences within striking distance of

Madrid. An intensely personal creation, Philip came increasingly to rely on its apartments, chapel and formal gardens for peace to reflect, and freedom to discharge the mountain of administration that pressed for his attention. The total cost of the works, revealed in the meticulously preserved accounts, was almost six million ducats.[4]

The Escorial was perhaps the most extreme example of what was a more general phenomenon in the sixteenth century: monarchy was becoming more static. Princes established a principal seat, or residence, if not always yet a capital city; their working regime involved steadily more attention to dispatches and administration, and less relentless an itinerary of travel than had been the lot of Charles V and Maximilian I. If the king could no longer be everywhere in person, more attention was given to the promotion of image by proxy. Likenesses of the prince were multiplied and distributed in a variety of different media. Most conventional was the mass-production of a favoured portrait. Henry IV of France, Elizabeth of England and others all promoted their image in this way, though the first fully documented case was that of Elector John Frederick of Saxony, who in 1532 ordered no fewer than 60 copies of a paired portrait of himself and his brother from the workshop of the court painter, Lucas Cranach.[5] Presumably these were intended for distribution both to favoured families within Saxony and to other German princes. The Saxon electors also made use of the more economical device of the portrait woodcut: some of Albrecht Dürer's finest work was in this medium.

A further flexible alternative to the painted image was the portrait medallion, a Renaissance fashion that spread in the sixteenth century through northern Europe. As a form of representation medals had much to recommend them, being portable, hardy and relatively easily mass produced. In fifteenth-century Italy most medals were cast from wax dies, and the fashion spread remarkably quickly after the technical applications had been mastered in the 1440s. Most subjects were the predictable popes, warriors and patrons, though the range of those immortalized in this way was at an early stage extended to the artists themselves: a professional indulgence common also in the world of portraiture. In the sixteenth century most crowned heads had medals struck, often associated with important milestones or famous victories, and it was not long before the form became widely parodied by their opponents. Each important turning point in the Dutch Revolt, for instance, was marked by a flurry of celebratory medallions on the part of the Spanish administration or the Dutch insurgents. But in these propaganda exchanges the state powers held most of the cards, not least because they disposed of the most powerful instrument for spreading the royal image throughout their dominions: the coinage. During the sixteenth century the custom of having a portrait head of the ruling monarch on the coinage became generalized through Europe, though there was little attempt to impose exclusive use of a nation's coinage for internal monetary transactions. Since coins still nominally contained quantities of precious metal equivalent to their exchange value, coins of many lands generally circulated freely together. But for all that, the rights to issue coinage were carefully controlled as an essential mark of lordship. Counterfeiting or clipping money was everywhere regarded as a most heinous crime, and often punished as treason or *lese majesté*.

Patrons and Artists

In the sixteenth-century world artists required their patrons, and most of the best-known figures did work to command. This is true of all the major composers, and most of the visual artists: Raphael and Michelangelo worked for Julius II and his successors in Rome, Holbein for Henry VIII, Lucas Cranach for Frederick the Wise. Few notable artists built a reputation without at some point attaching themselves to one of the major courts. For a young man at the beginning of a career this was the obvious way to both riches and reputation. The great princes could attract the best and reward most lavishly. The knowledge that they stood high in the favour of the great attracted further commissions from others at court eager to patronize the most esteemed artists.

In the course of the sixteenth century some of the great names succeeded, to a limited extent, in shifting the relationship in their favour. The greed and acquisitiveness of the Renaissance kings, above all their desire to bask in the glory of employing the greatest names, gave a small elite of artists a power never before accorded the artisan. Leonardo, like Erasmus, could pick and choose, and some of the Italians who accepted the eager patronage of Francis I gave little in return. Dürer, too, established a position of unusual independence. But these were very much the exception, men who through unusual talent, and generally only at the end of their careers, had earned themselves this degree of freedom.

A far more typical case is that of the German master, Hans Holbein. Holbein is best known today for his superb, insightful portraits of the leading figures of the court of Henry VIII. In fact, his position as the king's painter meant that he occupied most of his time in far more mundane work, devising and executing decorative schemes for the king's palaces: it was for this work that he drew his salary. No matter, for Holbein's status as the king's painter assured that his talents as a portrait artist wound not go unnoticed. Holbein's English career, in fact, is a masterly demonstration of the silky skills necessary for success in the volatile world of court politics. Convinced by the iconoclastic riots that accompanied the Reformation of the need to leave Basle, Holbein applied to his friend Erasmus for an introduction to the English court. The great Humanist was happy to oblige. 'The arts are freezing here', Erasmus reported of Holbein to his friend Pieter Gilles in Antwerp; so 'he is on his way to England to pick up some angels [gold coins]'.[6] In England, Holbein attached himself first to Erasmus's friend Thomas More, but as More's career languished with the failure of Henry's marriage to Catherine of Aragon, Holbein transferred his allegiance to More's great antagonist and tormentor, Thomas Cromwell. The two portraits of More and Cromwell that now face each other across a fireplace in the Frick collection in New York are a monument as much to Holbein's skill as a politician as his great talent as an artist. Through Cromwell Holbein passed into the service of the king, and hence to fame and prosperity. Having left Basle to escape the consequences of the Reformation, the artist settled happily to a career capturing the likenesses of the new Tudor elite, and any other tasks that came his way, such as a title-page design for the Coverdale Bible.

In this ideological flexibility Holbein was hardly unusual among sixteenth-century artists: most accommodated themselves easily to the prevailing religious ethos of their place of work. The German Erhard Altdorfer produced notable work in the Protestant tradition, while his brother, Albrecht, comfortably settled in Catholic Regensburg, produced pictures of unimpeachable orthodoxy. Holbein was also not unusual in his versatility. Artists would be expected to turn their skills to whatever their employer required, whether this was designs for wall decorations, artefacts or tableaux, woodcuts, altarpieces or family portraits. Lucas Cranach, court artist of Frederick the Wise of Saxony, did all of these, and more. His most reliable source of income was in fact the monopoly of spices and medicines he held for his apothecary business.

We can absorb several other important lessons from this examination of the career of Holbein and other contemporaries. Even when we accept that a man like Holbein was constrained in his choice of tasks, we tend to ascribe to the artist at least a principal role in the process of composition. This expectation has a lot to do with shifts in taste and a primary concentration on artists – rather than patrons – in art historical scholarship. This may leave a distorted view of their respective roles in the creative process. Renaissance patrons generally commissioned a work for a particular purpose, to hang in a specific place, or to tell a particular story. It would be naive to assume that they did not involve themselves fully in order to ensure that the end product met their expectations.

This certainly was the pattern established in the culture that incubated the art of the Renaissance, Italy. In Florence, artistic patronage was, as much else in this most orderly of bureaucratic societies, carefully regulated by both contract and custom. At the beginning of the fifteenth century the principal financiers of major public projects were the guilds. The rise of the Medici was accompanied by a far more confident and less inhibited patronage of art and buildings by private citizens of wealth. The Medici took the lead, but their use of the arts to reinforce their claim to leadership also inspired others and in the later half of the fifteenth century the public face of Florence was substantially rebuilt. The example of Florence was eagerly pursued in Venice, and in the new courts of the *condottieri* dukes, Mantua, Urbino and Ferrara. Here, as elsewhere, it was the patron who held the whip hand. Many took an active role in the design of their projects, whether architectural or decorative. Some were themselves talented architects or craftsmen. Cosimo de Medici is even said to have provided the original design adopted by King Alfonso of Naples for his villa at Poggioreale.

This fever of building and creativity indicated several important general principles in the relationship between those who commanded, and those who executed such works. First the power of the patron, the patron as creator. Not untypical was the attitude of Isabella d'Este, Duchess of Mantua, one of the most prolific collectors and patrons of the early sixteenth century. For her suite in the Palazzo Ducale she attempted to attract the best artists in Italy: her principal interest was the content of the paintings not harmony of style, and she issued exceptionally detailed instructions. Giovanni Bellini actually refused the commission because of its lack of flexibility; the contract signed by Perugino for a mythological group specified theme, figures, clothes, and what was to appear in the background. Painters would also be expected to accommodate their work to the political positions of those who commissioned them: a requirement that demanded acute sensitivity in a polity as turbulent as sixteenth-century Florence.

Modern taste also diverges from the values of the fifteenth and sixteenth-century cultural universe in the value we attach to different cultural artefacts. In general we now attach greater value to paintings than sculpture and architectural design. This was not the case then. In mediaeval craft society the cost of a work of art was assessed largely in terms of its materials and labour, and artists paid for their skill as an artisan: creative genius had no recognizable financial value. In the values of the time, bronze was costly, marble less so; the value of a panel painting might well be less than its elaborate gilded frame. Fresco (painting on walls) was the cheapest of them all. Tapestry was generally valued far more highly than panel-painting or fresco. Architecture, which offered the most obvious display of power and wealth (not least by its cost) was regarded as the highest of the arts; painting was more appropriate for the more private expression of religious duty.

The question that confronts us is how far the new age of the Renaissance challenged these pitiless mercantile values. Once again, Italy led the way, and certainly by the beginning of the sixteenth century a good painter was recognized as bringing an additional creative talent to his work. Here the growth of Humanism, and the experience of classical literature, had a profound impact on the perception of the artist. Those who read Cicero's praise of his collection of sculpture, or the works of the Elder and Younger Pliny, were introduced to a concept of beautiful art that gave aesthetic pleasure quite apart from any religious function or civic obligation. Implicit was the concept of the work of art as the creation of its artist. Such literary models made a tangible impact in Florence and beyond by the end of the fifteenth century, but the beneficiaries were those at the very peak of their profession. Most artists continued to be regarded as members – albeit skilled members – of an artisan trade.

By the later sixteenth century we see both models of the artist's role existing in parallel. A large number of artists, even those at the peak of their profession, continued to cling tightly to royal and princely courts. One could name here the Clouets in France, Pontormo in Florence (where Medici patronage kept him occupied on one project for the last decade of his life), Antonio Mor at the Habsburg court in Brussels, or Zuccaro, who journeyed from Italy to work on the interior decoration of the Escorial. Against this, the sixteenth century threw up a growing number of artists who won fame through the development of a highly individual style: one thinks of El Greco, Hieronymus Bosch or Pieter Breughel. Yet even in these cases the artists owe their fame to the fact that their talents were quickly recognized by powerful patrons, in all of these cases, the Habsburgs, who by this time had superseded the Italian cities and courts as the greatest patrons of European art. Most of Breughel's greatest paintings are divided between the three great Habsburg collections in Vienna, Brussels and Madrid, and to see the best of Hieronymus Bosch's one must also make the pilgrimage to the Prado, for Philip II showed an early fascination for the opaque and mysterious world of the great Flemish painter. El Greco, a native of Crete, was from 1577 permanently resident in Toledo, where his work too caught the eye of the royal patron.

In conclusion one might legitimately regard the sixteenth century as a transitional era on the road to the establishment of a commercial art market. In the seventeenth century the great patrons would still commission; but they, and other collectors, would also buy on the open market. Artists would increasingly paint for the market, a development that would inevitably lead, as they discovered which of their works were most marketable, to an increase in specialization, and narrowing of their range. One sees something of this already in such idiosyncratic painters as those last mentioned, Breughel and El Greco, who found fame and fortune in a specific style and genre. These developments would reach their apogee in the seventeenth-century Dutch Republic, a society exceptional in its social disposition of art, and the extent to which religion, as a motive or subject of painting, was relegated to a subsidiary place. But it was only here, and in these exceptional circumstances, that the artist was finally emancipated from the patron.

Medium and Message

Two questions confront any general survey of sixteenth-century culture. Was there any significant change in the media of cultural exchange during the sixteenth century? And if so, were these varied cultural forms expected to meet any substantially different needs? These questions are at least partly stimulated by an intuitive sense that the arts found a broader public as the century wore on, and that, in response to the new social and religious movements of the day, they were actively engaged to sway this new public as instruments of propaganda.

Both propositions indeed contain the germ of truth. While many manifestations of the higher arts remained an elite privilege, possession and purchase did come within the purview of a gradually expanding public. In the first decades of the sixteenth century only members of

Europe's highest aristocracies could aspire to have their likeness preserved, whether in the supporting wings of a religious painting, or in
the emerging field of the independent portrait. By the end of the
century many relatively modest bourgeois citizens could commission
such a portrait; their sense of pride still glows from the canvas in many
a museum collection, even if their identities are now lost again in the
anonymity they had sought to escape by this conspicuous investment.

Fundamentally, though, portrait painting remained a difficult skill,
and an expensive one, and this restricted potential ownership. This was
not the case with the woodcut. As with the transformation from
manuscript to print, so the application of woodcut technology made
possible a mass market in representational art. These were opportunities swiftly recognized in the sixteenth century, if not wholly grasped.
One of the first to seize the potential of the new medium was the
precociously talented German artist Albrecht Dürer. The son of a
goldsmith, Dürer seems to have imbibed the meticulous care and
attention to detail peculiar to that craft even as he embarked on his
career as a painter. His early apprenticeship included both travels in
Italy and work as a book illustrator in Basle and Strasbourg. He was
thus well placed to apply to the conventional religious painting of the
German masters both the new sophistication of the Renaissance and
the radical potential of the black/white medium of the woodcut.
Dürer excelled in all branches of his art, receiving commissions for
major altarpieces from across Germany. More elaborate decorative
designs were executed at the command of the emperor Maximilian,
an important patron. But Dürer found his widest public with the
magnificent cycles of woodcuts, two Passion series and an Apocalypse,
which he executed in his mature years. Dürer did not regard these as
the least of his artistic achievement. He kept careful control of the
numbers of copies printed, and they fetched a good price. From the
beginning of his career Dürer had shown a keen financial sense: already
by 1497 he had hired an agent to handle his foreign sales, and his
prints became the cornerstone of his prosperity. In August 1509 he
complained in a letter to the wealthy Frankfurt cloth merchant Jacob
Heller, for whom he had taken a year painting an altarpiece, that he
would have been better off if he had stuck to producing prints.[7] To a
master of Dürer's status and erudition, there was a world of difference
between this, the woodcut as artwork, and hack-work for cheap illustrations, either in books or broadsheets. But most of the great German
masters (including Holbein and Dürer himself) cut their teeth on such
schlechtes Holzwerk.

The woodcut as a form encouraged cleanness of line and didactic simplicity. There was less room for shade and subtleties of tone than in work with oils, or in metal-plate engraving. In this respect it was indeed the perfect tool for a polemical age.

The woodcut was well established in art and book culture before the Reformation. Indeed, some would argue that the height of technical accomplishment in the medium was already reached in the first two decades of the sixteenth century. They already had an important role in the first mature age of the printed book, both in supplying technical diagrams and illustrations (such as astrological charts and topographical panorama); the woodcut made possible the great strides in map-making that would follow in this century. But when the new religious controversies erupted in Germany, coincidentally home to the best developed and most widely disseminated woodcut culture, the protagonists were quick to recognize its potential. Woodcuts were soon being employed as illustrations in polemical and didactic literature, and independent broadsheets. The first known representation of Martin Luther was on the title-page of an edition of the Leipzig disputation of 1519, though it would be an exaggeration to describe it as a likeness. What we have is no more than a primitive outline of a preaching monk, no doubt designed by one who had not known the newly famous preacher. By the following year, though, Luther's features were becoming well known throughout Germany through the dissemination of a series of striking portraits by the Wittenberg artist Lucas Cranach. These combine physical realism with an messianic glorification of the reformer. This was a propaganda image of striking simplicity: the image of the simple monk, the man of the book, alone against the massed ranks of the pope and his minions, could not have been made more transparent.

This simplicity may have been the key to its success. In the years that followed, artists and printers combined with the Protestant theologians to produce a series of broadsheets and pictorial polemics much admired by posterity. Here, it has been argued, in the artful combination of picture and text, lay the elusive bridge between the literate and the broader public that the Reformation sought (in the 1520s successfully) to engage.[8] Personally, I have considerable doubts whether this is how things actually operated in a sixteenth-century context. The picture of the literate cobbler expounding the text to his less gifted companions is a beguiling one, and conforms to our modern sense of the greater accessibility of the visual. But many of these polemical illustrations are extremely complex, and hardly accessible to those of meaner education. In any case, the tradition of the satirical broadsheet was very largely confined to Germany, and does little to explain the equal success of the Protestant message in other cultures where religious polemic was scarcely ever accompanied in illustration. In due course we may come to recognize these illustrations as more akin to the modern cartoon (of which they were the first precursors): that is, polite diversion for the literate and educated, reinforcing an already received message. The primary mode of dissemination lay, as with any other message in this period, in the combination of text and the spoken word; spoken, that is, or sung, for the role of music and singing as a polemical tool is vastly undervalued.

Nevertheless, among the literate, book owners and readers (for most woodcuts were published in books) the woodcut did perform an important educational function. This was not primarily polemical. Most woodcuts appeared not in works of theology but in technical scientific books, works of astrology and astronomy, and in new genres that flourished largely thanks to the woodcut, such as travel books and works of botany, horticulture, topography and anatomy. In this technical sense the sixteenth century did take important steps towards the visual representation of knowledge. By the end of the sixteenth century the woodcut had begun to give ground to the more technically subtle medium of metal-plate engraving. In its capacity for fine line and shading this soon became an important artistic medium in its own right.

If the claims of the woodcut as an evangelical teaching tool must be downplayed, it is still necessary to consider the wider issue of the impact of the Reformation on the arts. Was the Reformation, as is often assumed, a disaster for the fine arts? At first sight, the charge sheet makes grim reading. In all the parts of Europe where the Reformation took root the visual arts underwent a significant transformation. From the beginning the reformers favoured an extremely strict interpretation of the biblical commandment against idolatry. In Wittenberg Luther's colleague Karlstadt took advantage of his absence in 1521–2 to purge the churches of statues and altarpieces, and such acts of iconoclasm became commonplace in the Reformation century. It was the ferocious attack on the church art of Basle that drove Holbein away in 1529, and several German cities experienced similar assaults.

While few mainstream reformers could approve such violent and disorderly proceedings the orderly removal of religious images became a high priority in many places where the Reformation attained an early supremacy. When the issue was debated in Zurich in 1523, Zwingli supported Karlstadt in advocating the removal of all paintings and sculptures. His precepts were followed so meticulously that in due course he could report, 'in Zurich we have churches which are positively luminous; the walls are beautifully white'.[9] In Strasbourg Martin Bucer had reached similar conclusions by 1524. Hostility towards images reached its height with the spreading influence of Calvin in the second half of the century. In his *Institutes of the Christian Religion* Calvin laid out with great clarity the depth of his hostility to any visual representation of God, and this theological understanding was given greater emphasis by smaller, polemical pamphlets in which he articulated his loathing for the polluting consequences of idolatry. At one point he compares idolaters to latrine cleaners. 'Hardened by habit, they sit in their own excrement, and yet believe they are surrounded by roses.'[10]

With this rhetorical background it is hardly surprising that the advance of all major Calvinist churches was accompanied by a holocaust of images: in Scotland, France, most famously in the Netherlands. In the process precious and irreplaceable objects of great value were lost forever. Iconoclasm was so widespread partly because it was so effective. In places where the magistrates dragged their feet, attacks on images were a highly effective way of forcing the issue; one could discuss later whether proper authority had been sought or granted, but the damage could not be undone. That of course, was another major weapon in the hands of the iconoclasts, that the changes wrought by the destruction of art could be made good only at enormous expense. Thus in countries that shifted back and forth between confessions, such as England in the reign of Mary, the Protestant stripping of the altars could only partially be repaired. There were other, deeper psychological forces at work as well. At one level the savage attack on the churches, the repudiation of a previously cherished tradition, mirrored the sudden drama of a conversion experience, a similarly traumatic event that reorientated understanding of God and severed ties with the past. Attacks on religious statues and pictures were also a direct challenge to the miraculous powers often attributed or implied for the holiest objects of veneration: for if these objects possessed such potency, why would they not defend themselves? In a culture where the miraculous played such an important role there was an expectation that those who laid sacrilegious hands on such holy things would not go unpunished; when they did, it was a telling blow against the old faith. Iconoclasts drove home their point by subjecting rejected images to ritual humiliations, or turning them to humdrum domestic use (a hollow painted statue might be reused as a pig trough). Even in cultures where, as in England, the removal of images was managed in an orderly manner, this was often accompanied by official demonstrations of the fraudulence of 'feigned miracles and false relics'.

Nevertheless, the consequences of the Reformation for the arts were by no means as monochrome or disastrous as these circumstances might suggest. Luther was not personally hostile to the arts; indeed, in one respect (in his love of music) he showed a high artistic sensibility. In theological terms he was far more concerned to effect change from wrong use than to destroy works of art, and the radicalism of Karlstadt violated his innate sense of order. Luther returned to Wittenberg in 1522 largely to put a stop to the changes initiated in his absence; the disgraced Karlstadt was exiled to a country parish. Luther's more benign sense that the pictorial arts were not in themselves harmful set the tone for the developing Lutheran tradition. Lutheran churches continued to favour a relatively ornate decorative style, and while certain forms of traditional religious painting lost ground new themes emerged to take their place. The development of a new and distinctive Protestant idiom in religious painting owed much to the personal co-operation of Luther, Melanchthon and Lucas Cranach, court painter of Frederick the Wise. Cranach has already been mentioned in connection with his important series of portraits of Luther, and his woodcut propaganda in favour of the Reformation. He also assisted the reformers in finding new visual representations for critical themes of Protestant theology. One of the most important of these new motifs was 'the Law and the Gospel', a juxtaposition of the old Law of Moses, and the new saving power of Christ's crucifixion and redemption. This theme found enduring success both as a theme in panel painting and as a book title-page. Cranach, a highly astute businessman who made a fortune through his various ventures, also made a major contribution to the Reformation through the provision of illustrative woodcuts for Bibles and other Wittenberg imprints.

The experience of Wittenberg set the tone for an extensive and generally harmonious engagement between Lutheranism and the arts. In other German cities that adopted reform, artists such as Bruyn, the brothers Beham and Dürer accommodated themselves easily to the change. Indeed, with the coming of the Reformation to Hungary, Poland and the wide expanses of northern Germany, German artists found themselves in increasing demand in these lands. The court and urban culture of places like Pomerania, Cracow and Wrocław manifest a fascinating *mélange* of existing indigenous

Figure 33 Augustin Cranach, Conversion of St Paul, *Epitaph for Vitus Oertel*, 1586. Courtesy Evangelische Stadtkirchen gemeinde, Lutherstadt Wittenberg.

artistic traditions and two new forces: German art and the Italian Renaissance. The results are a complex artistic heritage that deserves to be better known.

The Swiss Reformed tradition left less scope for purely religious art. Zwingli took pride in Zurich's severely whitewashed churches, and most Reformed cultures pursued the ideal of churches 'cleansed' of all internal decoration. Nevertheless, this did not mean that there was no room for artistic sensibility. Zwingli was most extreme in prohibiting the visual and musical arts from Christian worship, but even he did not disallow the arts altogether, limiting them to a non-reverential use in the home and public places: so long as they were merely historical representations, and not doctrinal aids. Calvin took a much more positive position. So long as idolatry was avoided, along with any representation of the Godhead, Calvin in fact showed a clear appreciation of the part refined aesthetic appreciation could play in the building of faith. Calvinist countries continued to be home to a robust artistic tradition. If official commissions for churches were no longer available (and sculptors suffered particularly) then domestic art flourished as prosperous citizens redeployed resources into the adornment of their homes. By the seventeenth century the Calvinist Dutch Republic was home to Europe's liveliest and most socially dispersed art market, and even in France an important fraction of the leading painters and graphic artists were Calvinists. More specifically, in two areas, music and architecture, Calvinism made a distinctive and original contribution to sixteenth-century culture.

Luther's love of music is well known, and he quickly discerned the important role it might play in spreading the Gospel message. His concern to involve the laity more in church worship led him towards important liturgical innovation of lasting impact. Most important was his promotion of the chorale (or hymn), German language verses in stanza form, set to music adapted from German secular tunes of the period and sung by the whole congregation. This gave the congregation a far more active role than had been customary in the Mass, where participation was limited to responses, and music would be the sole preserve of the priest (or, in more elaborate settings, the choir).

The Calvinist churches learned from Luther's innovation, but adapted it in significant ways. The core of the Calvinist musical tradition was the metrical psalms, that is, psalms set for congregational use, to be sung by the whole congregation in the vernacular, one note per syllable. The musical simplicity and lack of decoration encouraged the emphasis on the words that Calvin so favoured, but was also the basis of an extraordinary cultural phenomenon, for the different metre of the verse text meant that it was usually impossible to use a tune for more than one psalm. Once learned then, a tune became indelibly associated with a particular psalm, canticle, or prayer. As the movement spread the psalms followed, from the churches to the barns and other places of secret worship, out into the streets, and on to the battlefield. The metrical psalms became the mark of identity of the Calvinist insurgency. Calvinists sung their psalms as they were led to execution, in their demonstrations for freedom of conscience, as they went about building churches or smashing images. Psalm 68 became the song of battle; its rumbling metre could strike fear into the hearts of the enemy even before the Huguenot forces became visible. As time went on Protestant composers prepared four-part harmonizations for domestic parlour use. Their enduring appeal is demonstrated by the fact that the rural communities of the Protestant Cévennes in Southern France apparently developed no lullaby tradition: the mothers sang their babies to sleep with psalms.

We are faced here with two aspects of music not always sufficiently appreciated: its value as a teaching tool and its role in building group solidarity. Both have their echoes in modern life; the first is still recognized today in pre-school and primary education, the second most obviously in the chants and songs of sports' supporters. But in the sixteenth century, an age when many could still not read, this was a cultural phenomenon of first importance. Perhaps here lies the key to the success of Protestantism in building a mass movement spanning the literate and illiterate that historians have vainly sought in the illustrated woodcut.

The Protestant architectural tradition has proved less robust, partly through natural wastage of what were largely urban buildings (thus vulnerable to redevelopment), and partly through deliberate destruction. All the Huguenot temples in France, for instance, were destroyed as the local Catholic powers reasserted their authority, or at the latest after the Revocation of the Edict of Nantes by Louis XIV in 1685. Often it was the Catholic population themselves who took the initiative in erasing the hated symbol of the despised Calvinist faith. But in their own time these new Protestant churches evolved a new architectural style that was both striking and a radical addition to the urban townscape. In Germany, the opportunities to express the new theological and pastoral priorities of the Reformation through innovation in church design were minimal, since the Lutheran churches by and large simply appropriated existing buildings. The same was true of other state-sponsored Reformations such as England and Scandinavia.

In France and in the first phase of the Dutch Revolt, however, freedom of worship was normally made strictly conditional on the Calvinists vacating any churches they may have seized and ransacked. In return they were allowed to erect new buildings on designated sites. In retrospect this was probably a mistake, since the challenge of creating new churches from nothing not only gave the new congregations the opportunity for architectural innovation; it also gave them the chance to demonstrate their power and wealth through the speed with which they could gather the funds for such an enterprise. The results were often astonishing. When, in 1566, the Calvinists of Antwerp set about constructing their new church, they created a totally new form of building: an austere rectangle, closely patterned on the proportions of the temple of Solomon. The building, initially in wood, was finished within months, and its construction attracted the attention of large and curious crowds. One bystander, the Catholic patrician Marcus van Vaernewijck was moved to describe the scene in his diary; he added a sketch plan, the only tangible remains of the now lost building.[11]

The fate of so many of these Calvinist churches, torn down at the first opportunity by the vengeful Catholic authorities, demonstrates how alien was the new Protestant concept of a church: placing the pulpit rather than the altar in the central position, with a lack of architectural ornamentation providing for both visibility and audibility. As the religious warfare of the later sixteenth century established the limits of Calvinist expansion, and as the Counter-Reformation gathered pace, Catholics had the opportunity of a more concrete response. This, the reassertion of traditional visions of the sacred in architecture and art, was one of the most important cultural consequences of the Reformation, and one of the most enduring. The new artistic language found its first expression in lands that had scarcely wavered in allegiance to the old faith, Spain, Italy and Bavaria. But as the Catholic reconquest spread through central and eastern Europe, and took root in France, the art of the Baroque became ever more exuberant and triumphalist. Its very elaboration was a standing rebuke and challenge to the despised visual austerity of Calvinism. When the two cultures clashed directly, for instance with Charles I's patronage of Van Dyck in England, the results could be explosive.

As this example demonstrates, the full consequences of the Reformation challenge to the visual arts would only be manifest in the seventeenth century, the high point of the Baroque. But enough has been said to demonstrate that, far from introducing a period that was artistically barren, the Reformation provided an important new stimulus to the re-examination of developing cultural values and modes of expression, and one that was, in a number of fields, immensely invigorating.

Urban Culture

Most of the developments described above were played out as much in the towns and cities of Europe as in the royal courts. The sixteenth century was one of the great ages of urban culture. This at first rather surprising statement may seem hard to square with an age in which predatory princes were doing everything within their power to curb the cities' independence. This is the century, after all, when the city republic of Florence, the epitome of urban political values, was reborn as the Grand Duchy of Tuscany; when Swiss models of government found admirers but no imitators; and when for many of Europe's citizens exchanging rural life for a home in the city brought only poverty, disease and the prospect of an early death.

But through all of this the city, if less visible as an independent political unit, became ever more prominent as a focus for cultural and social institutions. The economic success of Europe's cities brought a substantial cultural dividend, and many were substantially rebuilt during the sixteenth century. The century as a whole witnessed a steady replacement of wooden buildings with stone and brick. This trend was a continuation of an imperative inherited from the mediaeval centuries, and a common reaction to the catastrophic fires that periodically devastated pre-industrial towns. A fire in Toulouse in 1463, for instance, that raged for a fortnight, destroyed two thirds of the city. Many urban authorities responded by insisting that new intramural buildings should only be of brick or stone; and though such building codes were flagrantly abused (wooden structures being merely disguised with a plaster facade) the proportion of brick buildings did increase steadily. In countries where Protestantism had prevailed the brick or stone employed in this rebuilding was often salvaged from demolished Catholic churches and monasteries.

This was by no means the extent of the Protestant impact on the face of urban society. Before the Reformation religious institutions had not only been among the cities' most numerous occupational groups; they had also owned a considerable proportion of urban property. The properties owned by churches, religious houses and hospitals together with their gardens often covered as much as one third or one half of the city. Dissolution brought much of this property into lay hands: indeed, a massive reorganization of urban property was often the first impact of evangelical change. In order to prevent this glut of new property causing a calamitous fall in house values magistrates often encouraged immigration, usually targeted at artisans with specific craft skills. At the same time town authorities took specific responsibility for previously religious institutions, such as schools and hospitals. Over the course of decades these new monuments to civic power were the focus of ambitious rebuilding; and this was true too in Catholic

Europe, as lay authority shouldered increasing responsibility in the fields of poor relief and care for the sick. The vast expansion in schooling provided further opportunities for the architectural manifestation of civic pride, particularly the prestige of Latin schools and academies. When such projects were in hand urban authorities would often intervene aggressively to buy up the adjacent plots necessary to fulfil their plans.

Much the most potent symbol of civic power was the town hall. In the sixteenth century town halls were remodelled or rebuilt across Europe: examples from central Europe include Poznań in Poland (*c.*1550), Pilsen in Bohemia (1554–9), Bratislava (1581), Danzig, Bremen and Constance (all in the 1590s). To some extent this was a response to the proliferating functions of government in a burgeoning administrative culture; but it may also have been a statement of symbolic defiance against the background of a steady decline of urban independence throughout the century. When the city fathers of Antwerp determined to erect a new city hall, they commissioned an exquisite Renaissance building of opulence and classical simplicity, a tangible demonstration of their new status as the major trade entrepôt of northern Europe. To underscore the polemical point they had emblazoned across the portal the cheeky Imperial motto, SPQA: *Senatus et populusque Antwerpiae*. In the following decade Antwerp lost some ground to the small north German port of Emden, briefly made rich by a temporary transfer of the English cloth staple, and the trade attracted by an influx of Netherlandish merchants. When in 1574 the Emden council built their new city hall, this was a close copy of the Antwerp building: even little Emden was not afraid to proclaim to the world its ambition to rival Antwerp as a major trading centre. The symbolism was not lost on the prickly Antwerp magistrates.

Other public buildings followed as the cities of Europe expanded the range of their public responsibilities: a weigh-house, usually on the market square, an arsenal, schools, in the largest cities a bourse. But often the most impressive new buildings were those of wealthy private citizens. In Italy the remodelling of the main thoroughfares in Florence and Venice had been largely completed by the end of the fifteenth century, as the wealthy patrician and merchant families competed to construct the most elegant palaces. These *palazzi* were often the work of many years, even generations, for it might take years to secure the necessary adjacent lots to build an appropriate monument to the family's new status. But in both cities the effort was impressive and the effect enduring. In north Europe the great urban rebuilding came

Figure 34   The town hall at Antwerp. Photo AKG London/Erich Lessing.

later, but by the mid-sixteenth century it was in midflow. Many of the most elegant townhouses show the influence of Dutch architects, who were active through much of central and northern Europe. The Polish port of Danzig enjoyed phenomenal prosperity in the last decades of the century as is attested by the numerous elegant sixteenth-century houses in the city centre, all in an unmistakably Dutch style. In the cities of Germany, vernacular, Renaissance and northern features competed for pre-eminence. The town centre of Wittenberg offers a fascinating contrast in the monumental classicism of the house constructed by Lucas Cranach, and the gables of the so-called Melanchthon house, built in 1536.[12] In France the new town houses of the bourgeoisie showed domestic echoes of the architectural style of the Loire châteaux.

The city streets framed by these noble new buildings were home to a varied and impressive cultural life. Of course much urban culture took place in private, at home. In the parlours of the larger town houses families would gather to read and be read to, and to share food and music with friends. The growing sophistication of this culture was a consequence of the ever-widening reach of education, even as it built on highly traditional elements. But the most visible face of urban culture was in the streets, where citizens gathered for the ceremonies and occasions that had for centuries given shape to their identity as a community, or communities. In sampling this cultural scene it may be helpful to distinguish between informal and formal entertainments. In towns and cities some form of entertainment would be available most days, whether travelling balladeers, tumblers and clowns, a fight at the market or an erring tradesman to mock in the pillory. The cornerstone of more formal entertainment culture was provided by the guilds. Guilds had their own patron saints, their own traditions and rituals. They played as important a part in the recreational culture of their members as in their working lives. They sponsored processions, feasts and special Masses. The religious plays performed on the feasts of Corpus Christi throughout mediaeval Europe were often organized on a guild basis. In England the guilds performed mystery plays, as did the guilds of Florence; the Spanish guilds staged pageants. In several European cultures dramatic entertainment often took the form of competitions between societies, often organized loosely on a guild basis. This was true of France, Germany (where the shoemaker Hans Sachs won enduring fame through his plays in support of the Reformation) and especially the Netherlands. Here the Chambers of Rhetoric (*rederijkerkamers*) were an integral part of urban life. There competitions were large public events, and the texts of the performances were often subsequently published as printed collections. In the Netherlands and also in France poems as well as plays were composed in the Chambers. The most famous and established poetry competitions (the French *puys*) attracted a cosmopolitan entry and some distinguished winners. Although the craft origins of such associations were gradually eroded, they continued to hold a position of importance in urban society, not least in preserving a degree of social interaction between different ranks of society.

Of course townspeople gathered in public for more than simply recreational purposes. They would congregate in large numbers in the market for trade, for sermons, in or outside the church, to hear proclamations, or to see justice executed. Sermons, it need hardly be said, could be a major part of entertainment culture. The reputation won by the Franciscans before the Reformation was consciously pursued by the Protestant reformers and preachers of the Catholic Reformation. Many aimed to move their audience with shameless theatrical tricks, and many clearly succeeded. The best preachers (and they were usually wooed to the towns) could often draw vast crowds. These regular parts of urban life were largely self-regulating, and generally proceeded with due solemnity and decorum. Other, more exuberant public gatherings also played an important part in civic life, though even here it was important that tradition imposed limits (for all that the appearance of the abolition of limits was essential to the recreation). Thus Carnival was a period of wild, drunken and excited festival. But it was not riot, nor looting, and contemporaries seem to have had a fairly clear view of where the limits lay. Significantly, urban elites were not afraid of Carnival: on the contrary they were often eager participants. In the early sixteenth century Nuremberg patricians played a prominent part in Carnival; in Paris in 1583 Henry III was moved to join the revelries.

Carnival was a ubiquitous part of European culture, though it seems to have played a more important role in southern Europe where the climate was more forgiving of outdoor festivities in the depth of winter. The Carnival season began in January, with mounting excitement as Lent approached. It culminated in massive eating, drinking, dancing and singing, accompanied by revelry in costumes and disguises, and special ceremonies (often the performance of a play of some kind) on the main square. Recurrent elements included a procession, often with parodies of more solemn urban rituals, and a competition, horse or foot races, or jousting. In Europe's colder reaches other summer and autumn festivals sometimes attained an equal importance: May Day, Midsummer, or the feast of St Bartholomew (24 August).

Urban elites were on the whole quite comfortable with festivals of this sort, which offered familiar and time-honoured relief from the day-to-day pressures of urban existence. They fretted more about casual dangers, such as the power of the priest or minister to stir up his flock with his sermons, for the pulpit was potentially a powerful organ of public criticism. Most dangerous of all was the everyday diet of rumour, scandal and song. The enormous versatility of song provided a potent vehicle for protest, ridicule and political comment. This spontaneous, inventive culture had a far greater contemporary importance than the patchy surviving evidence would necessarily suggest. During the latter days of the French Wars of Religion the Paris magistrate Pierre de l'Estoile took to strolling the streets and marketplaces, and when he returned home recording what he had heard in his journal. This diary, in consequence, is a fantastic repertoire of otherwise lost political ditties: all extremely contemporary in their comment on events, and all highly uncomfortable for the Paris ruling classes.[13]

This last example makes the point that urban culture, for all the reverence for tradition and time-honoured form, was in fact extremely sensitive to change. Over the course of the century the greatest challenge was that posed by the Reformation. In Protestant Europe the guilds were shorn of their most obvious religious functions. The transfer of property brought new responsibilities, but also new wealth into the hands of magistrates. Town government became more complex but more rewarding; those who undertook these charges became more conscious of their dignity, and elaborated a much richer and more complex civic ritual to dramatize their new estate. Against this, a contested Reformation often introduced, at least temporarily, huge tensions into the body politic: divisions among the citizens, even the magistrates themselves. This was more clearly manifested when cities attempted to execute justice against condemned heretics. Executions that had previously been an important communal act (and source of entertainment) became a source of discord and division, as crowds that had once booed and hooted now showed their sympathy for the victim, or even tried to rescue them from the stake. No wonder that many European cities after one or more such incidents did their best to avoid executions for religious causes at all, if possible: a further reminder of the timeless power of the martyr, or the religious fanatic.

Even in urban cultures not divided by such conflicts, economic change also produced more subtle, but arguably no less profound changes. The course of the sixteenth century witnessed the emergence of an upper bourgeoisie both affluent and educated, and some began to look with increasing distaste on the more plebeian public revels. There is some evidence that these urban elites began to withdraw into their own more exclusive culture. In the field of drama the amateur societies gradually gave way to a more professional theatre, which towards the end of the century was beginning to find its feet as an independent cultural form. This was most obvious in England with the great blossoming of dramatic talent at the close of the Elizabethan age. One must not exaggerate the extent to which this new urban theatre departed from established norms. Shakespeare worked under the patronage of the great, in his first days as an actor in Lord Pembroke's company, later in the Lord Chamberlain's Men, renamed the King's Men after the accession of James VI and I. In this aristocratic patronage the London theatre conformed to a pattern normal throughout Europe, where theatre flourished almost exclusively close to the court. But by the end of the century the London dramatists had taken a significant step beyond this, notably with the construction of the Globe in 1599. This was a commercial enterprise inspired by the actor impresario Richard Burbage with Shakespeare as a partner. The investors were sufficiently confident of their urban audience

– admittedly underpinned by Shakespeare's genius – to conceive of theatre as a commercial enterprise. In this field at least, the contrast with a hundred years before is stark. At the end of the fifteenth century those who made money from drama would be travelling players, moving their shows from fair to fair, living off their luck, and often scarcely distinguishable from the vagrants with whom they were often grouped in punitive legislation. By the end of the century theatre as a commercial entertainment culture was beginning to make the transition to respectability.

Country Pleasures

The recreational culture of the countryside lacked the refinement of the more sophisticated urban milieux. There was little trace of the more refined domestic entertainments: low levels of literacy limited access to books, and few country dwellings were sufficiently spacious to accommodate more than the most rudimentary family gatherings. When country people sought recreation they did so at the inn or outdoors.

Taverns were great centres of entertainment culture. It was here that people gathered to exchange news, make bargains, and while away long winter hours. Sometimes they might be entertained, or divert themselves with songs or storytelling. The long narrative tale was a feature of many European cultures, as were the travelling musicians, often blind, who scratched a bare living by the ballads and tales they held in their capacious memories. Inns were also important as a place to dance, especially at wedding feasts or festivals. Jan Steen, the Dutch genre painter who was also an innkeeper, has left us remarkable visual records of occasions such as these: exuberant, inclusive, apparently chaotic. Through his second occupation Steen would certainly have had first-hand experience of such occasions, though as a Catholic in the Protestant Dutch Republic he also undoubtedly relished the opportunity to point up the human frailties of his Calvinist neighbours.[14]

Few country inns would, in truth, have been as substantial as the structures painted by Steen. The largest festival occasions generally took place in the open air. For country folk the winter ribaldries of Carnival were often less important than the great festivals of May Day (a celebration of spring), midsummer, and harvest time. These occasions would be embellished by feasting, drinking and dancing. Country dances exhibited considerable regional variations, but fell into two main families: the round dance, normally performed in a ring and often at increasing whirling pace until the participants collapsed exhausted, or the sword dance. These dances of mock combat were more for display, and involved menfolk only. The English morris dance is a quaint residue of this tradition.

More occasional diversions might be games and festivities connected with religious rites of passage: baptisms, weddings or funerals. Football and stoolball (a primitive form of cricket) were both widely enjoyed in England by the sixteenth century, and Tudor kings continued the vain attempts of their mediaeval predecessors to stamp them out. Ball games were seen as a distraction from the more virtuous and militarily useful art of practising archery. Scotland and the Low Countries had a primitive form of golf, in the Netherlands it was played on ice and known as *kolf*. All European cultures enjoyed various sorts of animal fights, cockfighting or baiting bulls or bears. With hunting reserved for the rich this was all that remained for the more plebeian.

Baptisms, funerals and particularly weddings were encrusted with dense accretions of custom that enlivened the solemnity with feasting and celebration.[15] Although a wedding was not a wholly inclusive village entertainment the processions, from bridal house to church, from church to feast, provided spectacle and the feasting and dancing provided plentiful opportunities for mischief – far too plentiful for the Protestant ministers who tried to bring these customs under control. Finally, savage diversions were provided by what might be described as the rites of discipline, the 'rough ridings' or charivari with which communities singled out those who had overstepped the bounds of accepted social practice. Those selected for public humiliation might be old husbands who had married much younger girls, or a husband beaten by a dominant wife. They would be subjected to cruel public repudiation, with the village crowd collected outside their window beating pots and pans (this was known as 'rough music'). Such ceremonies were known across Europe from England to Portugal and Hungary; in societies where reputation was a precious asset and fiercely protected against defamation, the impact of such public shaming must have been devastating.

In sixteenth-century society the upholding of social norms frequently depended on customary institutions such as this – blunt, cruel, and arbitrary – but in a rough-and-ready way reflecting the cultural norms of society. Far more problems were encountered when attempts were made to regulate or tame popular culture from outside the community. There were many reasons why, during the sixteenth century, the authorities began to look less kindly on popular culture. Occasions of unbridled festivity might be a useful safety valve, but they also left a difficult legacy of quarrels, injuries and unwanted pregnancies. During the course of the sixteenth century several aspects of popular recreation culture came under sustained attack.

These criticisms are normally associated with the Reformation, but certainly pre-date it. The German lawyer Sebastian Brant considered drinking, gaming and dancing at church festivals the ruin of the country people, and the second edition of his *Ship of Fools* (1495) included a bold attack on Carnival. In Florence these sentiments were echoed by Savonarola, and Erasmus was also harshly critical of Carnival, which he regarded as unchristian. But these were generally isolated voices from the educated, or humanist elite; a more systematic assault would await the Protestant Reformation. The most obviously vulnerable were the multifarious festivals, feasts and processions associated with Catholic feast days, now doubly vulnerable both for their excess and the tarnished reputation of their patron saints. Many Protestant cultures swept away most of these holidays, a movement that reached its apogee with an attempt to popularize a new sanitized calendar.

As this example suggests, Calvinists proved to be the most resolute opponents of popular entertainment culture. Several Reformed churches, notably the Dutch, attempted to ban the theatre, and in Geneva the playing of cards was prohibited (an inhibition of which Calvin's own brother fell foul). But their most persistent, and perhaps most quixotic, campaign was against dancing. The Calvinist hatred of dancing was graphically illustrated by the Elizabethan Puritan writer Philip Stubbs. He attacked what he called 'the horrible vice of pestiferous dancing' for providing participants with opportunities for 'filthy groping and unclean handling', and so acting 'as an introduction to whoredom, a preparative to wantonness, a provocation to uncleanness, and an indroit to all kinds of lewdness'.[16] In this they took their lead from Calvin himself, who in 1546 had jeopardized his fragile regime in Geneva by pursuing a prominent member of one of Geneva's leading families who had danced at a family wedding. After much controversy the magistrate was forced to submit to an act of public repentance. The French Huguenot churches indeed proved the most unrelenting in their hostility to dancing, frequently bringing members of their congregations before the consistory or excluding them from communion.

Such moral austerity in due course found its echo in Catholic culture. The Council of Trent deprecated the fact that 'the celebration of saints and the visitation of relics be perverted by the people into boisterous festivals and drunkenness' and took steps to prevent this. Towards the end of the century Catholic reformers turned their fire on religious drama. But the fragmentary nature of such initiatives and their only partial success demonstrate the danger of reforming campaigns – in both confessions – that ran too far ahead of public opinion. To rein in excess was one thing, to attack the fundamentals of recreation culture quite another, particularly when these were recreations also enjoyed by the governing elites. The magistrates of the Dutch Republic gave the ministers little encouragement as they fulminated against the theatre, and the persistent assaults on lascivious dancing did little to stamp it out. In lands where the authorities assisted in the abolition of traditional festivals and saints' days, the people invented their own new occasions for bonfires, bell-ringing and feasting. In England these were comemorations of patriotic anniversaries connected with England's progress to Protestantism.[17] Such revelries were, in the last resort, an essential part of life.

15

Europe in 1600

The dawn of a new century brought resolution to some of the most stubborn conflicts of the departing era. In 1598 France and Spain made peace (the Peace of Vervins). This was a peace of exhaustion for the two giants of European politics, but one that proved surprisingly enduring: France and Spain would not find themselves at war again until 1635. The war with England drifted on for a few years yet, but in 1604, the new king, James VI and I, swiftly concluded terms. For Spain this left only the Dutch war, now largely confined to a privateering war in home waters, though the Dutch still relished the opportunity of preying on Spanish and Portuguese possessions overseas. On land, the frontier between the Spanish Netherlands (now settled under the benign and intelligent management of the Archdukes, Albert and Isabella) and the new Dutch state was effectively drawn. Few, on either side, invested hope in the outright victory that would reunite the 17 provinces of Charles V, either as Spanish territory or as an independent state. In the first years of the seventeenth century a cautious start was made on peace negotiations, though both sides were reluctant to settle: the Dutch still hoped to profit by war, and for Spain, recognition of an independent Dutch state was still a bitter pill. In the end all that could be achieved was a truce, for 12 years (1609–21); but that, in effect, concluded the Dutch war of independence.

For Spain, the cumulative resolution of these three conflicts, none on favourable terms, represented a shattering defeat. The bold strategies of Philip II, who in 1588 had seemed a single campaign away from decisive victory over his heretical enemies, had crumbled to nothing. Now, instead, Spain had to contend with three strong, independent powers, and the two decades of fighting since the Armada had achieved little but the progressive exhaustion of the Spanish treasury and an erosion of national self-confidence. Opinions vary as to whether the late sixteenth-century conflicts had done terminal damage to Spain's status as a great power. Contemporary travellers spoke of deserted villages and an exhausted countryside, and the new era would see the continuation of the familiar cycle of state bankruptcy and tax rises. But Spain was always a sparsely populated country, and modern studies suggest that the Castilian economy was still at this point relatively robust. The Spanish Crown continued through the seventeenth century to raise and equip huge armies; it was dynastic failure (the death of the childless Carlos II) that finally undid the Spanish Habsburgs, rather than military defeat. Nevertheless it is clear that with the Peace of Vervins and the passing of Philip II contemporaries sensed a shift in the balance of power. The re-emergence of France as a force promised equilibrium: the fear that Europe would be swamped by Habsburg expansionism, a strong possibility for much of the sixteenth century, was no longer a consideration. The Habsburg dream of European hegemony was buried for ever.

For France, the new century presented a far more optimistic perspective than would have been imaginable only two decades before. A strong, energetic, adult king, Henry IV, had settled both with foreign enemies and domestic opponents. A new marriage, to Mary of Medici in 1600, offered the prospect of dynastic continuity. The last piece in the domestic jigsaw came when Henry settled with his former Huguenot co-religionists in 1598 (the Edict of Nantes). At the time, of course, there was no way of knowing that this treaty would be any more enduring than the numerous similar agreements that had punctuated the 40 years of fighting. Indeed, one recent study of the Wars of Religion chooses to continue the story to 1629, when the Huguenots were forced to surrender their last military strongholds.[1] For all this the Edict of Nantes did provide a basis of security by which the two religious communities could go about their now increasingly separate lives. The Huguenots were fated to be a minority, largely concentrated in southern France, but a minority sufficiently privileged to convince the vast proportion of their number of the benefits of loyalty to the crown. The king, meanwhile, gave every evidence of the sincerity of his conversion to the majority religion by acting as the leading patron of an energetic campaign of Catholic renewal. It was a serious setback to the newly confident French state when he was assassinated in Paris in 1610.

Elizabeth of England had the satisfaction of outlasting her great contemporaries, but the era had run its course, and by 1603 there was a sense of general relief when the old queen's death made possible a peaceful transition to a new reign, and a new dynasty. However the Tudors had served England well, and it was not long before the clumsy vulgarity of James and his even more foolish and inept son Charles I had clothed memories of the Tudor century in a rosy glow. In truth, the English achievement was considerable. From dynastic turmoil and international irrelevance, England had emerged during the sixteenth century as a major force, Europe's principal Protestant kingdom, a maritime power on the brink of colonial empire. At times it had been a close-run thing, and who knows how stable Elizabeth's kingdom would have proved had Philip of Spain succeeded in landing his troops in 1588. But in the first decades of the seventeenth century England would be courted as arbiters in both theological (Synod of Dort, 1618) and political disputes, a measure of the kingdom's greatly enhanced status. Most important of all, the century had witnessed the progressive restructuring of the traditionally antagonistic relationship with the northern neighbour, Scotland. The personal union of crowns in 1603 was a sign that the tide had indeed turned, and that the political elites of the two kingdoms had recognized that there was more to be gained in co-operation than enmity and mutual provocation. Given that the first half of the century had been one of almost constant warfare this was a sea-change indeed, and the new relationship would be a cornerstone of the later British Empire.

In 1600 the major unresolved issues of European politics lay further east. The second half of the sixteenth century had been a time of persistent and destructive conflict in the Baltic region. In Scandinavia, the independence of Sweden established by Gustavus Vasa had never been fully acknowledged by the Danish crown; for their part the Swedes chafed at the obvious restriction on their freedom imposed by Danish control of both banks of the Sound.[2] Years of mutual provocation finally turned to open warfare in 1563, a brutal and destructive conflict that lasted seven years. Turbulence in the Swedish royal house – most specifically the madness of Erik XIV – forced the Swedes eventually to seek terms, but the main objectives that had brought Sweden to war, access to the North Sea and control of the trade routes to Russia, remained as ambitions to be revived in more propitious circumstances. In the last quarter of the century the house of Vasa was increasingly preoccupied by the consequences first of election to the throne of Poland and then the Catholicism of King Sigismund; his ambitious plan for the unification of the crowns of Sweden and Poland was thwarted only by his equal insistence on freedom of worship for non-Lutherans in Sweden. In the event an aristocratic rebellion secured the deposition of Sigismund in favour of his brother, Charles IX. The Swedish crown ended the century battling to restore its damaged authority against restless nobles at home, and restlessly pursuing the goal of a greater Baltic empire that had so far eluded them. This campaign would reach its apotheosis in the German military adventures of Gustavus Adolphus, but his ambitions were surprising only in their focus on the empire: Swedish ambition had been a destabilizing factor in regional politics for some time.

Here in the unsettled politics of Scandinavia lay one root of the Thirty Years' War; another lay in the false calm of the empire itself. The period of German history after 1555 has been comparatively neglected, but this was not a period without significant tensions and conflict. The Peace of Augsburg had provided for peaceful coexistence between the Catholic and Lutheran states of the empire, a striking achievement, and one admired elsewhere in Europe, where the German solution was often cited as a possible way forward in religious disputes. But the Peace provided a solution only for existing circumstances: it could not anticipate future events, and several times in the second half of the century it came close to collapse. The spread of Calvinism in the empire introduced a significant new source of tension, not least with the established Lutheran powers. The emergence of the Rhineland Palatinate as the principal, and ambitious spokesman of the new creed promised long term difficulties. The Peace also made no provision for cases where the head of an ecclesiastical state might convert: when this occurred the attempt of the Archbishop of Cologne to secularize his lands as a Protestant led to a five year war (1583–8). But most of all the tenuous peace in the empire could be maintained only so long as the Habsburgs were prepared to rule over lands which were, to all intents and purposes, Protestant. This was as true of their hereditary dominions in Austria as of the inherited kingdoms Bohemia and Hungary. When the Habsburgs embarked on a more aggressive campaign of conversion the effect was to unsettle the nervous Estates. Their rebellion in turn provoked an inevitable military response, and general European war.

The Thirty Years' War (1618–48) was in this respect the final resolution of the age of religious warfare brought about by the confrontation between Calvinism and Catholic renewal in the mid-sixteenth century. The general settlement of 1648 introduced a genuinely new era of European politics: an era of great power warfare, diplomacy and competition for colonial supremacy, fought out on a world stage. Never again would religion form a principal motive for conflict between nations within Europe. But if, for these reasons, the peace of 1648 was a truly epochal event, the outlines of this new world were already visible in the settlements of 1598–1609. Here were prefigured the rise of France, Britain and the Dutch Republic: the three great Atlantic powers of the coming age. It is also true that although religion was at the heart of the Thirty Years' War, this was nevertheless a war of armies, often mercenary armies made up of a hotchpotch of national contingents. Although brutal and destructive, it did not have the same passionate intensity of the first great age of religious war, where civilian populations had turned on their neighbours and former friends with such brutal intensity. The contrast in the two phases of the Dutch war is telling. The first decade of the Dutch Revolt, the war of independence from Spain (1572–1609) was disfigured by a series of horrific massacres, culminating in 1576 in the sack of Antwerp. In contrast when the war with Spain resumed after the expiration of the Twelve Year Truce in 1621, the war on land was pursued in a series of stately campaigns against border fortresses that did little damage and inflicted few casualties. This was now essentially an economic conflict, rather than a struggle to the death.[3]

All of this hints at a change in the temper of religious life within Europe. It would be too much to say that the end of the sixteenth century brought with it the resolution of the Reformation conflicts: the eager missionary efforts of the Jesuits in central Europe, and the reconquests of the Thirty Years' War, give the lie to that. But the last decades of the sixteenth century had at least brought a dawning recognition that neither Protestants nor Catholics could aspire to the complete subjugation of the other, and both confessions in their different ways began to accommodate to this new reality. Few states went as far as an open toleration, still less equality between the rival confessions. But in a number of countries penal legislation against minorities was less urgently pursued, with, or sometimes without, the connivance of government.

Such grudging freedom of conscience seldom amounted to toleration. The advocates of any principle of religious toleration remained lonely voices (and not always so principled).[4] But for the most ardent zealots Catholic and Protestant churches had by now opened up new missionary fields, both at home and abroad. For the Catholic Church the evangelization of the non-Christian populations of Asia and the New World presented a task of enormous magnitude, but one pursued with remarkable zeal and courage. The salvation of these millions of souls was an important psychological compensation for those lost to Protestantism nearer to home.

For all the mainstream churches the instruction of their own peoples in the new demands of their faith was a huge and daunting task. Scholars of sixteenth-century Protestantism now freely acknowledge that the reformers' early hopes that the end of the Roman obedience would permit them to create an informed and educated congregation of believers were naive and optimistic. In this they echo the pessimistic assessment of the reformers themselves, who poured out their sense of frustration with the apparent indifference of their flocks in countless sermons. To regard this, however, as the 'failure' of the Reformation goes too far. Sermons were never intended to be a historical document, certainly not as a critical report: to interpret them in this vein is to misunderstand their rhetorical, prophetic function. Even if they could not always recite their catechism, the populations of Protestant Europe had certainly developed a real loyalty to their creed; one they articulated not by an intellectual understanding of Justification by Faith Alone, but by a fierce loyalty to the customs and practice of their new church when this was under threat. To express this loyalty they developed their own new patriotic festivals, commemorations and customs. In England these included the celebrations of the accession of Elizabeth (Crownation Day, 17 November) and later the Gunpowder Plot (Guy Fawkes Day, 5 November).[5] In the Netherlands, the anniversary of the relief of Leiden in 1572 (3 October) became a day of similar patriotic festivity.

This picture of a slow but real Reformation, reorientating both behaviour and loyalties, makes more sense when set alongside the similarly laboured progress of religious renewal in Catholic lands. Although the Council of Trent finished its work in 1563, it was often a whole generation before the prescriptions for reform had even begun to be put into place. In the meantime the defence of Catholic Europe necessarily drew on more established loyalties: those of the Catholic populations (who in France effectively saved the country for Catholicism) and of those members of the ruling elites who remained loyal to the old faith. But there was a price to be paid. Not all Catholic rulers welcomed the provisions of Trent. In particular the provisions for clerical education cut across traditional patronage networks and so were hardly welcome even to the Catholic episcopate. In France and the Habsburg lands – both bulwarks of Catholic Europe – there were little signs that the winds of change had impacted on the make up of the episcopacy even late in the seventeenth century. The Archbishopric of Paris continued to be a family fiefdom of the Gondi family, and the bishops as a caste remained the king's faithful servants but hardly beacons of sanctity. The application of the spirit of Trent remained very much in the hands of committed individuals, and the educational initiatives of the new religious orders. In the parish, the impact of Catholic renewal would be felt only deep in the seventeenth century, if then. The war on traditional religious practices which reform-minded clergy regarded as superstitious or even semi-pagan was fought fitfully, and, in the depths of the Catholic countryside, with little success. The true monuments to Catholic Reformation were not in these country parishes, but in the great architectural creations of the Baroque: a triumphant reminder of how much of Europe's land mass had by 1648 been reclaimed from Protestantism.

Government and Society

The turbulent political and religious events of the sixteenth century left a considerable mark on Europe's emerging nation states. Contemporaries were fully aware how different was the new emerging political order of 1600 from that of a hundred years before. In 1500, one may remember, the Italian peninsula lay at the heart of European politics, its territories greatly desired by Europe's most ambitious rulers, its culture and intellectual life a beacon and model of excellence. By the end of the century much of this had changed. Though Italian art was still widely admired and collected, the cultural image of Italy had been badly tarnished during a century in which its internal politics had receded to the periphery of wider European concerns. Images of Italy in the popular press and theatre were now largely hostile and negative. The changing notion of Italian political culture is perhaps epitomized by the career of Catherine of Medici, arguably the most famous Italian to tread the wider European political stage during the course of the century. In her youth courted as a suitable bride by one of Europe's most prestigious ruling houses, in her later years she was reviled as the epitome of Italian duplicity and ruthlessness, a stock image later translated effortlessly on to the Elizabethan stage. To the extent that Italy enjoyed any continuing political influence in wider

European affairs in the later decades of the century it owed this to the resurgent papacy, now securely established as the guiding spirit behind the movement of Catholic renewal. This was a somewhat ironic consequence, given the low esteem in which the Renaissance papacy had been held at the beginning of the century.

This transformation of perspectives with regard to Italy is a reminder of how much of the state formation in Europe during the sixteenth century had been utterly unpredictable. The century had seen the emergence of important new powers, such as the Dutch Republic, but others equally or more promising had failed. The mediaeval power of Burgundy had disappeared into the larger Habsburg Empire, as had Portugal (in this case temporarily, as it turned out). While the northern Netherlands had effected a successful secession, the Huguenot strongholds of southern France had not; the state-building process had encompassed Spain, France and in Germany the major Protestant states, but not the Habsburg lands of southern Germany. Several potentially potent combinations of territories – such as the Anglo-Netherlandish state envisaged in the marriage treaty of Mary of England and Philip of Spain – had vanished and were never to be heard of again.

Such developments inevitably inspired reflective consideration from many of Europe's best minds. Those who reflected on theories of rulership in print (an expanding sixteenth-century genre) generally built on two models, both with strong classical and mediaeval roots. There were those who put their trust in princes, inspired by the contemporary success of Renaissance monarchy and evidence of the ever broadening reach of royal administration. This tradition produced some notable landmarks of European literature, whether the dispassionate *realpolitik* of Machiavelli's *The Prince*, or the more optimistic agenda of Erasmus in his *Education of the Christian Prince*: a prince must rule, but through enlightened Christian principles and a regard for the common good he might be a powerful force in the building of a Christian society. Europe's rulers did much to enhance the appeal of such an agenda by their energetic patronage of the cultural symbolism of power. In the second half of the century royal power seemed to many theorists the rock of security in the tribulation of social decay brought on by religious violence, a position epitomized by the great French jurist Jean Bodin, anticipating the triumphalist royal absolutism of the seventeenth century.

Yet alongside these hymns to royal authority existed a second strand which saw social authority in terms of a contract between the ruler and the ruled. This too drew on powerful roots, and during the course of the century found expression both in times of peace (as in the writings of the French thinker Claude de Seyssel) and social conflict. Contract theories found their most powerful articulation in the conflicts of the Reformation, first in justifying the resistance of the German states to the emperor Charles V, later in their most developed and radical form to justify the rebellion of the Calvinist minorities in France and the Netherlands.

By the end of the sixteenth century the royalist strand was emerging as the dominant mode of political thought, as contract theories fell into discredit through their association with the wilder consequences of resistance theory. But this development was not universal through-out Europe, and in any case the impact on the conduct of political affairs may greatly be doubted. Much sixteenth-century political thought was a combination of sycophancy, wishful thinking and wisdom after the event. Rulers liked to hear their authority given a pleasing Humanist veneer or comforting Ciceronian roots, but how much such writings influenced the day-to-day relationships between Europe's political elites is greatly to be doubted. Resistance theory, in particular, had a short and fitful existence. In both France and the Netherlands the major theoretical articulation of rights of resistance were published long after the rebellion was an established fact, effect-ively *ex post facto* rationalizations of uprisings that had complex and sometimes very conservative roots. In the Dutch case, the defence of communal liberties was essentially mediaeval in character, and found its characteristic expression in the claim that the crown had violated existing traditional rights.[6] In France the radical monarchomach tracts were the product of a brief moment of despair following the St Bartholomew's Day massacre. Their implications were uncomfortable even for the noble leaders of the French Huguenot leadership, and as the movement stabilized they were swiftly forgotten, except, ironically, by the radical polemicists of the Catholic League, who in the last decade of the century turned these arguments against the Protestant champion Henry IV. The Huguenot writings were resurrected again in a different political context during the English Civil War in the seven-teenth century; it is probably to this that they owe their subsequent historical renown, rather than any contemporary influence in France during their first lifetime.

The changes in government that did occur during the sixteenth century were incremental, and owed little to contemporary theoretical writings. For all this the century saw change of a far-reaching nature.

Throughout Europe government became more intensive. Spurred by the greater expense of waging war, and the length and indecisive nature of most military conflicts of the period, the state power demanded and received higher and more regular taxation. Sixteenth-century states all witnessed a consequent and commensurate increase in administration: all Europe's major powers employed more officials, and their powers reached further out into the provinces. Government, though still sporadic and somewhat arbitrary in its incidence, impacted more regularly and with greater force on the lives of Europe's citizens. Most European states enacted more legislation, and attempted to legislate in more areas of life. Economic legislation increased, as did attempts to lead and direct lives by statute. There was a general movement towards the codification of law, the replacement of local tradition with standard rules and processes. All of this in turn implied a massive growth in the size of the legal and administrative castes, accompanied by a progressive professionalization of their practice.

The implications of these profound changes for the relationship between the different orders within Europe's ruling elites were mixed. The growth of legislative activity did not always mean a greater importance for representative assemblies. Whereas in eastern Europe and England such assemblies enjoyed an enhanced role and reputation during the sixteenth century, in France the Estates General played little constructive role, being reduced to the role of a sounding board and safety valve in a time of national crisis. After meeting only sporadically during the sixteenth century it met one last time in 1614, and then not again until 1789. Such developments were an indication at least of the pretensions of Europe's ruling dynasties, many of which pursued during the century an ambitious vision of unfettered power, burnished by the prestige of the lavishly displayed accoutrements of kingship. But in fact the reality was often very different. England flourished despite the extinction of the Tudors, France despite the ending of the Valois dynasty; the most spectacularly successful of seventeenth-century societies, the Dutch Republic, had divested itself of monarchy altogether. That political maturity depended less than kings and political theorists might suggest on the personal capacities of an adult male king is indicated by the fact that many of Europe's most successful powers came through periods of extended dynastic turbulence, royal minorities, or the complete absence of male heirs. The fact that many of sixteenth-century Europe's most successful rulers were women was something with which the prevailing political orthodoxies scarcely came to terms at all.

Beneath the surface, sixteenth-century political society was characterized by two profound if slightly conflicting developments. Firstly,
there was a general broadening of the active political elite. This was a
product of sheer necessity, a result of the sheer weight of administration as government increased in size and complexity. Service and
administration would gradually come to rival (perhaps even overtake)
the church as an alternative route to power and wealth for those of
humble birth. While traditional elites hardly ceded their grip on power,
they were increasingly reliant on bourgeois bureaucrats to oil the
wheels of political society. These trends were reinforced by the growth
of education – now conceived as a necessity in secular society rather
than purely as an adjunct of the church – and by the growth of the
professions. By the end of the sixteenth century these professional
groups, lawyers, doctors, ministers of the church, had developed a
full range of the defensive mechanisms against unqualified interlopers
that had served mediaeval craft guilds so well: and would serve to
enhance and build the prestige of the liberal professions right down
to our own day.[7]

Importantly, all of this occurred without shaking the overwhelming
dominance in society of aristocratic values. In this respect the achievement of Europe's nobilities in the sixteenth century was impressive, for
while their traditional military functions and role in government were
progressively eroded they lost little of their social position, wealth, or
social prestige. Throughout Europe the rising bourgeois continued to
look up to Europe's nobilities, and indeed often sought to seal their
social success by ascending into the ranks of the nobility; in this, for all
the multiple social prejudice against new or 'robe' nobilities, they often
succeeded. Much of the success of Europe's nobilities in the sixteenth
century came from their giving the impression of being a closed caste,
while in fact being extremely open.

All sixteenth-century families struggled to ensure a succession
through the generations, and the nobility were as subject as any
other families to the harsh realities of pre-modern demographics.
Noble families died out. But as this occurred aristocracies were constantly renewed from the ranks of the mercantile urban patriciate, the
professions, and the gentry. All of these groups eagerly sought and
plotted their promotion into Europe's established elites, in the meantime aping noble manners, values, and ways of living. Such admiration
and aspirations secured the continuing social and political dominance
of Europe's aristocracies. The only truly closed aristocracy was that of
the Dutch Republic, where there was no power capable of conferring

new ennoblements; and here significantly the nobility quickly declined into political irrelevance.[8] Elsewhere the prestige of the aristocracy survived the sixteenth century triumphantly intact, and on into the glory days of the Ancien Régime. There would be no 'crisis of the aristocracy' in Europe until the French Revolution.

Living in Europe in 1600

The dawn of the new century is perhaps not the best moment to take a snapshot of European living conditions. The warfare of the 1590s had taken an exceptionally severe toll: this was a brutal decade in many parts of Europe. France had witnessed the most destructive and debilitating fighting of the entire Wars of Religion; and if the military tide had receded in the Netherlands, all of western Europe's powers were groaning under the cumulative burden of 40 years of war finance, debt and military action. Even those nations not directly afflicted by warfare were in the 1590s assailed by a run of exceptionally poor harvests and severe epidemics: plague and influenza decimated the population in areas of Europe as diverse as London and Castile.[9] And in many European places the worst was still to come. Parts of central Europe would suffer huge depopulation during the Thirty Years' War; in fractured societies such ill fortune brought terrified incomprehension, and the inevitable search for scapegoats. In 1600 the worst of the European witch-craze still lay ahead.

Even so, if one can step back from the immediacy of this tribulation, one can discern some marked shifts in the conditions of everyday life, at least for some of Europe's citizens, in the course of the sixteenth century. For many, conditions of life had shown a marked shift in the space of three generations, certainly in terms of the material conditions of existence.

In assessing the extent of this consumer culture one is faced with something of a conundrum. On the one hand it is frequently stated that average wages among working people declined during the sixteenth century, eroded by slow but steady monetary inflation. Against this, and in apparent contradiction, there is also plentiful evidence of greater sophistication of material things: in housing, furnishings, clothes and consumption. One should be cautious, however, before reaching for what at first sight seems the inexorable mathematical inference, that the sixteenth century simply witnessed greater inequalities of wealth, with more wealth concentrated in fewer hands. There are in fact other ways in which the circle can be squared. It has to be remembered that in social groups where there existed any surplus for spending beyond necessities, wealth was accumulated incrementally. Most conspicuous spending was for long-term benefit, and only clothes would be used to destruction over a short time period. Any such possessions were jealously guarded, and reverentially passed on to succeeding generations. One only has to read a sampling of sixteenth-century wills to realize how carefully material possessions were accumulated, cherished and disposed. The most precious furnishings, like jewels or books, were often specifically chosen as testamentary gifts; fine garments were frequently dispensed to servants. In this way consumer culture was spread even to those whose spending power was weak.

A few years ago I had the opportunity to investigate the consumer culture of a particular subgroup of European urban society: French and Dutch immigrants who had settled in London during the reign of Elizabeth I. To investigate how far they had succeeded in becoming assimilated into indigenous London society I compared the wills of several hundred immigrants who died in London in the last decade of the sixteenth century with those of a similar cohort a generation before.[10] In 1563–4 London was afflicted by a severe visitation of plague, and the immigrant population was not spared; many of these earlier wills were clearly made in great haste by men not long in London. But even those made with calm reflection seldom mention much tangible wealth. The beginning of Elizabeth's reign had seen a considerable movement of peoples to London, both religious exiles and economic migrants, most bringing skills and some liquid cash, but few possessions. Yet by the end of the century the economic situation of this community was transformed. Many of those who died in the 1590s left household stuff of great value: jewellery, silver plate, musical instruments, a Turkish rug, portraits and furniture.

The developments evident here are probably accelerated and accentuated by particular features of the immigrant experience, but that this accumulation of material wealth is a more general phenomenon is evident from widely spread evidence. The growth of household possessions can be charted in an invaluable run of Netherlandish household inventories, and in a slightly later period by a study of testamentary evidence in Metz.[11] By the end of the sixteenth century urban families had money to invest, albeit carefully, in leisure pursuits as well as material possessions. From another direction evidence for the steady growth of a consumer society comes from tax records, and in the duty raised on imports and exports, which in the case of England shows a steady proliferation of different classes of imports, many of which could scarcely be described as essentials. When the profits to be made in such trade became obvious, eager projectors sponsored attempts to set up new manufactures domestically, and then to have their investment protected by an exclusive right of sale (the detested monopolies). The hostility expressed to such schemes demonstrates a clear sense among the political nation that there was profit to be made in innovation.[12]

For all the hopes invested in new manufacturing techniques, by and large the growth of a consumer society depended on products and manufactures long familiar to Europe's elites. New World products, particularly foodstuffs, did not make any great impact in this period, nor would they in the seventeenth century. What one sees is the steady penetration of the middle ranges of European society of non-European products already familiar in the mediaeval world, such as sugar and spices. These become less wholly the preserve of the elite, and less expensive. But consumer products cherished for their value and utility, whose progress we can chart over the century, overwhelmingly originated within Europe, and generally in the local economy. Furniture would mostly be made domestically; glass, the use of which for windows and tableware expands steadily, might be imported (Italy was renowned for the finest glass) but would more likely be made at home. Fine and costly fabrics were an important component of overseas trade, but governments also gave considerable attention to securing their local manufacture. Only food that was climatically sensitive (such as wine, figs, olives and raisins) remained an unambiguous staple of the import – export trade.

To sum up some general trends: the great urban rebuilding of the sixteenth century had a considerable impact on living conditions. Progressively more houses were made of brick rather than wood, and increasingly partitioned into a larger number of separate rooms. They became more cluttered with possessions: for the first time many houses had more than one bed, allowing marginally greater privacy and dignity for the subsidiary members of a household. Dress consisted of more layers (this was the age in which the habit of wearing underclothes became more common) and greater attention was paid to variety and seasonal fashion. Consumer goods travelled further to reach a more sophisticated and varied market, facilitated (and necessitated) by a gradual growth in the money economy. In all of this there were, of course, strong regional differences. There were differences in housing materials: wood proved more tenacious in the north, stone replaced brick in the south. There were differences in culture between Catholic and Protestant lands; and there were pronounced differences between town and country.

No doubt that the greatest impact of the changes described above was felt in the towns. It was here that one witnesses the greatest concentrations of wealth, and it was to the cities that the ambitious and upwardly mobile tended to gravitate. In consequence the largest of Europe's cities witnessed substantial population growth during the course of the sixteenth century: London from 60,000 to 200,000, Paris reaching the same size from a higher base (100,000 in 1500). In the Netherlands all of Holland's cities enjoyed rapid growth, with Amsterdam beginning its rapid expansion to the status of an European colossus.

Cities were centres of trade, of education, of the most sophisticated leisure culture, increasingly of government and administration. Most of all, they were the centres of information culture. Here, without a doubt, lay one of the great transformations of the sixteenth century, and at its heart lay the culture of print. The printed book was an invention of the fifteenth century, and it would not be put to significantly new purposes until the rise of the newspaper in the eighteenth century. But there is no doubt that the sheer scale of publishing during the sixteenth century gave the book an ever more important social role: in consequence its reach and social impact increased profoundly during the course of the century.

In the first 50 years of the printed book, Europe's presses probably achieved a global output of some 10,000 editions.[13] By the end of the sixteenth century such totals were being published in Europe every year or 18 months. The book had also taken on some significantly different roles. In 1500 printed materials tended to be either elite objects, large format books, often in Latin and as expensive as the manuscript books they replaced, or pragmatic official documents: single sheet proclamations or indulgences. Both forms survived, and flourished during the sixteenth century, and one must not underestimate the continuing importance of books published purely for the social elites. Expensive books were important for the development of the art of illustration, and the sixteenth century saw the emergence of several significant new genres: technical manuals and scientific books, works of astrology and architectural handbooks, maps and atlases. But in the wider world of the printed book there were significant changes. Latin gave ground to books in vernacular languages. Most importantly there was an astonishing growth of publication of books in the middle size range, quartos and octavos, books that bore the weight of the vast increase in publication of pamphlets, religious polemic, catechisms, books of devotion, school textbooks, popular histories, poetry, almanacs and books of prodigies and sensations. These were the classes of literature that invaded the houses of Europe's middle orders. These were the books that changed the concept of a library, from being an accoutrement of the royal and ecclesiastical elite to something to which the relatively modest minister, lawyer or bourgeois householder could aspire. In the fifteenth century a fine library was still not that much more common than a menagerie of exotic beasts – that other status symbol of the highest social elites – or a formal garden. By the late sixteenth century some very ordinary individuals accumulated collections of several hundred books. These were still, by and large, the working collections of professional people. Books were collected for serious purposes, an aspect of working lives, rather than leisure. But people also read for enjoyment: history (a vastly expanding genre), poetry, romances, the Bible.

The influence of book culture on wider society was so manifold that one can pick out many examples of how books changed the way people thought and acted. Perhaps here we should look beyond the most obvious categories – the religious polemic of the German *Flugschriften* and the religious wars – to books whose influence was more subtle. The printing press, for instance, revolutionized the art of map-making, and with it, in due course, the ways in which the spatial world was conceived. The mediaeval world had also loved maps, but in the manuscript age maps, perhaps even more than texts, were necessarily characterized by great individuality. The dissemination of woodcut technology, allied to the printing press and followed by copper-plate engraving, was the vital technical ingredient of greater cartographical accuracy, just as the world was visibly expanding and taking shape. During the sixteenth century Europe witnessed a vogue for cartography, both maps of towns and nations, and ambitious attempts to represent the new continents being explored by Europeans in this era. Among Europe's elites in particular, the impact on spatial perception was profound.

A similarly profound and long-term effect can be discerned through the publication of grammars and dictionaries – another sixteenth century vogue. In this field, as with the codification of law, an interest in the structure of language often went along with the desire for greater standardization, particularly in written culture. In many parts of Europe such campaigns for linguistic purity sparked heated debates over rival theories and prescriptions, also battled out in print. But the overall effect of these and other parallel social pressures (such as the creeping influence of government) was the establishment of a leading dialect as the dominant linguistic form of the vernacular. While regional dialects would survive for many centuries in spoken form, dialect played little part in written culture, either in official documents or in the culture of the printed book. In France, for instance, where Occitan was the spoken language of the South and separate tongues survived in Britanny and the Basque country (Navarre), less than one-tenth of 1 per cent of printed books were in dialect. The socially ambitious from the regions necessarily mastered a bilingual command of their regional dialect and the master language of government.

The great book of the age was, as is widely recognized, the Bible. It is hard in a secular age to do justice to the potency of the Bible in the sixteenth century. But this was a remarkable and multifaceted book, a success in so many of the categories of print that sixteenth-century readers found so fascinating. It was a travelogue and a work of history; a work of literature and poetry; it provided the model for much of the most successful drama of the age. It was a work of prophecy in an age obsessed by prophecy. It was a treasure trove for botanists, for grammarians and etymologists, and a foundation text for students of the ancient languages. It was a work of jurisprudence, perhaps the sixteenth century's most influential legal text; it was certainly the century's most influential work of political thought. It provided role models for rulers and priests, for fathers and mothers, for soldiers and martyrs.

In this book the print culture of the sixteenth century was displayed in all its technical sophistication. It could be a handy pocket sized book in tiny print, or a glorious illustrated folio. The narrative illustrations in the Old Testament brought to life some of the greatest stories of the Christian tradition; even in the austere purged Protestant edition that text often came accompanied by maps, technical drawings, and ingenious diagrams of belief and unbelief. It is not too much to say that in this one volume is epitomized much of what sixteenth-century book culture had to offer.

The sixteenth century placed this compendious and many-sided work directly in the hands of unprecedented numbers of people. Throughout the century and in all European vernaculars there were published at least 5,000 whole or partial editions of the Bible: a total of at least five million copies. Many were in small formats, and used to destruction; others were a most cherished family possession, passed down through the generations. With catechisms, another huge publishing phenomenon of the age, the purpose was clearly defined, but with the Bible its many-sidedness made its impact unpredictable and extraordinarily various.

By the end of the sixteenth century, then, there is evidence at least in Europe's urban centres of a tangible enrichment both of material and intellectual culture. The final question that must be addressed is how the changes of the century, both these underlying social changes and the political and religious movements of the age, impacted on family life. This is a difficult question, not least because the evidence is patchy, and often derived more from theoretical texts, such as ordinances, sermons and conduct books, than from reliable demographic evidence. The survival of high-quality demographic evidence before 1600 is rare for any part of Europe.

It is certainly the case that the sixteenth century brought to familial relations new elements of regulation. This was in part an aspect of the general advance of a culture of legislation, but this trend was here

Figure 35 The holy Protestant household: Hans Hug Kluber, *Portrait of the Basel Guildmaster Hans Rudolf Faesch and his Family*, 1559. Courtesy Oeffentliche Kunstsammlung Basel, Kunstmuseum, photo Martin Bühler.

reinforced by the leaders of the reforming movements of the Protestant and Catholic churches. Protestant churches, for instance, placed
increasing emphasis on the importance of swift baptism, which discouraged major festive gatherings of kin and elaborate feasting. The
formalization of ceremonies of betrothal and insistence of prior paren-
tal consent before marriage also introduced cultural change. Protestant
societies generally were much less relaxed about marriages entered into
through the informal exchange of vows followed by consummation, a
type of marriage always recognized as valid in the established Catholic
tradition. The reformers waged an unrelenting battle to bring all
marriage into an orderly process presided over by the church.

In this, as in their disapproval of dancing, they moved some way
ahead of contemporary social custom, and progress was slow. But this
was an area where the Reformation could and did make a difference.
Historians are now much more cautious about sweeping assertions of a
consequent fundamental reorientation of the family unit. It used, for
instance, to be thought that the sixteenth century marked a significant
stage in the progress from the model of an extended family (including
servants and collateral kin) to a nuclear model (father, mother and
children). The construction of such a case relied heavily on reading of
printed literature, sermons and conduct books that harked constantly
on the familial responsibilities of father and mother, husband and wife.
But such limited demographic evidence as there is does not in fact
support a general assertion that family units became smaller or less
complex. There is plentiful incidental evidence that the extended
family of kinsfolk and servants (often themselves younger relations)
continued to be important parts of larger families. Grandparents and
older relatives continued to support the family within their power, and
relied on younger relatives for help in indigent old age.

The Reformation reordered the household especially in the case of
the clergy family. In replacing the unmarried priest, who might or
might not live in an informal liaison with his housekeeper, with the
clergy family, Protestantism introduced an important new ingredient
into urban and village society. Perhaps this was most important in the
village, where the clergy always enjoyed an especially elevated (or
exposed) social position as one of the few educated members of the
local community. Now they brought with them a wife, often from their
own social milieu, and children as well. This development was not
universally popular. Although the new clergy family meant that the
carnal lusts of the priest would be constrained, it also meant more
mouths to feed; precious clerical income would necessarily be re-

deployed from caring for church fabric and works of charity to domestic necessities. This adjustment was most obvious in those Protestant traditions that retained bishops, for these bishops often in their anxiety to provide for their children showed the finely tuned nepotistic instincts of the Renaissance popes (and with far less political justification).[14] Among the broader ranks of the Protestant clergy, families bred professional dynasties, generations of sons who followed their fathers into clerical office. Often they would marry the daughters of clergy families too.

Perceptions of the impact of sixteenth-century change on the role of women, in the family and the workplace, have also undergone a process of refinement in recent years. The sixteenth-century reformers articulated a model of the female vocation as wife and mother, and as women's history first emerged as an independent strand of research a generation ago such pronouncements were harshly judged. To many, the emphasis on a feminine vocation to the household was viewed as extremely prejudicial, particularly in an era when evolving patterns of work constrained female initiative in the workplace. In fact here, as with household structure more generally, contemporary reality was various and inconsistent, and the swiftly moving populations of Europe's towns and villages had room for every variant of household unit. Protestant preachers, in this as so much else, proposed a model that had only a faint echo in reality.

In so far as the Reformation impacted on relations between husband and wife within the home, it was to bring greater order and regulation; and such regulations were predicated, as in any age, on the assumption that the cornerstone of any successful domestic relationship was love and mutual respect. Indeed, the Protestant promotion of marriage as a social ideal often brought with it an overt concern for proper behaviour on the part of both parties. An examination of the regulatory activity of Calvinist consistories, for instance, suggests that the ministers and elders devoted a good deal of time to mending strained relationships. Reconciliation was far more important than judgement or punishment. Drunken, neglectful or violent husbands were dealt with severely, and there was no sense that violent or adulterous conduct was more tolerable in the husband than the wife. A successful marriage, then as now, bred respect and love, and this resonates from much of the surviving documentation touching on family affairs. Anyone reading large quantities of sixteenth-century wills, for instance, will be struck by how often a dying husband expressed confidence in the surviving spouse, to raise the family but also to run the business.

The evidence is equally strong that sixteenth-century parents loved their children. There is no sense that frequency of loss, in childbirth or through infant diseases, diminished human affection. Domestic bereavements were keenly felt, whether that was the loss of a spouse, an infant, or a growing child. The books of consolation that addressed this issue counselled resignation and acceptance of God's will, but did nothing to suggest that the loss should not be mourned; the emotional intensity of a sudden family death is vividly expressed in surviving family correspondence and diaries.[15]

The truth is that the general lot of sixteenth-century men and women remained hard. A growing material prosperity, measured in carefully gathered material possessions, could do nothing to mitigate the frightful arbitrary quality of sudden misfortune. At the end of the sixteenth century the perils of existence had in no way receded. Epidemics still struck with equal force; in fact the growth of cities may even have intensified their incidence. The everyday hazards of travel, work and unbalanced diet (no less unbalanced for the spread of certain luxuries) took their toll on life and health. People continued to live, as they had in 1500, with pain and disability as the common lot. Death reached among them with sudden and pitiless capriciousness. And so it would be until the birth of modern medicine, still centuries away. Such medical advances as there were in the period were more of a theoretical than practical nature. In any case they could hardly keep pace with the rapidly increasing power of weapons of war to maim and kill, or even with the new biological killers exchanged between Europe and the New World. So, if people in 1600 had a wider range of goods to comfort their earthly lives, their departure to the next world could neither be anticipated nor, when illness struck, much delayed.

The Place of the Sixteenth Century

If this is how Europe looked in 1600, how should this survey of the conditions of material existence affect how we place the sixteenth century in the wider scheme of things? All of what has been said thus far suggests that the study of the sixteenth century is ill served by what one might call progress-orientated terminology. This particularly applies to the umbrella term 'early modern', usually used to describe the two or three centuries that are seen to bridge the mediaeval and the modern worlds. This term is especially unhelpful because it seems to suggest that we should search the sixteenth century for the first green shoots of developments crucial to the creation of modern European society. Nothing could be more wrong-headed or misleading. If one articulates the crucial developments that made the modern world, I would think one should concentrate on five main strands. These are: (1) the advance of secularization, and the retreat of God; (2) the harnessing of new sources of energy for the creation of industrial society, and mass, cheap transportation; (3) the subjugation of the non-European world; (4) the transformation of agriculture that, together with modern medicine, made possible the huge population growth of the last two centuries; and (5) the replacement of an aristocratic with a meritocratic and finally democratic ethos.

If one examines each of these in turn, one is drawn to the conclusion that none of these developments had even really begun in the sixteenth century; certainly none had made a significant impact. God was still universally believed to exist, and to exist as an active force in human existence. Superstition was scarcely eroded; belief in devils and witches was well nigh universal. The sixteenth century witnessed no fundamental innovation in transportation, or the exploitation of energy: human, animal and wind power remained the fundamental resources available to human ingenuity. Grain yields remained low. The normal ratio of 1 : 3 or 1 : 5 that is generally reckoned for the return on each grain sown could be improved to 1 : 7 by careful husbandry in agriculturally advanced areas; but this was nowhere near the 1 : 30 ratio that became the norm with the impact of modern agricultural science.

If fundamental change must be denied, such advances as we do see are more often refinements of the existing mediaeval technologies. There is no denying that the book took a great leap forward from the manuscript age with the domestication of printing. But this was still largely within a context familiar from the mediaeval world: the university, the school, urban culture. It would require the spread of the newspaper, an eighteenth century invention, before the book was fully liberated from its mediaeval origins. Even the growth of government and administration, a highly significant development, was underpinned by largely traditional values. The aristocratic ethos of society survived largely unscathed, and such innovations as there were in the realm of political thought (such as resistance theory and absolutism) proved in the longer term to be false directions. We still of course live with the legacy of the Renaissance and Reformation, though perhaps if the major Christian confessions eventually reunite their dwindling congregations in the twenty-first century, the Reformation too may seem a diminished and less significant event. This would be much as the end of the Cold War has readjusted our perspective on Eastern Europe.

The sixteenth century is a period of European history of great charm and allure. Those of us who study it are always tempted to look beyond its undoubted cruelty and arbitrary brutality, because it generated so much excitement, so many great individuals, so many extraordinary moments. It is a century that has left a rich monument of beautiful and imposing buildings, fine paintings and books; and of course it is these that endure rather than the filth, the smells, the deformity and suffering. It is the historian's difficult task to do justice to all these diverse, starkly contrasting, and often contradictory elements; but that is what keeps drawing us back.

Appendix: Lists of the Major European Rulers and their Consorts

Note: when no date of death is given for consorts, this is because they outlived their husbands.

Holy Roman Emperors

Maximilian I (1493–1519)
b.   1459, Wiener Neustadt
m. (1) 1477, Mary of Burgundy; d. 1482
    (2) 1494, Bianca Maria Sforza; d. 1510

Charles V (1519–56)
b.   1500, Ghent
m. 1526, Isabella of Portugal, daughter of King Manuel I; d. 1539

Ferdinand I (1556–64)
b.   1503, Alcalá de Henares (Spain)
m. 1521, Anne of Bohemia and Hungary; d. 1547

Maximilian II (1564–76)
b.   1527, Vienna
m. 1548, Maria of Habsburg

Rudolph II (1576–1612)
b.   1552, Vienna

Spain (Aragon and Castile)

Isabella (1474–1504)
b.   1451, Madrigal de las Altas Torres
m.   1469, Ferdinand of Aragon

Ferdinand (1479–1516)
b.   1452, Sos (Aragon)
m.   (1) 1469, Isabella of Castile; d. 1504
     (2) 1506, Germaine de Foix

Charles I (1516–56)
(see Emperor Charles V)

Philip II (1556–98)
b.   1527, Vallodolid
m.   (1) 1543, Maria, infanta of Portugal; d. 1545
     (2) 1554, Mary, Queen of England; d. 1558
     (3) 1559, Elizabeth of Valois, daughter of King Henry II; d. 1568
     (4) 1570, Anna of Austria, daughter of Maximilian II; d. 1580

Philip III (1598–1621)
b.   1578, Madrid
m.   1599, Margaret of Austria; d. 1611

Portugal

Manuel I (1495–1521)
b.   1469, Alochete
m.   (1) 1497, Isabella, daughter of Ferdinand of Aragon; d. 1498
     (2) 1498, Maria, daughter of Ferdinand of Aragon; d. 1517
     (3) 1518, Eleanor, sister of Charles V

Joao III (1521–57)
b.   1502, Lisbon
m.   1525, Catalina sister of Charles V

Sebastian (1557–78)
b.   1554, Lisbon

Henry, Cardinal of Archbishop of Lisbon (1578–80)
b.   1512, Lisbon

Philip II of Spain (1580–98)

France

Louis XII (1498–1515)
b. 1462, Blois
m. (1) 1476, Jeanne of France; dissolved 1498
    (2) 1499, Anne of Britanny; d. 1514
    (3) 1514, Mary Tudor, daughter of Henry VIII

Francis I (1515–47)
b. 1494, Cognac
m. (1) 1514, Claude of France; d. 1524
    (2) 1530, Eleanor of Austria, sister of Charles V

Henry II (1547–59)
b. 1519, Saint-Germain-en-Laye
m. 1533, Catherine of Medici, niece of Pope Clement VII

Francis II (1559–60)
b. 1544, Fontainebleau
m. 1558, Mary, Queen of Scots, 1558

Charles IX (1560–74)
b. 1550, Saint-Germain-en-Laye
m. 1570, Elizabeth of Austria

Henry III (1574–89)
b. 1551, Fontainebleau
m. 1575, Louise de Vaudémont

Henry IV (1589–1610)
b. 1553, Pau
m. (1) 1572, Margaret of Valois; dissolved 1599
    (2) 1600, Mary of Medici

England

Henry VII (1485–1509)
b. 1457, Pembroke
m. 1486, Elizabeth of York, daughter of Edward IV; d. 1503

Henry VIII (1509–47)
b. 1491, Greenwich
m. (1) 1509, Catherine of Aragon; divorced
    (2) 1533, Anne Boleyn; exec. 1536
    (3) 1536, Jane Seymour; d. 1537
    (4) 1540, Anne of Cleves; divorced 1540

(5) 1540, Catherine Howard; exec. 1542
(6) 1543, Catherine Parr

Edward VI (1547–53)
b.   1537, Hampton Court

Mary I (1553–58)
b.   1516, Greenwich
m.   1554, Philip II of Spain

Elizabeth I (1558–1603)
b.   1533, Greenwich

Scotland

James IV (1488–1513)
b.   1473
m.   1503, Margaret Tudor, daughter of Henry VII of England

James V (1513–42)
b.   1512, Linlithgow
m.   (1) Madeleine of France; d. 1537
     (2) 1538, Mary of Guise

Mary, Queen of Scots (1542–67)
b.   1542, Linlithgow
m.   (1) 1558, Francis, son of Henry II of France; died 1559
     (2) 1565 Henry, Lord Darnley; murdered 1567
     (3) 1567 James, Earl of Bothwell
     deposed; exec. 1587

James VI (1567–1625)
b.   1566, Edinburgh
m.   1589, Anne of Denmark

Denmark and Sweden

Hans (1481–1513)
b.   1455

Christian II (1513–23)
b.   1481, Nyborg
m.   1515, Isabella, sister of Charles V; d. 1526
     deposed; d. 1559

Denmark/Norway

Frederick I (1523–33)
b. 1471
m. 1518, Sofie of Pomerania

Christian III (1534–59)
b. 1503, Gottorp
m. 1525, Dorothea of Saxony-Lauenburg

Frederick II (1559–88)
b. 1534, Hadeslev
m. 1572, Sofie of Mecklenburg

Christian IV (1588–1648)
b. 1577, Frederiksborg
m. (1) 1597, Anna Katrine of Brandenburg, d. 1612.
   (2) 1615, Kirsten Munk; divorced 1630

Sweden/Finland

Gustavus Vasa (1523–60)
b. 1496
m. (1) Katarina of Saxony-Lunenburg
   (2) 1536, Margareta Leijanhufvud

Erik XIV (1560–8)
b. 1533, Stockholm; d. 1577
m. 1568, Karin Månsdotter

John III (1568–92)
b. 1537, Stegeborg
m. (1) 1562, Katarina Jagiellonica
   (2) 1585, Gunilla Bielke

Sigismund I (1592–9)
b. 1566, Gripsholm; d. 1632
m. (1) 1592, Anna, daughter of Archduke
   Charles of Austria; d. 1598
   (2) 1605, Constance of Austria (her sister)

Netherlands

Habsburg regents and Governors General

Margaret of Austria (1507–15; 1519–30)
daughter of Maximilian I

Mary of Hungary (1531–55)
sister of Charles V

Margaret of Parma (1559–67)
illegitimate daughter of Charles V

Duke of Alva (1567–73)

Don Luis de Requesens (1573–6)

Don John of Austria (1576–8)

Alexandro Farnese, Duke of Parma (1578–92)

Stadholders of Holland after the revolt

William of Orange (1572–84)

Maurice of Nassau (1584–1625)

Poland

Jan Olbracht (1492–1501)
b.   1459, Cracow

Alexander (1501–6)
b.   1461, Cracow
m.   Helena, daughter of Tzar Ivan III

Sigismund I (1506–48)
b.   1467
m.   (1) 1512, Barbara Zápolya of Hungary; d. 1512
      (2) 1518, Bona Sforza

Sigismund Augustus (1548–72)
b.   1520, Cracow
m.   (1) Elizabeth of Habsburg; d. 1545
      (2) 1547, Barbara Radzill; d. 1551

(3) 1553, Catherine of Habsburg

Henry Valois (1573–4)
(see Henry III of France)

Stefan Batory (1576–86)
m. Anna Jagiellonka

Sigismund III Vasa (1587–1632)
m. (1) 1592, Anna of Austria; d. 1598
(2) 1605, Constance of Austria

Muscovy

Ivan III ('The Great') (1462–1505)
b. Moscow, 1440
m. (1) 1452, Maria of Tver; d. 1467
(2) 1472, Sophia Palaeologue; d. 1503

Vasily III (1505–33)
b. Moscow, 1479
m. (1) Solomonia Saburova; annulled 1525
(2) 1526, Yelena Gliskaya

Ivan IV ('The Terrible') (1533–84)
b. Kolomenskoe, 1530
m. (1) 1547, Anastastasia Romanovna Zakharina; d. 1560
(2) 1561, Kucheney; d. 1569
(3) 1571, Marfa Sobakina; d. 1571
(4) 1572, Anna Boltovskaya; banished 1575
(5) 1575, Anna Vassilchikova; d. 1577
(6) 1576, Vassilissa Melentievna; banished 1577
(7) 1580, Maria Nagaya

Feodor I (1584–98)
b. Moscow, 1577
m. 1580, Irina Godunova

Boris Godunov (1598–1605)
b. 1552
m. 1570, Maria Grigoroevna Skuratova; d. 1605

Popes

Alexander VI (1492–1503)

b. 1431, Valencia, Rodrigo Borgia

Pius III (1503)
b. 1439, Siena, Francesco Todeschini

Julius II (1503–13)
b. 1453, Albissola, Guiliano della Rovere

Leo X (1513–21)
b. 1475, Florence, Giovanni de Medici

Adrian VI (1522–3)
b. 1459, Utrecht, Adrian Florensz Dedel

Clement VII (1523–34)
b. 1479, Florence, Giulio de Medici

Paul III (1534–49)
b. 1468, Canino, Alessandro Farnese

Julius III (1550–5)
b. 1487, Rome, Giovanni del Monte

Marcellus II (1555)
b. 1501, Montepulciano, Marcello Cervini

Paul IV (1555–9)
b. 1476, Benevento, Giampietro Caraffa

Pius IV (1559–65)
b. 1499, Milan, Giovanni Angelo Medici

Pius V (1566–72)
b. 1504, Bosco, Michele Ghislieri

Gregory XIII (1572–85)
b. 1502, Bologna, Ugo Buoncompagno

Sixtus V (1585–90)
b. 1520, Grottammare, Felice Peretti

Urban VII (1590)
b. 1521, Rome, Giambattista Castagna

Gregory XIV (1590–1)
b. 1535, Somma, Niccolo Sfondrati

Innocent IX (1591)
b. 1519, Bologna, Giovanni Antonio Faccinetti

Clement VIII (1592–1605)
b. 1536, Fano, Ippolito Aldobrandini

Timelines

Timeline 1: The Early Reformation – Church Reform and Habsburg Politics

Year	Protestant reform movement	Politics in Germany	Habsburg Politics beyond Germany	Catholic Church / Italy
1514				Pope Leo X renews the indulgence for the reconstruction of St Peter's in Rome
1515				
1516			Accession of Charles V in Spain	
1517	31 Oct.: 95 theses published			
1518	L. answers questions from Cajetan, Diet of Augsburg			
1519	Leipzig disputation /Johannes Eck	Jan.: Maximilian I dies	Accession of Charles V in Germany	
1520	June: Papal Bull *Exsurge Domine*		1520–2 *comuneros* revolt in Spain	
1521	April: Diet of Worms – Luther banned by imperial edict; unrest in Wittenberg	Diet of Worms – Charles V delegates power in Germany to Ferdinand I		Charles V wages war with Francis I of France, the battleground being Italy
1522	Publication of German NT; Luther intervenes against the	1522/3: Rising of the Imperial Knights		

Timeline 1: (contd.)

Year	Protestant reform movement	Politics in Germany	Habsburg Politics beyond Germany	Catholic Church / Italy
1523/4	Zwickau prophets in Wittenberg			
1525		Peasants' War	Battle of Pavia: Charles V takes Francis I prisoner	Peace of Madrid. Francis I loses Milan and Genoa to Charles V
1526	German Mass	1st Diet of Speyer – local determination of confession	Battle of Mohács – Hungarian inheritance	
1527			Sack of Rome by imperial forces	
1528				
1529	German catechisms, marriage and baptismal booklets	2nd Diet of Speyer – German Catholic states vote to enforce Edict of Worms	– Treaty of Cambrai (Ladies Peace) – Habsburg/French temporary settlement – 1st siege of Vienna by Ottomans	
1530		Diet of Augsburg – Protestant states formulate Augsburg confession	Charles V: imperial coronation at Bologna	
1531	Oct.: Battle of Kappel (d. of Zwingli)	Formation of Protestant Schmalkaldic League		Ferdinand I Crowned King of The Romans
1532	– establishment of reformed civic government in Geneva	Religious Peace of Nuremberg to unite against the Ottoman threat	Charles V relieves Vienna	

1533				
1534	*Affair of the placards* in France – Henry VIII declared supreme head of church in England			
1535	Defeat of Anabaptists in Münster		Charles V seizes Tunis	
1536	Jean Calvin arrives in Geneva: *Institutio Religionis Christianae*		Francis I allies with Ottomans against the empire	
1537	Declaration of Danish Lutheran church order			
1538	Calvin expelled from Geneva (to Strasbourg)		'Holy League' reformed – Charles V, Ferdinand I, Rome and Venice against the Ottomans	
1539/40				Confirmation of Jesuits by Pope Paul III
1541	Calvin recalled to Geneva	Colloquy of Regensburg	Failure of Charles V at Algiers; loss of Hungary to the Ottomans	
1542				Re-establishment of the Roman Inquisition
1543				
1544			Peace of Crespy – Francis I to help Charles V v. Schmalkaldic League	

Timeline 1: (contd.)

Year	Protestant reform movement	Politics in Germany	Habsburg Politics beyond Germany	Catholic Church / Italy
1545				1545–8 1st period Council of Trent
1546	d. of Luther			
1547		Battle of Mühlberg –	defeat of Schmalkaldic League – d. of Francis I	
1548/9/50	*Book of Common Prayer*			
1551		– Augsburg interim		– Edict of Châteaubriand against heresy in France 1551–2 2nd period Council of Trent
1552		Charles V loses Metz to Henry II of France		
1553	d. Edward VI in England			
1554				
1555		Religious peace of Augsburg	25 Oct.: Charles V abdicates	

Timeline 2: Wars of Religion on the Atlantic Seaboard

Year	British Isles	France	Netherlands	Spain
1557		defeat at battle St Quentin		Philip II victory at St Quentin (death of Charles V)
1558	Jan.: loss of Calais to France Nov.: accession Elizabeth I			
1559		– Peace of Cateau-Cambrésis – Henry II dies in a joust		Peace of Cateau-Cambrésis
1560	English aid to Scottish Calvinist rebel Lords	– Conspiracy of Amboise Dec.: d. Francis II		Spanish fleet take Djerba, then defeated by Ottoman navy (May)
1561				
1562		March: massacre of Vassy		1562–3 3rd period Council of Trent
1563		– Murder Duc de Guise – Peace of Amboise		
1564			Count of Egmont sent to Philip II by Dutch Estates	
1565				Spring: Ottoman attack on Malta; Sept: relief of Malta by Spanish fleet
1566			Aug.: outbreak Dutch revolt	
1567	Darnley assassinated: civil war in Scotland, Mary Stuart overthrown	Escapade of Meaux – Huguenot leaders attempt to seize King Charles IX from the Guise faction	Duke of Alva moves troops to Netherlands: Council of Troubles	
1568		March: Edict of Longjumeau – temporary settlement	Execution of Egmont and Hornes	Dec.: revolt of Granada

Timeline 2: (contd.)

Year	British Isles	France	Netherlands	Spain
1569	Rising of the Northern Earls (England)	March: battle of Jarnac (d. Condé)		
1570	Elizabeth I excommunicated	Aug.: Edict of St Germain		Ottoman occupation of Cyprus; Holy League (Venice, Spain and Rome) joint expedition
1571	Ridolfi plot against Eliz. I		Sea Beggar raids intensify	Battle of Lepanto – Ottoman navy defeated
1572	Duke of Norfolk executed	St Bartholomew's Day massacre	William of Orange enters Netherlands with army	
1573		Siege of La Rochelle	– Fall of Haarlem – Requesens sent to Spain (73–6)	
1574–5			Siege of Leiden	
1576			Nov.: sack of Antwerp; Pacification of Ghent	
1577	77–80: Drake's global circumnavigation			
1578				Portuguese king and army destroyed at Alcazar-el-Kebir; Spanish/Ottoman truce
1579	79–80 Spanish expeditions to Ireland		Southern Catholic provinces form the Union of Arras; Northern states form Union of Utrecht	

1580/1	Philip II accession in Portugal	Estates General declare Philip II deposed		
1582				
1583				
1584	Treaty of Joinville with French Catholic League	Assassination William of Orange; Fall of Antwerp to Spain	Treaty of Joinville – French Catholic League with Spain	
1585				Treaty of Nonsuch – English aid for Dutch revolt; Raleigh's Roanoke adventure
1586				
1587	Cadiz raided by Drake			Mary Stuart executed
1588	Armada against England defeated		Dec.: Henry of Guise and Cardinal of Guise assassinated by Henry III	Armada defeated
1589	English defeated in Lisbon		Henry III assassinated Siege of Paris	Defeat in Lisbon
1590/1		Parma aids Catholic League in France		English aid to Henry IV in France
1592			Siege of Rouen	
1593			Henry IV reconverts to Catholicism	
1594		Groningen surrenders to Dutch		
1595			Henry IV declares war on Spain	
1596/7				
1598	d. Philip II; Peace of Vervins		– Peace of Vervins (with Spain) – Edict of Nantes home settlement	

Notes

1. Time and Space: Living in Sixteenth-Century Europe

1   Harry Miskimin, *The Economy of Later Renaissance Europe, 1460–1600* (Cambridge, 1977), pp. 21–4. The population of Europe in the year 2000 (excluding Russia) was projected as 527 million. The discrepancy between these figures and those given in table 4.3 (derived from Jan de Vries, *European Urbanization*), arises from the fact that de Vries excludes Turkish Europe (approximately 5 million inhabitants), Lithuania and Muscovy from his calculations.

2   A. L. E. Verheyden, 'Une correspondance inédite adressé par les familles protestantes des Pays-Bas à leurs coreligionnaires d'Angleterre', *Bulletin de la commission royale d'histoire*, 120 (1955), pp. 95–292.

3   Quoted in Gerhard Dohrn-van Rossum, *History of the Hour: Clocks and Modern Temporal Order* (Chicago, 1996), p. 155.

4   Piero Camporesi, *Bread of Dreams: Food and Fantasy in Early Modern Europe* (London, 1989).

5   Quoting Amanda Eurich, *The Economics of Power: The Private Finances of the House of Foix-Navarre-Albret during the Wars of Religion* (Kirksville, Mo., 1994), pp. 128 ff.

6   Henry Kamen, *The Iron Century* (London, 1976), p. 15.

7   William G. Naphy, 'Plague-spreading and a magisterially controlled fear', in Naphy and Penny Roberts, *Fear in Early Modern Society* (Manchester, 1997), pp. 28–43.

8   Charles L. Cooke, 'Calvin's illnesses and their relation to vocation', in Timothy George (ed.), *John Calvin and the Church* (Louisville, 1990), pp. 59–70. Gerhard Benecke, *Maximilian I* (London, 1982), p. 10.

9   Quoted in Steven Ozment, *Flesh and Spirit: Private Life in Early Modern Germany* (New York, 1999), p. 53. Note also the double reckoning by clock and hour time.

10   Quoted in Robert Jütte, *Poverty and Deviance in Early Modern Europe* (Cambridge, 1994), p. 30.

11   Heiko A. Oberman, *Luther: Man between God and the Devil* (New Haven, 1989).

12   Bodo Nischan, 'Lutheran confessionalization, preaching and the Devil', in his *Lutherans and Calvinists in the Age of Confessionalism* (Aldershot, 1999).

13   Bruce Gordon and Peter Marshall (eds), *The Place of the Dead: Death and Remembrance in Late Mediaeval and Early Modern Europe* (Cambridge, 2000).

2.   Europe in 1500: Political Organization

1   Geoffrey Parker, *The World Is Not Enough. The Messianic Vision of Philip II* (Waco, 2001).

2   For collectors of such curiosities other member of the exclusive 'two kings club' were Margaret Tudor, successively wife of Louis XII of France and James IV of Scotland, and Eleanor, sister of Charles V and successively wife of Manuel of Portugal and Francis I of France.

3   Indeed it would have come close to recreating the middle kingdom, Lotharingia, of the ninth-century Carolingian inheritance; another reminder of how real were distant mediaeval models in this period.

4   The seven were the four secular electors, the electors of Brandenburg, and the Palatinate, the Duke of Saxony and the King of Bohemia, and the three archbishops of Cologne, Trier and Mainz.

5   Thomas A. Brady, *Turning Swiss: Cities and Empire, 1450–1550* (Cambridge, 1985).

3.   The Struggle for Italy

1   Jonathan Wolfson, *Padua and the Tudors: English Students in Italy, 1485–1603* (Cambridge, 1998).

2   The concept of the empire still had sufficient reality for the republic of Venice to invest 200,000 ducats to pay the emperor Charles V for formal investiture of title of its mainland possessions in 1523. Maximilian had earlier vowed to reduce the republic to a status of a free imperial city.

3   As quoted in Denys Hay and John Law, *Italy in the Age of the Renaissance, 1380–1530* (London, 1989), p. 12.

4. The Winds of Change

1 Raingard Esser, 'Fear of water and floods in the Low Countries', in William G. Naphy and Penny Roberts, *Fear in Early Modern Society* (Manchester, 1997), pp. 62–77.
2 See here Felipe Fernández-Armesto, *Columbus* (Oxford, 1991), pp. 35–9.
3 Jan de Vries, *European Urbanisation, 1500–1800* (London, 1984), p. 28.
4 Steven Ozment, *Flesh and Spirit: Private Life in Early Modern Germany* (New York, 1999), pp. 4–5. As a point of comparison, a journeyman in the cloth trade, at the top of the artisan wage level, might make 100 gulden a year.
5 Geoffrey Parker, *The Dutch Revolt* (London, 1977), p. 21
6 George Hubbert, *Public Schools in Renaissance France* (Chicago, 1984).
7 Figures taken from R. A. Houston, *Literacy in Early Modern Europe: Culture and Education, 1500–1800* (Harlow, 1988), p. 32.
8 Vellum, made from cleaned and scraped calfskin, was a durable and reliable surface for the inscription of text, and a staple of the manuscript age. Its expense largely confined its use to luxury presentation copies by the sixteenth century. Parchment was made of the cheaper sheepskin.
9 For a thoughtful and clear-minded introduction see now Richard Rex, 'Humanism', in Andrew Pettegree (ed.), *The Reformation World* (London, 2000), pp. 51–70.

5. The Reformation

1 Bernd Moeller, 'Religious life in Germany on the eve of the Reformation', in Gerald Strauss (ed.), *Pre-Reformation Germany* (London, 1972), p. 16.
2 Mark Edwards, *Printing, Propaganda and Martin Luther* (Berkeley, 1994), p. 17.
3 The editions are listed in Heimo Reinitzer, *Biblia deutsch: Luthers Bibelübersetzung und ihre Tradition* (Wolfenbüttel, 1983), pp. 116–27.
4 The Twelve Articles of the German Peasantry, art. 3. Text in Peter Blickle, *The Revolution of 1525* (Baltimore, 1981), pp. 195–201.
5 *The Letters of Sir John Hackett, 1526–1534*, ed. E.F. Rogers (Morgantown, Va., 1977), p. 81.

6. Charles V and the Defence of Catholic Europe

1 For a variety of speculations (though mostly on twentieth-century subjects) see Niall Ferguson (ed.), *Virtual History: Alternatives and Counterfactuals* (London, 1997). For my own modest contribution to the genre

see Andrew Pettegree, 'The execution of Martin Luther', *History Review,* (March 1996), pp. 20–5.

2 Franche-Comté was excluded from this abdication, lest France should use this as a pretext to invade. The abdication of his sovereignty over the Hispanic dominions took place on 16 January 1556 in a small private ceremony. The formal abdication of the empire was not accepted by the imperial diet until February 1558.

7. The Age of Religious War

1 Natalie Zemon Davis, 'The rites of violence', in her *Society and Culture in Early Modern France* (London, 1975), pp. 152–87.

2 David Bagchi, *Luther's Earliest Opponents: Catholic Controversialists, 1518–1525* (Minneapolis, 1991).

3 H. J. Schroeder (ed.), *The Canons and Decrees of the Council of Trent* (Illinois, 1978), Canons 12, 32.

4 Quoted in R. Po-Chia Hsia, *The World of Catholic Renewal, 1540–1770* (Cambridge, 1998), p. 18.

5 John O'Malley, *The First Jesuits* (Cambridge, Mass., 1993).

6 A. Lynn Martin, *The Jesuit Mind* (Ithaca, 1988).

7 See, for a powerful exploration of this theme, Christopher Elwood, *The Body Broken: The Calvinist Doctrine of the Eucharist and the Symbolization of Power in Sixteenth-Century France* (New York, 1999).

8 Alastair Duke, Gillian Lewis and Andrew Pettegree (eds), *Calvinism in Europe, 1540–1610: A Collection of Documents* (Manchester, 1992), pp. 37–8.

9 William G. Naphy, *Calvin and the Consolidation of the Genevan Reformation* (Manchester, 1994).

10 Jean-François Gilmont, *Jean Calvin et le livre imprimé* (Geneva, 1997), p. 362.

11 John Calvin, *Institutes of the Christian Religion*, Book 1, ch. 16, pt 3.

12 Letter to Sturm, December 1560, cited in Duke, Lewis and Pettegree, *Calvinism in Europe*, p. 80.

13 An admirable survey of the debate is Jeremy Black, *A Military Revolution? Military Change and European Society 1550–1800* (Basingstoke, 1991).

14 Geoffrey Parker, *The Military Revolution: Military Innovation and the Rise of the West, 1500–1800* (Cambridge, 1988).

15 Mark Greengrass, 'Financing the cause: Protestant mobilization and accountability in France (1562–1589)', in Henk van Nierop et al., (eds), *Reformation, Revolt and Civil War in France and the Netherlands, 1555–1585* (Amsterdam, 1999), pp. 233–54; James B. Wood, *The King's Army: Warfare, Soldiers and Society during the Wars of Religion in France, 1562–1576* (Cambridge, 1996).

8. The French Wars of Religion

1 Francis II was married to Mary, Queen of Scots, whose mother, Mary of Guise, was the sister of the Duke and Cardinal.
2 Chantilly, Musée Condé, Papiers de Condé (I), Série L, vol. xix. F. 59. Translated by R. J. Knecht, and quoted in his *The French Wars of Religion* (London, 1989), p. 107.
3 Quoted in Mack P. Holt, *The French Wars of Religion, 1562–1629* (Cambridge, 1995), p. 95.

9. The Dutch Revolt

1 Clough to Richard Gresham, printed in J. M. B. C. Kervyn de Lettenhove, *Relations politiques des Pays-Bas et de l'angleterre sous le règne de Philippe II* (10 vols, Brussels, 1882–1900), vol. 4, pp. 337–8.
2 William's new wife embarked on a series of flagrant affairs, including with Jan Rubens, father of the painter.
3 For an acute discussion of the importance of fear of the Inquisition in the opposition to Spain, see Alastair Duke, 'Salvation by coercion: the controversy surrounding the Inquisition in the Low Countries on the eve of the revolt', in his *Reformation and Revolt in the Low Countries* (London, 1990), pp. 152–74.

10. The Making of Protestant Britain

1 The sixth of Scotland and the first of England; hence the careful double enumeration which is insisted upon by scholars who write from a Scottish perspective, and carelessly ignored by some historians south of the border.
2 A school of writing best represented by Christopher Haigh, *English Reformations: Religion, Politics and Society under the Tudors* (Oxford, 1993); J. J. Scarisbrick, *The Reformation and the English People* (Oxford, 1984).
3 These refinements, such as the joining of the words of institution at the Eucharist from the 1549 Prayer Book ('The Body of Christ, given to you') with the words of the 1552 Book ('Do this in remembrance of me') have often been interpreted as a suspiciously conservative development. In fact, the two together represent mainstream Calvinist theology far better than the 1552 words alone.
4 Norman L. Jones, *Faith by Statute: Parliament and the Settlement of Religion 1559* (London, 1982).

5 Kenneth R. Andrews, *Trade, Plunder and Settlement: Maritime Enterprise and the Genesis of the British Empire, 1480–1630* (Cambridge, 1984), p. 146.

6 As is suggested by Geoffrey Parker in the fascinating contrafactual essay 'If the Armada had landed', in his *Spain and the Netherlands, 1559–1659* (London, 1979), pp. 135–47.

7 David Cressy, *Bonfires and Bells: National Memory and the Protestant Calendar in Elizabethan and Stuart England* (London, 1989).

8 Quoted in J. A. van Dorsten, *The Radical Arts: The First Decade of an Elizabethan Renaissance* (Leiden, 1573), p. 12.

11. Philip II and the Resolution of the Reformation Conflict

1 Quoted in Henry Kamen, *Philip of Spain* (Yale, 1997), p. 81.

2 Instructions issued to Cardinal Caetani, legate in France, 1589. Quoted in John Lynch, *Spain under the Habsburgs. Vol. I: Empire and Absolutism, 1516–1598* (Oxford, 1981), p. 273. The pope's distrust of Philip was fully reciprocated. In 1581, frustrated by the lack of support for his campaign to reclaim the Netherlands, Philip unburdened himself to Granvelle: 'I assure you that [the pope] is wearing me out and has me on the point of losing my patience, great though it is.... It is clear to me that if the Netherlands were ruled by someone else, the pope would have performed miracles to prevent them being lost to the church, but because they are my states, I believe he is prepared to see them lost, because they will thus be lost to me.' Quoted in Geoffrey Parker, *Philip II* (Boston, 1978), p. 58.

3 Contrast Kamen, *Philip of Spain*, and Geoffrey Parker, *The Grand Strategy of Philip II* (New Haven, 1998). M. J. Rodriguez-Salgado, *The Changing Face of Empire: Charles V, Philip II and Habsburg Authority, 1551–1559* (Cambridge, 1988), is a sympathetic portrait of Philip's conduct of government in his first years.

4 Philip and Anna had four sons, though only Philip, born 1578, would survive to succeed his father as Philip III.

12. New Worlds

1 By way of comparison, there are some 600 manuscripts of the most popular devotional text, the *Imitation of Christ*, surviving from the fifteenth century.

2 Silvio A. Bedini, *The Pope's Elephant* (Nashville, 1998), is a charming and beautifully constructed narration of this little known tale.

3 Hernando Cortés, *5 Letters of Cortés to the Emperor* (New York, 1962). J. H. Elliott, 'The mental world of Hernán Cortés', in his *Spain and its World, 1500–1700* (New Haven, 1989), pp. 27–41.
4 Lyle N. McAlister, *Spain and Portugal in the New World, 1492–1700* (Minneapolis, 1984), p. 131.

13. Eastern Europe

1 I was in Leiden in the autumn of 1989, watching the demolition of the Berlin Wall on German television. The wall was first breached on a Thursday, and I can vividly remember that on the preceding Monday no-one had an inkling what was going to happen.
2 Alodia Kawecka-Gryczowa and Januz Tazbir, 'The book and the Reformation in Poland', in Jean-François Gilmont (ed.), *The Reformation and the Book* (Aldershot, 1998), p. 413.
3 Some 150 of the 3,000 letters of the collected correspondence of Erasmus are either from or to correspondents in Poland, Bohemia or Hungary.
4 R. J. W. Evans, *The Making of the Habsburg Monarchy, 1550–1700* (Oxford, 1979), p. 28.
5 Quoted in Gordon Rupp, 'Luther against "The Turk, the Pope and the Devil"', in Peter Newman Brooks (ed.), *Seven-Headed Luther* (Oxford, 1983), pp. 255–74.
6 The unconscious echo of this system in the Spanish *encomienda* was a comparison neither state would have recognized or particularly welcomed.
7 Robert Bideleux and Ian Jeffries, *A History of Eastern Europe* (London, 1998), p. 70.
8 The astrologers were equally relieved since Ivan had promised to have them executed by burning if their prophecy was inaccurate.
9 Maria Craciun, 'Protestantism and Orthodoxy in sixteenth-century Moldavia', in Karin Maag (ed.), *The Reformation in Eastern and Central Europe* (Aldershot, 1997), pp. 126–35.

14. Culture

1 Peter Burke, *Popular Culture in Early Modern Europe* (London, 1978).
2 Isabelle Cazeaux, *French Music in the Fifteenth and Sixteenth Centuries* (New York, 1975), pp. 19–20.
3 Thomas DaCosta Kaufmann, *Court, Cloister and City: The Art and Culture of Central Europe, 1450–1800* (London, 1995), pp. 143–4.
4 George Kubler, *Building the Escorial* (Princeton, 1982), p. 153.

5   Carl C. Christensen, *Princes and Propaganda: Electoral Saxon Art of the Reformation* (Kirksville, 1992), p. 39.

6   Quoted in Andrew Pettegree, 'Art', in his *The Reformation World* (London, 2000), p. 480.

7   Giulia Bartrum, *German Renaissance Prints, 1490–1550* (London, 1995), p. 9.

8   The best study of these images remains Robert Scribner, *For the Sake of Simple Folk: Popular Propaganda for the German Reformation* (Cambridge, 1981).

9   Charles Garside, *Zwingli and the Arts* (New Haven, 1966), p. 160.

10 Jean Calvin, *Excuse a MM les Nicodémites*, quoted in Carlos Eire, *War against the Idols: The Reformatio of Worship from Erasmus to Calvin* (Cambridge, 1986), p. 220.

11 The sketch is reproduced in Alastair Duke, Gillian Lewis and Andrew Pettegree, *Calvinism in Europe, 1540–1610: A collection of Documents* (Manchester, 1992), p. 154.

12 The Cranachhaus is illustrated in Pettegree, *Reformation World*, p. 473.

13 A sampling (from a later period) of the diary is available in English as Nancy Roelker (ed.), *The Paris of Henry of Navarre as Seen by Pierre de l'Estoile* (Harvard, 1958).

14 H. Perry Chapman et al., *Jan Steen, Painter and Storyteller* (Washington, 1996).

15 See particularly Susan Karant-Nunn, *The Reformation of Ritual: An Interpretation of Early Modern Germany* (London, 1997).

16 Quoted in Burke, *Popular Culture*, p. 212.

17 David Cressy, *Bonfires and Bells: National Memory and the Protestant Calendar in Elizabethan and Stuart England* (London, 1989).

15. Europe in 1600

1   Mack Holt, *The French Wars of Religion, 1562–1629* (Cambridge, 1995).

2   The Sound, the narrow passage between present day Sweden and Denmark at the entry to the North Sea and Baltic, is less than two miles across. After Swedish independence Denmark retained the most southerly province of what is now mainland Sweden, Scania, and thus controlled both banks of the narrow entry to the Baltic.

3   Jonathan Israel, *The Dutch Republic and the Hispanic World, 1606–1661* (Oxford, 1982).

4   I explore the use of toleration as a partisan tool in an article, 'The politics of toleration in the Free Netherlands', in Ole Peter Grell and Robert Scribner (eds), *Tolerance and Intolerance in the European Reformation* (Cambridge, 1996), pp. 182–98.

5 David Cressy, *Bonfires and Bells: National Memory and the Protestant Calendar in Elizabethan and Stuart England* (London, 1989).

6 Martin van Gelderen, *The Political Thought of the Dutch Revolt, 1555–1590* (Cambridge, 1992).

7 Wilfred Prest (ed.), *The Professions in Early Modern England* (London, 1987).

8 H. F. K. van Nierop, *The Nobility of Holland from Knights to Regents, 1500–1650* (Cambridge, 1993).

9 Peter Clark (ed.), *The European Crisis of the 1590s* (London, 1985), makes a convincing case for the exceptional difficulties of these years.

10 Andrew Pettegree, 'Thirty Years on: Progress towards integration amongst the immigrant population of Elizabethan London', in John Chartres and David Hey (eds), *English Rural Society, 1500–1800: Essays in Honour of Joan Thirsk* (Cambridge, 1990), pp. 297–312.

11 Philip Benedict, 'Towards the comparative study of the popular market for art: The ownership of paintings in seventeenth-century Metz', in his *The Faith and Fortunes of a Religious Minority* (Aldershot, 2001).

12 Joan Thirsk, *Economic Policy and Projects: The Development of a Consumer Society in Early Modern England* (Oxford, 1978).

13 Books published in the fifteenth century are known as incunabula: obviously they are among the rarest items of any library collection. But the total bulk is still impressive.

14 Felicity Heal, *Of Prelates and Princes: A Study of the Economic and Social Position of the Tudor Episcopate* (Cambridge, 1980); idem, *Hospitality in Early Modern England* (Oxford, 1990).

15 Steven Ozment, *Ancestors: The Loving Family in Old Europe* (Cambridge, Mass., 2001).

Further Reading

Other than in exceptional circumstances, these notes on further reading are confined to works available in English. In the case of works translated from another language, the date given is that of the English edition, rather than the foreign original.

1. Time and Space: Living in Sixteenth-Century Europe

For the conditions of everyday existence, nothing matches the magnificent sweep of Fernand Braudel, *Civilization and Capitalism. Vol. I: The Structures of Everyday Life* (London, 1982). See also Catharine Lis and Hugo Soly, *Poverty and Capitalism in Pre-Industrial Europe* (Hassocks, 1979), now supplemented by Robert Jütte, *Poverty and Deviance in Early Modern Europe* (Cambridge, 1994). Massimo Livi-Bacci, *Population and Nutrition: An Essay on European Demographic History* (Cambridge, 1991). Otherwise, the best work is often to be found in the study of specific localities. Bob Scribner, *Germany: A New Social and Economic History. Vol. I: 1450–1630* (London, 1996); Emmanuel le Roy Ladurie, *The French Peasantry, 1450–1660* (Aldershot, 1987).

The problems and politics of time are dealt with in Gerhard Dohrn-van Rommum, *History of the Hour: Clocks and the Modern Temporal Order* (Chicago, 1996); David Ewing Duncan, *Calendar* (New York, 1998). On diet, Maguelonne Toissaint-Samat, *History of Food* (Oxford, 1992), is massive and idiomatic. For a more radical interpretation, see Piero Camporesi, *Bread of Dreams: Food and Fantasy in Early Modern Europe* (Cambridge, 1989). See also Stephen Mennell, *All Manner of Food: Eating and Taste in England and France from the Middle Ages to the Present* (Oxford,

1985); Alexander Fenton and Ester Kizbán, *Food in Change: Eating Habits from the Middle Ages to the Present Day* (Edinburgh, 1986). Robert I. Rotberg and Theodore K. Rabb (eds), *Hunger and History: The Impact of Changing Food Production and Consumption Patterns on Society* (Cambridge, 1985).

On sickness and disease, see especially Charles Webster (ed.), *Health, Medicine and Mortality in the Sixteenth Century* (Cambridge, 1979); L. I. Conrad, et al., *The Western Medical Tradition, 800 BC to AD 1800* (Cambridge, 1995). Of all diseases, plague was the most feared. A. Lynn Martin, *Plague? Jesuit Accounts of Epidemic Disease in the Sixteenth Century* (Kirksville, Mo., 1994); Paul Slack, *The Impact of Plague in Tudor and Stuart England* (London, 1985). J. Arrizabalaga et al., *The Great Pox: The French Disease in Renaissance Europe* (Yale, 1997), deals with the traumatic impact of syphilis. On the healers, the magnificent Keith Thomas, *Religion and the Decline of Magic* (London, 1973), has a great deal on magical healing. The scarcely more useful 'learned' medicine is the subject of Ole Grell and A. Cunningham (eds), *Medicine and the Reformation* (London, 1993); N. Siraisi, *Mediaeval and Early Renaissance Medicine* (Chicago, 1990); A. Wear, et al., *The Medical Renaissance of the Sixteenth Century* (Cambridge, 1995); Marie-Christine Pouchelle, *The Body and Surgery in the Middle Ages* (Cambridge, 1989). On childbirth, Jean Towler and Joan Bramall, *Midwives in History and Society* (London, 1986).

On the relationship between this World and the next see two excellent recent collections: Bruce Gordon and Peter Marshall, *The Place of the Dead: Death and Remembrance in Late Mediaeval and Early Modern Europe* (Cambridge, 2000). William G. Naphy and Penny Roberts, *Fear in Early Modern Society* (Manchester, 1997). These build on classic works such as Piero Camporesi, *The Fear of Hell: Images of Damnation and Salvation in Early Modern Europe* (Cambridge, 1990).

2. Europe in 1500: Political organization

Good studies of the late Middle Ages include Steven Ozment, *The Age of Reform, 1200–1500* (New Haven, 1980). Johann Huizinga's classic *Waning of the Middle Ages* is now reissued in a new translation as *The Autumn of the Middle Ages* (London, 1996).

J. H. Burns, *Lordship, Kingship and Empire: The Idea of Monarchy, 1400–1525* (Oxford, 1992), provides the intellectual context for new monarchy. See also M. S. Anderson, *The Origins of the Modern European State System, 1495–1618* (London, 1998).

On Spain, J. F. O'Callaghan, *A History of Mediaeval Spain* (London, 1975); J. N. Hillgarth, *The Spanish Kingdoms, 1250–1516* (2 vols, Oxford, 1978); Peggy K. Liss, *Isabel the Queen* (Oxford, 1992). A. W. Lovett, *Early Habsburg Spain* (Oxford, 1986), has an excellent chapter on Ferdinand and Isabella. H. V. Livermore, *A New History of Portugal* (2nd edn, Cambridge, 1976).

On France, Frederic J. Baumgartner, *Louis XII* (Stroud, 1994); R.J. Knecht, *The Rise and Fall of Renaissance France* (London, 1996); his *Renaissance Warrior and Patron: The Reign of Francis I* (Cambridge, 1994) is the second, revised edition of his classic study of *Francis I* (1982).

On England, Steven Gunn, *Early Tudor Government, 1485–1558* (Basingstoke, 1995); John Guy, *Tudor England* (London, 1988), is now the standard textbook. G. R. Elton, *Reform and Reformation* (London, 1977), is the most accessible account of his view of the Tudor 'Revolution' in government. See also Diarmaid MacCulloch, *The Reign of Henry VIII: Politics, Policy and Piety* (Basingstoke, 1995). Michael Lynch, *Scotland: A New History* (London, 1991).

On Northern Europe, T. K. Derry, *A History of Scandinavia* (London, 1979). On the Empire, Michael Hughes, *Early Modern Germany, 1477–1806* (Basingstoke, 1992). There is no good modern English-language study of Maximilian I. Gerhard Benecke, *Maximilian I* (London, 1982) is idiosyncratic. Jean Bérenger, *History of the Habsburg Empire, 1273–1700* (London, 1994), provides the long view.

On states that failed to be, C. A. J. Armstrong, *England, France and Burgundy in the Fifteenth Century* (London, 1983); R. Vaughan, *Valois Burgundy* (London, 1975); Thomas A. Brady, *Turning Swiss: Cities and Empire, 1450–1550* (Cambridge, 1985), is a fascinating exploration of what might have been for the Habsburgs.

3.   The Struggle for Italy

On Italy, see for introduction, Denys Hay and John Law, *Italy in the Age of the Renaissance, 1380–1530* (London, 1989). Eric Cochrane, *Italy, 1530–1630* (London, 1988). On the states of northern Italy more specifically, Robert Finlay, *Politics in Renaissance Venice* (London, 1980). Eric Cochrane, *Florence in the Forgotten Centuries, 1527–1800* (Chicago, 1973).

Rome and the papacy are well served in the literature. See Peter Partner, *Renaissance Rome, 1500–1559: A Portrait of a Society* (Berkeley, 1976). Paoplo Prodi, *The Papal Prince* (Cambridge, 1987). Christine Shaw, *Julius II: The Warrior Pope* (Oxford, 1993), is a fine biography. Silvio A. Bedini,

The Pope's Elephant (Nashville, 1998), is a splendid evocation of the world of Leo X.

For the French perspective on the Valois–Habsburg struggle, Knecht, *Francis I* (above); Frederic Baumgartner, *Henry II* (Durham, NC, 1988); David Potter, *War and Government in the French Provinces: Picardy, 1470–1560* (Cambridge, 1993). R. J. Knecht, *The Rise and Fall of Renaissance France* (London, 1996). David Abulafia (ed.), *The French Descent into Renaissance Italy, 1494–95: Antecedents and Effects* (Aldershot, 1995), is an excellent collection of specialist work.

4. The Winds of Change

On the European city Jan de Vries, *European Urbanization, 1500–1800* (London, 1984), provides the indispensable statistical and analytical basis which had been the point of departure for all other work in the field. Modern and accessible recent surveys are Christopher R. Friedrichs, *The Early Modern City, 1450–1750* (London, 1995), and Alexander Cowan, *Urban Europe, 1500–1700* (London, 1988).

On navigation and ship technology, Richard Unger (ed.), *Cogs, Caravels, and Galleons: The Sailing Ship 1000–1650* (London, 1994). This contains a comprehensive and up-to-date bibliography. Unger's *The Ship in the Medieval Economy, 600–1600* (London and Montreal, 1980) is also useful. J. H. Parry, *The Age of Reconnaissance* (New York, 1963), though in places dated, remains a readable account of global exploration/exploitation, while C. R Boxer, *The Portuguese Seaborne Empire 1415–1825* (London 1969), is a classic. A couple of more recent works with technical information on the operation of ships, including pilotage and navigation, are Gillian Hutchinson, *Medieval Ships and Shipping* (Leicester, 1994), and Ian Friel, *The Good Ship: Ships, Shipbuilding and Technology in England 1200–1520* (London, 1995). The bible on navigation is D. W. Waters, *The Art of Navigation in Elizabethan and Early Stuart Times* (London, 1958).

On printing, Elizabeth Eisenstein, *The Printing Revolution in Early Modern Europe* (Cambridge, 1983), is a valuable abridgement of her longer classic, *The Printing Press as an Agent of Change* (2 vols, Cambridge, 1979). For a more accessible introduction, Lucien Febvre and Henri-Jean Martin, *The Coming of the Book: The Impact of Printing, 1450–1800* (London, 1976). Albert Kapr, *Johann Gutenberg: The Man and his Invention* (Aldershot, 1996), catches the excitement of the pioneering years. For the impact of printing in the religious sphere, Jean-François Gilmont, *The Reformation and the Book* (Aldershot, 1998), is excellent. Philip Gaskell, *A New Introduction to Bibliography* (Oxford, 1972), is an invaluable technical handbook. Changes in literacy are surveyed in R. A. Houston, *Literacy in Early Modern Europe* (1988).

On Humanism, Charles G. Nauert, *Humanism and the Culture of Renaissance Europe* (Cambridge, 1995). For Italian Humanism, John F. D'Amico, *Renaissance Humanism in Papal Rome* (Baltimore, 1983); Paul F. Grendler, *Schooling in Renaissance Italy: Literacy and Learning, 1300–1600* (Baltimore, 1989). A. Goodman and A. Mackay, *The Impact of Humanism on Western Europe* (London, 1990), takes the long view. See also Albert Rabil (ed.), *Renaissance Humanism, Foundations, Forms and Legacy* (3 vols, Philadelphia, 1988); Roy Porter and Mikuslás Teich (eds), *The Renaissance in National Context* (Cambridge, 1992). L.-E. Halkin, *Erasmus: A Critical Biography* (Oxford, 1993), is arguably the best of the recent biographies of Erasmus. Peter G. Bietenholz, *Contemporaries of Erasmus* (3 vols, Toronto, 1985–7), is an invaluable handbook of those who knew, admired or opposed the great Dutchman. The ongoing new translation of the *Correspondence of Erasmus*, ed. Peter G. Bietenholz (Toronto, 1974–), is also a fantastic resource. On Erasmus's manipulation of image see Lisa Jardine, *Erasmus, Man of Letters* (Princeton, 1993).

5. The Reformation

On the pre-Reformation Church, R. N. Swanson, *Religion and Devotion in Europe, c.1215–c.1515* (Cambridge, 1995), is excellent. For a more thematic approach, Joseph H. Lynch, *The Mediaeval Church* (London, 1992). See also Miri Rubin, *Corpus Christi: The Eucharist in Late Mediaeval Culture* (Cambridge, 1991). On England, see now Eamon Duffy, *The Stripping of the Altars* (New Haven, 1992). For the Renaissance papacy, Charles Stinger, *The Renaissance in Rome* (Bloomington, 1985); Christine Shaw, *Julius II: The Warrior Pope* (Oxford, 1993); for mediaeval reform, Antony Black, *Council and Commune: The Conciliar Movement and the Council of Basle* (London, 1979).

Recent general treatments of the Reformation include Euan Cameron, *The European Reformation* (Oxford, 1991), and Carter Lindberg, *The European Reformations* (Oxford, 1996). See also now Andrew Pettegree (ed.), *The Reformation World* (London, 1999). On Luther and Germany, the classic A. G. Dickens, *The German Nation and Martin Luther* (London, 1974), is stimulating and readable; Heiko Oberman, *Luther, Man between God and the Devil* (New Haven, 1989), is the best (and certainly most original) biography of Luther. On the Reformation controversies, Mark Edwards, *Luther and the False Brethren* (Stanford, 1975); and on Luther's public appeal, Steven Ozment, *The Reformation in the Cities* (New Haven, 1975), Robert Scribner, *For the Sake of Simple Folk* (Cambridge, 1981). For the impact of printed polemic, Mark U. Edwards, *Printing, Propaganda and Martin Luther* (Berkeley, 1994), and Miriam Chrisman, *Conflicting Visions of Reform: German Lay Propaganda Pamphlets, 1519–1530* (London, 1996). R. Po-Chia Hsia, *The German People and the Reformation* (Ithaca, 1988), is an outstandingly useful collection.

For the German Peasants' War and its consequences, Peter Blickle, *The Revolution of 1525* (Baltimore, 1981). Relevant documents are collected in Tom Scott and Bob Scribner, *The German Peasants' War: A History in Documents* (London, 1991). See also Tom Scott, *Thomas Müntzer: Theology and Revolution in the German Reformation* (Basingstoke, 1989). Hans-Jürgen Goertz, *The Anabaptists* (London, 1996), is an excellent treatment of the radical movement. Peter Blickle, *Communal Reformation: The Quest for Salvation in Sixteenth-Century Germany* (London, 1992), is an interesting attempt to provide a new conceptional framework which has not yet achived general acceptance. On the rural and princely Reformation more generally, C. Scott Dixon, *The Reformation and Rural Society: The Parishes of Brandenburg-Ansbach-Kulmbach* (Cambridge, 1996); Thomas Robisheaux, *Rural Society and the Search for Order in Early Modern Germany* (Cambridge, 1989). The best introduction to imperial politics and the Schmalkaldic League is Thomas A. Brady, *Protestant Politics: Jacob Sturm (1489–1553) and the German Reformation* (London, 1995).

For the Swiss Reformation, see now Bruce Gordon, *The Swiss Reformation* (Manchester, 2002). Still useful is the classic G. R. Potter, *Zwingli* (Cambridge, 1976). The early impact of the Reformation outside Germany is examined in Andrew Pettegree (ed.), *The Early Reformation in Europe* (Cambridge, 1992); Ole Grell, *The Scandinavian Reformation* (Cambridge, 1995). On the early evangelical movements in France and the Netherlands, Mark Greengrass, *The French Reformation* (Oxford, 1987); Francis Higman, *Censorship and the Sorbonne* (Geneva, 1979), and his *Piety and the People: French Vernacular Evangelical Literature, 1511–1551* (Aldershot, 1996); Alastair Duke, *Reformation and Revolt in the Low Countries* (London, 1990).

6. Charles V and the Defence of Catholic Europe

On Charles V, A. W. Lovett, *Early Habsburg Spain* (Oxford, 1986). Manuel Fernandez Alvarez, *Charles V* (London, 1975), is splendid, and the classic work of Karl Brandi, *The Emperor Charles V* (London, 1939), still has considerable merit. The anniversary year 2000 produced some new work of merit, especially Hugo Soly (ed.), *Charles V 1500–1558 and his Time* (Antwerp, 2000). On Spain, Stephen Haliczer, *The Communeros of Castile* (Madison, 1981), describes the last gasp of feudal resistance. The last stages of the Habsburg – Valois war are analysed in M. J. Rodriguez-Salgado, *The Changing Face of Empire: Charles V, Philip II and Habsburg Authority, 1551–1559* (Cambridge, 1988).

For the war with the Ottomans, P. Coles, *The Ottoman Impact on Europe* (London, 1968); S. Fischer-Galati, *Ottoman Imperialism and German Protestantism, 1521–1555* (New York, 1959).

7. The Age of Religious War

The Catholic Reformation still requires a definitive study. N. S. Davidson, *The Catholic Reformation* (Oxford, 1987), and R. Po-Chia Hsia, *The World of Catholic Renewal, 1540–1770* (Cambridge, 1998), are useful as an introduction. There is no modern study of the Council of Trent, but see *The Canons and Decrees of the Council of Trent*, ed. H. J. Schroeder (Rockford, Ill., 1978), for a good edition of the text.

Against this, a host of important local studies now chart the progress of Catholic Reform at a local level. See especially Marc Forster, *The Counter-Reformation in the Villages: Religion and Reform in the Bishopric of Speyer* (Ithaca, 1992); David Gentilcore, *From Bishop to Witch: The System of the Sacred in Early Modern Terra d'Otranto* (Manchester, 1992); and the works on Spain cited for chapter 11. On the new religious orders and missions, A. D. Wright, *The Counter-Reformation: Catholic Europe and the Non-Christian World* (London, 1982); John W. O'Malley, *The First Jesuits* (Cambridge, Mass., 1993).

On Calvinism, William G. Naphy, *Calvin and the Consolidation of the Reformation in Geneva* (Manchester, 1994), is a bold revisionist portrait. T. H. L. Parker, *Calvin* (London, 1975), and William Monter, *Calvin's Geneva* (New York, 1967), are still valuable. Andrew Pettegree, Alastair Duke and Gillian Lewis, *Calvinism in Europe, 1540–1620* (Cambridge, 1994), offers an introduction to Calvinism as an international movement. Raymond Mentzer, *Sin and the Calvinists* (Kirksville, 1994), is the best introduction to Calvinist social discipline. See also R. Po-Chia Hsia, *Social Discipline in the Reformation: Central Europe 1550–1650* (London, 1989).

The impact of warfare as an agent of change is debated back and forth in J. R. Hale, *War and Society in Renaissance Europe, 1450–1620* (London, 1985); Geoffrey Parker, *The Military Revolution: Military Innovation and the Rise of the West, 1500–1800* (Cambridge, 1988); and Jeremy Black, *A Military Revolution?* (Basingstoke, 1991). A shrewd local study is David Potter, *War and Government in the French Provinces: Picardy, 1470–1560* (Cambridge, 1993).

8.   The French Wars of Religion

On France, for introduction, Mack Holt, *The French Wars of Religion* (Cambridge, 1995); R. J. Knecht, *The French Civil Wars* (London, 2000).

On the rise of Protestantism, Philip Benedict, *Rouen during the French Wars of Religion* (Cambridge, 1981); Nicola Sutherland, *The Huguenot Struggle for Recognition* (New Haven, 1980). Donald Kelley, *The Beginnings of Ideology: Consciousness and Society in the French Reformation* (Cambridge, 1981), examines French Protestant thought. N. Z. Davis, *Society and Culture in Early Modern France* (London, 1975), contains a number of highly influential articles. Kevin C. Robbins, *City of the Ocean Sea: La Rochelle, 1530–1650* (Leiden, 1997), is a superb analysis of a new Protestant society. For the period after the massacre, Robert M. Kingdon, *Myths about the St. Bartholomew's Day Massacres, 1572–1576* (Cambridge, Mass., 1988); Scott M. Manetsch, *Theodore Beza and the Quest for Peace in France, 1572–1598* (Leiden, 2000).

James B. Wood, *The King's Army: Warfare, Soldiers and Society during the Wars of Religion in France, 1562–1576* (Cambridge, 1996), deals with the military conflict. On French Catholicism, Christopher Elwood, *The Body Broken: The Calvinist Doctrine of the Eucharist and the Symbolization of Power in Sixteenth-Century France* (Oxford, 1999); Larissa Juliet Taylor, *Heresy and Orthodoxy in Sixteenth-Century Paris: François Le Picart and the Beginnings of the Catholic Reformation* (Leiden, 1999). Barbara Diefendorf, *Beneath the Cross: Catholics and Huguenots in Sixteenth-Century Paris* (New York, 1991), is a splendid interpretation of the causes of the massacre of St Bartholomew's Day. On the end of the wars, Michael Wolfe, *The Conversion of Henri IV* (Cambridge, Mass., 1993).

9.   The Dutch Revolt

For the Netherlands, Jonathan Israel, *The Dutch Republic, its Rise, Greatness and Fall, 1477–1806* (Oxford, 1995), provides a splendid introduction. Geoffrey Parker, *The Dutch Revolt* (London, 1977), is still indispensable. On the politics and warfare, Geoffrey Parker *Spain and the Netherlands, 1559–1659: Ten Studies* (London, 1979), and his *The Army of Flanders and the Spanish Road, 1567–1659* (Cambridge, 1972). William S. Maltby, *Alba* (Berkeley, 1983), is a sympathetic study of an unsympathetic character. For the religious aspect of the struggle, see Alastair Duke, *Reformation and Revolt in the Low Countries* (London, 1990); for the contribution of the exiles, Andrew Pettegree, *Emden and the Dutch Revolt: Exile and the Development of Reformed Protestantism* (Oxford, 1992); and for the role of the leading metropolis, Guido Marnef, *Antwerp in the Age of Reformation: Underground Protestantism in a Commercial Metropolis, 1550–1577* (Baltimore, 1996). For political thought, Martin Van Gelderen, *The Political Thought of the Dutch Revolt, 1555–1590* (Cambridge, 1992), and his collection of texts, *The Dutch Revolt* (Cambridge, 1993). For a useful survey of the most recent writing, Philip Benedict et al. (eds), *Reformation, Revolt and Civil War in France and the Netherlands, 1555–1585* (Amsterdam, 1999).

10. The Making of Protestant Britain

For introduction, John Guy, *Tudor England* (Oxford, 1988). Penry Williams, *The Tudor Regime* (Oxford, 1979), is good on the mechanics of government. On the Elizabethan settlement, Norman Jones, *Faith by Statute: Parliament and the Settlement of Religion, 1559* (1982), and *The Dawn of the Elizabethan Age* (Oxford, 1993). For emerging Protestant culture, Patrick Collinson, *The Birthpangs of English Protestantism* (Basingstoke, 1988). Ian Green, *The Christian's ABC: Catechisms and Catechizing in England, c.1530–1740* (Oxford, 1996), and *Print and Protestantism in Early Modern England* (Oxford, 2000) are the first two parts of a monumental study of Protestant book culture.

On English foreign policy Charles Wilson, *Elizabeth and the Revolt of the Netherlands* (London, 1970), is provocative and polemical; R. B. Wernham, *The Making of Elizabethan Foreign Policy* (Berkeley, 1980), is an introduction to his two deeply researched books *After the Armada: Elizabethan England and the Struggle for Western Europe, 1588–1595* (Oxford, 1984) and *The Return of the Armadas: The Last Years of the Elizabethan Wars against Spain, 1595–1603* (Oxford, 1994).

Kenneth R. Andrews, *Trade, Plunder and Settlement: Maritime Enterprise and the Genesis of the British Empire, 1480–1630* (Cambridge, 1984), is excellent on the English encroachment which stirred Anglo-Spanish conflict. Colin Martin and Geoffrey Parker, *The Spanish Armada* (London, 1988), is the best study of the expedition itself.

11. Philip II and the Resolution of the Reformation Conflict

Peter Pierson, *Philip II of Spain* (London, 1975), and Geoffrey Parker, *Philip II* (Boston, 1978), are both very readable. Two recent, but contrasting views of Philip's personality, are available in Henry Kamen, *Philip of Spain* (New Haven, 1997), and Geoffrey Parker, *The Grand Strategy of Philip II*

(New Haven, 1998). On warfare, I. A. A. Thompson, *War and Government in Habsburg Spain, 1560–1620* (London, 1976), is a classic, as is Geoffrey Parker, *The Army of Flanders and the Spanish Road, 1567–1659* (Cambridge, 1972). Fernand Braudel, *The Mediterranean and the Mediterranean World in the Age of Philip II* (2 vols, London, 1972) is still indispensable.

For Spanish culture and society see William A. Christian, *Local Religion in Sixteenth-Century Spain* (Princeton, 1981); Henry Kamen, *The Phoenix and the Flame: Catalonia and the Counter-Reformation* (New Haven, 1993); Richard L. Kagan, *Lucrecia's Dreams: Politics and Prophecy in Sixteenth-Century Spain* (Berkeley, 1990). Recent research had also permitted a more realistic evaluation of the work and impact of the Inquisition. See particularly, Stephen Haliczer, *Inquisition and Society in the Kingdom of Valencia, 1478–1834* (Berkeley, 1990); William Monter, *Frontiers of Heresy: The Spanish Inquisition from the Basque Lands to Sicily* (Cambridge, 1990).

12. New Worlds

G. V. Scammell, *The First Imperial Age: European Overseas Expansion, 1400–1715* (London, 1989), is a fine introduction. J. H. Parry, *The Age of Reconnaissance* (Berkeley, 1963), is still useful. Felipe Fernandez-Armesto, *Columbus* (1991), is a good recent narrative; the explorer's own voice can be heard in *The Journal of Christopher Columbus*, trans. Cecil Jane (rev. edn, London, 1960). William D. Philips and Carla Rahn Phillips, *The Worlds of Christopher Columbus* (Cambridge, 1992), place him in context. C. R. Boxer, *The Portuguese Seaborne Empire, 1415–1825* (London, 1969), deals with the first discoveries. If this is inevitably slightly dated, an excellent and more recent synthesis is A. J. R. Russell-Wood, *The Portuguese Empire, 1415–1808* (Baltimore, 1992). See also Wolfgang Schivelbusch, *Tastes of Paradise: A Social History of Spices, Stimulants and Intoxicants* (New York, 1993).

On the Americas, J. H. Elliott, *Spain and its World, 1500–1700* (New Haven, 1989). Ross Hassig, *Mexico and the Spanish Conquest* (London, 1994). Herman Cortés, *Letters from Mexico*, ed. Anthony Pagden (New Haven, 1986). For the impact on Europe, Alfred W. Crosby, *The Columbian Exchange: Biological and Cultural Consequences of 1492* (Westport, Conn., 1972).

The collision of cultures is the primary theme of S. Greenblatt, *Marvellous Possessions: The Wonder of the New World* (Oxford, 1991); see also the essays collected in his *New World Encounters* (Berkeley, 1993). R. F. Townsend, *Sex and Conquest: Gendered Violence, Political Order, and the European Conquest of the Americas* (Ithaca, 1995). D. A. Brading, *The First America:*

The Spanish Monarchy, Creole Patriots, and the Liberal State (Cambridge, 1991), studies the emergence of Hispanic American identity.

For the organization of New World societies, P. K. Liss, *Mexico under Spain, 1521–1556: Society and the Origins of Nationality* (Chicago, 1975); Charles Gibson, *The Aztecs under Spanish Rule* (Stanford, 1964); Alonso de Zorita, *The Lords of New Spain* (London, 1965). James Lockhart, *Spanish Peru, 1532–1560* (Madison, 1968). The defence of the colonial monopoly is the subject of Paul E. Hoofman, *The Spanish Crown and the Defense of the Caribbean, 1535–1585* (Baton Rouge, La., 1980). On the vital silver production, Harry E. Cross, 'Colonial silver mining: Mexico and Peru', *Hispanic American Historical Review*, 52 (1972), provides the data; Jeffrey A. Cole, *The Potosí Mita, 1573–1700: Compulsory Indian Labour in the Andes* (Stanford, 1985), spells out the grim facts. Carl Ortwin Sauer, *Sixteenth Century North America* (Berkeley, 1971), studies early contacts between Europeans and native Americans. For the ecological impact of contact, Carl Ortwin Sauer, *The Early Spanish Main* (Berkeley, 1966), is a classic regional study, and Alfred W. Crosby, *The Columbian Exchange* (Westport, Conn., 1972), a seminal work.

13. Eastern Europe

Eastern Europe is now only beginning to make the impact it deserves on the English-language literature. On the Habsburg lands see J. Bérenger, *A History of the Habsburg Empire*; R. J. W. Evans, *The Making of the Habsburg Monarchy, 1500–1700* (Oxford, 1977). P. S. Fichtner, *Ferdinand I of Austria: The Problems of Dynasticism in the Age of Reformation* (New York, 1982), concentrates mostly on the Habsburg inheritance in Hungary and Bohemia. See also K. J. Dillon, *King and Estates in the Bohemian Lands, 1526–1564* (Brussels, 1976). R. J. W. Evans and T. V. Thomas (eds), *Crown, Church and Estates: Central European Politics in the Sixteenth and Seventeen Centuries* (London, 1991), is a valuable collection. On the economy, Antoni Maczak, Henryk Samsonowicz and Peter Burke, *East-Central Europe in Transition: From the Fourteenth to the Seventeenth Century* (Cambridge, 1975). Robert Bideleux and Ian Jeffries, *A History of Eastern Europe* (London, 1998), has valuable remarks, though the main focus is on a later period.

For the impact of the Reformation in eastern Europe, the essays in Andrew Pettegree, *The Early Reformation in Europe* (Cambridge, 1992), and Robert Scribner, *The Reformation in National Context* (Cambridge, 1994). See now especially, Karin Maag (ed.), *The Reformation in Eastern and Central Europe* (Aldershot, 1997), and Graeme Murdock, 'Eastern Europe', in Pettegree (ed.), *The Reformation World* (London, 2000).

Thomas Fudge, *The Magnificent Ride* (Aldershot, 1998), is a new and original study of the Hussite movement. For the later proliferation of Protestant sects, G. H. Williams, *The Radical Reformation* (3nd edn, Kirksville, Mo., 1992). J. Lecler, *Toleration and the Reformation* (London, 1960), is a classic study with important sections on Poland and eastern Europe.

On Hungary, V. Zimányi, *Economy and Society in Sixteenth and Seventeenth Century Hungary, 1526–1650* (Budapest, 1987); J. M. Bak and B. M. Birály (eds), *From Hunyadi to Rákóczi: War and Society in Late Mediaeval and Early Modern Hungary* (New York, 1982). For Poland, Norman Davies, *God's Playground: A History of Poland* (2 vols, Oxford, 1981), is an accessible introduction. See also A. Maczak, et. al (eds), *East Central Europe in Transition* (Cambridge, 1985).

For the Ottoman Empire and its engagement with European society, Justin McCarthy, *The Ottoman Turks* (London, 1997); Matin Kunt and Christine Woodhead (eds), *Suleiman the Magnificent and his Age* (London, 1995); P. Coles, *The Ottoman Impact on Europe* (1968). For an excellent recent survey, Cemel Kafadar, 'The Ottomans and Europe', in Thomas A. Brady et al., *Handbook of European History*, vol. I, pp. 589–636; S. Fischer-Galati, *Ottoman Imperialism and German Protestantism, 1511–1555* (1959).

14. Culture

On Court Culture, John Adamson (ed.), *The Princely Courts of Europe, 1500–1750* (London, 1999), sets the scene. R. J. Knecht, *Francis I* (Cambridge, (1982), is excellent for the cultural patronage of Francis I. On the Habsburgs, Hugh Trevor-Roper, *Princes and Artists: Patronage and Ideology at Four Habsburg Courts, 1517–1633* (London, 1976); Thomas DaCosta Kaufmann, *Court, Cloister and City: The Art and Culture of Central Europe, 1450–1800* (London, 1995), deals with Habsburg patronage in central Europe, and much else besides. George Kubler, *Building the Escorial* (Princeton, 1982), is an exhaustive struggle of an architectural Odyssey.

Among the extensive literature on sixteenth-century Italian art, Mary Hollingsworth, *Patronage in Sixteenth-Century Italy* (London, 1996), is fresh and stimulating. Alison Cole, *Art of the Italian Renaissance Courts* (London, 1995), provides an accessible introduction to the fifteenth-century context. On music, Iain Fenlon (ed.), *Man and Music: The Renaissance* (Basingstoke, 1989), offers an excellent series of introductory essays, taking the major cultural centres of Europe by turn. See also G. Abrahams (ed.), *The New Oxford History of Music. Vol. IV: The Age of Humanism,*

1540–1630 (London, 1968); Isabelle Cazeaux, *French Music in the Fifteenth and Sixteenth Centuries* (New York, 1975). On Protestant music the most comprehensive study is Freidrich Blume and Ludwig Finscher (eds), *Protestant Church Music: A History* (New York, 1974). On Renaissance medals, Sir George Hill, *Medals of the Renaissance* (2nd rev. edn, J. G. Pollard, London, 1978); Stephen K. Scher, *The Currency of Fame: Portrait Medals of the Renaissance* (London, 1994); G. F. Hill and Graham Pollard, *Renaissance Medals from the Samuel H. Kress Collection at the National Gallery of Art* (London, 1967), is lavishly illustrated. On coinage, Joe Cribb et al. (eds), *The Coin Atlas* (London, 1970), is a compendious and well-illustrated book.

For the Protestant Reformation's radical reorganization of the visual arts, Carl Christiansen, *Art and the Reformation in Germany* (Athens, OH, 1979), and his *Princes and Propaganda: Electoral Saxon Art of the Reformation* (Kirksville, 1992). Sergiusz Michalski, *The Reformation and the Visual Arts: The Protestant Image Question in Western and Eastern Europe* (London, 1993), is a study which strays over the normal boundaries. On England, Margaret Aston, *England's Iconoclasts* (Oxford, 1988), and Tessa Watt, *Cheap Print and Popular Piety, 1550–1640* (Cambridge, 1991) deal intelligently with popular religious culture. For the more problematic case of Calvinism, Paul Corby Finney (ed.), *Seeing beyond the Word: Visual Arts and the Calvinist Tradition* (Grand Rapids, 1999). For the Catholic response, Philip Soergel, *Wondrous in his Saints, Counter-Reformation Propaganda in Bavaria* (Berkeley, 1993).

15. Europe in 1600

Peter Clark (ed.), *The European Crisis of the 1590s* (London, 1985), takes a pessimistic view. For the general strategic situation, Richard Bonney, *The European Dynastic States, 1494–1660* (Oxford, 1991). The unresolved politico-religious tensions are explored in Geoffrey Parker, *The Thirty Years' War* (London, 1984). On England, John Guy (ed.), *The Reign of Elizabeth I: Court and Culture in the Last Decade* (Cambridge, 1995). On France, Mark Greengrass, *France in the Age of Henri IV* (London, 1984).

On conditions of life, Steven Ozment, *Where Fathers Ruled: Family Life in Reformation Europe* (Cambridge, Mass., 1983), and *Flesh and Spirit: Private Life in Early Modern Germany* (New York, 1999); Merry Wiesner, *Women and Gender in Early Modern Europe* (Cambridge, 1993). Ralph Houlbrooke, *English Family Life, 1576–1716* (Oxford, 1988), is an anthology of contemporary sources. Long term social trends are the subject of M. L. Bush (ed.), *Social Orders and Social Classes in Europe since 1500*

(London, 1992). Henry Kamen, *European Society, 1500–1700* (London, 1984), is wide-ranging and stimulating.

The effect of the Reformation on familial relations is probed in Joel F. Harrington, *Reordering Marriage and Society in Reformation Germany* (Cambridge, 1995); Robert M. Kingdon, *Adultery and Divorce in Calvin's Geneva* (Cambridge, Mass., 1995). A pessimistic view of the impact of the Reformation on women's place in society is taken by Lyndal Roper, *The Holy Household: Women and Morals in Reformation Augsburg* (Oxford, 1989).

For the diversification of diet, particularly among the more affluent, Roger Chartier, *A History of Private Life* (Cambridge, Mass., 1989). General patterns of consumption are traced most authoritatively in a special issue of the French journal *Annales*, 30 (1975). The birth of a consumer society in England is the subject of Joan Thirsk, *Economic Policy and Projects* (Oxford, 1978).

For the Reformation attitude to the poor, Calter Lindberg, *Beyond Charity: Reformation Initiatives for the Poor* (Minneapolis, 1993). See also, on Catholic societies, Brian Pullan, *Rich and Poor in Renaissance Venice: The Social Institutions of a Catholic State* (Cambridge, 1971); Linda Martz, *Poverty and Welfare in Habsburg Spain: The Example of Toledo* (Cambridge, 1983); Maureen Flynn, *Sacred Charity: Confraternities and Social Welfare in Spain, 1400–1700* (Ithaca, 1989). The social mores of the post-Reformation community are explored in Martin Ingram, *Church Courts, Sex and Marriage in England, 1570–1640* (Cambridge, 1987); James R. Farr, *Hands of Honor: Artisans and Their World in Dijon, 1550–1650* (Ithaca, 1988).

Village society is the focus of David Sabean, *Power in the Blood: Popular Culture and Village Discourse in Early Modern Germany* (Cambridge, 1984). The terrors awaiting those who strayed into criminality are laid out in Richard van Dülmen, *Theatre of Horror: Crime and Punishment in Early Modern Germany* (London, 1990). Pieter C. Spierenburg, *The Spectacle of Suffering: Executions and the Evolution of Repression from a Preindustrial Metropolis to the European Experience* (Cambridge, 1984).

Index